Advanced Information and Knowledge Processing

Series Editors
Professor Lakhmi Jain
lakhmi.jain@unisa.edu.au

Professor Xindong Wu
wu@cs.uvm.edu

Also in this series

Gregoris Mentzas, Dimitris Apostolou, Andreas Abecker and Ron Young
Knowledge Asset Management
1-85233-583-1

Michalis Vazirgiannis, Maria Halkidi and Dimitrios Gunopulos
Uncertainty Handling and Quality Assessment in Data Mining
1-85233-655-2

Asunción Gómez-Pérez, Mariano Fernández-López and Oscar Corcho
Ontological Engineering
1-85233-551-3

Arno Scharl (Ed.)
Environmental Online Communication
1-85233-783-4

Shichao Zhang, Chengqi Zhang and Xindong Wu
Knowledge Discovery in Multiple Databases
1-85233-703-6

Jason T.L. Wang, Mohammed J. Zaki, Hannu T.T. Toivonen and Dennis Shasha (Eds)
Data Mining in Bioinformatics
1-85233-671-4

C.C. Ko, Ben M. Chen and Jianping Chen
Creating Web-based Laboratories
1-85233-837-7

Manuel Graña, Richard Duro, Alicia d'Anjou and Paul P. Wang (Eds)
Information Processing with Evolutionary Algorithms
1-85233-886-0

Colin Fyfe
Hebbian Learning and Negative Feedback Networks
1-85233-883-0

Yun-Heh Chen-Burger and Dave Robertson
Automating Business Modelling
1-85233-835-0

Sanghamitra Bandyopadhyay, Ujjwal Maulik,
Lawrence B. Holder and Diane J. Cook (Eds)

Advanced Methods for Knowledge Discovery from Complex Data

With 120 Figures

 Springer

Sanghamitra Bandyopadhyay, PhD
Machine Intelligence Unit, Indian Statistical Institute, Kolkata, India

Ujjwal Maulik, PhD
Department of Computer Science & Engineering, Jadavpur University, Kolkata, India

Lawrence B. Holder, PhD
Diane J. Cook, PhD
Department of Computer Science & Engineering, University of Texas at Arlington, USA

British Library Cataloguing in Publication Data
A catalogue record for this book is available from the British Library

AI&KP ISSN 1610-3947

ISBN 978-1-84996-991-8   e-ISBN 978-1-84628-284-3
Springer Science+Business Media
springeronline.com

Printed in the United States of America
34-543210 Printed on acid-free paper

To our parents, for their unflinching support, and
to Utsav, for his unquestioning love.
S. Bandyopadhyay and U. Maulik

To our parents, for their constant love and support.
L. Holder and D. Cook

Contents

Part II Applications

Contributors

Sanghamitra Bandyopadhyay
Machine Intelligence Unit
Indian Statistical Institute
Kolkata, India
sanghami@isical.ac.in

Bhabatosh Chanda
Electronics and Communication Sciences Unit
Indian Statistical Institute
Kolkata, India
chanda@isical.ac.in

Jeff Coble
Department of Computer Science and Engineering
University of Texas at Arlington
Arlington, Texas USA
coble@cse.uta.edu

Diane J. Cook
Department of Computer Science and Engineering
University of Texas at Arlington
Arlington, Texas USA
cook@cse.uta.edu

Melba M. Crawford
The University of Texas at Austin
Austin, Texas USA
crawford@csr.utexas.edu

Amit K. Das
Computer Science and Technology Department
Bengal Engineering College (Deemed University)
Kolkata, India
amit@becs.ac.in

Mohamed M. Gaber
School of Computer Science and Software Engineering
Monash University
Australia
Mohamed.Medhat.Gaber@infotech.monash.edu.au

Thomas Gärtner
Fraunhofer Institut Autonome Intelligente Systeme
Germany
thomas.gaertner@ais.fraunhofer.de

Lise Getoor
Department of Computer Science and UMIACS
University of Maryland, College Park
Maryland, USA
getoor@cs.umd.edu

Joydeep Ghosh
The University of Texas at Austin
Austin, Texas USA
ghosh@ece.utexas.edu

Jiawei Han
University of Illinois at Urbana-Champaign
Urbana-Champaign, Illinois USA
hanj@uiuc.edu

Lawrence B. Holder
Department of Computer Science and Engineering
University of Texas at Arlington
Arlington, Texas USA
holder@cse.uta.edu

Tao Jiang
School of Computer Engineering
Nanyang Technological University
Nanyang Avenue, Singapore
jian0006@ntu.edu.sg

Shonali Krishnaswamy
School of Computer Science and Software Engineering
Monash University
Australia
Shonali.Krishnaswamy@infotech.monash.edu.au

Shailesh Kumar
Fair Isaac Corporation
San Diego, California USA
shaileshkumar@fairisaac.com

Ujjwal Maulik
Department of Computer Science and Engineering
Jadavpur University
Kolkata, India
drumaulik@jdvu.ac.in

Srinivas Mukkamala
Department of Computer Science
New Mexico Tech, Socorro, USA
srinivas@cs.nmt.edu

Joseph Potts
Department of Computer Science and Engineering
University of Texas at Arlington
Arlington, Texas USA
potts@cse.uta.edu

Sanjoy K. Saha
Department of Computer Science and Engineering
Jadavpur University
Kolkata, India
sks@becs.ac.in

Sunita Sarawagi
Department of Information Technology
Indian Institute of Technology
Mumbai, India
sunita@iitb.ac.in

Andrew H. Sung
Department of Computer Science
Institute for Complex Additive Systems Analysis
New Mexico Tech, Socorro, USA
sung@cs.nmt.edu

Ah-Hwee Tan
School of Computer Engineering
Nanyang Technological University
Nanyang Avenue, Singapore
asahtan@ntu.edu.sg

Jason T. L. Wang
Department of Computer Science
New Jersey Institute of Technology
University Heights
Newark, New Jersey USA
wangj@njit.edu

Wei Wang
University of North Carolina at Chapel Hill
Chapel Hill, North Carolina USA
weiwang@cs.unc.edu

Xifeng Yan
University of Illinois, Urbana-Champaign
Urbana-Champaign, Illinois USA
xyan@uiuc.edu

Jiong Yang
Case Western Reserve University
Cleveland, Ohio USA
jiong@eecs.cwru.edu

Mohammed J. Zaki
Computer Science Department
Rensselaer Polytechnic Institute
Troy, New York USA
zaki@cs.rpi.edu

Arkady Zaslavsky
School of Computer Science and Software Engineering
Monash University
Australia
Arkady.Zaslavsky@infotech.monash.edu.au

Sen Zhang
Department of Mathematics, Computer Science and Statistics,
State University of New York, Oneonta
Oneonta, New York USA
ZHANGS@oneonta.edu

Preface

The growth in the amount of data collected and generated has exploded in recent times with the widespread automation of various day-to-day activities, advances in high-level scientific and engineering research and the development of efficient data collection tools. This has given rise to the need for automatically analyzing the data in order to extract knowledge from it, thereby making the data potentially more useful.

Knowledge discovery and data mining (KDD) is the process of identifying valid, novel, potentially useful and ultimately understandable patterns from massive data repositories. It is a multi-disciplinary topic, drawing from several fields including expert systems, machine learning, intelligent databases, knowledge acquisition, case-based reasoning, pattern recognition and statistics.

Many data mining systems have typically evolved around well-organized database systems (e.g., relational databases) containing relevant information. But, more and more, one finds relevant information hidden in unstructured text and in other complex forms. Mining in the domains of the world-wide web, bioinformatics, geoscientific data, and spatial and temporal applications comprise some illustrative examples in this regard. Discovery of knowledge, or potentially useful patterns, from such complex data often requires the application of advanced techniques that are better able to exploit the nature and representation of the data. Such advanced methods include, among others, graph-based and tree-based approaches to relational learning, sequence mining, link-based classification, Bayesian networks, hidden Markov models, neural networks, kernel-based methods, evolutionary algorithms, rough sets and fuzzy logic, and hybrid systems. Many of these methods are developed in the following chapters.

In this book, we bring together research articles by active practitioners reporting recent advances in the field of knowledge discovery, where the information is mined from complex data, such as unstructured text from the world-wide web, databases naturally represented as graphs and trees, geoscientific data from satellites and visual images, multimedia data and bioinformatic data. Characteristics of the methods and algorithms reported here include the use of domain-specific knowledge for reducing the search space, dealing with uncertainty, imprecision and concept drift, efficient linear and/or sub-linear scalability, incremental approaches to knowledge discovery, and increased level and intelligence of interactivity with human experts and decision makers. The techniques can be sequential, parallel or stream-based in nature.

The book has been divided into two main sections: foundations and applications. The chapters in the foundations section present general methods for mining complex data. In Chapter 1, Bandyopadhyay and Maulik present an overview of the field of data mining and knowledge discovery. They discuss the main concepts of the field, the issues and challenges, and recent trends in data mining, which provide the context for the subsequent chapters on methods and applications.

In Chapter 2, Ghosh, Kumar and Crawford address the issue of high dimensionality in both the attributes and class values of complex data. Their approach builds a binary hierarchical classifier by decomposing the set of classes into smaller partitions and performing a two-class learning problem between each partition. The simpler two-class learning problem often allows a reduction in the dimensionality of the attribute space. Their approach shows improvement over other approaches to the multi-class learning problem and also results in the discovery of knowledge in the form of the class hierarchy.

Cook, Holder, Coble and Potts describe techniques for mining complex data represented as a graph in Chapter 3. Many forms of complex data involve entities, their attributes, and their relationships to other entities. It is these relationships that make appropriate a graph representation of the data. The chapter describes numerous techniques based on the core Subdue methodology that uses data compression as a metric for interestingness in mining knowledge from the graph data. These techniques include supervised and unsupervised learning, clustering and graph grammar learning. They address efficiency issues by introducing an incremental approach to processing streaming graph data. They also introduce a method for mining graphs in which relevant examples are embedded, possibly overlapping, in one large graph. Numerous successes are documented in a number of domains.

In Chapter 4, Gärtner also presents techniques for mining graph data, but these techniques are based on kernel methods which implicitly map the graph data to a higher-dimensional, non-relational space where learning is easier, thus avoiding the computational complexity of graph operations for matching and covering. While kernel methods have been applied to single graphs, Gärtner introduces kernels that apply to sets of graphs and shows their effectiveness on problems from the fields of relational reinforcement learning and molecular classification.

While graphs represent one of the most expressive forms of complex data representations, some specializations of graphs (e.g., trees) still allow the representation of significant relational information, but with reduced computational cost. In Chapter 5, Zaki presents a technique called TreeMiner for finding all frequent subtrees in a forest of trees and compares this approach to a pattern-matching approach. Zaki shows results indicating a significant increase in speed over the pattern-matching approach and applies the new technique to the problem of mining usage patterns from real logs of website browsing behavior.

Another specialized form in which complex data might be expressed is a sequence. In Chapter 6, Sarawagi discusses several methods for mining sequence data, i.e., data modeled as a sequence of discrete multi-attribute records. She reviews state-of-the-art techniques in sequence mining and applies these to two real applications: address cleaning and information extraction from websites.

In Chapter 7, Getoor returns to the more general graph representation of complex data, but includes probabilistic information about the distribution of links (or relationships) between entities. Getoor uses a structured logistic regression model to learn patterns based on both links and entity attributes. Results in the domains of web browsing and citation collections indicate that the use of link distribution information improves classification performance.

The remaining chapters constitute the applications section of the book. Significant successes have been achieved in a wide variety of domains, indicating the potential benefits of mining complex data, rather than applying simpler methods on simpler transformations of the data. Chapter 8 begins with a contribution by Zhang and Wang describing techniques for mining evolutionary trees, that is, trees whose parent–child relationships represent actual evolutionary relationships in the domain of interest. A good example, and one to which they apply their approach, is phylogenetic trees that describe the evolutionary pathways of species at the molecular level. Their algorithm efficiently discovers "cousin pairs," which are two nodes sharing a common ancestor, in a single tree or a set of trees. They present numerous experimental results showing the efficiency and effectiveness of their approach in both synthetic and real domains, namely, phylogenic trees.

In Chapter 9, Jiang and Tan apply a variant of the *Apriori*-based association rule-mining algorithm to the relational domain of Resource Description Framework (RDF) documents. Their approach treats RDF relations as items in the traditional association-rule mining framework. Their approach also takes advantage of domain ontologies to provide generalizations of the RDF relations. They apply their technique to a synthetically-generated collection of RDF documents pertaining to terrorism and show that the method discovers a small set of association rules capturing the main associations known to be present in the domain.

Saha, Das and Chanda address the task of content-based image retrieval by mapping image data into complex data using features based on shape, texture and color in Chapter 10. They also develop an image retrieval similarity measure based on human perception and improve retrieval accuracy using feedback to establish the relevance of the various features. The authors empirically validate the superiority of their method over competing methods of content-based image retrieval using two large image databases.

In Chapter 11, Mukkamala and Sung turn to the problem of intrusion detection. They perform a comparative analysis of three advanced mining methods: support vector machines, multivariate adaptive regression splines, and linear genetic programs. Overall, they found that the three methods performed similarly on the intrusion detection problem. However, they also found that a significant increase in performance was possible using feature selection, where the above three mining methods were used to rank features by relevance. Their conclusions are empirically validated using the DARPA intrusion detection benchmark database.

One scenario affecting the above methods for mining complex data is the increasing likelihood that data will be collected via a continuous stream. In Chapter 12, Gaber, Krishnaswamy and Zaslavsky present a theoretical framework for mining algorithms applied to this scenario based on a model of on-board, resource-constrained mining. They apply their model to the task of on-board mining of data streams in sensor networks. In addition to this general framework they have also developed lightweight mining algorithms for clustering, classification and frequent itemset discovery. Their model and algorithms are empirically validated using synthetic streaming data and the resource-constrained environment of a common handheld computer.

Finally, in Chapter 13, Yang, Yan, Han and Wang also consider the task of mining data streams. They specifically focus on the constraints that the mining algorithm scan the data only once and adapt to evolving patterns present in the data stream. They develop an evolutionary classifier based on a naive Bayesian classifier and employ a train-and-test method combined with a divergence measure to detect evolving characteristics of the data stream. They perform extensive empirical testing based on synthetic data to show the efficiency and effectiveness of their approach.

In summary, the chapters on the foundations and applications of mining complex data provide a representative selection of the available methods and their evaluation in real domains. While the field is rapidly evolving into new algorithms and new types of complex data, these chapters clearly indicate the importance and potential benefit of developing such algorithms to mine complex data. The book may be used either in a graduate level course as part of the subject of data mining, or as a reference book for research workers working in different aspects of mining complex data.

We take this opportunity to thank all the authors for contributing chapters related to their current research work that provide the state of the art in advanced methods for mining complex data. We are grateful to Mr S. Santra of Machine Intelligence Unit, Indian Statistical Institute, Kolkata, India, for providing technical assistance during the preparation of the final manuscript. Finally, a vote of thanks to Ms Catherine Drury of Springer Verlag London Ltd. for her initiative and constant support.

January, 2005

Sanghamitra Bandyopadhyay
Ujjwal Maulik
Lawrence B. Holder
Diane J. Cook

Part I

Foundations

1

Knowledge Discovery and Data Mining

Sanghamitra Bandyopadhyay and Ujjwal Maulik

Summary. Knowledge discovery and data mining has recently emerged as an important research direction for extracting useful information from vast repositories of data of various types. This chapter discusses some of the basic concepts and issues involved in this process with special emphasis on different data mining tasks. The major challenges in data mining are mentioned. Finally, the recent trends in data mining are described and an extensive bibliography is provided.

1.1 Introduction

The sheer volume and variety of data that is routinely being collected as a consequence of widespread automation is mind-boggling. With the advantage of being able to store and retain immense amounts of data in easily accessible form comes the challenge of being able to integrate the data and make sense out of it. Needless to say, this raw data potentially stores a huge amount of information, which, if utilized appropriately, can be converted into knowledge, and hence wealth for the human race. Data mining (DM) and knowledge discovery (KD) are related research directions that have emerged in the recent past for tackling the problem of making sense out of large, complex data sets.

Traditionally, manual methods were employed to turn data into knowledge. However, sifting through huge amounts of data manually and making sense out of it is slow, expensive, subjective and prone to errors. Hence the need to automate the process arose; thereby leading to research in the fields of data mining and knowledge discovery. Knowledge discovery from databases (KDD) evolved as a research direction that appears at the intersection of research in databases, machine learning, pattern recognition, statistics, artificial intelligence, reasoning with uncertainty, expert systems, information retrieval, signal processing, high performance computing and networking.

Data stored in massive repositories is no longer only numeric, but could be graphical, pictorial, symbolic, textual and linked. Typical examples of some such domains are the world-wide web, geoscientific data, VLSI chip layout and routing, multimedia, and time series data as in financial markets. More-over, the data may be very high-dimensional as in the case of text/document representation. Data pertaining to the same object is often stored in different forms. For example, biologists routinely sequence proteins and store them in files in a symbolic form, as a string of amino acids. The same protein may also be stored in another file in the form of individual atoms along with their three dimensional co-ordinates. All these factors, by themselves or when taken to-gether, increase the complexity of the data, thereby making the development of advanced techniques for mining complex data imperative. A cross-sectional view of some recent approaches employing advanced methods for knowledge discovery from complex data is provided in the different chapters of this book. For the convenience of the reader, the present chapter is devoted to the de-scription of the basic concepts and principles of data mining and knowledge discovery, and the research issues and challenges in this domain. Recent trends in KDD are also mentioned.

1.2 Steps in the Process of Knowledge Discovery

Essentially, the task of knowledge discovery can be classified into data prepa-ration, data mining and knowledge presentation. Data mining is the core step where the algorithms for extracting the useful and interesting patterns are applied. In this sense, data preparation and knowledge presentation can be considered, respectively, to be preprocessing and postprocessing steps of data mining. Figure 1.1 presents a schematic view of the steps involved in the pro-cess of knowledge discovery. The different issues pertaining to KDD are now described.

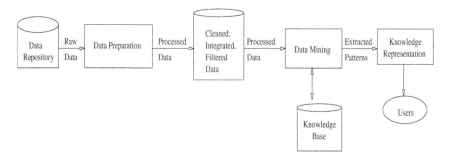

Fig. 1.1. The knowledge discovery process.

1.2.1 Database Theory and Data Warehousing

An integral part of KDD is the database theory that provides the necessary tools to store, access and manipulate data. In the data preparation step, the data is first cleaned to reduce noisy, erroneous and missing data as far as possible. The different sub tasks of the data preparation step are often performed iteratively by utilizing the knowledge gained in the earlier steps in the subsequent phases. Once the data is cleaned, it may need to be integrated since there could be multiple sources of the data. After integration, further redundancy removal may need to be carried out. The cleaned and integrated data is stored in databases or data warehouses.

Data warehousing [40, 66] refers to the tasks of collecting and cleaning transactional data to make them available for online analytical processing (OLAP). A data warehouse includes [66]:

- Cleaned and integrated data: This allows the miner to easily look across vistas of data without bothering about matters such as data standardization, key determination, tackling missing values and so on.
- Detailed and summarized data: Detailed data is necessary when the miner is interested in looking at the data in its most granular form and is necessary for extracting important patterns. Summary data is important for a miner to learn about the patterns in the data that have already been extracted by someone else. Summarized data ensures that the miner can build on the work of others rather than building everything from scratch.
- Historical data: This helps the miner in analyzing past trends/seasonal variations and gaining insights into the current data.
- Metadata: This is used by the miner to describe the context and the meaning of the data.

It is important to note that data mining can be performed without the presence of a data warehouse, though data warehouses greatly improve the efficiency of data mining. Since databases often constitute the repository of data that has to be mined, it is important to study how the current database management system (DBMS) capabilities may be utilized and/or enhanced for efficient mining [64].

As a first step, it is necessary to develop efficient algorithms for implementing machine learning tools on top of large databases and utilizing the existing DBMS support. The implementation of classification algorithms such as C4.5 or neural networks on top of a large database requires tighter coupling with the database system and intelligent use of coupling techniques [53, 64]. For example, clustering may require efficient implementation of the nearest neighbor algorithms on top of large databases.

In addition to developing algorithms that can work on top of existing DBMS, it is also necessary to develop new knowledge and data discovery management systems (KDDMS) to manage KDD systems [64]. For this it is necessary to define KDD objects that may be far more complex than database objects (records or tuples), and queries that are more general than SQL and that can operate on the complex objects. Here, KDD objects may be rules, classifiers or a clustering [64]. The KDD objects may be pre-generated (e.g., as a set of rules) or may be generated at run time (e.g., a clustering of the data objects). KDD queries may now involve predicates that can return a classifier, rule or clustering as well as database objects such as records or tuples. Moreover, KDD queries should satisfy the concept of closure of a query language as a basic design paradigm. This means that a KDD query may take as argument another compatible type of KDD query. Also KDD queries should be able to operate on both KDD objects and database objects. An example of such a KDD query may be [64]: "Generate a classifier trained on a user defined training set generated though a database query with user defined attributes and user specified classification categories. Then find all records in the database that are wrongly classified using that classifier and use that set as training data for another classifier." Some attempts in this direction may be found in [65, 120].

1.2.2 Data Mining

Data mining is formally defined as the process of discovering *interesting, previously unknown* and *potentially useful* patterns from large amounts of data. Patterns discovered could be of different types such as associations, subgraphs, changes, anomalies and significant structures. It is to be noted that the terms *interesting* and *potentially useful* are relative to the problem and the concerned user. A piece of information may be of immense value to one user and absolutely useless to another. Often data mining and knowledge discovery are treated as synonymous, while there exists another school of thought which considers data mining to be an integral step in the process of knowledge discovery.

Data mining techniques mostly consist of three components [40]: a model, a preference criterion and a search algorithm. The most common model functions in current data mining techniques include classification, clustering, regression, sequence and link analysis and dependency modeling. Model representation determines both the flexibility of the model for representing the underlying data and the interpretability of the model in human terms. This includes decision trees and rules, linear and nonlinear models, example-based techniques such as NN-rule and case-based reasoning, probabilistic graphical dependency models (e.g., Bayesian network) and relational attribute models.

The preference criterion is used to determine, depending on the underlying data set, which model to use for mining, by associating some measure of goodness with the model functions. It tries to avoid overfitting of the underlying data or generating a model function with a large number of degrees of freedom. Finally, once the model and the preference criterion are selected, specification of the search algorithm is defined in terms of these along with the given data.

1.2.3 Knowledge Presentation

Presentation of the information extracted in the data mining step in a format easily understood by the user is an important issue in knowledge discovery.

Since this module communicates between the users and the knowledge discovery step, it goes a long way in making the entire process more useful and effective. Important components of the knowledge presentation step are data visualization and knowledge representation techniques. Presenting the information in a hierarchical manner is often very useful for the user to focus attention on only the important and interesting concepts. This also enables the users to *see* the discovered patterns at multiple levels of abstraction. Some possible ways of knowledge presentation include:

- rule and natural language generation,
- tables and cross tabulations,
- graphical representation in the form of bar chart, pie chart and curves,
- data cube view representation, and
- decision trees.

The following section describes some of the commonly used tasks in data mining.

1.3 Tasks in Data Mining

Data mining comprises the algorithms employed for extracting patterns from the data. In general, data mining tasks can be classified into two categories, descriptive and predictive [54]. The descriptive techniques provide a summary of the data and characterize its general properties. The predictive techniques learn from the current data in order to make predictions about the behavior of new data sets. The commonly used tasks in data mining are described below.

1.3.1 Association Rule Mining

The root of the association rule mining problem lies in the market basket or transaction data analysis. A lot of information is hidden in the thousands of transactions taking place daily in supermarkets. A typical example is that if a customer buys butter, bread is almost always purchased at the same time. Association analysis is the discovery of rules showing attribute–value associations that occur frequently.

Let $I = \{i_1, i_2, \ldots, i_n\}$ be a set of n items and X be an itemset where $X \subset I$. A k-itemset is a set of k items. Let $T = \{(t_1, X_1), (t_2, X_2) \ldots, (t_m, X_m)\}$ be a set of m transactions, where t_i and X_i, $i = 1, 2, \ldots, m$, are the transaction identifier and the associated itemset respectively. The *cover* of an itemset X in T is defined as follows:

$$cover(X, T) = \{t_i | (t_i, X_i) \in T, X \subset X_i\}. \tag{1.1}$$

The *support* of an itemset X in T is

$$support(X, T) = |cover(X, T)| \tag{1.2}$$

and the *frequency* of an itemset is

$$frequency(X, T) = \frac{support(X, T)}{|T|}. \tag{1.3}$$

In other words, support of an itemset X is the number of transactions where all the items in X appear in each transaction. The frequency of an itemset represents the probability of its occurrence in a transaction in T. An itemset is called frequent if its support in T is greater than some threshold min_sup. The collection of frequent itemsets with respect to a minimum support min_sup in T, denoted by $\mathcal{F}(T, min\_sup)$ is defined as

$$\mathcal{F}(T, min\_sup) = \{X \subset I, support(X, T) > min\_sup\}. \tag{1.4}$$

The objective in association rule mining is to find all rules of the form $X \Rightarrow Y$, $X \bigcap Y = \emptyset$ with probability $c\%$, indicating that if itemset X occurs in a transaction, the itemset Y also occurs with probability $c\%$. X is called the *antecedent* of the rule and Y is called the *consequent* of the rule. Support of a rule denotes the percentage of transactions in T that contains both X and Y. This is taken to be the probability $P(X \bigcup Y)$. An association rule is called *frequent* if its support exceeds a minimum value min_sup.

The confidence of a rule $X \Rightarrow Y$ in T denotes the percentage of the transactions in T containing X that also contains Y. It is taken to be the conditional probability $P(X|Y)$. In other words,

$$confidence(X \Rightarrow Y, T) = \frac{support(X \bigcup Y, T)}{support(X, T)}. \tag{1.5}$$

A rule is called *confident* if its confidence value exceeds a threshold min_conf. The problem of association rule mining can therefore be formally stated as follows: *Find the set of all rules R of the form $X \Rightarrow Y$ such that*

$$R = \{ X \Rightarrow Y | X, Y \subset I, X \bigcap Y = \emptyset, X \bigcup Y = \mathcal{F}(T, min\_sup),$$
$$confidence(X \Rightarrow Y, T) > min\_conf\}. \tag{1.6}$$

Other than support and confidence measures, there are other measures of interestingness associated with association rules. Tan *et al.* [125] have presented an overview of various measures proposed in statistics, machine learning and data mining literature in this regard.

The association rule mining process, in general, consists of two steps:

1. Find all frequent itemsets,
2. Generate strong association rules from the frequent itemsets.

Although this is the general framework adopted in most of the research in association rule mining [50, 60], there is another approach to immediately generate a large subset of all association rules [132].

The task of generating frequent itemsets is a challenging issue due to the huge number of itemsets that must be considered. The number of itemsets grows exponentially with the number of items $|I|$. A commonly used algorithm for generating frequent itemsets is the *Apriori* algorithm [3, 4]. It is based on the observation that if an itemset is frequent, then all its possible subsets are also frequent. Or, in other words, if even one subset of an itemset X is not frequent, then X cannot be frequent. Thus starting from all 1 itemsets, and proceeding in a recursive fashion, if any itemset X is not frequent, then that branch of the tree is pruned, since any possible superset of X can never be frequent. Chapter 9 describes an approach based on the *Apriori* algorithm for mining association rules from resource description framework documents, which is a data modeling language proposed by the World Wide Web Consortium (W3C) for describing and interchanging metadata about web resources.

1.3.2 Classification

A typical pattern recognition system consists of three phases. These are *data acquisition, feature extraction* and *classification*. In the data acquisition phase, depending on the environment within which the objects are to be classified, data are gathered using a set of sensors. These are then passed on to the feature extraction phase, where the dimensionality of the data is reduced by measuring/retaining only some characteristic features or properties. In a broader perspective, this stage significantly influences the entire recognition process. Finally, in the classification phase, the extracted features are passed on to the classifier that evaluates the incoming information and makes a final decision. This phase basically establishes a transformation between the features and the classes.

The problem of classification is basically one of partitioning the feature space into regions, one region for each category of input. Thus it attempts to assign every data point in the entire feature space to one of the possible (say, k) classes. Classifiers are usually, but not always, designed with labeled data, in which case these problems are sometimes referred to as *supervised classification* (where the parameters of a classifier function D are learned). Some common examples of the *supervised* pattern classification techniques are the nearest neighbor (NN) rule, Bayes maximum likelihood classifier and perceptron rule [7, 8, 31, 36, 45, 46, 47, 52, 105, 127]. Figure 1.2 provides a block diagram showing the supervised classification process. Some of the related classification techniques are described below.

NN Rule [36, 46, 127]

Let us consider a set of n pattern points of known classification $\{\mathbf{x}_1, \mathbf{x}_2, \ldots, \mathbf{x}_n\}$, where it is assumed that each pattern belongs to one of the classes $C_1, C_2, \ldots, C_k$. The NN classification rule then assigns a pattern $\mathbf{x}$ of unknown classification to the class of its nearest neighbor, where $\mathbf{x}_i \in \{\mathbf{x}_1, \mathbf{x}_2, \ldots, \mathbf{x}_n\}$ is defined to be the nearest neighbor of $\mathbf{x}$ if

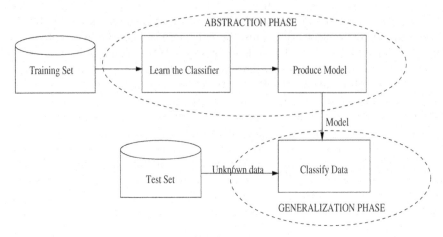

Fig. 1.2. The supervised classification process.

$$D(\mathbf{x}_i, \mathbf{x}) = \min_l\{D(\mathbf{x}_l, \mathbf{x})\}, \qquad l = 1, 2, \ldots, n \qquad (1.7)$$

where D is any distance measure definable over the pattern space.

Since the aforesaid scheme employs the class label of only the nearest neighbor to $\mathbf{x}$, this is known as the 1-NN rule. If k neighbors are considered for classification, then the scheme is termed as the k-NN rule. The k-NN rule assigns a pattern $\mathbf{x}$ of unknown classification to class C_i if the majority of the k nearest neighbors belongs to class C_i. The details of the k-NN rule along with the probability of error is available in [36, 46, 127].

The k-NN rule suffers from two severe limitations. Firstly, all the n training points need to be stored for classification and, secondly, n distance computations are required for computing the nearest neighbors. Some attempts at alleviating the problem may be found in [14].

Bayes Maximum Likelihood Classifier [7, 127]
In most of the practical problems, the features are usually noisy and the classes in the feature space are overlapping. In order to model such systems, the feature values $x_1, x_2, \ldots, x_j, \ldots, x_N$ are considered as random values in the probabilistic approach. The most commonly used classifier in such probabilistic systems is the Bayes maximum likelihood classifier, which is now described.

Let P_i denote the *a priori* probability and $p_i(\mathbf{x})$ denote the class conditional density corresponding to the class C_i ($i = 1, 2, \ldots, k$). If the classifier decides $\mathbf{x}$ to be from the class C_i, when it actually comes from C_l, it incurs a loss equal to L_{li}. The expected loss (also called the conditional average loss or risk) incurred in assigning an observation $\mathbf{x}$ to the class C_i is given by

$$r_i(\mathbf{x}) = \sum_{l=1}^{k} L_{li}\, p(C_l/\mathbf{x}), \qquad (1.8)$$

where $p(C_l/\mathbf{x})$ represents the probability that $\mathbf{x}$ is from C_l. Using Bayes formula, Equation (1.8) can be written as,

$$r_i(\mathbf{x}) = \frac{1}{p(\mathbf{x})} \sum_{l=1}^{k} L_{li}\, p_l(\mathbf{x}) P_l, \qquad (1.9)$$

where

$$p(\mathbf{x}) = \sum_{l=1}^{k} p_l(\mathbf{x}) P_l.$$

The pattern $\mathbf{x}$ is assigned to the class with the smallest expected loss. The classifier which minimizes the total expected loss is called the *Bayes classifier*.

Let us assume that the loss (L_{li}) is zero for correct decision and greater than zero but the same for all erroneous decisions. In such situations, the expected loss, Equation (1.9), becomes

$$r_i(\mathbf{x}) = 1 - \frac{P_i p_i(\mathbf{x})}{p(\mathbf{x})}. \qquad (1.10)$$

Since $p(\mathbf{x})$ is not dependent upon the class, the Bayes decision rule is nothing but the implementation of the decision functions

$$D_i(\mathbf{x}) = P_i p_i(\mathbf{x}), \qquad i = 1, 2, \ldots, k, \qquad (1.11)$$

where a pattern $\mathbf{x}$ is assigned to class C_i if $D_i(\mathbf{x}) > D_l(\mathbf{x})$, $\forall l \neq i$. This decision rule provides the minimum probability of error. It is to be noted that if the *a priori* probabilities and the class conditional densities are estimated from a given data set, and the Bayes decision rule is implemented using these estimated values (which may be different from the actual values), then the resulting classifier is called the *Bayes maximum likelihood classifier*.

Assuming normal (Gaussian) distribution of patterns, with mean vector μ_i and covariance matrix $\sum_i$, the Gaussian density $p_i(\mathbf{x})$ may be written as

$$p_i(\mathbf{x}) = \frac{1}{(2\pi)^{\frac{N}{2}} |\sum_i|^{\frac{1}{2}}} \exp\left[-\frac{1}{2}(\mathbf{x} - \mu_i)' \sum_i{}^{-1} (\mathbf{x} - \mu_i) \right], \qquad (1.12)$$

$$i = 1, 2, \ldots, k.$$

Then, $D_i(\mathbf{x})$ becomes (taking log)

$$D_i(\mathbf{x}) = \ln P_i - \tfrac{1}{2}\ln|\sum_i| - \frac{1}{2}(\mathbf{x} - \mu_i)' \sum_i{}^{-1}(\mathbf{x} - \mu_i) \qquad (1.13)$$

$$i = 1, 2, \ldots, k$$

Note that the decision functions in Equation (1.13) are hyperquadrics, since no terms higher than the second degree in the components of **x** appear in it. It can thus be stated that the Bayes maximum likelihood classifier for normal distribution of patterns provides a second-order decision surface between each pair of pattern classes. An important point to be mentioned here is that if the pattern classes are truly characterized by normal densities, then, on average, no other surface can yield better results. In fact, the Bayes classifier designed over known probability distribution functions, provides, on average, the best performance for data sets which are drawn according to the distribution. In such cases, no other classifier can provide better performance, on average, because the Bayes classifier gives minimum probability of misclassification over all decision rules.

Decision Trees

A decision tree is an acyclic graph, of which each internal node, branch and leaf node represents a test on a feature, an outcome of the test and classes or class distribution, respectively. It is easy to convert any decision tree into classification rules. Once the training data points are available, a decision tree can be constructed from them from top to bottom using a recursive divide and conquer algorithm. This process is also known as decision tree induction. A version of ID3 [112] , a well known decision-tree induction algorithm, is described below.

Decision_tree_induction (training data points, features)

1. Create a node N.
2. If all training data points belong to the same class (C) then return N as a leaf node labelled with class C.
3. If cardinality (features) is NULL then return N as a leaf node with the class label of the majority of the points in the training data set.
4. Select a feature (F) corresponding to the highest information gain label node N with F.
5. For each known value f_i of F, partition the data points as s_i.
6. Generate a branch from node N with the condition feature = f_i.
7. If s_i is empty then attach a leaf labeled with the most common class in the data points.
8. Else attach the node returned by Decision_tree_induction(s_i,(features-F)).

The information gain of a feature is measured in the following way. Let the training data set (D) have n points with k distinct class labels. Moreover, let n_i be the number of data points belonging to class C_i (for $i = 1, 2, \ldots, k$). The expected information needed to classify the training data set is

$$I(n_1, n_2, \ldots, n_k) = -\sum_{i=1}^{k} p_i \log_b(p_i) \qquad (1.14)$$

where p_i $(= \frac{n_i}{n})$ is the probability that a randomly selected data point belongs to class C_i. In case the information is encoded in binary the base b of the log function is set to 2. Let the feature space be d-dimensional, i.e., F has d distance values $\{f_1, f_2, \ldots, f_d\}$, and this is used to partition the data points D into s subsets $\{D_1, D_2, \ldots, D_s\}$. Moreover, let n_{ij} be the number of data points of class C_i in a subset D_j. The entropy or expected information based on the partition by F is given by

$$E(A) = \sum_{j=1}^{s} (\frac{n_{1j}, n_{2j} \ldots n_{kj}}{n}) I(n_{1j}, n_{2j} \ldots n_{kj}), \qquad (1.15)$$

where

$$I(n_{1j}, n_{2j} \ldots n_{kj}) = -\sum_{j=1}^{j=k} p_{ij} log_b(p_{ij}). \qquad (1.16)$$

Here, p_{ij} is the probability that a data point in D_i belongs to class C_i. The corresponding information gain by branching on F is given by

$$Gain(F) = I(n_1, n_2, \ldots, n_k) - E(A). \qquad (1.17)$$

The ID3 algorithm finds out the feature corresponding to the highest information gain and chooses it as the test feature. Subsequently a node labelled with this feature is created. For each value of the attribute, branches are generated and accordingly the data points are partitioned.

Due to the presence of noise or outliers some of the branches of the decision tree may reflect anomalies causing the overfitting of the data. In these circumstances tree-pruning techniques are used to remove the least reliable branches, which allows better classification accuracy as well as convergence.

For classifying unknown data, the feature values of the data point are tested against the constructed decision tree. Consequently a path is traced from the root to the leaf node that holds the class prediction for the test data.

Other Classification Approaches
Some other classification approaches are based on learning classification rules, Bayesian belief networks [68], neural networks [30, 56, 104], genetic algorithms [17, 18, 19, 20, 21, 100] and support vector machines [29]. In Chapter 2, a novel binary hierarchical classifier is built for tackling data that is high-dimensional in both the attributes and class values. Here, the set of classes is decomposed into smaller partitions and a two-class learning problem between each partition is performed. The simpler two-class learning problem often allows a reduction in the dimensionality of the attribute space.

1.3.3 Regression

Regression is a technique used to learn the relationship between one or more independent (or, *predictor*) variables and a dependent (or, *criterion*) variable.

The simplest form of regression is linear regression where the relationship is modeled with a a straight line learned using the training data points as follows.

Let us assume that for the input vector X $(x_1, x_2, \ldots, x_n)$ (known as the predictor variable), the value of the vector Y (known as the response variable) $(y_1, y_2, \ldots, y_n)$ is known. A straight line through the vectors X, Y can be modeled as $Y = \alpha + \beta X$ where α and β are the regression coefficients and slope of the line, computed as

$$\beta = \frac{\sum_{i=1}^{n}(x_i - x^*)(y_i - y^*)}{\sum_{i=1}^{n}(x_i - x^*)^2} \tag{1.18}$$

$$\alpha = y^* - \beta x^* \tag{1.19}$$

where x^* and y^* are the average of $(x_1, x_2, \ldots, x_n)$ and $(y_1, y_2, \ldots, y_n)$.

An extension of linear regression which involves more than one predictor variable is multiple regression. Here a response variable can be modeled as a linear function of a multidimensional feature vector. For example

$$Y = \alpha + \beta_1 X_i + \beta_2 X_2 + \ldots + \beta_n X_n \tag{1.20}$$

is a multiple regression model based on n predictor variables $(X_1, X_2, \ldots X_n)$. For evaluating α, β_1 and β_2, the least square method can be applied.

Data having nonlinear dependence may be modeled using polynomial regression. This is done by adding polynomial terms to the basic linear model. Transformation can be applied to the variable to convert the nonlinear model into a linear one. Subsequently it can be solved using the method of least square. For example consider the following polynomial

$$Y = \alpha + \beta_1 X + \beta_2 X^2 + \ldots + \beta_n X^n \tag{1.21}$$

The above polynomial can be converted to the following linear form by defining the new variables $X_1 = X, X_2 = X^2, \ldots, X_n = X^n$ and can be solved using the method of least squares.

$$Y = \alpha + \beta_1 X_1 + \beta_2 X_2 + \ldots + \beta_n X_n \tag{1.22}$$

1.3.4 Cluster Analysis

When the only data available are unlabelled, the classification problems are sometimes referred to as *unsupervised classification*. Clustering [6, 31, 55, 67, 127] is an important unsupervised classification technique where a set of patterns, usually vectors in a multidimensional space, are grouped into clusters in such a way that patterns in the same cluster are similar in some sense and patterns in different clusters are dissimilar in the same sense. For this it is necessary to first define a measure of similarity which will establish a rule for assigning patterns to a particular cluster. One such measure of similarity may be the Euclidean distance $\mathbf{D}$ between two patterns $\mathbf{x}$ and $\mathbf{z}$ defined by $\mathbf{D} = \|\mathbf{x} - \mathbf{z}\|$. The smaller the distance between $\mathbf{x}$ and $\mathbf{z}$, the greater is the similarity between the two and vice versa.

Clustering in N-dimensional Euclidean space $I\!\!R^N$ is the process of partitioning a given set of n points into a number, say K, of groups (or, clusters) based on some similarity/dissimilarity metric. Let the set of n points $\{\mathbf{x}_1, \mathbf{x}_2, \ldots, \mathbf{x}_n\}$ be represented by the set S and the K clusters be represented by $C_1, C_2, \ldots, C_K$. Then

$$C_i \neq \emptyset \qquad for\ i = 1, \ldots, K,$$
$$C_i \cap C_j = \emptyset \quad for\ i = 1, \ldots, K, \quad j = 1, \ldots, K \text{ and } i \neq j, \text{ and}$$
$$\textstyle\bigcup_{i=1}^{K} C_i = S.$$

Clustering techniques may be hierarchical or non-hierarchical [6]. In hierarchical clustering, the clusters are generated in a hierarchy, where every level of the hierarchy provides a particular clustering of the data, ranging from a single cluster (where all the points are put in the same cluster) to n clusters (where each point comprises a cluster). Among the non-hierarchical clustering techniques, the K-means algorithm [127] has been one of the more widely used ones; it consists of the following steps:

1. Choose K initial cluster centers $\mathbf{z}_1, \mathbf{z}_2, \ldots, \mathbf{z}_K$ randomly from the n points $\{\mathbf{x}_1, \mathbf{x}_2, \ldots, \mathbf{x}_n\}$.
2. Assign point $\mathbf{x}_i, \quad i = 1, 2, \ldots, n$ to cluster $C_j, j \in \{1, 2, \ldots, K\}$ iff

$$\|\mathbf{x}_i - \mathbf{z}_j\| < \|\mathbf{x}_i - \mathbf{z}_p\|, \quad p = 1, 2, \ldots, K, \text{ and } j \neq p.$$

   Ties are resolved arbitrarily.
3. Compute new cluster centers $\mathbf{z}_1^*, \mathbf{z}_2^*, \ldots, \mathbf{z}_K^*$ as follows :

$$\mathbf{z}_i^* = \frac{1}{n_i} \Sigma_{x_j \in C_i} \mathbf{x}_j \quad i = 1, 2, \ldots, K,$$

   where n_i is the number of elements belonging to cluster C_i.
4. If $\mathbf{z}_i^* = \mathbf{z}_i, \quad i = 1, 2, \ldots, K$ then terminate. Otherwise continue from Step 2.

Note that if the process does not terminate at Step 4 normally, then it is executed for a maximum fixed number of iterations.

It has been shown in [119] that the K-means algorithm may converge to values that are not optimal. Also global solutions of large problems cannot be found within a reasonable amount of computation effort [122]. It is because of these factors that several approximate methods, including genetic algorithms and simulated annealing [15, 16, 91], are developed to solve the underlying optimization problem. These methods have also been extended to the case where the number of clusters is variable [13, 92], and to fuzzy clustering [93].

The K-means algorithm is known to be sensitive to outliers, since such points can significantly affect the computation of the centroid, and hence the resultant partitioning. K-medoid attempts to alleviate this problem by using the medoid, the most centrally located object, as the representative of the cluster. Partitioning around medoid (PAM) [75] was one of the earliest K-medoid algorithms introduced. PAM finds K clusters by first finding a representative object for each cluster, the medoid. The algorithm then repeatedly tries to make a better choice of medoids analyzing all possible pairs of objects such that one object is a medoid and the other is not. PAM is computationally quite inefficient for large data sets and large number of clusters. The CLARA algorithm was proposed by the same authors [75] to tackle this problem. CLARA is based on data sampling, where only a small portion of the real data is chosen as a representative of the data and medoids are chosen from this sample using PAM. CLARA draws multiple samples and outputs the best clustering from these samples. As expected, CLARA can deal with larger data sets than PAM. However, if the best set of medoids is never chosen in any of the data samples, CLARA will never find the best clustering. Ng and Han [96] proposed the CLARANS algorithm which tries to mix both PAM and CLARA by searching only the subset of the data set. However, unlike CLARA, CLARANS does not confine itself to any sample at any given time, but draws it randomly at each step of the algorithm. Based upon CLARANS, two spatial data mining algorithms, the spatial dominant approach, SD(CLARANS), and the nonspatial dominant approach, NSD(CLARANS), were developed. In order to make CLARANS applicable to large data sets, use of efficient spatial access methods, such as R*-tree, was proposed [39]. CLARANS had a limitation that it could provide good clustering only when the clusters were mostly equisized and convex. DBSCAN [38], another popularly used density clustering technique that was proposed by Ester *et al.*, could handle nonconvex and non-uniformly-sized clusters. Balanced Iterative Reducing and Clustering using Hierarchies (BIRCH), proposed by Zhang *et al.* [138], is another algorithm for clustering large data sets. It uses two concepts, the clustering feature and the clustering feature tree, to summarize cluster representations which help the method achieve good speed and scalability in large databases. Discussion on several other clustering algorithms may be found in [54].

Deviation Detection

Deviation detection, an inseparably important part of KDD, deals with identifying if and when the present data changes significantly from previously measured or normative data. This is also known as the process of detection of outliers. Outliers are those patterns that are distinctly different from the normal, frequently occurring, patterns, based on some measurement. Such deviations are generally infrequent or rare. Depending on the domain, deviations may be just some noisy observations that often mislead the standard classification or clustering algorithms, and hence should be eliminated. Alternatively, they may become more valuable than the average data set because they contain useful information on the abnormal behavior of the system, described by the data set.

The wide range of applications of outlier detection include fraud detection, customized marketing, detection of criminal activity in e-commerce, network intrusion detection, and weather prediction. The different approaches for outlier detection can be broadly categorized into three types [54]:

- Statistical approach: Here, the data distribution or the probability model of the data set is considered as the primary factor.
- Distance-based approach: The classical definition of an outlier in this context is: An object O in a data set T is a $DB(p, D)$-outlier if at least fraction p of the objects in T lies greater than distance D from O [77].
- Deviation-based approach: Deviation from the main characteristics of the objects are basically considered here. Objects that "deviate" from the description are treated as outliers.

Some algorithms for outlier detection in data mining applications may be found in [2, 115].

1.3.5 Major Issues and Challenges in Data Mining

In this section major issues and challenges in data mining regarding underlying data types, mining techniques, user interaction and performance are described [54].

Issues Related to the Underlying Data Types

- *Complex and high dimensional data*
  Databases with very large number of records having high dimensionality (large numbers of attributes) are quite common. Moreover, these databases may contain complex data objects such as, hypertext and multimedia, graphical data, transaction data, and spatial and temporal data. Consequently mining these data may require exploring combinatorially explosive search space and may sometimes result in spurious patterns. Therefore, it is important that the algorithms developed for data mining tasks are very efficient and can also exploit the advantages of techniques such as dimensionality reduction, sampling, approximation methods, incorporation of domain specific prior knowledge, etc. Moreover, it is essential to develop different techniques for mining different databases, given the diversity of the data types and the goals. Some such approaches are described in different chapters of this book. For example,
  - hybridization of several computational intelligence techniques for feature selection from high-dimensional intrusion detection data is described in Chapter 11,

- complex data that is modeled as a sequence of discrete multi-attribute records is tackled in Chapter 6, with two real applications, viz., address cleaning and information extraction from websites,
- mining complex data represented as graphs forms the core of Chapters 3, 4 and 7, and
- tree mining is dealt with in Chapters 5 and 8.

- *Missing, incomplete and noisy data*
Sometime data stored in a database either may not have a few important attributes or may have noisy values. These can result from operator error, actual system and measurement failure, or from a revision of the data collection process. These incomplete or noisy objects may confuse the mining process causing the model to overfit/underfit the data. As a result, the accuracy of the discovered patterns can be poor. Data cleaning techniques, more sophisticated statistical methods to identify hidden attributes and their dependencies, as well as techniques for identifying outliers are therefore required.

- *Handling changing data and knowledge*
Situations where the data set is changing rapidly (e.g., time series data or data obtained from sensors deployed in real-life situations) may make previously discovered patterns invalid. Moreover, the variables measured in a given application database may be modified, deleted or augmented with time. Incremental learning techniques are required to handle these types of data.

Issues Related to Data Mining Techniques

- *Parallel and distributed algorithms*
The very large size of the underlying databases, the complex nature of the data and their distribution motivated researchers to develop parallel and distributed data mining algorithms.

- *Problem characteristics*
Though a number of data mining algorithms have been developed, there is none that is equally applicable to a wide variety of data sets and can be called the universally best data mining technique. For example, there exist a number of classification algorithms such as decision-tree classifiers, nearest-neighbor classifiers, neural networks, etc. When the data is high-dimensional with a mixture of continuous and categorical attributes, decision-tree-based classifiers may be a good choice. However they may not be suitable when the true decision boundaries are nonlinear multivariate functions. In such cases, neural networks and probabilistic models may be a better choice. Thus, the particular data mining algorithm chosen is critically dependent on the problem domain.

Issues Related to Extracted Knowledge

- *Mining different types of knowledge*

Different users may be interested in different kinds of knowledge from the same underlying database. Therefore, it is essential that the data mining method allows a wide range of data analysis and knowledge discovery tasks such as data characterization, classification and clustering.

- *Understandability of the discovered patterns*
  In most of the applications, it is important to represent the discovered patterns in more human understandable form such as natural language, visual representation, graphical representation, rule structuring. This requires the mining techniques to adopt more sophisticated knowledge representation techniques such as rules, trees, tables, graphs, etc.

Issues Related to User Interaction and Prior Knowledge

- *User interaction*
  The knowledge discovery process is interactive and iterative in nature as sometimes it is difficult to estimate exactly what can be discovered from a database. User interaction helps the mining process to focus the search patterns, appropriately sampling and refining the data. This in turn results in better performance of the data mining algorithm in terms of discovered knowledge as well as convergence.
- *Incorporation of* a priori knowledge
  Incorporation of *a priori* domain-specific knowledge is important in all phases of a knowledge discovery process. This knowledge includes integrity constraints, rules for deduction, probabilities over data and distribution, number of classes, etc. This *a priori* knowledge helps with better convergence of the data mining search as well as the quality of the discovered patterns.

Issues Related to Performance of the Data Mining Techniques

- *Scalability*
  Data mining algorithms must be scalable in the size of the underlying data, meaning both the number of patterns and the number of attributes. The size of data sets to be mined is usually huge, and hence it is necessary either to design faster algorithms or to partition the data into several subsets, executing the algorithms on the smaller subsets, and possibly combining the results [111].
- *Efficiency and accuracy*
  Efficiency and accuracy of a data mining technique is a key issue. Data mining algorithms must be very efficient such that the time required to extract the knowledge from even a very large database is predictable and acceptable. Moreover, the accuracy of the mining system needs to be better than or as good as the acceptable range.

- *Ability to deal with minority classes*
  Data mining techniques should have the capability to deal with minority
  or low-probability classes whose occurrence in the data may be rare.

1.4 Recent Trends in Knowledge Discovery

Data mining is widely used in different application domains, where the data is
not necessarily restricted to conventional structured types, e.g., those found in
relational databases, transactional databases and data warehouses. Complex
data that are nowadays widely collected and routinely analyzed include:

- Spatial data – This type of data is often stored in Geographical Information Systems (GIS), where the spatial coordinates constitute an integral
  part of the data. Some examples of spatial data are maps, preprocessed
  remote sensing and medical image data, and VLSI chip layout. Clustering
  of geographical points into different regions characterized by the presence
  of different types of land cover, such as lakes, mountains, forests, residen-
  tial and business areas, agricultural land, is an example of spatial data
  mining.
- Multimedia data – This type of data may contain text, image, graphics,
  video clips, music and voice. Summarizing an article, identifying the content of an image using features such as shape, size, texture and color,
  summarizing the melody and style of a music, are some examples of multimedia data mining.
- Time series data – This consists of data that is temporally varying. Examples of such data include financial/stock market data. Typical applications
  of mining time series data involve prediction of the time series at some future time point given its past history.
- Web data – The world-wide web is a vast repository of unstructured information distributed over wide geographical regions. Web data can typically
  be categorized into those that constitute the *web content* (e.g., text, images, sound clips), those that define the *web structure* (e.g., hyperlinks,
  tags) and those that monitor the *web usage* (e.g., http logs, application
  server logs). Accordingly, web mining can also be classified into web content mining, web structure mining and web usage mining.
- Biological data – DNA, RNA and proteins are the most widely studied
  molecules in biology. A large number of databases store biological data
  in different forms, such as sequences (of nucleotides and amino acids),
  atomic coordinates and microarray data (that measure the levels of gene
  expression). Finding homologous sequences, identifying the evolutionary
  relationship of proteins and clustering gene microarray data are some examples of biological data mining.

In order to deal with different types of complex problem domains, specialized algorithms have been developed that are best suited to the particular

problem that they are designed for. In the following subsections, some such complex domains and problem solving approaches, which are currently widely used, are discussed.

1.4.1 Content-based Retrieval

Sometimes users of a data mining system are interested in one or more patterns that they want to retrieve from the underlying data. These tasks, commonly known as content-based retrieval, are mostly used for text and image databases. For example, searching the web uses a page ranking technique that is based on link patterns for estimating the relative importance of different pages with respect to the current search. In general, the different issues in content-based retrieval are as follows:

- Identifying an appropriate set of features used to index an object in the database;
- Storing the objects, along with their features, in the database;
- Defining a measure of similarity between different objects;
- Given a query and the similarity measure, performing an efficient search in the database;
- Incorporating user feedback and interaction in the retrieval process.

Text Retrieval

Text retrieval is also commonly referred to as information retrieval (IR). Content-based text retrieval techniques primarily exploit the semantic content of the data as well as some distance metric between the documents and the user queries. IR has gained importance with the advent of web-based search engines which need to perform this task extensively. Though most of the users or text retrieval systems would want to retrieve documents closest in meaning to their queries (i.e., on the basis of semantic content), practical IR systems usually ignore this aspect in view of the difficulty of the problem (this is an open and extremely difficult problem in natural language processing). Instead, the IR systems typically match terms occurring in the query and the stored documents. The content of a document is generally represented as a term vector (which typically has very high dimensionality). A widely used distance measure between two term vectors V_1 and V_2 is the cosine distance, which is defined as

$$D_c(V_1, V_2) = \frac{\sum_{j=1}^{T} \sum_{i=1}^{T} v_{1i} v_{2j}}{\sqrt{\sum_{i=1}^{T} v_{1i}^2 \sum_{i=1}^{T} v_{2i}^2}}, \tag{1.23}$$

where $V_k = \{v_{k1} v_{k2} \ldots v_{kT}\}$. This represents the inner product of the two term vectors after they are normalized to have unit length, and it reflects the similarity in the relative distribution of their term components.

The term vectors may have Boolean representation where 1 indicates that the corresponding term is present in the document and 0 indicates that it is not. A significant drawback of the Boolean representation is that it cannot be used to assign a relevance ranking to the retrieved documents. Another commonly used weighting scheme is the Term Frequency–Inverse Document Frequency (TF–IDF) scheme [24]. Using TF, each component of the term vector is multiplied by the frequency of occurrence of the corresponding term. The IDF weight for the ith component of the term vector is defined as $\log(N/n_i)$, where n_i is the number of documents that contain the ith term and N is the total number of documents. The composite TF–IDF weight is the product of the TF and IDF components for a particular term. The TF term gives more importance to frequently occurring terms in a document. However, if a term occurs frequently in most of the documents in the document set then, in all probability, the term is not really that important. This is taken care of by the IDF factor.

The above schemes are based strictly on the terms occurring in the documents and are referred to as vector space representation. An alternative to this strategy is latent semantic indexing (LSI). In LSI, the dimensionality of the term vector is reduced using principal component analysis (PCA) [31, 127].

PCA is based on the notion that it may be beneficial to combine a set of features in order to obtain a single composite feature that can capture most of the variance in the data. In terms of text retrieval, this could identify the similar pattern of occurrences of terms in the documents, thereby capturing the hidden semantics of the data. For example, the terms "data mining" and "knowledge discovery" have nothing in common when using the vector space representation, but could be combined into a single principal component term since these two terms would most likely occur in a number of related documents.

Image Retrieval

Image and video data are increasing day by day; as a result content-based image retrieval is becoming very important and appealing. Developing interactive mining systems for handling queries such as *Generate the N most similar images of the query image* is a challenging task. Here image data does not necessarily mean images generated only by cameras but also images embedded in a text document as well as handwritten characters, paintings, maps, graphs, etc.

In the initial phase of an image retrieval process, the system needs to understand and extract the necessary features of the query images. Extracting the semantic contents of a query image is a challenging task and an active research area in pattern recognition and computer vision. The features of an image are generally expressed in terms of color, texture, shape. These features of the query image are computed, stored and used during retrieval. For example, QBIC (Query By Image Content) is an interactive image mining system developed by the scientists in IBM. QBIC allows the user to search a large image database with content descriptors such as color (a three-dimensional color feature vector and k-dimensional color histogram where the value of k is dependent on the application), texture (a three-dimensional texture vector with features that measure coarseness, contrast and directionality) as well as the relative position and shape (twenty-dimensional features based on area, circularity, eccentricity, axis orientation and various moments) of the query image. Subsequent to the feature-extraction process, distance calculation and retrieval are carried out in multidimensional feature space. Chapter 10 deals with the task of content-based image retrieval where features based on shape, texture and color are extracted from an image. A similarity measure based on human perception and a relevance feedback mechanism are formulated for improved retrieval accuracy.

Translations, rotations, nonlinear transformation and changes of illumination (shadows, lighting, occlusion) are common distortions in images. Any change in scale, viewing angle or illumination changes the features of the distorted version of the scene compared to the original version. Although the human visual system is able to handle these distortions easily, it is far more challenging to design image retrieval techniques that are invariant under such transformation and distortion. This requires incorporation of translation and distortion invariance into the feature space.

1.4.2 Web Mining

The web consists of a huge collection of widely distributed and inter-related files on one or more web servers. Web mining deals with the application of data mining techniques to the web for extracting interesting patterns and discovering knowledge. Web mining, though essentially an integral part of data mining, has emerged as an imporant and independent research direction due to the typical characteristics, e.g., the diversity, size, dynamic and link-based nature, of the web. Some reviews on web mining are available in [79, 87].

As already mentioned, the information contained in the web can be broadly categorized into:

- *Web content* – the component that consists of the stored facts, e.g., text, images, sound clips and structured records such as lists and tables,
- *Web structure* – the component that defines the connections within the content of the web, e.g., hyperlinks and tags, and
- *Web usage* – the components that describes the user's interaction with the web, e.g., http logs and application server logs.

Depending on which category of web data is being mined, web mining has been classified as:

- *Web content mining,*
- *Web structure mining,* or

- *Web usage mining.*

Web content mining (WCM) is the process of analyzing and extracting information from the contents of web documents. Research in this direction involves using techniques of other related fields, e.g., information retrieval, text mining, image mining, natural language processing.

In WCM, the data is preprocessed to extract text from HTML documents, eliminating the stop words, and identifying the relevant terms and computing some measures such as the term frequency (TF) and document frequency (DF). The next issue in WCM involves adopting a strategy for representing the documents in such a way that the retrieval process is facilitated. Here the common information retrieval techniques are used. The documents are generally represented as a sparse vector of term weights; additional weights are given to terms appearing in title or keywords. The common data mining techniques applied on the resulting representation of the web content are:

- Classification, where the documents are assigned to one or more exising categories,
- Clustering, where the documents are grouped based on some similarity measure (the dot product between two document vectors being the more commonly used measure of similarity), and
- Association, where association between the documents is identified.

Other issues in WCM include topic identification, tracking and drift analysis, concept hierarchy creation and computing the relevance of the web content.

In web structure mining (WSM) the structure of the web is analyzed in order to identify important patterns and inter-relations. For example, WSM may reveal information about the quality of a page, ranking, page classification according to topic and related/similar pages.

Typically, the web may be viewed as a directed graph as shown in Figure 1.3. Here the nodes represent the web pages, and the edges represent the hyperlinks. The hyperlinks contain important information which can be utilized for efficient information retrieval. For example, in Figure 1.3 the information that several hyperlinks (edges) point to page A may indicate that A is an *authority* [76] on some topic. Again, based on the structure of the web graph, it may be possible to identify web communities [41]. A web community is described as a collection of web pages, such that each member of the collection contains many more links to other members in the community than outside it.

The web pages are typically maintained on web servers, which are accessed by different users in client–server transactions. The access patterns, user profiles and other data are maintained at the servers and/or the clients. Web usage mining (WUM) deals with mining such data in order to discover meaningful patterns such as associations among the web pages and categorization of users. An example of discovered associations could be that 60% of users who accessed some site www.isical.ac.in/~sanghami, also accessed

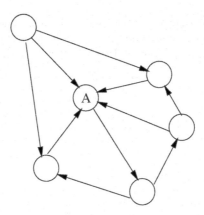

Fig. 1.3. Example of a part of the web viewed as a directed graph

www.isical.ac.in/∼sanghami/pub_pointer.htm. WUM can be effectively utilized in commercial applications, for designing new product promotions and evaluating existing ones, determining the value of clients and predicting user behavior based on users' profiles. It can also be used in reorganizing the web more rationally.

Resource Description Framework (RDF) is becoming a popular encoding language for describing and interchanging metadata of web resources. Chapter 9 describes an *Apriori*-based algorithm for mining association rules from RDF documents. User behavior analysis, distributed web mining, web visualization and web services [88, 89, 95, 124] are some of the recent research directions in web mining. Semantic webs, where the stored documents have attached semantics, are also a recent development, and hence semantic web mining is also a promising area.

1.4.3 Mining Biological Data

Over the past few decades, major advances in the field of molecular biology, coupled with advances in genomic technology, have led to an explosive growth in the biological information generated by the scientific community. Bioinformatics, viewed as the use of computational methods to make biological discoveries, has evolved as a major research direction in response to this deluge of information. The main purpose is to utilize computerized databases to store, organize and index the data and to use specialized tools to view and analyze the data. The ultimate goal of the field is to enable the discovery of new biological insights as well as to create a global perspective from which unifying principles in biology can be derived. Sequence analysis, phylogenetic/evolutionary trees, protein classification and analysis of microarray data constitute some typical problems of bioinformatics where mining techniques are required for extracting meaningful patterns. A broad classification of *some* (not all) bioinformatic tasks is provided in Figure 1.4. The mining tasks often used for biological data include clustering, classification, prediction and frequent pattern identification [130]. Applications of some data mining techniques in bioinformatics and their requirements are mentioned below.

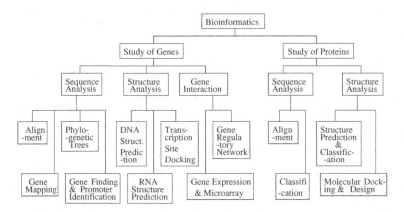

Fig. 1.4. Broad classification of certain bioinformatic tasks.

The huge amount of biological data stored in repositories distributed all around the globe is often noisy. Moreover, the same information may be stored in different formats. Therefore data preprocessing tasks such as cleaning and integration is important in this domain [130]. Clustering and classification of gene-expression profiles or microarray data is performed in order to identify the genes that may be responsible for a particular trait [22]. Determining or modeling the evolutionary history of a set of species from genomic DNA or amino acid sequences using phylogenetic trees is widely studied in bioinformatics [32]. Mining such trees to extract interesting information forms the basis of study in Chapter 8. Classification of proteins and homology modeling are two important approaches for predicting the structure of proteins, and may be useful in drug design [11, 28, 34]. Motif-based classification of proteins is also another important research direction [62]. A motif is a conserved element of a protein sequence that usually correlates with a particular function. Motifs are identified from a local multiple sequence alignment of proteins corresponding to a region whose function or structure is known. Motif identification from a number of protein sequences is another mining task that is important in bioinformatics.

Data analysis tools used earlier in bioinformatics were mainly based on statistical techniques such as regression and estimation. Recently, computational intelligence techniques such as genetic algorithms and neural networks are being widely used for solving certain bioinformatics problems with the need to handle large data sets in biology in a robust and computationally efficient manner [101, 116]. Some such techniques are discussed later in this chapter.

1.4.4 Distributed Data Mining

Sometimes the data to be mined may not be available in a centralized node; rather, it is distributed among different sites with network connections. Distributed data mining (DDM) algorithms are designed to analyse these distributed data without necessarily downloading everything to a single site, due to the following reasons:

- Network cost and traffic
  Downloading large volumes of data from different sites to a single node requires higher bandwidth of the network system with the problem of associated traffic congestion.
- Privacy preservation
  Sometimes, privacy may be a key consideration that precludes the transfer of data from one site to another. For example, credit card companies may not want to share their databases with other users, though they would want to extract meaningful and potentially useful information from the data.

In general, data may be distributed either homogeneously or heterogeneously. For a homogeneous (or heterogeneous) distributed system one can assume the whole data set is horizontally (or vertically) fragmented and the fragmented modules are kept in different sites. An example of homogeneously distributed data is a banking database where the different sites have the same attributes related to customer accounts but for different customers. An example of heterogeneously distributed data is astronomy data in which different sites observe the same region of the sky, but take readings corresponding to different properties, e.g., in different frequency bands.

In general the goal of DDM algorithms [69, 70, 73] is to analyze homogeneously or heterogeneously distributed data efficiently using the network and resources available in different sites. Several distributed algorithms have been developed in recent times. Principal component analysis is a useful technique for feature extraction that has been used successfully to design DDM algorithms [72]. In [35] a decision-tree-based classifier has been designed from distributed data. The idea of the K-means clustering algorithm has been extended for clustering distributed data [12, 37, 129].

1.4.5 Mining in Sensor and Peer-to-Peer Networks

In recent times, data that are distributed among different sites that are dispersed over a wide geographical area are becoming more and more common. In particular, sensor networks, consisting of a large number of small, inexpensive sensor devices, are gradually being deployed in many situations for monitoring the environment. The nodes of a sensor network collect time-varying streams of data, have limited computing capabilities, small memory storage, and low communication and battery power capabilities. One of the modes of communication among the nodes in a sensor network is of the peer-to-peer style. Here each node exchanges messages only with its direct neighbors. Mining in such a scenario offers many challenges, including:

- limited communication bandwidth,
- constraints on computing resources,
- limited power supply,
- the need for fault-tolerance, and
- the asynchronous nature of the network.

Chapters 12 and 13 describe some mining techniques for data streams in a sensor network scenario where memory constraints, speed and the dynamic nature of the data are taken into consideration. In designing algorithms for sensor networks, it is imperative to keep in mind that power consumption has to be minimized. Even gathering the distributed sensor data in a single site could be expensive in terms of battery power consumed. LEACH, LEACH-C, LEACH-F [58, 59], and PEGASIS [84] are some of the attempts towards making the data collection task energy efficient. The issue of the energy–quality trade-off has been studied in [121] along with a discussion on energy–quality scalability of three categories of commonly used signal-processing algorithms viz., filtering, frequency domain transforms and classification. In [114], Radivojac et al. develop an algorithm for intrusion detection in a supervised framework, where there are far more negative instances than positive (intrusions). A neural-network-based classifier is trained at the base station using data where the smaller class is over-sampled and the larger class is under-sampled [25]. An unsupervised approach to the outlier detection problem in sensor networks is presented in [103], where kernel density estimators are used to estimate the distribution of the data generated by the sensors, and then the outliers are detected depending on a distance-based criterion. Detecting regions of interesting environmental events (e.g., sensing which regions in the environment have a chemical concentration greater than a threshold) has been studied in [81] under the assumption that faults can occur in the equipment, though they would be uncorrelated, while environmental conditions are spatially correlated.

Clustering the nodes of the sensor networks is an important optimization problem. Nodes that are clustered together can easily communicate with each other. Ghiasi et al. [48] have studied the theoretical aspects of this problem with application to energy optimization. They illustrate an optimal algorithm for clustering the sensor nodes such that each cluster (that is characterized by a master) is balanced and the total distance between the sensor nodes and the master nodes is minimized. Some other approaches in this regard are available in [26, 135].

Algorithms for clustering the data spread over a sensor network are likely to play an important role in many sensor-network-based applications. Segmentation of data observed by the sensor nodes for situation awareness and detection of outliers for event detection are only two examples that may require clustering algorithms. The distributed and resource-constrained nature of the sensor networks demands a fundamentally distributed algorithmic solution to the clustering problem. Therefore, distributed clustering algorithms may come in handy [71] when it comes to analyzing sensor network data or data streams.

1.4.6 Mining Techniques Based on Soft Computing Approaches

Soft computing [137] is a consortium of methodologies that works synergistically and provides, in one form or another, flexible information processing capability for handling real-life ambiguous situations. Its aim is to exploit the tolerance for imprecision, uncertainty, approximate reasoning, and partial truth in order to achieve tractability, robustness, and low-cost solutions. The guiding principle is to devise methods of computation that lead to an *acceptable solution at low cost*, by seeking an approximate solution to an imprecisely or precisely formulated problem. In data mining, it is often impractical to expect the optimal or exact solution. Moreover, in order for the mining algorithms to be useful, they must be able to provide good solutions reasonably fast. As such, the requirements of a data mining algorithm are often found to be the same as the guiding principle of soft computing, thereby making the application of soft computing in data mining natural and appropriate.

Some of the main components of soft computing include fuzzy logic, neural networks and probabilistic reasoning, with the latter subsuming belief networks, evolutionary computation and genetic algorithms, chaos theory and parts of learning theory [1]. Rough sets, wavelets, and other optimization methods such as tabu search, simulated annealing and ant colony optimization are also considered to be components of soft computing. In the following subsections, some of the major components in the soft computing paradigm, viz., fuzzy sets, genetic algorithms and neural networks, are discussed followed by a brief description of their applications in data mining.

Fuzzy Sets

Fuzzy set theory was developed in order to handle uncertainties, arising from vague, incomplete, linguistic or overlapping patterns, in various problem-solving systems. This approach is developed based on the realization that an object may belong to more than one class, with varying degrees of class membership. Uncertainty can result from the incomplete or ambiguous input information, the imprecision in the problem definition, ill-defined and/or overlapping boundaries among the classes or regions, and the indefiniteness in defining or extracting features and relations among them.

Fuzzy sets were introduced in 1965 by Lotfi A. Zadeh [136, 137], as a way to represent vagueness in everyday life. We almost always speak in fuzzy terms, e.g., *he is more or less tall, she is very beautiful.* Hence, concepts of *tall* and *beautiful* are fuzzy, and the *gentleman* and *lady* have membership values to these fuzzy concepts indicating their degree of belongingness. Since this theory is a generalization of the classical set theory, it has greater flexibility to capture various aspects of incompleteness, imprecision or imperfection in information about a situation. It has been applied successfully in computing with words or the matching of linguistic terms for reasoning.

Fuzzy set theory has found a lot of applications in data mining [10, 107, 134]. Examples of such applications may be found in clustering [82, 106, 128], association rules [9, 133], time series [27], and image retrieval [44, 94].

Evolutionary Computation

Evolutionary computation (EC) is a computing paradigm comprising problem-solving techniques that are based on the principles of biological evolution. The essential components of EC are a strategy for representing or encoding a solution to the problem under consideration, a criterion for evaluating the fitness or goodness of an encoded solution, and a set of biologically in-spired operators applied on the encoded solutions. Because of the robustness and effectiveness of the techniques in the EC family, they have widespread applications in various engineering and scientific circles such as pattern recognition, image processing, VLSI design, and embedded and real-time systems. The commonly known techniques in EC are genetic algorithms (GAs) [51], evolutionary strategies [118] and genetic programming [80]. Of these, GAs appear to be the most well-known and widely used technique in this computing paradigm.

GAs, which are efficient, adaptive and robust search and optimization processes, use biologically-inspired operators to guide the search in very large, complex and multimodal search spaces. In GAs, the genetic information of each individual or potential solution is encoded in structures called *chromosomes*. They use some domain or problem-dependent knowledge for directing the search into more promising areas; this is known as the *fitness function*. Each individual or chromosome has an associated fitness function, which indicates its degree of goodness with respect to the solution it represents. Various biologically-inspired operators such as *selection, crossover* and *mutation* are applied on the chromosomes to yield potentially better solutions. GAs represent a form of multi-point, stochastic search in complex landscapes. Applications of genetic algorithms and related techniques in data mining include extraction of association rules [85], predictive rules [42, 43, 97], clustering [13, 15, 16, 91, 92, 93], program evolution [117, 126] and web mining [98, 99, 108, 109, 110].

Neural Networks

Neural networks can be formally defined as *massively-parallel interconnections of simple (usually adaptive) processing elements that interact with objects of the real world in a manner similar to biological systems.* Their origin can be traced to the work of Hebb [57], where a local learning rule is proposed. The benefit of neural nets lies in the high computation rate provided by their inherent massive parallelism. This allows real-time processing of huge data sets with proper hardware backing. All information is stored distributed among the various connection weights. The redundancy of interconnections produces a high degree of robustness resulting in a *graceful degradation* of performance in the case of noise or damage to a few nodes/links.

Neural network models have been studied for many years with the hope of achieving human-like performance (artificially), particularly in the field of pattern recognition, by capturing the key ingredients responsible for the remarkable capabilities of the human nervous system. Note that these models are extreme simplifications of the actual human nervous system. Some commonly used neural networks are the multi-layer perceptron, Hopfield network, Kohonen's self organizing maps and radial basis function network [56].

Neural networks have been widely used in searching for patterns in data [23] because they appear to bridge the gap between the generalization capability of human beings and the deterministic nature of computers. More important among these applications are rule generation and classification [86], clustering [5], data modeling [83], time series analysis [33, 49, 63] and visualization [78]. Neural networks may be used as a direct substitute for autocorrelation, multivariable regression, linear regression, trigonometric and other regression techniques [61, 123]. Apart from data mining tasks, neural networks have also been used for data preprocessing, such as data cleaning and handling missing values. Various applications of supervised and unsupervised neural networks to the analysis of the gene expression profiles produced using DNA microarrays has been studied in [90]. A hybridization of genetic algorithms and perceptrons has been used in [74] for supervised classification in microarray data. Issues involved in the research on the use of neural networks for data mining include model selection, determination of an appropriate architecture and training algorithm, network pruning, convergence and training time, data representation and tackling missing values. Hybridization of neural networks with other soft computing tools such as fuzzy logic, genetic algorithms, rough sets and wavelets have proved to be effective for solving complex problems.

1.4.7 Case-Based Reasoning

Case-based reasoning (CBR) is a model of reasoning where the systems expertise is embodied in a library of past *cases* (stored as a case base) already experienced by the system, rather than being encoded explicitly as rules, or implicitly as decision boundaries. In CBR, a problem is solved by first matching it to problems encountered in the past and retrieving one or a small set of similar cases. The retrieved cases are used to suggest a solution to the present problem, which is tested, and, if necessary, revised. The present problem and its solution is updated in the case base as a new case.

All case-based systems iterate in the following manner:

1. Retrieve the most similar case (or a small set of cases) by comparing the current case to the cases in the case base.
2. Reuse the retrieved case (or cases) to formulate a mechanism for solving the current problem.
3. Revise and adapt the proposed solution if necessary.
4. Update the case base by storing the current problem and the final solution as part of a new case.

The major tasks in CBR are case representation and indexing, case retrieval, case adaptation, case learning and case-base maintenance [102]. The representation of a case in a case base usually includes specification of the problem, relevant attributes of the environment that describe the circumstances of the problem, and a description of the solution that was adopted when the case was encountered. The cases stored in the case base should be stored in such a way that future retrieval and comparison tasks are facilitated. The issue of case indexing refers to this. A good choice of indexing strategy is one that reflects the important features of a case and the attributes that influence the outcome of the case, and also describes the circumstances in which a case is expected to be retrieved in the future.

Case retrieval refers to the process of finding the cases most similar to the current query case. The important issues involved are the case base search mechanism and the selection/match criteria. Several criteria, e.g., the number of cases to be searched and the availability of domain knowledge, are used for determining a suitable retrieval technique. The most commonly used retrieval approaches are the nearest neighbor and decision-tree-based methods.

Once a matching case is retrieved, case adaptation is used to transform the solution for the retrieved case to one that is suitable for the current problem. Some common approaches of case adaptation are to use the retrieved solution, derive a consensus solution, or provide multiple solutions, if multiple cases are retrieved.

Case learning deals with the issue of adding any new information that is gained while processing the current case into the case base, so that its information content is increased. This will be beneficial when processing future cases. One common learning method is to add the new problem, its solution, and the outcome to the case base. Case-base maintenance refers to the task of pruning the case base so that redundant and noisy information is removed, while important information is retained. Some important considerations here are the coverage and reachability [113]. While coverage refers to the set of problems that each could solve, reachability refers to the set of cases that could provide solutions to the current problem.

Case-based reasoning first appeared in commercial tools in the early 1990s and since then has been applied in a wide range of domains. These include medical diagnosis, product/service help desk, financial/marketing assessments, decision-support systems and assisting human designers in architectural and industrial design. Details about CBR may be found in [131] and more recently in [102].

1.5 Conclusions

This chapter presented the basic concepts and issues in KDD, and also discussed the challenges that data mining researchers are facing. Such challenges arise due to different reasons, such as very high dimensional and extremely large data sets, unstructured and semi-structured data, temporal and spatial patterns and heterogeneous data. Some important application domains where data mining techniques are heavily used have been elaborated. These include web mining, bioinformatics, and image and text mining. The recent trends in KDD have also been summarized, including brief descriptions of some common mining tools. An extensive bibliography is provided.

Traditional data mining generally involved well-organized database systems such as relational databases. With the advent of sophisticated technology, it is now possible to store and manipulate very large and complex data. The data complexity arises due to several reasons, e.g., high dimensionality, semi- and/or un-structured nature, and heterogeneity. Data related to the world-wide web, the geoscientific domain, VLSI chip layout and routing, multimedia, financial markets, sensor networks, and genes and proteins constitute some typical examples of complex data. In order to extract knowledge from such complex data, it is necessary to develop advanced methods that can exploit the nature and representation of the data more efficiently. The following chapters report the research work of active practitioners in this field, describing recent advances in the field of knowledge discovery from complex data.

References

[1] The Berkeley Initiative in Soft Computing. URL: www-bisc.cs.berkeley.edu/
[2] Agrawal, C. C., and Philip S. Yu, 2001: Outlier detection for high dimensional data. *Proccedings of the SIGMOD Conference.*
[3] Agrawal, R., T. Imielinski and A. N. Swami, 1993: Mining association rules between sets of items in large databases. *Proceedings of the 1993 ACM SIGMOD International Conference on Management of Data,* P. Buneman and S. Jajodia, eds., Washington, D.C., 207–16.
[4] Agrawal, R., and R. Srikant, 1994: Fast algorithms for mining association rules. *Proc. 20th Int. Conf. Very Large Data Bases, VLDB,* J. B. Bocca, M. Jarke, and C. Zaniolo, eds., Morgan Kaufmann, 487–99.
[5] Alahakoon, D., S. K. Halgamuge, and B. Srinivasan, 2000: Dynamic self organizing maps with controlled growth for knowledge discovery. *IEEE Transactions on Neural Networks,* **11**, 601–14.

[6] Anderberg, M. R., 1973: *Cluster Analysis for Application*. Academic Press.

[7] Anderson, T. W., 1958: *An Introduction to Multivariate Statistical Analysis*. Wiley, New York.

[8] Andrews, H. C., 1972: *Mathematical Techniques in Pattern Recognition*. Wiley Interscience, New York.

[9] Au, W. H. and K. Chan, 1998: An effective algorithm for discovering fuzzy rules in relational databases. *Proceedings of IEEE International Conference on Fuzzy Systems FUZZ IEEE*, IEEE Press, Alaska, USA, 1314–19.

[10] Baldwin, J. F., 1996: Knowledge from data using fuzzy methods. *Pattern Recognition Letters*, **17**, 593–600.

[11] Bandyopadhyay, S., 2005: An Efficient Technique for Superfamily Classification of Amino Acid Sequences: Feature Extraction, Fuzzy Clustering and Prototype Selection. *Fuzzy Sets and Systems (accepted)*.

[12] Bandyopadhyay, S., C. Giannella, U. Maulik, H. Kargupta, K. Liu and S. Datta, 2005: Clustering distributed data streams in peer-to-peer environments. *Information Sciences (accepted)*.

[13] Bandyopadhyay, S., and U. Maulik, 2001: Non-parametric genetic clustering: Comparison of validity indices. *IEEE Transactions on Systems, Man and Cybernetics Part-C*, **31**, 120–5.

[14] — 2002: Efficient prototype reordering in nearest neighbor classification. *Pattern Recognition*, **35**, 2791–9.

[15] — 2002: An evolutionary technique based on k-means algorithm for optimal clustering in r^n. *Information Sciences*, **146**, 221–37.

[16] Bandyopadhyay, S., U. Maulik and M. K. Pakhira, 2001: Clustering using simulated annealing with probabilistic redistribution. *International Journal of Pattern Recognition and Artificial Intelligence*, **15**, 269–85.

[17] Bandyopadhyay, S., C. A. Murthy and S. K. Pal, 1995: Pattern classification using genetic algorithms. *Pattern Recognition Letters*, **16**, 801–8.

[18] — 1998: Pattern classification using genetic algorithms: Determination of H. *Pattern Recognition Letters*, **19**, 1171–81.

[19] — 1999: Theoretical performance of genetic pattern classifier. *J. Franklin Institute*. **336**, 387–422.

[20] Bandyopadhyay, S., and S. K. Pal, 1997: Pattern classification with genetic algorithms: Incorporation of chromosome differentiation. *Pattern Recognition Letters*, **18**, 119–31.

[21] Bandyopadhyay, S., S. K. Pal and U. Maulik, 1998: Incorporating chromosome differentiation in genetic algorithms. *Information Science*, **104**, 293–319.

[22] Ben-Dor, A., R. Shamir and Z. Yakhini, 1999: Clustering gene expression patterns. *Journal of Computational Biology*, **6**, 281–97.

[23] Bigus, J. P., 1996: *Data Mining With Neural Networks: Solving Business Problems from Application Development to Decision Support*. McGraw-Hill.

[24] Chakrabarti, S., 2002: *Mining the Web: Discovering Knowledge from Hypertext Data*. Morgan Kaufmann.

[25] Chawla, N. V., K. W. Bowyer, L. O. Hall and W. P. Kegelmeyer, 2002: Smote: Synthetic minority over-sampling technique. *Journal of Artificial Intelligence Research*, **16**, 321–57.

[26] Chen, W., J. C. Hou and L. Sha, 2004: Dynamic clustering for acoustic target tracking in wireless sensor networks. *IEEE Transactions on Mobile Computing*, **3**, 258–71.

[27] Chiang, D. A., L. R. Chow and Y. F. Wang, 2000: Mining time series data by a fuzzy linguistic summary system. *Fuzzy Sets and Systems*, **112**, 419–32.

[28] Chiba, S., K. Sugawara, and T. Watanabe, 2001: Classification and function estimation of protein by using data compression and genetic algorithms. *Proc. Congress on Evolutionary Computation*, **2**, 839–44.

[29] Cristianini, N. and J. Shawe-Taylor, 2000: *An Introduction to Support Vector Machines (and other kernel-based learning methods)*. Cambridge University Press, UK.

[30] Dayhoff, J. E., 1990: *Neural Network Architectures: An Introduction*. Van Nostrand Reinhold, New York.

[31] Devijver, P. A. and J. Kittler, 1982: *Pattern Recognition: A Statistical Approach*. Prentice-Hall, London.

[32] Dopazo, H., J. Santoyo and J. Dopazo, 2004: Phylogenomics and the number of characters required for obtaining an accurate phylogeny of eukaryote model species. *Bioinformatics*, **20, Suppl 1**, I116–I121.

[33] Dorffner, G., 1996: Neural networks for time series processing. *Neural Network World*, **6**, 447–68.

[34] Dorohonceanu, B. and C. G. Nevill-Manning, 2000: Accelerating protein classification using suffix trees. *Proceedings of the 8th International Conference on Intelligent Systems for Molecular Biology (ISMB)*, 128–33.

[35] Du, W. and Z. Zhan, 2002: Building decision tree classifier on private data. *Proceedings of the IEEE International Conference on Data Mining Workshop on Privacy, Security, and Data Mining*, Australian Computer Society, **14**, 1–8.

[36] Duda, R. O. and P. E. Hart, 1973: *Pattern Classification and Scene Analysis*. John Wiley, New York.

[37] Eisenhardt, M., W. Muller and A. Henrich, 2003: Classifying Documents by Distributed P2P Clustering. *Proceedings of Informatik 2003, GI Lecture Notes in Informatics, Frankfurt, Germany*.

[38] Ester, M., H.-P. Kriegel, J. Sander and X. Xu, 1996: Density-based algorithm for discovering clusters in large spatial databases. *Proc. of the Second International Conference on Data Mining KDD-96*, Portland, Oregon, 226–31.

[39] Ester, M., H.-P. Kriegel and X. Xu, 1995: Knowledge discovery in large spatial databases: Focusing techniques for efficient class identification.

Proc. 4th Int. Symp. on Large Spatial Databases (SSD'95), Portland, Maine, 67–82.

[40] Fayyad, U., G. Piatetsky-Shapiro and P. Smyth, 1996: The KDD process for extracting useful knowledge from volumes of data. *Communications of the ACM*, **39**, 27–34.

[41] Flake, G. W., S. Lawrence and C. L. Giles, 2000: Efficient identification of the web communities. *Proceedings on the 6th ACM SIGKDD Conference on Knowledge Discovery and Data Mining*, 150–160.

[42] Flockhart, I. W., 1995: GA-MINER: Parallel data mining with hierarchical genetic algorithms–final report. Technical Report EPCC-AIKMS-GA-MINER-REPORT 1.0, University of Edinburgh, UK.

[43] Flockhart, I. W. and N. J. Radcliffe, 1996: A genetic algorithm-based approach to data mining. *Proceedings of the Second International Conference on Knowledge Discovery and Data Mining (KDD-96)*, E. Simoudis, J. W. Han and U. Fayyad, eds., AAAI Press, Portland, Oregon, USA, 299–302.

[44] Frigui, H., 1999: Adaptive image retrieval using the fuzzy integral. *Proceedings of NAFIPS 99*, IEEE Press, New York, USA, 575–9.

[45] Fu, K. S., 1982: *Syntactic Pattern Recognition and Applications*. Academic Press, London.

[46] Fukunaga, K., 1972: *Introduction to Statistical Pattern Recognition*. Academic Press, New York.

[47] Gelsema, E. S. and L. N. Kanal, eds., 1986: *Pattern Recognition in Practice II*. North Holland, Amsterdam.

[48] Ghiasi, S., A. Srivastava, X. Yang and M. Sarrafzadeh, 2002: Optimal energy aware clustering in sensor networks. *Sensors*, **2**, 258–69.

[49] Giles, C. L., S. Lawrence and A. C. Tsoi, 2001: Noisy time series prediction using a recurrent neural network and grammatical inference. *Machine Learning*, **44**, 161–83.

[50] Goethals, B., 2002: *Efficient Frequent Pattern Mining*. Ph.D. thesis, University of Limburg, Belgium.

[51] Goldberg, D. E., 1989: *Genetic Algorithms: Search, Optimization and Machine Learning*. Addison-Wesley, New York.

[52] Gonzalez, R. C. and M. G. Thomason, 1978: *Syntactic Pattern Recognition: An Introduction*. Addison-Wesley, Reading, MA.

[53] Hammond, K., R. Burke, C. Martin and S. Lytinen, 1995: FAQ finer: A case-based approach to knowledge navigation. *Working notes of the AAAI Spring Symposium: Information gathering from heterogeneous, distributed environments*, AAAI Press, Stanford University, 69–73.

[54] Han, J. and M. Kamber, 2000: *Data Mining: Concepts and Techniques*. Morgan Kaufmann, San Francisco, USA.

[55] Hartigan, J. A., 1975: *Clustering Algorithms*. John Wiley.

[56] Haykin, S., 1994: *Neural Networks, A Comprehensive Foundation*. McMillan College Publishing Company, New York.

[57] Hebb, D. O., 1949: *The Organization of Behavior*. John Wiley, New York.

[58] Heinzelman, W., A. Chandrakasan and H. Balakrishnan, 2000: Energy-efficient communication protocol for wireless microsensor networks. *Proceedings of the Hawaii Conference on System Sciences*.

[59] — 2002: An application-specific protocol architecture for wireless microsensor networks. *IEEE Transactions on Wireless Communications*, **1**, 660–70.

[60] Hipp, J., U. Güntzer and G. Nakhaeizadeh, 2000: Algorithms for association rule mining – a general survey and comparison. *SIGKDD Explorations*, **2**, 58–64.

[61] Hoya, T. and A. Constantidines, 1998: A heuristic pattern correction scheme for GRNNS and its application to speech recognition. *Proceedings of the IEEE Signal Processing Society Workshop*, 351–9.

[62] Hu, Y.-J., S. Sandmeyer, C. McLaughlin and D. Kibler, 2000: Combinatorial motif analysis and hypothesis generation on a genomic scale. *Bioinformatics*, **16**, 222–32.

[63] Hüsken, M. and P. Stagge, 2003: Recurrent neural networks for time series classification. *Neurocomputing*, **50(C)**.

[64] Imielinski, T. and H. Mannila, 1996: A database perspective on knowledge discovery. *Communications of the ACM*, **39**, 58–64.

[65] Imielinski, T., A. Virmani and A. Abdulghani, 1996: A discovery board application programming interface and query language for database mining. *Proceedings of KDD 96*, Portland, Oregon, 20–26.

[66] Inmon, W. H., 1996: The data warehouse and data mining. *Communications of the ACM*, **39**, 49–50.

[67] Jain, A. K. and R. C. Dubes, 1988: *Algorithms for Clustering Data*. Prentice-Hall, Englewood Cliffs, NJ.

[68] Jensen, F. V., 1996: *An Introduction to Bayesian Networks*. Springer-Verlag, New York, USA.

[69] Kargupta, H., S. Bandyopadhyay and B. H. Park, eds., 2005: *Special Issue on Distributed and Mobile Data Mining, IEEE Transactions on Systems, Man, and Cybernetics Part B*. IEEE.

[70] Kargupta, H. and P. Chan, eds., 2001: *Advances in Distributed and Parallel Knowledge Discovery*. MIT Press.

[71] Kargupta. H, R. Bhargava, K. Liu, M. Powers, P. Blair and M. Klein, 2004: VEDAS: A mobile distributed data stream mining system for real-time vehicle monitoring. *Proceedings of the 2004 SIAM International Conference on Data Mining*.

[72] Kargupta, H., W. Huang, S. Krishnamoorthy and E. Johnson, 2000: Distributed clustering using collective principal component analysis. *Knowledge and Information Systems Journal*, **3**, 422–48.

[73] Kargupta, H., A. Joshi, K. Sivakumar and Y. Yesha, eds., 2004: *Data Mining: Next Generation Challenges and Future Directions*. MIT/AAAI Press.

[74] Karzynski, M., A. Mateos, J. Herrero and J. Dopazo, 2003: Using a genetic algorithm and a perceptron for feature selection and supervised class learning in DNA microarray data. *Artificial Intelligence Review*, **20**, 39–51.

[75] Kaufman, L. and P. J. Rousseeuw, 1990: *Finding Groups in Data: An introduction to cluster analysis*. John Wiley.

[76] Kleinberg, J. M., 1998: Authoritative sources in a hyperlinked environment. *Proceedings of the ninth annual ACM-SIAM symposium on discrete algorithms*.

[77] Knorr, E. M. and R. T. Ng, 1998: Algorithms for mining distance-based outliers in large datasets. *Proceedings of the 24th International Conference on Very Large Data Bases, VLDB*, 392–403.

[78] Koenig, A., 2000: Interactive visualization and analysis of hierarchical projections for data mining. *IEEE Transactions on Neural Networks*, **11**, 615–24.

[79] Kosala, R. and H. Blockeel, 2000: Web mining research: A survey. *SIGKDD Explorations*, **2**, 1–15.

[80] Koza, J. R., 1992: *Genetic Programming: On the programming of computers by means of natural selection*. MIT Press, Cambridge, USA.

[81] Krishnamachari, B. and S. Iyengar, 2004: Distributed Bayesian algorithms for fault tolerant event region detection in wireless sensor networks. *IEEE Trans. Comp.*, **53**, 241–50.

[82] Krishnapuram, R., A. Joshi, O. Nasraoui and L. Yi, 2001: Low complexity fuzzy relational clustering algorithms for web mining. *IEEE Transactions on Fuzzy Systems*, **9**, 595–607.

[83] Lin, Y. and G. A. Cunningham III, 1995: A new approach to fuzzy-neural system modeling. *IEEE Transactions on Fuzzy Systems*, **3**, 190–8.

[84] Lindsey, S., C. Raghavendra and K. M. Sivalingam, 2002: Data gathering algorithms in sensor networks using energy metrics. *IEEE Transactions on Parallel and Distributed Systems, special issue on Mobile Computing*, **13**, 924–35.

[85] Lopes, C., M. Pacheco, M. Vellasco and E. Passos, 1999: Rule-evolver: An evolutionary approach for data mining. *Proceedings of RSFDGrC 99*, Yamaguchi, Japan, 458–62.

[86] Lu, H. J., R. Setiono and H. Liu, 2003: Effective data mining using neural networks. *IEEE Transactions on Knowledge and Data Engineering*, **15**, 14–25.

[87] Madria, S. K., S. S. Bhowmick, W. K. Ng and E. P. Lim, 1999: Research issues in web data mining. *Proceedings of First International Conference on data warehousing and knowledge discovery DaWaK*, M. K. Mohania and A. M. Tjoa, eds., Springer, volume 1676 of *Lecture Notes in Computer Science*, 303–12.

[88] Masand, B., M. Spiliopoulou, J. Srivastava and O. Zaiane, 2002: We-bkdd 2002: Web mining for usage patterns & profiles. *SIGKDD Explor. Newsl.*, **4**, 125–7, URL: doi.acm.org/10.1145/772862.772888.

[89] — eds., 2003: *WEBKDD 2002 – Mining Web Data for Discovering Usage Patterns and Profiles, Proceedings of 4th International Workshop*, volume 2703 of *Lecture Notes in Artificial Intelligence*. Springer, Edmonton, CA.

[90] Mateos, A., J. Herrero, J. Tamames and J. Dopazo, 2002: Supervised neural networks for clustering conditions in DNA array data after reducing noise by clustering gene expression profiles. *Microarray data analysis II*, Kluwer Academic Publishers, 91–103.

[91] Maulik, U. and S. Bandyopadhyay, 2000: Genetic algorithm-based clustering technique. *Pattern Recognition*, **33**, 1455–65.

[92] — 2002: Performance evaluation of some clustering algorithms and validity indices. *IEEE Transactions on Pattern Analysis and Machine Intelligence*, **24**, 1650–4.

[93] — 2003: Fuzzy partitioning using a real-coded variable-length genetic algorithm for pixel classification. *IEEE Trans. Geoscience and Remote Sensing*, **41**, 1075– 81.

[94] Medasani, S. and R. Krishnapuram, 1999: A fuzzy approach to complex linguistic query based image retrieval. *Proceedings of NAFIPS 99*, IEEE Press, New York, USA, 590–4.

[95] Mohan, C., 2002: Dynamic e-business: Trends in web services. Invited talk at the 3rd VLDB Workshop on Technologies for E-Services (TES).

[96] Ng, R. and J. Han, 1994: Efficient and effective clustering method for spatial data mining. *Proc. 1994 Int. Conf. Very Large Data Bases*, Santiago, Chile, 144–55.

[97] Noda, E., A. A. Freitas and H. S. Lopes, 1999: Discovering interesting prediction rules with a genetic algorithm. *Proceedings of IEEE Congress on Evolutionary Computation CEC 99*, Washington D. C., USA, 1322– 9.

[98] Oliver, A., N. Monmarché and G. Venturini, 2002: Interactive design of websites with a genetic algorithm. *Proceedings of the IADIS International Conference WWW/Internet*, Lisbon, Portugal, 355–62.

[99] Oliver, A., O. Regragui, N. Monmarché and G. Venturini, 2002: Genetic and interactive optimization of websites. *Eleventh International World Wide Web Conference*, Honolulu, Hawaii.

[100] Pal, S. K., S. Bandyopadhyay and C. A. Murthy, 1998: Genetic algorithms for generation of class boundaries. *IEEE Transactions on Systems, Man and Cybernetics, Part B*, **28**, 816–28.

[101] Pal, S. K., S. Bandyopadhyay and S. S. Ray: Evolutionary computation in bioinformatics: A review. *IEEE Transactions on Systems, Man and Cybernetics, Part B* (communicated).

[102] Pal, S. K. and S. C. K. Liu, 2004: *Foundations of Soft Case-Based Reasoning*. Wiley Series on Intelligent Systems, USA.

[103] Palpanas, T., D. Papadopoulos, V. Kalogeraki and D. Gunopulos, December, 2003: Distributed deviation detection in sensor networks. *SIGMOD Record*, **32**, 77–82.

[104] Pao, Y. H., 1989: *Adaptive Pattern Recognition and Neural Networks*. Addison-Wesley, New York.

[105] Pavilidis, T., 1977: *Structural Pattern Recognition*. Springer-Verlag, New York.

[106] Pedrycz, W., 1996: Conditional fuzzy c-means. *Pattern Recognition Letters*, **17**, 625–32.

[107] — 1998: Fuzzy set technology in knowledge discovery. *Fuzzy Sets and Systems*, **98**, 279–90.

[108] Picarougne, F., C. Fruchet, A. Oliver, N. Monmarché and G. Venturini, 2002: Recherche d'information sur Internet par algorithme gènètique. *Actes des quatrièmes journèes nationales de la ROADEF*, Paris, France, 247–8.

[109] — 2002: Web searching considered as a genetic optimization problem. *Local Search Two Day Workshop*, London, UK.

[110] Picarougne, F., N. Monmarché, A. Oliver and G. Venturini, 2002: Web mining with a genetic algorithm. *Eleventh International World Wide Web Conference*, Honolulu, Hawaii.

[111] Provost, F. and V. Kolluri, 1999: A survey of methods for scaling up inductive algorithms. *Data Mining and Knowledge Discovery*, **2**, 131–69.

[112] Quinlan, J. R. and R. L. Rivest, 1989: Inferring decision trees using the minimum description length principle. *Information and Computation*, **80**, 227–48.

[113] Racine, K. and Q. Yang, 1997: Maintaining unstructured case bases. *Proceedings of the Second International Conference on Case-Based Reasoning (ICCBR-97)*, Springer-Verlag, Berlin, 553–64.

[114] Radivojac, P., U. Korad, K. M. Sivalingam and Z. Obradovic, October, 2003: Learning from class-imbalanced data in wireless sensor networks. *58th IEEE Semiannual Conf. Vehicular Technology Conference (VTC)*, Orlando, FL, **5**, 3030–4.

[115] Ramaswamy, S., R. Rastogi and K. Shim, 2000: Efficient algorithms for mining outlier from large data sets. *Proceedings of the ACM conference on Management of Data*, 427–38.

[116] Ray, S. S., S. Bandyopadhyay, P. Mitra and S. K. Pal, 2005: Bioinformatics in neurocomputing framework, *IEE Proceedings Circuits, Devices and Systems* (accepted).

[117] Raymer, M. L., W. F. Punch, E. D. Goodman and L. A. Kuhn, 1996: Genetic programming for improved data mining: An application to the biochemistry of protein interactions. *Proceedings of First Annual Conference on Genetic Programming*, MIT Press, Stanford University, CA, USA, 375–80.

[118] Schwefel, H. P., 1981: *Numerical Optimization of Computer Models*. John Wiley, Chichester.

[119] Selim, S. Z. and M. A. Ismail, 1984: *K*-means type algorithms: A generalized convergence theorem and characterization of local optimality. *IEEE Transactions on Pattern Analysis and Machine Intelligence*, **6**, 81–7.

[120] Shen, W. M., K. Ong, B. Mitbander and C. Zaniolo, 1996: Metaqueries for data mining. *Advances in Knowledge Discovery and Data Mining*, U. M. Fayyad, G. Piatetsky-Shapiro, P. Smyth and R. Uthurusamy, eds., AAAI Press, 375–98.

[121] Sinha, A., A. Wang and A. Chandrakasan, 2000: Algorithmic transforms for efficient energy scalable computation. *Proc. of the International Symposium on Low Power Electronics and Design (ISLPED)*.

[122] Spath, H., 1989: *Cluster Analysis Algorithms*. Ellis Horwood, Chichester, UK.

[123] Specht, D. F., 1991: A general regression neural network. *IEEE Transactions on Neural Networks*, **2**, 568–76.

[124] Sperberg-McQueen, C. M., 2003: Web services and W3C.
URL: `w3c.dstc.edu.au/presentations/2003-08-21-web-ser`
`vices-interop/msm-ws.html`

[125] Tan, P.-N., V. Kumar and J. Srivastava, 2002: Selecting the right interestingness measure for association patterns. *Proceedings of the eighth ACM SIGKDD international conference on Knowledge discovery and data mining*, ACM Press, New York, USA, 32–41.

[126] Teller, A. and M. Veloso, 1995: Program evolution for data mining. *The International Journal of Expert Systems*, **8**, 216–36.

[127] Tou, J. T. and R. C. Gonzalez, 1974: *Pattern Recognition Principles*. Addison-Wesley, Reading, MA.

[128] Turksen, I. B., 1998: Fuzzy data mining and expert system development. *Proceedings of IEEE International Conference on Systems, Man, and Cybernetics*, IEEE Press, San Diego, CA, 2057–61.

[129] Vaidya, J., and C. Clifton, 2003: Privacy preserving *K*-means clustering over vertically partitioned data. *Proceedings of the ninth ACM SIGKDD International Conference on Knowledge Discovery and Data Mining*, ACM Press, New York, USA, 206–15.

[130] Wang, J. T. L., M. J. Zaki, H. Toivonen and D. E. Shasha, eds., 2005: *Data Mining in Bioinformatics*. Advanced Information and Knowledge Processing, Springer, USA.

[131] Watson, I., 1997: *Applying Case-Based Reasoning: Techniques for Enterprise Systems*. Morgan Kaufmann, San Francisco, USA.

[132] Webb, G. I., 2000: Efficient search for association rules. *Proceedings of the Sixth ACM SIGKDD International Conference on Knowledge Discovery and Data Mining*, The Association for Computing Machinery, 99–107.

[133] Wei, Q. and G. Chen, 1999: Mining generalized association rules with fuzzy taxonomic structures. *Proceedings of NAFIPS 99*, IEEE Press, New York, USA, 477–81.

[134] Yager, R. R., 1996: Database discovery using fuzzy sets. *International Journal of Intelligent Systems*, **11**, 691–712.

[135] Younis, O. and S. Fahmy, 2004 (to appear): Heed: A hybrid, energy-efficient, distributed clustering approach for ad-hoc sensor networks. *IEEE Transactions on Mobile Computing*, **3**.

[136] Zadeh, L. A., 1965: Fuzzy sets. *Information and Control*, **8**, 338–53.

[137] — 1994: Fuzzy logic, neural networks and soft computing. *Communications of the ACM*, **37**, 77–84.

[138] Zhang, T., R. Ramakrishnan and M. Livny, 1996: Birch: an efficient data clustering method for very large databases. *Proceedings of the 1996 ACM SIGMOD international conference on management of data*, ACM Press, 103–114.

2

Automatic Discovery of Class Hierarchies via Output Space Decomposition

Joydeep Ghosh, Shailesh Kumar and Melba M. Crawford

Summary. Many complex pattern classification problems involve high-dimensional inputs as well as a large number of classes. In this chapter, we present a modular learning framework called the BINARY HIERARCHICAL CLASSIFIER (BHC) that takes a coarse-to-fine approach to dealing with a large number of output classes. BHC decomposes a C-class problem into a set of $C-1$ two-(meta)class problems, arranged in a binary tree with C leaf nodes and $C-1$ internal nodes. Each internal node is comprised of a feature extractor and a classifier that discriminates between the two meta-classes represented by its two children. Both *bottom-up* and *top-down* approaches for building such a BHC are presented in this chapter. The BOTTOM-UP BINARY HIERARCHICAL CLASSIFIER (BU-BHC) is built by applying agglomerative clustering to the set of C classes. The TOP-DOWN BINARY HIERARCHICAL CLASSIFIER (TD-BHC) is built by recursively partitioning a set of classes at any internal node into two disjoint groups or meta-classes. The coupled problems of finding a good partition and of searching for a linear feature extractor that best discriminates the two resulting meta-classes are solved simultaneously at each stage of the recursive algorithm. The hierarchical, multistage classification approach taken by the BHC also helps with dealing with high-dimensional data, since simpler feature spaces are often adequate for solving the two-(meta)class problems. In addition, it leads to the discovery of useful domain knowledge such as class hierarchies or ontologies, and results in more interpretable results.

2.1 Introduction

A classification problem involves identifying a set of objects, each represented in a suitable common input space, using one or more class labels taken from a pre-determined set of possible labels. Thus it may be described as a four-tuple: $(\mathcal{I}, \mathbf{\Omega}, P_{X \times \Omega}, \mathcal{X})$, where $\mathcal{I}$ is the *input space*, in which the raw data is available (e.g. the image of a character), $\mathbf{\Omega}$ is the *output space*, comprised of all the class labels that can be assigned to an input pattern (e.g. the set of 26 alphabetic characters in English), $P_{X \times \Omega}$ is the *unknown* joint probability density function over random variables $X \in \mathcal{I}$ and $\Omega \in \mathbf{\Omega}$, and $\mathcal{X} \subset \mathcal{I} \times \mathbf{\Omega}$ is the training set sampled from the distribution $P_{X \times \Omega}$. The goal is to determine the relationship between the input and output spaces, a full specification of which is given by modeling the joint probability density function $P_{X \times \Omega}$.

Complexity in real-world classification problems can arise from multiple causes. First, the objects (and their representation) may themselves be complex, e.g. XML trees, protein sequences with 3-D folding geometry, variable length sequences, etc. [18]. Second, the data may be very noisy, the classes may have significant overlap and the optimal decision boundaries may be highly nonlinear. In this chapter we concentrate simultaneously on complexity due to high-dimensional inputs and a large number of class labels that can be potentially assigned to any input. Recognition of characters from the English alphabet ($C = 26$ classes) based on a (say) 64×64 binary input image and labeling of a piece of land into one of 10–12 land-cover types based on 100+ dimensional hyperspectral signatures are two examples that exhibit such complex characteristics.

There are two main approaches to simplifying such problems:

- **Feature extraction**: A feature extraction process transforms the input space, $\mathcal{I}$, into a lower-dimensional *feature space*, $\mathcal{F}$, in which discrimination among the classes Ω is high. It is particularly helpful given finite training data in a high-dimensional input space, as it can alleviate fundamental problems arising from the *curse of dimensionality* [2, 15]. Both domain knowledge and statistical methods can be used for feature extraction [4, 9, 12, 16, 27, 33]. Feature selection is a specific case of linear feature extraction [33].
- **Modular learning**: Based on the divide-and-conquer precept that "learning a large number of simple local concepts is both easier and more useful than learning a single complex global concept" [30], a variety of modular learning architectures have been proposed by the pattern recognition and computational intelligence communities [28, 36, 47]. In particular, multi-classifier systems develop a set of M classifiers instead of one, and subsequently combine the individual solutions in a suitable way to address the overall problem. In several such architectures, each individual classifier addresses a simpler problem. For example, it may specialize in only part of the feature space as in the mixture of experts framework [26, 41]. Alternatively, a simpler input space may effectively be created per classifier by sampling/re-weighting (as in bagging and boosting), using one module for each data source [48]; different feature subsets for different classes (input decimation) [49], etc. Advantages of modular learning include the ease and efficiency in learning, scalability, interpretability, and transparency [1, 21, 36, 38, 42].

This chapter focuses on yet another type of modularity which is possible for multi-class problems, namely, the decomposition of a C-class problem into a set of binary problems. Such decompositions have attracted much interest recently because of the popularity of certain powerful binary classifiers, most notably the support vector machine (SVM), which was originally formulated for binary dichotomies [50]. Although several extensions of SVMs to multi-class problems have been subsequently suggested (see papers referred to in [25]), the results of [25] show that such direct approaches are inferior to de-composing the multiclass problem into several binary classification problems, each addressed by a binary SVM.

Over the years, several approaches to decomposing the output space have been proposed. The most popular approaches, described in more detail in Section 2.2, are: (i) solving C "one-versus-rest" two-class problems; (ii) examining $\binom{C}{2}$ pairwise classifications; (iii) sequentially looking for or eliminating a single class at a time and (iv) applying error correcting output codes [10]. These approaches have been met with varying degrees of success. For the moment, we note that they typically do not take into account the natural affinities among the classes, or simultaneously determine simpler feature spaces that are tailored for specific output decompositions.

In this chapter, we propose an alternative approach to problem decomposition in output space that involves building a BINARY HIERARCHICAL CLASSIFIER (BHC) in which a C-class problem is addressed using a set of $M = C-1$ two-(meta)class feature extractor/classifier modules. These modules are arranged to form the $C-1$ internal nodes of a binary tree with C leaf nodes, one for each class. At each internal node, the partitioning of the parent meta-class into two child meta-classes is done simultaneously with the identification of an appropriately small but discriminating feature space for the corresponding classification problem. This is unlike the commonly used decision trees in which there may be several leaf nodes per class and the partitionings are explicitly done only in the *input* space. Instead the BHC can be considered as an example of a *coarse-to-fine* approach to multi-class problems. In earlier pattern recognition literature, several multistage approaches, including hierarchical ones were considered in which classes were progressively eliminated for an unlabelled sample [8, 43]. One of the goals of this work is to motivate the reader to reconsider such approaches as they often provide valuable domain information as a side-effect.

In addition to reducing the number of binary classifiers from $\mathcal{O}(C^2)$ in the pairwise classifier framework to $\mathcal{O}(C)$, the BHC framework also generates a class taxonomy that often provides useful domain knowledge. Indeed, the hierarchical problem decomposition viewpoint was motivated by the observation that many real-world classification problems have inherent taxonomies associated with them. Examples of such hierarchically structured classes can be found in domains as diverse as Biology, where all life forms are arranged in a multilevel taxonomy, and Internet portals such as YAHOO!, where all articles are arranged in a hierarchical fashion for ease of navigation and organization.

In fact, the BHC was developed by us while attempting to produce effective solutions to classification of land cover from remotely sensed hyperspectral imagery. Land covers have natural hierarchies and inter-class affinities, which the BHC was able to automatically infer and exploit. Figure 2.1 shows an example of a simple two-level hierarchy of various land-cover types

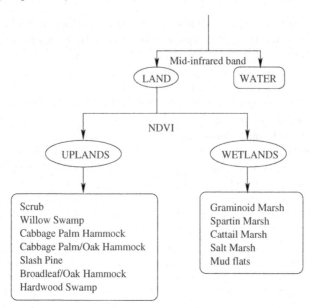

Fig. 2.1. A simple two-level hierarchy for a site with one WATER class and 12 LAND classes divided into seven UPLANDS and five WETLANDS meta-classes. The land versus water distinction is made by the response in the mid-infrared band while the distinction between uplands and wetlands is made using the Normalized Difference Vegetation Index (NDVI).

in the Bolivar peninsula [7]. In this example, 13 original (base) classes are first decomposed into two groups, LAND and WATER. WATER and LAND "meta-classes" can be readily separated based on the pixel responses in the mid-infrared frequency bands. WATER is one of the 13 base classes, while the LAND meta-class comprises 12 classes and is thus further partitioned into UPLANDS and WETLANDS meta-classes comprised of seven and five base classes respectively. The distinction between the UPLANDS and WETLANDS is made using the Normalized Difference Vegetation Index (NDVI) [45]. Instead of solving a 13-class problem, the hierarchy shown in Figure 2.1 can be used to first solve a binary problem (separating WATER from LAND), and then solve another binary problem to separate UPLANDS from WET-LANDS. Note that both the feature space as well as the output space of the two problems are different. The seven-class problem of discriminating among the UPLANDS classes and the five-class problem of discriminating among the WETLANDS classes can be further addressed in appropriate feature spaces using appropriate classifiers. Thus, a 13-class problem is decomposed using an *existing hierarchy* into simpler classification problems in terms of their output spaces.

Section 2.2 summarizes existing approaches to solving multi-class problems through output space decomposition. The BHC framework is formally defined in Section 2.3. The BOTTOM-UP BINARY HIERARCHICAL CLASSIFIER (BU-BHC) algorithm for building the BHC using ideas from agglomerative clustering [11] in a bottom-up fashion is described in Section 2.4. The TOP-DOWN BINARY HIERARCHICAL CLASSIFIER (TD-BHC) algorithm for building the BHC using ideas from our GAMLS framework [30] in a top-down approach is described in Section 2.5. Section 2.6 discusses both hard and soft ways of combining the results from individual binary classifiers to solve the original multi-class problem, for both top-down and bottom-up approaches. An experimental evaluation of the BHC framework over several large classification tasks follows in Section 2.7, and several class hierarchies extracted from the data are displayed in Section 2.8.

2.2 Background: Solving Multi-Class Problems

In this section we summarize and compare four main types of approaches that have been developed over the years to address multi-class problems using binary classifiers.

2.2.1 One-versus-rest

The traditional approach to multiclass problems is to develop C classifiers, each focussed on distinguishing one particular class from the rest. Often this is achieved by developing a discriminant function for each of the C classes. A new data point is assigned the class label corresponding to the discriminant function that gives the highest value for that data point. For example, in Nilsson's classic linear machine [37], the discriminant functions are linear, so the decision boundaries are constrained to be hyperplanes that intersect at a point. This is an example of the *discriminant analysis* family of algorithms, that includes *Quadratic Discriminant Analysis* [22, 34], *Regularized Discriminant Analysis* [13], and *Kernel Discriminant Analysis* [6, 20]. The essential difference among different discriminant analysis methods is the nature and bias of the discriminant function used.

2.2.2 Pairwise classification

Also known as round robin classification [17], these approaches learn one classifier for each pair of classes (employing a total of $\binom{C}{2}$ classifiers in the process) and then combine the outputs of these classifiers in a variety of ways to determine the final class label. This approach has been investigated by several researchers [14, 23, 39, 46]. Typically the binary classifiers are developed and examined in parallel, a notable exception being the efficient DAG-structured ordering given in [39]. A straightforward way of finding the winning class is through a simple voting scheme used for example in [14], which evaluates pairwise classification for two versions of CART and for the nearest neighbor rule. Alternatively, if the individual classifiers provide good estimates of the two-class posterior probabilities, then these estimates can be combined using an iterative hill-climbing approach suggested by [23].

Our first attempts at output space decomposition [7, 31] involved applying a pairwise classifier framework for land-cover prediction problems involving hyperspectral data. Class-pair-specific feature extraction was used to obtain superior classification accuracies. It also provided important domain knowledge with regard to what features were more useful for discriminating specific pairs of classes. While such a modular-learning approach for decomposing a C-class problem is attractive for a number of reasons including focussed feature extraction, interpretability of results and automatic discovery of domain knowledge, the fact that it requires $\mathcal{O}(C^2)$ pairwise classifiers might make it less attractive for problems involving a large number of classes. Further, the combiner that integrates the results of all the $\binom{C}{2}$ classifiers must resolve the couplings among these outputs that might increase with the number of classes.

2.2.3 Error correcting output codes (ECOC)

Inspired by distributed output representations in biological systems, as well as by robust data communication ideas, ECOC is one of the most innovative and popular approaches to have emerged recently to deal with multi-class problems [10]. A C-class problem is encoded as $\bar{C}$ binary problems. For each binary problem, one subset of the classes serves as the positive class (target $= 1$) while the rest form the negative class (target $= 0$). As a consequence, each original class is encoded into a $\bar{C}$-dimensional binary vector. The $C \times \bar{C}$ binary matrix is called the coding matrix. A given test input is labelled as belonging to the class whose code is closest to the code formed by the outputs of the $\bar{C}$ classifiers in response to that input.

2.2.4 Sequential methods

These approaches impose an ordering among the classes, and the classifiers are developed in sequence rather than in parallel. For example, one can first discriminate between class "1" and the rest. Then for data classified as "rest", a second classifier is designed to separate class "2" from the other remaining classes, and so on. Problem decomposition in the output space can also be accomplished implicitly by having C classifiers, each trying to solve the complete C-class problem, but with each classifier using input features most correlated with only one of the classes. This idea was used in [49] for creating an ensemble of classifiers, each using different *input decimations*. This method not only reduces the correlation among individual classifiers in an ensemble, but also reduces the dimensionality of the input space for classification problems. Significant improvements in misclassification error together with reductions in the number of features used were obtained on various public-domain data sets using this approach.

2.2.5 Comments and comparisons

A common characteristic of the approaches described above is that they do not take into account the underlying affinities among the individual classes (for example, how close or separated they are) while deciding on class selection/grouping for binary classification. Both one-versus-rest and pairwise methods treat each class the same way while, in ECOC, design of the code matrix is based on the properties of this matrix rather than the classes they represent. That is why it is helpful to have a strong base learner when applying ECOC since some of the groupings may lead to complicated decision boundaries. In contrast, the groupings in BHC are determined by the properties of the class distributions. Not being agnostic to class affinities helps us in determining natural groupings that facilitate both the discrimination process and the interpretation of results.

Three noteworthy studies have emerged recently that compare the three major approaches. Furnkranz [17] shows that the $\binom{C}{2}$ learning problems of pairwise classification can be learned more efficiently than the C problems of the one-versus-rest technique. His analysis is independent of the base learning algorithm. He also observes that both these approaches are more efficient than ECOC. A large number of empirical results are shown using RIPPER and C5.0 as base classifiers. The BHC uses only $C-1$ classifiers, similar to one-versus-rest, but since the class groupings are based on affinities, the binary classifications are simpler in general. Hence BHCs do not compromise much on efficiency in the process of reducing the number of classifiers needed. Hsu and Lin [25] did a detailed study comparing one-versus-rest and pairwise classification, both using the SVM as base classifier, to two approaches for directly generalizing the SVM algorithm to multi-class problems. The pairwise method performed best both in terms of accuracy and training time. One-versus-rest was second and both methods were better than the direct generalizations of SVM. Finally, a recent intriguing study [44] shows that no one of these methods performs significantly better than any other as far as test errors are concerned. The study is carefully done, but it is not clear whether the results are affected by the choice of SVMs with Gaussian kernels as the base classifiers.

2.3 The BINARY HIERARCHICAL CLASSIFIER Framework

Definition 1 A binary hierarchical classifier for a C-class problem $\mathcal{P}(\mathcal{I}, \Omega, P_{X \times \Omega}, \mathcal{X})$ is defined as an ensemble of $C-1$ two-(meta)class problems, arranged as a binary tree $\mathcal{T}(\Omega_1)$, $(\Omega_1 = \Omega)$ recursively defined as follows:

$$T(\mathbf{\Omega}_n) = \begin{cases} \left[\mathcal{P}(\mathcal{F}_n, \tilde{\mathbf{\Omega}}_n, P_{Y_n \times \tilde{\Omega}_n}, \mathcal{Y}_n), T(\mathbf{\Omega}_{2n}), T(\mathbf{\Omega}_{2n+1}) \right] & \text{if } |\mathbf{\Omega}_n| > 1 \\ \mathbf{\Omega}_n & \text{if } |\mathbf{\Omega}_n| = 1, \end{cases}$$

(2.1)

in which each internal node n (i.e. $n : |\mathbf{\Omega}_n| > 1$) has an associated two-(meta)class problem:

$$\mathcal{P}(\mathcal{F}_n, \tilde{\mathbf{\Omega}}_n, P_{Y_n \times \tilde{\Omega}_n}, \mathcal{Y}_n) \qquad (2.2)$$

where n is the index of a node in the tree. For each node n, $\mathbf{\Omega}_n$ is a set of classes in the associated meta-class. For each *internal* node n, $\{2n, 2n+1\}$ are indices of the left and right children, $\tilde{\mathbf{\Omega}}_n = \{\mathbf{\Omega}_{2n}, \mathbf{\Omega}_{2n+1}\}$, $\mathcal{F}_n$ is the feature space for the binary problem, Y_n are random variables in $\mathcal{F}_n$, and $\tilde{\Omega}_n$ are random variables in $\tilde{\mathbf{\Omega}}_n$. Further, each internal node n is comprised of meta-class feature extractors $\psi_n : \mathcal{I} \to \mathcal{F}_n$, such that discrimination between $\mathbf{\Omega}_{2n}$ and $\mathbf{\Omega}_{2n+1}$ is high in $\mathcal{F}_n$, and meta-class classifiers ϕ_n for classes $\tilde{\mathbf{\Omega}}_n$. Finally, a tree combiner Ξ integrates the outputs of all the internal node classifiers $\{\phi_n\}$ into a single output. The classifiers ϕ_n can be *hard classifiers* defined by the mapping $\phi_n^H : \mathcal{F}_n \to \tilde{\mathbf{\Omega}}_n$, or *soft classifiers* given by the mapping $\phi_n^S : \mathcal{F}_n \to P_n(\tilde{\Omega}_n = \mathbf{\Omega}_{2n}|Y_n)$. (Note that $P_n(\tilde{\Omega}_n = \mathbf{\Omega}_{2n+1}|\mathbf{y}_n(\mathbf{x}))$ is simply $1 - P_n(\tilde{\Omega}_n = \mathbf{\Omega}_{2n}|\mathbf{y}_n(\mathbf{x}))$.)
Correspondingly the combiner Ξ can be a *hard combiner* $\Xi_H : \{\tilde{\Omega}_n\}_{n:|\mathbf{\Omega}_n|>1} \to \mathbf{\Omega}$, where inputs to Ξ_H are the $C-1$ (meta)class labels and output is one of the C class labels in $\mathbf{\Omega}$, or a *soft combiner* $\Xi_S : \{P_n(\tilde{\Omega}_n|Y_n)\}_{n:|\mathbf{\Omega}_n|>1} \to \{P(\omega|X)\}_{\omega \in \mathbf{\Omega}}$, where inputs to Ξ_S are the meta-class posterior probabilities generated by the $C-1$ classifiers.

Figure 2.2 shows an example of a five-class BHC with four internal nodes and five leaf nodes. In general, the BHC tree $T(\mathbf{\Omega})$ contains $C = |\mathbf{\Omega}|$ leaf nodes and $C-1$ internal nodes. Each internal node n has its own feature extractor and classifier that discriminates the two meta-classes $\mathbf{\Omega}_{2n}$ and $\mathbf{\Omega}_{2n+1}$. The decomposition of the set of classes $\mathbf{\Omega}_n$ into two disjoint subsets $\mathbf{\Omega}_{2n}$ and $\mathbf{\Omega}_{2n+1}$ is an NP problem with $\mathcal{O}(2^{|\mathbf{\Omega}_n|})$ possible alternatives. Further, the feature space $\mathcal{F}_n$ depends on the decomposition of $\mathbf{\Omega}_n$. Hence the two coupled problems of finding the best possible decomposition of $\mathbf{\Omega}_n$ and the best feature space that discriminates the two resulting meta-classes must be solved simultaneously. The bottom up and top-down approaches of building such binary hierarchical classifiers are described next.

2.4 Bottom-up BHC

The BOTTOM-UP BINARY HIERARCHICAL CLASSIFIER (BU-BHC) algorithm is analogous to hierarchical agglomerative clustering [11]. Instead of merging data points or clusters at each stage,] classes or meta-classes are merged in the BU-BHC algorithm. Starting from the set of C meta-classes $\Pi_C = \{\mathbf{\Omega}^{(c)}\}_{c=1}^C$, where $\mathbf{\Omega}^{(c)} = \{\omega_c\}$, a sequence $\Pi_C \to \Pi_{C-1} \to \dots \Pi_2 \to \Pi_1$ with

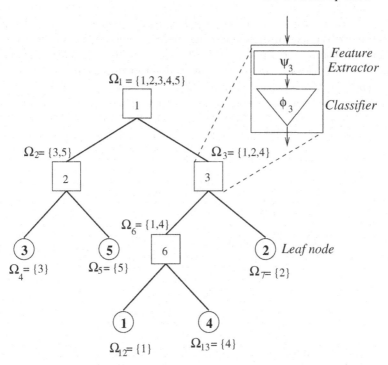

Fig. 2.2. An example of a BINARY HIERARCHICAL CLASSIFIER for a $C = 5$ class problem with four internal nodes and five leaf nodes. Each internal node n comprises a feature extractor ψ_n and a classifier ϕ_n. Each node n is associated with a set of classes Ω_n. The left and right children of internal node n are indexed $2n$ and $2n+1$, respectively.

an associated decreasing number of meta-classes is generated by merging two meta-classes Ω_α and Ω_β in Π_K to obtain the set Π_{K-1}.

In order to decide which of the K meta-classes in Π_K are to be merged to obtain Π_{K-1}, a "distance" between every pair of meta-classes, $\vartheta(\Omega_\alpha, \Omega_\beta)$ is defined as the *separation between the two meta-classes in the most discrimina-tory feature space* $\mathcal{F}(\Omega_\alpha, \Omega_\beta)$. Any suitable family of feature extractors can be used to quantify the distance between two meta-classes. In this chapter, since we are largely concerned with numeric data, two variants of the Fisher discriminant based linear feature extractors are proposed: FISHER(1), in which a one-dimensional projection of the D-dimensional input space is sought for the two-meta class problem, and FISHER(m), in which an m-dimensional feature space where $m = \min\{D, |\Omega_\alpha| + |\Omega_\beta| - 1\}$ is sought.

2.4.1 FISHER(1) Feature Extraction

The dimensionality of the Fisher projection space for a C-class problem with a D-dimensional input space is $\min\{D, C-1\}$. At each internal node in the

BHC, a two-class problem is solved, and hence only a one-dimensional feature space can be obtained for discriminating these two meta-classes. The distance function and the feature space obtained by the FISHER(1) feature extractor for the two meta-classes Ω_α and Ω_β are defined in this section.

Let $\{\mu^\rho \in \Re^{D \times 1}, \rho \in \{\alpha, \beta\}\}$ and $\{\Sigma^\rho \in \Re^{D \times D}, \rho \in \{\alpha, \beta\}\}$ be the means and covariances of the two meta-classes and let $\{P(\Omega_\rho), \rho \in \{\alpha, \beta\}\}$ be their priors. The statistics of meta-class Ω_ρ can be defined in terms of the estimated mean vectors, $\{\hat{\mu}_\omega \in \Re^{D \times 1}, \omega \in \Omega_\rho\}$, covariance matrices, $\{\hat{\Sigma}_\omega \in \Re^{D \times D}, \omega \in \Omega_\rho\}$ and class priors $\{\hat{P}(\omega), \omega \in \Omega_\rho\}$ as follows:

$$\hat{P}(\Omega_\rho) = \sum_{\omega \in \Omega_\rho} \hat{P}(\omega) = \frac{\sum_{\omega \in \Omega_\rho} |X_\omega|}{\sum_{\gamma \in \Omega} |X_\gamma|}, \quad \rho \in \{\alpha, \beta\}, \tag{2.3}$$

$$\hat{\mu}^\rho = \frac{\sum_{\omega \in \Omega_\rho} \sum_{\mathbf{x} \in \mathcal{X}_\omega} \mathbf{x}}{\sum_{\omega \in \Omega_\rho} |X_\omega|} = \frac{\sum_{\omega \in \Omega_\rho} \hat{P}(\omega) \hat{\mu}_\omega}{\sum_{\omega \in \Omega_\rho} \hat{P}(\omega)}, \quad \rho \in \{\alpha, \beta\}, \tag{2.4}$$

$$\begin{aligned} \hat{\Sigma}^\rho &= \frac{\sum_{\omega \in \Omega_\rho} \sum_{\mathbf{x} \in \mathcal{X}_\omega} (\mathbf{x} - \hat{\mu}^\rho)(\mathbf{x} - \hat{\mu}^\rho)^T}{\sum_{\omega \in \Omega_\rho} |X_\omega|} \\ &= \frac{\sum_{\omega \in \Omega_\rho} \hat{P}(\omega)\left[\hat{\Sigma}_\omega + (\hat{\mu}^\rho - \hat{\mu}_\omega)(\hat{\mu}^\rho - \hat{\mu}_\omega)^T\right]}{\sum_{\omega \in \Omega_\rho} \hat{P}(\omega)} \end{aligned} \tag{2.5}$$

The Fisher discriminant depends on the $D \times D$ symmetric within class covariance matrix $\mathbf{W}_{\alpha,\beta}$ given by:[1]

$$\mathbf{W}_{\alpha,\beta} = P(\Omega_\alpha)\Sigma^\alpha + P(\Omega_\beta)\Sigma^\beta, \tag{2.6}$$

and the $D \times D$, rank 1, between class covariance matrix $\mathbf{B}_{\alpha,\beta}$ given by:

$$\mathbf{B}_{\alpha,\beta} = P(\Omega_\alpha)P(\Omega_\beta)(\mu^\alpha - \mu^\beta)(\mu^\alpha - \mu^\beta)^T. \tag{2.7}$$

The corresponding one-dimensional Fisher projection is given by:

$$\mathbf{v}_{\alpha\beta} = \arg \max_{\mathbf{v} \in \Re^{D \times 1}} \frac{\mathbf{v}^T \mathbf{B}_{\alpha,\beta} \mathbf{v}}{\mathbf{v}^T \mathbf{W}_{\alpha,\beta} \mathbf{v}} \propto \mathbf{W}_{\alpha,\beta}^{-1} \left(\mu^\alpha - \mu^\beta\right). \tag{2.8}$$

Thus, the FISHER(1) feature extractor $\psi_{fisher}^{(1)}(X|\Omega_\alpha, \Omega_\beta) = \mathbf{v}_{\alpha\beta}^T \mathbf{x}$, where $\mathbf{x} \in \Re^{D \times 1}$ and $y \in \Re$ is a one-dimensional feature. The distance between the two meta-classes Ω_α and Ω_β is the FISHER(1) discriminant along the Fisher projection $\mathbf{v}_{\alpha\beta}$ of Equation (2.8).

2.4.2 FISHER(m) Feature Extraction

The basic assumption in Fisher's discriminant is that the two classes are unimodal. Even if this assumption is true for individual classes, it is not true

---

[1]Substituting estimated parameters for expected ones (e.g. $\hat{P} \equiv P$, $\hat{\mu} \equiv \mu$, and $\hat{\Sigma} \equiv \Sigma$).

for meta-classes comprised of two or more classes. Moreover, as the number of classes in the meta-classes Ω_α and Ω_β increases, the dimensionality of the feature space should also increase to compensate for the more complex decision boundaries between the two meta-classes. In the FISHER(1) feature extractor, irrespective of the sizes of the two meta-classes (in terms of the number of original classes), the Fisher projection is always one-dimensional because the rank of the between-class covariance matrix $\mathbf{B}_{\alpha,\beta}$ defined in Equation (2.7) is 1.

To alleviate this problem, we replace $\mathbf{B}_{\alpha,\beta}$ by a pairwise between-class covariance matrix $\tilde{\mathbf{B}}_{\alpha,\beta}$ that is defined in terms of the between-class covariances $\mathbf{B}_{\omega,\omega'} = P(\omega)P(\omega')(\mu_\omega - \mu_{\omega'})(\mu_\omega - \mu_{\omega'})^T$, $\forall (\omega, \omega' \in \Omega_\alpha \times \Omega_\beta$ as follows:

$$\tilde{\mathbf{B}}_{\alpha,\beta} = \sum_{\omega \in \Omega_\alpha} \sum_{\omega' \in \Omega_\beta} P(\omega)P(\omega')(\mu_\omega - \mu_{\omega'})(\mu_\omega - \mu_{\omega'})^T = \sum_{\omega \in \Omega_\alpha} \sum_{\omega' \in \Omega_\beta} \mathbf{B}_{\omega,\omega'}.$$
(2.9)

The rank of $\tilde{\mathbf{B}}_{\alpha,\beta}$ is $m_{\alpha\beta} = \min\{D, |\Omega_\alpha| + |\Omega_\beta| - 1\}$. The within-class covariance matrix for FISHER(m) is the same as in Equation (2.6). The Fisher projection matrix $\mathbf{V}_{\alpha\beta} \in \Re^{D \times m_{\alpha\beta}}$ for the FISHER(m) feature extractor is given by:

$$\mathbf{V}_{\alpha\beta} = \arg \max_{\mathbf{V} \in \Re^{D \times m_{\alpha\beta}}} \mathrm{tr}\left\{ \left(\mathbf{V}^T \mathbf{W}_{\alpha,\beta} \mathbf{V}\right)^{-1} \left(\mathbf{V}^T \mathbf{B}_{\alpha,\beta} \mathbf{V}\right) \right\}.$$
(2.10)

The optimal solution is the first $m_{\alpha\beta}$ eigenvectors of $\left(\mathbf{W}_{\alpha,\beta}^{-1} \mathbf{B}_{\alpha,\beta}\right)$. Thus, the FISHER($m$) feature extractor $\psi_{fisher}^{(m)}(X|\Omega_\alpha, \Omega_\beta) = \mathbf{V}_{\alpha\beta}^T \mathbf{x}$, where $\mathbf{y} \in \Re^{m_{\alpha\beta} \times 1}$ is an $m_{\alpha\beta}$-dimensional feature vector. The distance between the two meta-classes Ω_α and Ω_β is the FISHER(m) discriminant along the projection $\mathbf{V}_{\alpha\beta}$ of Equation (2.10).

The dimensionality of the feature space using the FISHER(m) feature extractor depends on the size of the meta-classes that are merged. In terms of the notation of the BHC introduced in Definition 1, the dimensionality of the feature space $\mathcal{F}_n$ at the internal node n is $\min\{D, |\Omega_n| - 1\}$. In particular, the dimensionality at the root node $n = 1$ is $\min\{D, |\Omega_1| - 1\} = \min\{D, C - 1\}$. This is the same as the dimensionality of the Fisher projection of the original C-class problem, the key difference being that in BHC, a two meta-class problem is solved in this space instead of the C-class problem. The tradeoff between the reduction in the number of classes from C to two and the increase in the complexity of the two meta-classes determines the utility of such a feature space.

2.4.3 Merging the Meta-Classes

Let Ω_α and Ω_β be the two closest (in terms of the Fisher projected distances defined in Sections 2.4.1 and 2.4.2) classes that are merged to form the meta-class $\Omega_{\alpha\beta} = \mathrm{MERGE}(\Omega_\alpha, \Omega_\beta)$. The estimated mean vector $\hat{\mu}^{\alpha\beta} \in \Re^{D \times 1}$, covariance matrix $\hat{\Sigma}^{\alpha\beta} \Re^{D \times D}$, and prior probability $\hat{P}(\Omega_{\alpha\beta})$ of the meta-class $\Omega_{\alpha\beta}$ are related to the means, covariances, and priors of the two merged meta-classes as follows:

$$\hat{P}(\Omega_{\alpha\beta}) = \sum_{\omega \in \Omega_{\alpha\beta}} \hat{P}(\omega) = \hat{P}(\Omega_\alpha) + \hat{P}(\Omega_\beta), \qquad (2.11)$$

$$\hat{\mu}^{\alpha\beta} = \frac{\sum_{\omega \in \Omega_{\alpha\beta}} \sum_{\mathbf{x} \in \mathcal{X}_\omega} \mathbf{x}}{\sum_{\omega \in \Omega_{\alpha\beta}} |\mathcal{X}_\omega|} = \frac{\hat{P}(\Omega_\alpha)\hat{\mu}^\alpha + \hat{P}(\Omega_\beta)\hat{\mu}^\beta}{\hat{P}(\Omega_\alpha) + \hat{P}(\Omega_\beta)}, \qquad (2.12)$$

$$
\begin{aligned}
\hat{\Sigma}^{\alpha\beta} &= \frac{\sum_{\omega \in \Omega_{\alpha\beta}} \sum_{\mathbf{x} \in \mathcal{X}_\omega} (\mathbf{x} - \hat{\mu}^{\alpha\beta})(\mathbf{x} - \hat{\mu}^{\alpha\beta})^T}{\sum_{\omega \in \Omega_{\alpha\beta}} |\mathcal{X}_\omega|} \\
&= \frac{\sum_{\rho \in \{\alpha,\beta\}} \hat{P}(\Omega_\rho)\left[\hat{\Sigma}^\rho + (\hat{\mu}^\rho - \hat{\mu}^{\alpha\beta})(\hat{\mu}^\rho - \hat{\mu}^{\alpha\beta})^T\right]}{\hat{P}(\Omega_\alpha) + \hat{P}(\Omega_\beta)}.
\end{aligned}
\qquad (2.13)
$$

Once the mean and covariance of the new meta-class $\Omega_{\alpha\beta}$ are obtained, its distance from the remaining classes $\Omega_\gamma \in \Pi_K - \{\Omega_\alpha, \Omega_\beta\}$ is computed as follows. The within-class covariance $\mathbf{W}_{\alpha\beta,\gamma}$ is given by:[2,3]

$$
\begin{aligned}
\mathbf{W}_{\alpha\beta,\gamma} &= P(\Omega_{\alpha\beta})\Sigma^{\alpha\beta} + P(\Omega_\gamma)\Sigma^\gamma \\
&= \tfrac{1}{2}\left[\mathbf{W}_{\alpha,\gamma} + \mathbf{W}_{\beta,\gamma} + \mathbf{W}_{\alpha,\beta}\right] + \frac{\mathbf{B}_{\alpha,\beta}}{P(\Omega_\alpha) + P(\Omega_\beta)}.
\end{aligned}
\qquad (2.14)
$$

Similarly, the between-class covariance $\mathbf{B}_{\alpha\beta,\gamma}$ for the FISHER(1) case is defined as:

$$
\begin{aligned}
\mathbf{B}_{\alpha\beta,\gamma} &= P(\Omega_{\alpha\beta})P(\Omega_\gamma)\left(\mu^{\alpha\beta} - \mu^\gamma\right)\left(\mu^{\alpha\beta} - \mu^\gamma\right)^T \mathbf{B}_{\alpha\beta,\gamma} \\
&= \mathbf{B}_{\alpha,\gamma} + \mathbf{B}_{\beta,\gamma} - \frac{P(\Omega_\gamma)}{P(\Omega_\alpha) + P(\Omega_\beta)}\mathbf{B}_{\alpha,\beta}.
\end{aligned}
\qquad (2.15)
$$

Finally, the pairwise between-class covariance $\tilde{\mathbf{B}}_{\alpha\beta,\gamma}$ for FISHER(m) case is defined as:

$$\tilde{\mathbf{B}}_{\alpha\beta,\gamma} = \sum_{\omega \in \Omega_{\alpha\beta}} \sum_{\omega' \in \Omega_\gamma} P(\omega)P(\omega')\left(\mu_\omega - \mu_{\omega'}\right)\left(\mu_\omega - \mu_{\omega'}\right)^T = \tilde{\mathbf{B}}_{\alpha,\gamma} + \tilde{\mathbf{B}}_{\beta,\gamma} \qquad (2.16)$$

The recursive updates of $\mathbf{W}_{\alpha\beta,\gamma}$, $\mathbf{B}_{\alpha\beta,\gamma}$ and $\tilde{\mathbf{B}}_{\alpha\beta,\gamma}$ can be used to efficiently compute the distance $\vartheta(\Omega_{\alpha\beta}, \Omega_\gamma)$ and continue to build the tree bottom-up efficiently.

2.5 Top-down BHC

The bottom-up BHC algorithm is $\mathcal{O}(C^2)$ as the distance between all pairs of classes must be computed at the very first stage. Each of the $C-1$ subsequent stages is $\mathcal{O}(C)$. For a large number of classes this might make the

---

[2]Substituting estimated parameters for expected ones (e.g. $\hat{P} \equiv P$, $\hat{\mu} \equiv \mu$, and $\hat{\Sigma} \equiv \Sigma$).

[3]See [29] for details of simplifications.

BU-BHC algorithm less attractive. In this section, we propose an alternate approach to building the BHC, i.e., the TOP-DOWN BINARY HIERARCHI-CAL CLASSIFIER (TD-BHC) algorithm. This algorithm is motivated by our GAMLS framework [30]. In TD-BHC, starting from a single meta-class set Π_1 at the root node comprising of all the C classes, an increasing sequence $\Pi_1 \to \Pi_2 \to \ldots \Pi_{C-1} \to \Pi_C$ of meta-classes is obtained. At each stage, Π_K, one of the meta-classes is partitioned into two disjoint subsets leading to Π_{K+1}. Using the notation introduced in Definition 1, the basic TD-BHC algorithm, BUILDTREE($\boldsymbol{\Omega}_n$), can be written as follows:

1. Partition $\boldsymbol{\Omega}_n$ into two meta-classes $(\boldsymbol{\Omega}_{2n}, \boldsymbol{\Omega}_{2n+1}) \leftarrow$ PARTITIONNODE($\boldsymbol{\Omega}_n$)
2. Recurse on each child:
   - if $|\boldsymbol{\Omega}_{2n}| > 1$ then BUILDTREE($\boldsymbol{\Omega}_{2n}$)
   - if $|\boldsymbol{\Omega}_{2n+1}| > 1$ then BUILDTREE($\boldsymbol{\Omega}_{2n+1}$)

The purpose of the PARTITIONNODE function is to find a partition of the set of classes $\boldsymbol{\Omega}_n$ into two disjoint subsets such that the discrimination between the two meta-classes $\boldsymbol{\Omega}_{2n}$ and $\boldsymbol{\Omega}_{2n+1}$ is high. The feature space that best discriminates between the two meta-classes is also discovered simultaneously. FISHER(1) and FISHER(m) are two examples of such feature extractors. The two problems of finding a partition, as well as the feature extractor that maximizes discrimination between the meta-classes obtained as a result of this partition, are coupled. These coupled problems are solved simultaneously using association and specialization ideas of the GAMLS framework [30].

2.5.1 The PARTITIONNODE Algorithm

When partitioning a set of classes into two meta-classes, initially each class is associated with both the meta-classes. The update of these associations and meta-class parameters is performed alternately while gradually decreasing the temperature, until a hard partitioning is achieved. The complete PAR-TITIONNODE algorithm which forms the basis of the TD-BHC algorithm is described in this section.

Let $\Omega = \boldsymbol{\Omega}_n$ be some meta-class at internal node n with $K = |\boldsymbol{\Omega}_n| > 2$ classes that needs to be partitioned into two meta-classes, $\Omega_\alpha = \boldsymbol{\Omega}_{2n}$ and $\Omega_\beta = \boldsymbol{\Omega}_{2n+1}$. The "association" $\mathbf{A} = [a_{\omega,\rho}]$ between class $\omega \in \Omega$ and meta-class Ω_ρ, $(\rho \in \{\alpha, \beta\})$ is interpreted as the posterior probability of ω belonging to Ω_ρ: $P(\Omega_\rho|\omega)$. The *completeness constraint* of GAMLS [30] implies that $P(\Omega_\alpha|\omega) + P(\Omega_\beta|\omega) = 1$, $\forall \omega \in \Omega$.

PARTITIONNODE(Ω)

1. **Initialize associations** $\{a_{\omega,\alpha} = P(\Omega_\alpha|\omega), \omega \in \Omega\}$ $(a_{\omega,\beta} = 1 - a_{\omega,\alpha})$:

$$P(\Omega_\alpha|\omega) = \begin{cases} 1 & \text{for some } \omega = \omega_{(1)} \in \Omega \\ 0.5 & \forall \, \omega \in \Omega - \{\omega_{(1)}\} \end{cases} \qquad (2.17)$$

The association of one of the classes $\omega_{(1)} \in \Omega$ with the meta-class Ω_α is fixed to 1, while all other classes are associated equally with both the meta-classes. This deterministic, non-symmetric and unbiased association initialization is possible only because PARTITIONNODE seeks to divide Ω into two meta-classes only and not more. As a result of this initialization, the TD-BHC algorithm always yields the same partition for a given data set and learning parameters, irrespective of the choice of $\omega_{(1)}$. The temperature parameter T is initialized to 1 in this chapter, and then decayed geometrically, as indicated in Step 6 of the algorithm below. Although the partition is not affected by the choice of the class $\omega_{(1)}$, the class that is "farthest" (in terms of e.g. Bhattacharya distance) from the meta-class Ω should be chosen for faster convergence.

2. **Find the most discriminating feature space** $\mathcal{F}(\Omega_\alpha, \Omega_\beta)$: For the current set of "soft" meta-classes $(\Omega_\alpha, \Omega_\beta)$ defined in terms of the associations $\mathbf{A}$, the feature extractor $\psi(X|\mathbf{A}) : \mathcal{I} \to \mathcal{F}(\Omega_\alpha, \Omega_\beta)$ that maximally discriminates the two meta-classes is sought. This step depends on the the feature extractor used. Section 2.5.3 describes how the FISHER(1) and FISHER(m) feature extractors can be extended to *soft meta-classes*.

3. **Compute the mean log-likelihoods** of classes $\omega \in \Omega$ in the feature space $\mathcal{F}(\Omega_\alpha, \Omega_\beta)$:

$$\mathcal{L}(\omega|\Omega_\rho) = \frac{1}{N_\omega} \sum_{\mathbf{x} \in \mathcal{X}_\omega} \log p(\psi(\mathbf{x}|\mathbf{A})|\Omega_\rho), \quad \rho \in \{\alpha, \beta\}, \quad \forall\, \omega \in \Omega, \quad (2.18)$$

where the PDF $p(\psi(\mathbf{x}|\mathbf{A})|\Omega_\rho)$ can be modeled using any distribution function. A single Gaussian per class is used in this chapter.

4. **Update the meta-class posteriors** by optimizing Gibb's free energy [30]:

$$a_{\omega,\alpha} = P(\Omega_\alpha|\omega) = \frac{\exp(\mathcal{L}(\omega|\Omega_\alpha)/T)}{\exp(\mathcal{L}(\omega|\Omega_\alpha)/T) + \exp(\mathcal{L}(\omega|\Omega_\beta)/T)}. \quad (2.19)$$

5. Repeat Steps 2 through 4 until the increase in Gibb's free energy is insignificant.

6. If $\left(\frac{1}{|\Omega|} \sum_{\omega \in \Omega} \mathcal{H}(\mathbf{a}_\omega)\right) < \theta_H$ (user-defined threshold) stop, otherwise:
   - Cool temperature: $T \leftarrow T\theta_T$ ($\theta_T < 1$ is a user-defined cooling parameter).
   - Go to Step 2.

As the temperature cools sufficiently and the entropy decreases to near zero ($\theta_\mathcal{H} = 0.01$ in our implementation), the associations or the posterior probabilities $\{P(\Omega_\alpha|\omega), \omega \in \Omega\}$ become close to 0 or 1. The meta-class $\Omega = \Omega_n$ is then split as follows:

$$\begin{aligned} \Omega_{2n} &= \{\omega \in \Omega_n | a_{\omega,\alpha} = P(\Omega_\alpha|\omega) > P(\Omega_\beta|\omega) = a_{\omega,\beta}\} \\ \Omega_{2n+1} &= \{\omega \in \Omega_n | a_{\omega,\beta} = P(\Omega_\beta|\omega) > P(\Omega_\alpha|\omega) = a_{\omega,\alpha}\} \end{aligned}. \quad (2.20)$$

2.5.2 Soft Meta-Class Parameter Updates

For any set of associations $\mathbf{A}$, the estimates of the meta-class mean vectors $\{\hat{\mu}^\rho \in \Re^{D \times 1}, \rho \in \{\alpha, \beta\}\}$, the covariance matrices $\{\hat{\Sigma}^\rho \in \Re^{D \times D}, \rho \in \{\alpha, \beta\}\}$, and priors $\{\hat{P}(\Omega_\rho), \rho \in \{\alpha, \beta\}\}$ are updated using the mean vectors $\{\hat{\mu}_\omega \in \Re^{D \times 1}, \omega \in \Omega\}$, covariance matrices $\{\hat{\Sigma}_\omega \in \Re^{D \times D}, \omega \in \Omega\}$, and class priors $\{\hat{P}(\omega), \omega \in \Omega\}$, of the classes in Ω. Let $\mathcal{X}_\omega$ denote the training set comprising $N_\omega = |\mathcal{X}_\omega|$ examples of class ω. For any given associations or posterior probabilities $\mathbf{A} = \{a_{\omega,\rho} = P(\Omega_\rho|\omega), \rho \in \{\alpha, \beta\}, \omega \in \Omega\}$, the estimate of the mean is computed by $\hat{\mu}^\rho = \sum_{\omega \in \Omega} P(\omega|\Omega_\rho)\hat{\mu}_\omega$, $\rho \in \{\alpha, \beta\}$. The corresponding covariance is:

$$
\begin{aligned}
\hat{\Sigma}^\rho &= \sum_{\omega \in \Omega} \frac{P(\omega|\Omega_\rho)}{N_\omega} \left[\sum_{\mathbf{x} \in \mathcal{X}_\omega} (\mathbf{x} - \hat{\mu}^\rho)(\mathbf{x} - \hat{\mu}^\rho)^T \right] \\
&= \sum_{\omega \in \Omega} P(\omega|\Omega_\rho) \left[\hat{\Sigma}_\omega + (\hat{\mu}_\omega - \hat{\mu}^\rho)(\hat{\mu}_\omega - \hat{\mu}^\rho)^T \right], \quad \rho \in \{\alpha, \beta\}.
\end{aligned}
\tag{2.21}
$$

Using Bayes theorem, $P(\omega|\Omega_\rho) = \frac{\hat{P}(\omega)P(\Omega_\rho|\omega)}{\hat{P}(\Omega_\rho)}$, where

$$
\hat{P}(\Omega_\rho) = \frac{1}{\hat{P}(\Omega)} \sum_{\omega \in \Omega} P(\Omega_\rho|\omega)\hat{P}(\omega) \quad : \rho \in \{\alpha, \beta\}.
\tag{2.22}
$$

2.5.3 Soft FISHER-Based Feature Extractor

The FISHER(1) feature extractor is computed exactly as described in Section 2.4.1. The only difference is that in the soft meta-classes case the mean and covariance of the two meta-classes are estimated as shown in the previous section. Using these, the within-class covariance $\mathbf{W}_{\alpha,\beta}$ and the between-class covariance $\mathbf{B}_{\alpha,\beta}$ are computed as in Equation (2.6) and Equation (2.7) respectively. The one-dimensional Fisher projection is given by Equation (2.8). The one-dimensional projection obtained by FISHER(1) may not be sufficient for discriminating meta-classes with a large number of classes. Thus, the FISHER(m) feature extractor proposed in Section 2.4.2 is also extended to the soft meta-classes case.

In the BU-BHC algorithm at any merge step, each class belongs to either of the two meta-classes while in the TD-BHC, at any stage of the PARTITION-NODE algorithm, a class $\omega \in \Omega$ partially belongs to *both* the meta-classes. To reflect this soft assignment of classes to the two meta-classes, the pairwise between-class covariance matrix $\tilde{\mathbf{B}}_{\alpha,\beta}$ used in FISHER(m) is modified as follows:

$$
\begin{aligned}
\tilde{\mathbf{B}}_{\alpha,\beta} &= \tfrac{1}{2} \sum_{\omega \in \Omega} \sum_{\omega' \in \Omega - \{\omega\}} |a_{\omega,\alpha} - a_{\omega',\alpha}| P(\omega)P(\omega')(\mu_\omega - \mu_{\omega'})(\mu_\omega - \mu_{\omega'})^T \\
&= \tfrac{1}{2} \sum_{\omega \in \Omega} \sum_{\omega' \in \Omega - \{\omega\}} |a_{\omega,\alpha} - a_{\omega',\alpha}| \mathbf{B}_{\omega,\omega'},
\end{aligned}
\tag{2.23}
$$

where $|a_{\omega,\alpha} - a_{\omega',\alpha}|$ is large if the associations of ω and ω' with the two meta-classes are different. Thus, the weight corresponding to the between-class covariance component is large only when the associations with the respective classes are different. In the limiting case, when the associations become hard i.e. 0 or 1, then Equation (2.23) reduces to Equation (2.9). The rank of the pairwise between-class covariance matrix is $\min\{D, |\Omega| - 1\}$ and hence the dimensionality of the feature space $\mathcal{F}_n$ at internal node n remains $\min\{D, |\Omega_n| - 1\}$ as it was in the BU-BHC algorithm. Either FISHER(1) or FISHER(m) can be used as the feature extractors $\psi(X|\mathbf{A})$ in Step 2 of the PARTITIONNODE algorithm.

If the original class densities are Gaussian ($\mathcal{G}(\mathbf{x}|\mu, \Sigma)$), the class density functions in Step 3 of the PARTITIONNODE algorithm in Equation (2.18) for FISHER(1) is:

$$p(\psi_{fisher}^{(1)}(\mathbf{x}|\mathbf{A})|\Omega_\rho) = \mathcal{G}\left(\mathbf{v}_{\alpha\beta}^T\mathbf{x}|\mathbf{v}_{\alpha\beta}^T\mu^\rho, \mathbf{v}_{\alpha\beta}^T\Sigma^\rho\mathbf{v}_{\alpha\beta}\right), \quad \rho \in \{\alpha, \beta\}, \quad (2.24)$$

where $\mathbf{v}_{\alpha\beta}$ is defined in Equation (2.8). Similarly the class density functions for the FISHER(m) feature extractor can be defined as a multivariate ($m_{\alpha\beta}$-dimensional) Gaussians,

$$p(\psi_{fisher}^{(m)}(\mathbf{x}|\mathbf{A})|\Omega_\rho) = \mathcal{G}\left(\mathbf{V}_{\alpha\beta}^T\mathbf{x}, \mathbf{V}_{\alpha,\beta}^T\mu^\rho, \mathbf{V}_{\alpha\beta}^T\Sigma^\rho\mathbf{V}_{\alpha\beta}\right), \quad \rho \in \{\alpha, \beta\}, \quad (2.25)$$

where $\mathbf{V}_{\alpha\beta}$ is defined in Equation (2.10).

2.6 Combining in BHCs

As mentioned in Definition 1, either a hard or a soft classifier can be used at each internal node in the BHC, leading to two types of combiners: hard and soft. In this section both the hard and soft combining schemes are presented. The *hard combiner* Ξ_H essentially uses ideas from decision tree classifiers [3] to propagate a novel example to one of the leaf nodes based on the outputs of all the internal nodes, while the *soft combiner* Ξ_S estimates the true posteriors of the leaf-node classes from the posteriors of the internal node classifiers.

2.6.1 The Hard Combiner

A novel test example is classified by the hard combiner Ξ_H of BHC by pushing it from the root node to a leaf node. The output of the hard classifier at internal node n, $\phi_n^H(\psi_n(\mathbf{x}))$, is a class label Ω_{2n} or Ω_{2n+1}. Depending on the output at node n, $\mathbf{x}$ is pushed either to the left child or the right child. The basic hard combiner is implemented as follows:

1. Initialize $n = 1$ (start at root node).
2. while node n is an internal node, recursively push point $\mathbf{x}$ to the appropriate child:

$$n \leftarrow \begin{cases} 2n & \text{if } \phi_n^H(\psi_n(\mathbf{x})) = \Omega_{2n} \\ 2n + 1 & \text{if } \phi_n^H(\psi_n(\mathbf{x})) = \Omega_{2n+1} \end{cases} \quad (2.26)$$

3. Assign the (unique) class label Ω_n at the leaf node n to $\mathbf{x}$.

2.6.2 The Soft Combiner

If a soft classifier is used at each internal node, the results of these hierarchically arranged classifiers can be combined by first computing the overall posteriors $\{P(\omega|\mathbf{x}), \omega \in \mathbf{\Omega}\}$ and then applying the maximum *a posteriori* probability (MAP) rule: $\omega(\mathbf{x}) = \arg\max_{\omega \in \mathbf{\Omega}} P(\omega|\mathbf{x})$, to assign the class label $\omega(\mathbf{x})$ to $\mathbf{x}$. The posteriors $P(\omega|\mathbf{x})$ can be computed by multiplying the posterior probabilities of all the internal node classifiers on the path to the corresponding leaf node.

Theorem 1. *The posterior probability $P(\omega|\mathbf{x})$ for any input $\mathbf{x}$ is the product of the posterior probabilities of all the internal classifiers along the unique path from the root node to the leaf node $n(\omega)$ containing the class ω, i.e.*

$$P(\omega|\mathbf{x}) = \prod_{\ell=0}^{\mathcal{D}(\omega)-1} P(\Omega_{n(\omega)}^{(\ell+1)}|\mathbf{x}, \Omega_{n(\omega)}^{(\ell)}), \tag{2.27}$$

where $\mathcal{D}(\omega)$ is the depth of $n(\omega)$ (depth of the root node is 0), $\Omega_n^{(\ell)}$ is the metaclass at depth ℓ in the path from the root node to $n(\omega)$, such that $\Omega_{n(\omega)}^{(\mathcal{D}(\omega))} = \{\omega\}$ and $\Omega_{n(\omega)}^{(0)} = \Omega_1 = $ root node. (See [32] for proof.)

Remark 1 *The posterior probabilities $P_n(\mathbf{\Omega}_k|\mathbf{x}, \mathbf{\Omega}_n)$, $k \in \{2n, 2n+1\}$ are related to the overall posterior probabilities $\{P(\omega|\mathbf{x}), \omega \in \mathbf{\Omega}\}$ as follows:[4]*

$$P_n(\mathbf{\Omega}_k|\mathbf{x}, \mathbf{\Omega}_n) = \frac{\sum_{\omega \in \mathbf{\Omega}_k} P(\omega|\mathbf{x})}{\sum_{\omega \in \mathbf{\Omega}_n} P(\omega|\mathbf{x})}, \quad k \in \{2n, 2n+1\} \tag{2.28}$$

2.7 Experiments

Both BU-BHC and TD-BHC algorithms are evaluated in this section on public-domain data sets available from the UCI repository [35] and National Institute of Standards and Technology (NIST) and two additional hyperspectral data sets. The classification accuracies of eight different combinations of the BHC classifiers (bottom-up vs top-down, FISHER(1) vs FISHER(m) feature extractor and soft vs hard combiners) are compared with multilayered perceptron-based and maximum likelihood classifiers. The class hierarchy that is automatically discovered from both the BU-BHC and TD-BHC for these data sets are shown for some of these data sets to provide concrete examples of the domain knowledge discovered by the BHC algorithms.

2.7.1 Data Sets Used

The BHC was originally formulated by us to tackle the challenging problem of labeling land cover based on remotely-sensed hyperspectral images, but it

---

[4]This relationship can also be used to indirectly prove Theorem 1.

Table 2.1. The twelve classes in the AVIRIS/KSC hyperspectral data set

Num	Class Name
	Upland Classes
1	Scrub
2	Willow Swamp
3	Cabbage palm hammock
4	Cabbage oak hammock
5	Slash pine
6	Broad leaf/oak hammock
7	Hardwood swamp
	Wetland Classes
8	Graminoid marsh
9	Spartina marsh
10	Cattail marsh
11	Salt marsh
12	Mud flats

clearly has broader applicability. Therefore in this section we shall evaluate it on five public-domain data sets in addition to two hyperspectral data sets. The four public-domain data sets obtained from the UCI repository [35] consist of two 26-class English letter recognition data sets (LETTER-I and LETTER-II) with classes A–Z, a 10-class DIGITS data set with classes 0–9 and a six-class SATIMAGE data set with the following classes: red soil, cotton crop, gray soil, damp gray soil, soil with vegetation stubble, and very damp gray soil. See [29] for more details about these data sets.

The two high-dimensional hyperspectral data sets are AVIRIS and HYMAP, both obtained from NASA. AVIRIS covers 12 classes or land-cover types, and we used a 183-band subset of the 224 bands (excluding water absorption bands) acquired by NASA's Airborne Visible/Infrared Imaging Spectrometer (AVIRIS) sensor over Kennedy Space Center in Florida. The seven upland and five wetland cover types identified for classification are listed in Table 2.1. Classes 3–7 are all trees. Class 4 is a mixture of Class 3 and oak hammock. Class 6 is a mixture of broad leaf trees (maples and laurels) and oak hammock. Class 7 is also a broad leaf tree. These classes have similar spectral signatures and are very difficult to discriminate in multispectral, and even hyperspectral, data using traditional methods.

The HYMAP data set represents a nine-class land-cover prediction problem, where the input is 126 bands across the reflective solar wavelength region of 0.441–2.487 μm with contiguous spectral coverage (except in the atmospheric water vapor bands) and bandwidths between 15 and 20 nm. This data set was obtained over Stover Point (South Texas) in September of 1999. The vegetation here consists of common high estuarine marsh species including *Spartina spartinae*, *Borrichia frutescens*, *Monanthochloa littoralis*, and *Batis*

Table 2.2. The nine classes in the STOVER/HYMAP data set.

Num	Class Name
1	Water
2	*Spartina Spartinae*
3	*Batis maritima*
4	*Borrichia frutescens* + *Spartina spartinae* + *Monanthocloa littoralis*
5	Sand flats (bare soil)
6	Pure *Borrichia frutescens*
7	Trees
8	Dense bushes
9	*Borrichia frutescens* + *Spartina spartinae*

maritima. Adjacent to the resaca (which is a generic term that refers to an old river bed which has been cut off by the meandering of the river resulting in an ox-bow) is an almost impregnable layer of dense shrubs and trees. The nine classes determined for Stover Point are listed in Table 2.2.

2.7.2 Classification Results

The eight versions of the BHC framework that are evaluated on the data sets described in the previous section are generated by the following sets of choices:

- **Building the tree**: The BHC tree can be built either bottom-up or top-down. The biases of the BU-BHC and the TD-BHC algorithms are different. The BU-BHC tries to find the most similar meta-classes from the available set and hence is more greedy at each step than the TD-BHC, which attempts to partition a meta-class into two subsets with a more global perspective. As a result of the differences of these biases, different BHC trees and therefore different classification accuracies can be obtained.
- **Feature extractor used**: Both the FISHER(1) and FISHER(m) feature extractors based on Fisher's discriminant are investigated. While the tree structure for the two Fisher projections may be different, the discrimination between classes at any internal node using FISHER(m) projections is higher than the discrimination with FISHER(1) projection and therefore FISHER(m)-based BHC performs better in general than the corresponding BHC with FISHER(1) feature extractor.
- **Nature of combiner**: Both hard and soft combiners were investigated. In general, the soft combiner performs slightly better than the hard combiner, as is expected.

The classification accuracy averaged over 10 experiments on each data set is reported in Table 2.3. In each experiment, stratified sampling was used to partition the data set into training and test sets of equal size.[5] Eight versions

---

[5] 10-fold cross validation is currently in vogue in some circles but is an overkill for fairly large data sets.

of the BHC classifiers were compared to two standard classifiers leading to the following 10 classifiers for each data set:

- MLP: a finely-tuned multilayered perceptron-based classifier for each data set;
- MLC: a maximum-likelihood classifier using a full covariance matrix wherever possible and using a diagonal covariance matrix if the full covariance matrix is ill-conditioned due to high input dimensionality;
- BU-BHC(1,H): BU-BHC with FISHER(1) and hard combiner;
- BU-BHC(1,S): BU-BHC with FISHER(1) and soft combiner;
- BU-BHC(m,H): BU-BHC with FISHER(m) and hard combiner;
- BU-BHC(m,S): BU-BHC with FISHER(m) and soft combiner;
- TD-BHC(1,H): TD-BHC with FISHER(1) and hard combiner;
- TD-BHC(1,S): TD-BHC with FISHER(1) and soft combiner;
- TD-BHC(m,H): TD-BHC with FISHER(m) and hard combiner;
- TD-BHC(m,S): TD-BHC with FISHER(m) and soft combiner.

Table 2.3. Classification accuracies on public-domain data sets from the UCI repository [35] (SATIMAGE, DIGITS, LETTER-I) and NIST(LETTER-II) and remote-sensing data sets from the Center for Space Research, The University of Texas at Austin (HYMAP, AVIRIS). The input dimensions and number of classes are also indicated for each data set.

	SATIMAGE	DIGITS	LETTER-I	LETTER-II	HYMAP	AVIRIS
Dimensions	36	64	16	30	126	183
Classes	6	10	26	26	9	12
MLP	79.77	82.33	79.28	76.24	78.21	74.54
MLC	77.14	74.85	82.73	79.48	82.73	72.66
BU-BHC(1,H)	83.26	88.87	71.29	78.45	95.18	94.97
BU-BHC(1,S)	84.48	89.00	72.81	79.93	95.62	95.31
BU-BHC(m,H)	85.29	91.71	76.55	80.94	95.12	95.51
BU-BHC(m,S)	85.35	91.95	78.41	81.11	95.43	95.83
TD-BHC(1,H)	83.77	90.11	70.45	74.59	95.31	96.33
TD-BHC(1,S)	84.02	90.24	72.71	75.83	95.95	97.09
TD-BHC(m,H)	84.70	91.44	77.85	81.48	96.48	97.15
TD-BHC(m,S)	84.95	91.61	79.13	81.99	96.64	97.93

The finely tuned MLP classifiers and the MLC classifiers are used as benchmarks for evaluating the BHC algorithms. Almost all the BHC versions performed significantly better than the MLP and MLC classifiers on all data sets except LETTER-I and LETTER-II. In general the TD-BHC was slightly better than the BU-BHC mainly because its global bias leads to less greedy trees than the BU-BHC algorithm. Further, the FISHER(m) feature extractor consistently yields slightly better results than the FISHER(1) feature extractor, as expected. Finally, the soft combiner also performed sightly better than the hard combiner. This again is an expected result as the hard combiner loses some information as it thresholds the posteriors at each internal node.

2.7.3 Discussion of Results and Further Comparative Studies

From Table 2.3, we see that the BHC classifiers did not perform as well on the LETTER-I data set. This turns out to be due to the presence of some bimodal classes in this data set, which is problematic for the simple Fisher discriminant. For such data sets it is preferable to use more powerful binary classifiers at the internal nodes of the BHC, i.e. use the BHC framework only to obtain the class hierarchy and then use other, more appropriate, feature-extractors/classifiers for the two-class problems at each internal node. This intuition is borne out in our recent work [40] where gaussian-kernel based SVMs were used for the internal nodes, leading to statistically significant performance improvements for all the nine data sets considered. Also of interest is the comparison of this BHC-SVM architecture with an ECOC-based ensemble (using well-tuned SVMs as the base classifiers) given in this work. The outcome of this comparison is not obvious since two very different philosophies are being encountered. While the BHC groups the classes according to their natural affinities in order to make each binary problem easier, it cannot exploit the powerful error correcting properties of an ECOC ensemble that can provide good results even when individual classifiers are weak. This empirical study showed that while is no clear advantage to either technique in terms of classification accuracy, the BHCs typically achieve this performance using fewer classifiers. Note that each dichotomy in an ECOC setup can be addressed using all the training data, while for the BHC the data available decreases as one moves away from the root since only a subset of the classes are involved in lower-level dichotomies. Thus one may expect the ECOC approach to be less affected by a paucity of training data. However the experiments in [40] showed that BHC was competitive even for small sample sizes, indicating that the reduction in data is compensated for by the simpler dichotomies resulting from affinity-based grouping of classes.

All the results above assume equal penalty for each type of misclassification. In many real applications, classification into a nearby class is less costly than being labeled as a distant class. For example, wet gray soil being classified as damp gray soil is not as costly as being labeled as red, dry soil. If such asymmetric costs are considered, the coarse-to-fine approach of the BHC framework provides an additional advantage over all the other methods considered.

2.8 Domain Knowledge Discovery

One of the important aspects of the BHC classifiers is the domain knowledge that is discovered by the automatic BU-BHC and TD-BHC tree construction algorithms. The trees constructed by the BU-BHC(m) and TD-BHC(m) are shown in Figures 2.3 to 2.10 for the most common of the trees obtained in the ten experiments for each data set. The numbers at the internal nodes of the binary trees represent the mean training and test set classification accuracies at that internal node over all the experiments for which this tree is obtained.

- **IRIS**: It is well known that Iris Versicolour and Virginica are "closer" to each other than Iris Setosa. So, not surprisingly, the first split for both BU-BHC(m) and TD-BHC(m) algorithms invariably separates Setosa from the other two classes.
- **SATIMAGE**: Figures 2.3 and 2.4 show the BU-BHC(m) and TD-BHC(m) trees generated for the SATIMAGE data set. In the BU-BHC tree, the Classes 4 (damp gray soil) and 6 (very damp gray soil) merged first. This was followed by Class 3 (gray soil) merging in the meta-class (4,6). The right child of the root node contains the remaining three classes out of which the vegetation classes i.e. Class 2 (cotton crop) and Class 5 (soil with vegetation stubble) were grouped first. The tree formed in the TD-BHC is even more informative as it separates the four bare soil classes from the two vegetation classes at the root node and then separates the four soil classes into *red-soil* (Class 1) and *gray-soil* (Classes 3, 4, and 6) meta-classes. The *gray-soil* meta-class is further partitioned into *damp-gray-soil* (Classes 4 and 6) and *regular-gray-soil* (Class 3). Thus reasonable class hierarchies are discovered by the BHC framework for the SATIMAGE data set.

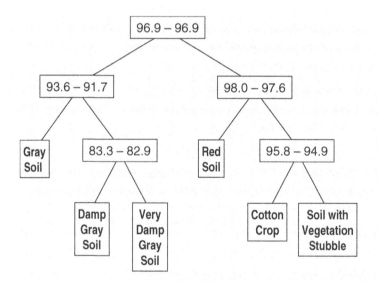

Fig. 2.3. BU-BHC(m) class hierarchy for the SATIMAGE data set.

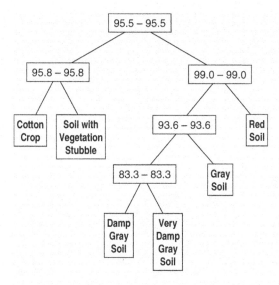

Fig. 2.4. TD-BHC(m) class hierarchy for the SATIMAGE data set.

- **LETTER**: The 26-class LETTER-I data set is only 16-dimensional. Although relatively lower dimensionality makes it an "easier" problem from the curse of dimensionality perspective, the fact that the number of classes is more than the dimensionality makes it a "harder" problem from the problem decomposition perspective. As seen in Table 2.3, the performance of BHC classifiers actually is poorer than other approaches, the reasons for which have already been discussed. Nevertheless, it is interesting to see the trees obtained by the BHC algorithms for such a large (in terms of output space) classification problem (Figures 2.5 and 2.6). Several interesting groups of characters are merged in the BU-BHC tree. For example meta-classes like {M,W,N,U} {F,P}, {V,Y,T}, {S,Z,B,E}, {I,J}, {K,R}, and {G,Q,C} are discovered. These conform well with the shapes of the letters. The TD-BHC tree is different from the BU-BHC tree but also has several interesting meta-classes like {M,W,U,H,N}, {K,R}, {V,Y,T}, {F,P}, {S,Z}, {C,G,O}, and {B,D,E}. Even for a small dimensional input space, as compared to the number of classes, the BHC algorithm was able to discover a meaningful class hierarchy for this 26-class problem. However, note that one could have obtained other reasonable hierarchies as well, and it is difficult to quantify the quality of a specific hierarchy other than through its corresponding classification accuracy.
- **LETTER-II**: Since the output space is still the same, the BHC trees for LETTER-II should be similar to the LETTER-I trees. In our experiments, similar interesting meta-classes such as {M,W,N,U}, {F,P}, {V,T}, {S,Z,B,E}, {I,J} and {G,Q,C} were discovered in the BU-BHC tree. The

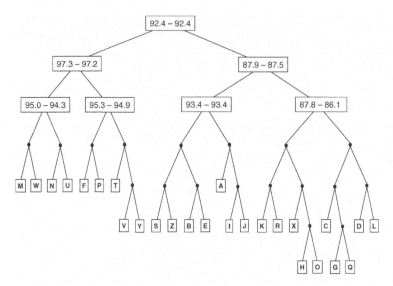

Fig. 2.5. BU-BHC(m) class hierarchy for the LETTER-I data set.

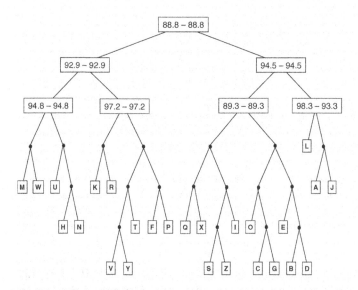

Fig. 2.6. TD-BHC(m) class hierarchy for the LETTER-I data set.

TD-BHC classifier for LETTER-II data set resulted in a few new groupings as well, including {O,Q}, {H,K,A,R} and {P,D}.

- **Hyperspectral data**: Figures 2.7, 2.8, 2.9 and 2.10 show the bottom-up and top-down trees obtained for AVIRIS and HYMAP. By considering the meaning of the class labels it is evident that this domain provided the most useful knowledge. Invariably, when water was present, it was the first to be split off. Subsequent partitions would, for example, distinguish between marshy wetlands and uplands, as in Figure 2.1. Note that the trees shown are representative results. While there are sometimes small variations in the trees obtained by perturbing the data, invariably all the trees produce hierarchies that are meaningful and reasonable to a domain expert [24].

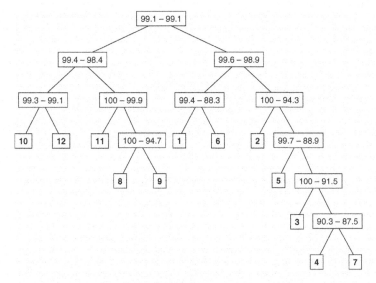

Fig. 2.7. BU-BHC(m) class hierarchy for the AVIRIS data set.

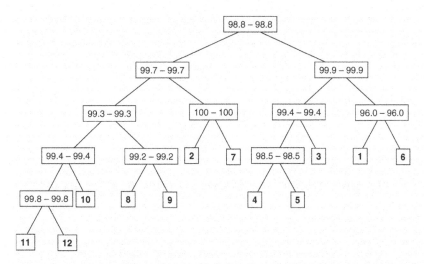

Fig. 2.8. TD-BHC(m) class hierarchy for the AVIRIS data set.

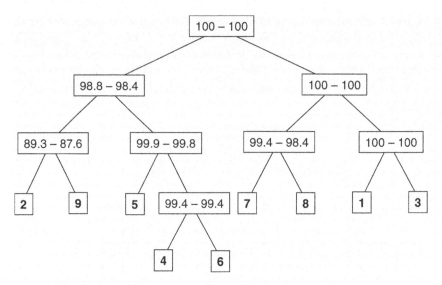

Fig. 2.9. BU-BHC(m) class hierarchy for the HYMAP data set.

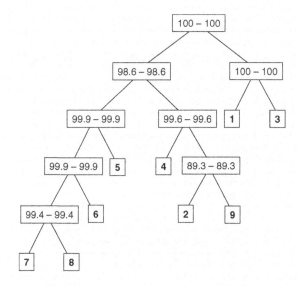

Fig. 2.10. TD-BHC(m) class hierarchy for the HYMAP data set.

2.9 Conclusions

This chapter presented a general framework for certain difficult classification problems in which the complexity is primarily due to having several classes as well as high-dimensional inputs. The BHC methodology relies on progressively partitioning or grouping the set of classes based on their affinities with one another. The BHC, as originally conceived, uses a custom Fisher's discriminant feature extraction for each partition, which is quite fast as it only involves summary class statistics. Moreover, as a result of the tree building algorithms, a class taxonomy is automatically discovered from data, which often leads to useful domain knowledge. This property was particularly helpful in our analysis of hyperspectral data.

The hierarchical BHC approach is helpful only if some class affinities are actually present, i.e. it will not be appropriate if all the classes are essentially "equidistant" from one another. In practice, this is not very restrictive since many applications involving multiple class labels, such as those based on biological or text data, do have natural class affinities, quite often reflected in class hierarchies or taxonomies. In fact it has been shown that exploiting a *known* hierarchy of text categories substantially improves text classification [5]. In contrast, the BHC attempts to induce a hierarchy directly from the data where no pre-existing hierarchy is available. Another recent approach with a similar purpose is presented in [19] where Naive Bayes is first used to quickly generate a confusion matrix for a text corpus. The classes are then clustered based on this matrix such that classes that are more confused with one another tend to be placed in the same group. Then SVMs are used in a "one-versus-all" framework within each group of classes to come up with the final result. Thus this approach produces a two-level hierarchy of classes. On text benchmarks, this method was three to six times faster than using "one-vs-all" SVMs directly, while producing comparable or better classification results.

We note that one need not be restricted to our choices of a Fisher discriminant and a simple Bayesian classifier at each internal node of the class-partitioning tree. In Section 2.7.3, we summarized our related work on using SVMs as the internal classifiers on a tree obtained via the Fisher discriminant/Bayesian classifier combination. The feature extraction step itself can also be customized for different domains such as image or protein sequence classification. In this context, recollect that the trees obtained for a given problem can vary somewhat depending on the specific training set or classifier design, indicative of the fact that that there are often multiple reasonable ways of grouping the classes. The use of more powerful binary classifiers provides an added advantage in that the overall results are more tolerant to the quality of the tree that is obtained.

The design space for selecting an appropriate feature extractor–classifier combination is truly rich and needs to be explored further. A well-known trade-off exists between these two functions. For example, a complex feature extraction technique can compensate for a simple classifier. With this viewpoint, let us compare the top-down BHC with decision trees such as C5.0, CART and CHAID. One can view the action at each internal node of a decision tree as the selection of a specific value of exactly one variable (feature extraction stage), followed by a simple classifier that just performs a simple comparison against this value. Thus the BHC node seems more complex. However, the demands on a single node in a decision tree are not that strong, since samples from the same class can be routed to different branches of the tree and still be identified correctly at later stages. In contrast, in the hard version of BHC, all the examples of a given class have to be routed to the same child at each internal node visited by them.

Acknowledgments: This research was supported in part by NSF grant IIS-0312471, the Texas Advanced Technology Research Program (CSRA-ATP-009), and a grant from Intel Corp. We thank members of CSR, and in particular Jisoo Ham and Alex Henneguelle, for helpful comments.

References

[1] Ballard, D., 1987: Modular learning in neural networks. *Proc. AAAI-87*, 279–84.

[2] Bellman, R. E., ed., 1961: *Adaptive Control Processes*. Princeton University Press.

[3] Breiman, L., J. H. Friedman, R. Olshen and C. J. Stone, 1984: *Classification and Regression Trees*. Wadsworth and Brooks, Pacific Grove, California.

[4] Brill, F. Z., D. E. Brown and W. N. Martin, 1992: Fast genetic selection of features for neural network classifiers. *IEEE Transactions on Neural Networks*, **3**, 324–28.

[5] Chakrabarti, S., B. Dom, R. Agrawal and P. Raghavan, 1998: Scalable feature selection, classification and signature generation for organizing large text databases into hierarchical topic taxonomies. *VLDB Journal*, **7**, 163–78.

[6] Chakravarthy, S., J. Ghosh, L. Deuser and S. Beck, 1991: Efficient training procedures for adaptive kernel classifiers. *Neural Networks for Signal Processing*, IEEE Press, 21–9.

[7] Crawford, M. M., S. Kumar, M. R. Ricard, J. C. Gibeaut and A. Neuenshwander, 1999: Fusion of airborne polarimetric and interferometric SAR for classification of coastal environments. *IEEE Transactions on Geoscience and Remote Sensing*, **37**, 1306–15.

[8] Dattatreya, G. R. and L. N. Kanal, 1985: Decision trees in pattern recognition. *Progress in Pattern Recognition 2*, L. N. Kanal and A. Rosenfeld, eds., Elsevier Science, 189–239.

[9] Deco, G. and L. Parra, 1997: Nonlinear feature extraction by redundancy reduction in an unsupervised stochastic neural network. *Neural Networks*, **10**, 683–91.

[10] Dieterich, T. G. and G. Bakiri, 1995: Solving multiclass learning problems via error-correcting output codes. *Journal of Artificial Intelligence Research*, **2**, 263–86.

[11] Duda, R. and P. Hart, 1973: *Pattern Classification and Scene Analysis*. Addison-Wesley.

[12] Etemad, K. and R. Chellappa, 1998: Separability-based multiscale basis selection and feature extraction for signal and image classification. *IEEE Transactions on Image Processing*, **7**, 1453–65.

[13] Friedman, J., 1989: Regularized discriminant analysis. *Journal of the American Statistical Association*, **84**, 165–75.

[14] — 1996: Another approach to polychotomous classification. Technical report, Stanford University.

[15] — 1996: On bias, variance, 0/1 loss, and the curse-of-dimensionality. Technical report, Department of Statistics, Stanford University.

[16] Fukunaga, K., 1990: *Introduction to Statistical Pattern Recognition* (2nd Ed.), Academic Press, NY.

[17] Furnkranz, J., 2002: Round robin classification. *Jl. Machine Learning Research*, **2**, 721–47.

[18] Ghosh, J., 2003: Scalable clustering. *The Handbook of Data Mining*, N. Ye, ed., Lawrence Erlbaum Assoc., 247–77.

[19] Godbole, S., S. Sarawagi and S. Chakrabarti, 2002: Scaling multi-class support vector machines using inter-class confusion. *Proceedings of the 8th International Conference on Knowledge Discovery and Data Mining (KDD-02)*, 513–18.

[20] Hand, D., 1982: *Kernel Discriminant Analysis*. Research Studies Press, Chichester, UK.

[21] Happel, B. and J. Murre, 1994: Design and evolution of modular neural network architectures. *Neural Networks*, **7:6/7**, 985–1004.

[22] Hastie, T. and R. Tibshirani, 1996: Discriminant adaptive nearest neightbor classification. *IEEE Transactions on Pattern Analysis and Machine Intelligence*, **PAMI-18**, 607–16.

[23] — 1998: Classification by pairwise coupling. *Advances in Neural Information Processing Systems*, M. J. K. Michael, I. Jordan and S. A. Solla, eds., MIT Press, Cambridge, Massachusetts, **10**, 507–13.

[24] Henneguelle, A., J. Ghosh and M. M. Crawford, 2003: Polyline feature extraction for land cover classification using hyperspectral data. *Proc. IICAI-03*, 256–69.

[25] Hsu, C. W. and C. J. Lin, 2002: A comparison of methods for multiclass support vector machines. *IEEE Transactions on Neural Networks*, **13**, 415–25.

[26] Jordan, M. and R. Jacobs, 1994: Hierarchical mixture of experts and the EM algorithm. *Neural Computation*, **6**, 181–214.

[27] Khotanzad, A. and Y. Hong, 1990: Invariant image recognition by zernike moments. *IEEE Transactions on Pattern Analysis and Machine Intelligence*, **12**, 28–37.

[28] Kittler, J. and F. Roli, eds., 2001: *Multiple Classifier Systems*. LNCS Vol. 1857, Springer.

[29] Kumar, S., 2000: *Modular learning through output space decomposition*. Ph.D. thesis, Dept. of ECE, Univ. of Texas at Austin, USA.

[30] Kumar, S. and J. Ghosh, 1999: GAMLS: A generalized framework for associative modular learning systems (invited paper). *Proceedings of the Applications and Science of Computational Intelligence II*, Orlando, Florida, 24–34.

[31] Kumar, S., J. Ghosh and M. M. Crawford, 1999: A versatile framework for labeling imagery with a large number of classes. *Proceedings of the International Joint Conference on Neural Networks*, Washington, D.C.

[32] — 2002: Hierarchical fusion of multiple classifiers for hyperspectral data analysis. *Pattern Analysis and Applications, splecial issue on Fusion of Multiple Classifiers*, **5**, 210–20.

[33] Mao, J. and A. K. Jain, 1995: Artificial neural networks for feature extraction and multivariate data projection. *IEEE Transactions on Neural Networks*, **6 (2)**, 296–317.

[34] McLachlan, G. J., 1992: *Discriminant Analysis and Statistical Pattern Recognition*. John Wiley, New York.

[35] Merz, C. and P. Murphy, 1996: UCI repository of machine learning databases. URL: `www.ics.uci.edu/~mlearn/MLRepository.html`.

[36] Murray-Smith, R. and T. A. Johansen, 1997: *Multiple Model Approaches to Modelling and Control*. Taylor and Francis, UK.

[37] Nilsson, N. J., 1965: *Learning Machines: Foundations of Trainable Pattern-Classifying Systems*. McGraw Hill, NY.

[38] Petridis, V. and A. Kehagias, 1998: *Predictive Modular Neural Networks: Applications to Time Series*. Kluwer Academic Publishers, Boston.

[39] Platt, J. C., N. Cristianini and J. Shawe-Taylor, 2000: Large margin DAGs for multiclass classification. MIT Press, **12**, 547–53.

[40] Rajan, S. and J. Ghosh, 2004: An empirical comparison of hierarchical vs. two-level approaches to multiclass problems. *Multiple Classifier Systems*, F. Roli, J. Kittler and T. Windeatt, eds., LNCS Vol. 3077, Springer, 283–92.

[41] Ramamurti, V. and J. Ghosh, 1998: On the use of localized gating in mixtures of experts networks (invited paper), *SPIE Conf. on Applications and Science of Computational Intelligence, SPIE Proc. Vol. 3390*, 24–35.

[42] — 1999: Structurally adaptive modular networks for nonstationary environments. *IEEE Trans. on Neural Networks*, **10**, 152–60.

[43] Rasoul Safavian, S. and D. Landgrebe, 1991: A survey of decision tree classifier methodology. *IEEE Transactions on Systems, Man, and Cybernetics*, **21**, 660–74.

[44] Rifkin, R. and A. Klautau, 2004: In defense of one-vs-all classification. *Jl. Machine Learning Research*, **5**, 101–41.

[45] Sakurai-Amano, T., J. Iisaka and M. Takagi, 1997: Comparison of land cover indices of AVHRR data. *International Geoscience and Remote Sensing Symposium*, 916–18.

[46] Schölkopf, B., C. Burges and A. J. Smola, eds., 1998: *Advances in Kernel Methods: Support Vector Learning*. MIT Press.

[47] Sharkey, A., 1999: *Combining Artificial Neural Nets*. Springer-Verlag.

[48] Sharkey, A. J. C., N. E. Sharkey, and G. O. Chandroth, 1995: Neural nets and diversity. *Proceedings of the 14th International Conference on Computer Safety, Reliability and Security*, Belgirate, Italy.

[49] Tumer, K. and N. C. Oza, 1999: Decimated input ensembles for improved generalization. *Proceedings of the International Joint Conference on Neural Networks*, Washington, D.C.

[50] Vapnik, V., 1995: *The Nature of Statistical Learning Theory*. Springer.

Graph-based Mining of Complex Data

Diane J. Cook, Lawrence B. Holder, Jeff Coble and Joseph Potts

Summary. We describe an approach to learning patterns in relational data represented as a graph. The approach, implemented in the Subdue system, searches for patterns that maximally compress the input graph. Subdue can be used for supervised learning, as well as unsupervised pattern discovery and clustering.

Mining graph-based data raises challenges not found in linear attribute–value data. However, additional requirements can further complicate the problem. In particular, we describe how Subdue can incrementally process structured data that arrives as streaming data. We also employ these techniques to learn structural concepts from examples embedded in a single large connected graph.

3.1 Introduction

Much of current data-mining research focuses on algorithms to discover sets of attributes that can discriminate data entities into classes, such as shopping or banking trends for a particular demographic group. In contrast, we are developing data-mining techniques to discover patterns consisting of complex relationships between entities. The field of relational data mining, of which graph-based relational learning is a part, is a new area investigating approaches to mining relational information by finding associations involving multiple tables in a relational database.

Two main approaches have been developed for mining relational information: logic-based approaches and graph-based approaches. Logic-based approaches fall under the area of inductive logic programming (ILP) [16]. ILP embodies a number of techniques for inducing a logical theory to describe the data, and many techniques have been adapted to relational data mining [6]. Graph-based approaches differ from logic-based approaches to relational mining in several ways, the most obvious of which is the underlying representation. Furthermore, logic-based approaches rely on the prior identification of the predicate or predicates to be mined, while graph-based approaches are more data-driven, identifying any portion of the graph that has high support. However, logic-based approaches allow the expression of more complicated patterns involving, e.g., recursion, variables, and constraints among variables. These representational limitations of graphs can be overcome, but at a computational cost.

Our research is particularly applicable to domains in which the data is event-driven, such as counter-terrorism intelligence analysis, and domains where distinguishing characteristics can be object attributes or relational attributes. This ability has also become a crucial challenge in many security-related domains. For example, the US House and Senate Intelligence Committees' report on their inquiry into the activities of the intelligence community before and after the September 11, 2001 terrorist attacks revealed the necessity for "connecting the dots" [18], that is, focusing on the relationships between entities in the data, rather than merely on an entity's attributes. A natural representation for this information is a graph, and the ability to discover previously-unknown patterns in such information could lead to significant improvement in our ability to identify potential threats. Similarly, identifying characteristic patterns in spatial or temporal data can be a critical component in acquiring a foundational understanding of important research in many of the basic sciences.

Problems of such complexity often present additional challenges, such as the need to assimilate incremental data updates and the need to learn models from data embedded in a single input graph. In this article we review techniques for graph-based data mining and focus on a method for graph-based relational learning implemented in the Subdue system. We describe methods of enhancing the algorithm to handle challenges associated with complex data, such as incremental discovery of streaming structural data and learning models from embedded instances in supervised graphs.

3.2 Related Work

Graph-based data mining (GDM) is the task of finding novel, useful, and understandable graph-theoretic patterns in a graph representation of data. Several approaches to GDM exist, based on the task of identifying frequently occurring subgraphs in graph transactions, i.e., those subgraphs meeting a minimum level of support. Kuramochi and Karypis [15] developed the FSG system for finding all frequent subgraphs in large graph databases. FSG starts by finding all frequent single and double edge subgraphs. Then, in each iteration, it generates candidate subgraphs by expanding the subgraphs found in the previous iteration by one edge. In each iteration the algorithm checks how many times the candidate subgraph occurs within an entire graph. The candidates whose frequency is below a user-defined level are pruned. The algorithm returns all subgraphs occurring more frequently than the given level.

Yan and Han [19] introduced gSpan, which combines depth-first search and lexicographic ordering to find frequent subgraphs. Their algorithm starts from all frequent one-edge graphs. The labels on these edges, together with labels on incident vertices, define a code for every such graph. Expansion of these one-edge graphs maps them to longer codes. The codes are stored in a tree structure such that if $\alpha = (a_0, a_1, ..., a_m)$ and $\beta = (a_0, a_1, ..., a_m, b)$, the β code is a child of the α code. Since every graph can map to many codes, the codes in the tree structure are not unique. If there are two codes in the code tree that map to the same graph and one is smaller than the other, the branch with the smaller code is pruned during the depth-first search traversal of the code tree. Only the minimum code uniquely defines the graph. Code ordering and pruning reduces the cost of matching frequent subgraphs in gSpan.

Inokuchi *et al.* [12] developed the *Apriori*-based Graph Mining (AGM) system, which uses an approach similar to Agrawal and Srikant's [2] *Apriori* algorithm for discovering frequent itemsets. AGM searches the space of frequent subgraphs in a bottom-up fashion, beginning with a single vertex, and then continually expanding by a single vertex and one or more edges. AGM also employs a canonical coding of graphs in order to support fast subgraph matching. AGM returns association rules satisfying user-specified levels of support and confidence.

We distinguish graph-based relational learning (GBRL) from graph-based data mining in that GBRL focuses on identifying novel, but not necessarily the most frequent, patterns in a graph representation of data [10]. Only a few GBRL approaches have been developed to date. Subdue [4] and GBI [20] take a greedy approach to finding subgraphs, maximizing an information theoretic measure. Subdue searches the space of subgraphs by extending candidate subgraphs by one edge. Each candidate is evaluated using a minimum description length metric [17], which measures how well the subgraph compresses the input graph if each instance of the subgraph were replaced by a single vertex. GBI continually compresses the input graph by identifying frequent triples of vertices, some of which may represent previously-compressed portions of the input graph. Candidate triples are evaluated using a measure similar to information gain. Kernel-based methods have also been used for supervised GBRL [14].

3.3 Graph-based Relational Learning in Subdue

The Subdue graph-based relational learning system[1] [4, 5] encompasses several approaches to graph-based learning, including discovery, clustering and supervised learning, which will be described in this section. Subdue uses a labeled graph $G = (V, E, L)$ as both input and output, where $V = \{v_1, v_2, \ldots, v_n\}$ is a set of vertices, $E = \{(v_i, v_j) | v_i, v_j \in V\}$ is a set of edges, and L is a set of labels that can appear on vertices and edges. The graph G can contain directed edges, undirected edges, self-edges (i.e., $(v_i, v_i) \in E$), and multi-edges (i.e.,

---

[1]Subdue source code, sample data sets and publications are available at ailab.uta.edu/subdue.

more than one edge between vertices v_i and v_j). The input graph need not be connected, but the learned patterns must be connected subgraphs (called substructures) of the input graph. The input to Subdue can consist of one large graph or several individual graph transactions and, in the case of supervised learning, the individual graphs are classified as positive or negative examples.

3.3.1 Substructure Discovery

Subdue searches for a substructure that best compresses the input graph. Subdue uses a variant of beam search for its main search algorithm. A substructure in Subdue consists of a subgraph definition and all its occurrences throughout the graph. The initial state of the search is the set of substructures consisting of all uniquely labeled vertices. The only operator of the search is the *ExtendSubstructure* operator. As its name suggests, it extends a substructure in all possible ways by a single edge and a vertex, or by only a single edge if both vertices are already in the subgraph.

The search progresses by applying the *ExtendSubstructure* operator to each substructure in the current state. The resulting state, however, does not contain all the substructures generated by the *ExtendSubstructure* operator. The substructures are kept on a queue and are ordered based on their description length (sometimes referred to as value) as calculated using the MDL principle described below.

The search terminates upon reaching a user-specified limit on the number of substructures extended, or upon exhaustion of the search space. Once the search terminates and Subdue returns the list of best substructures found, the graph can be compressed using the best substructure. The compression procedure replaces all instances of the substructure in the input graph by single vertices, which represent the substructure definition. Incoming and outgoing edges to and from the replaced instances will point to, or originate in the new vertex that represents the instance. The Subdue algorithm can be invoked again on this compressed graph. This procedure can be repeated a user-specified number of times, and is referred to as an iteration.

Subdue's search is guided by the minimum description length (MDL) [17] principle, which seeks to minimize the description length of the entire data set. The evaluation heuristic based on the MDL principle assumes that the best substructure is the one that minimizes the description length of the input graph when compressed by the substructure [4]. The description length of the substructure S given the input graph G is calculated as $DL(S) + DL(G|S)$, where $DL(S)$ is the description length of the substructure, and $DL(G|S)$ is the description length of the input graph compressed by the substructure. Description length $DL()$ is calculated as the number of bits in a minimal encoding of the graph. Subdue seeks a substructure S that maximizes compression as calculated in Equation (3.1).

$$Compression = \frac{DL(S) + DL(G|S)}{DL(G)} \tag{3.1}$$

As an example, Figure 3.1a shows a collection of geometric objects described by their shapes and their "ontop" relationship to one another. Figure 3.1b shows the graph representation of a portion ("triangle on square") of the input graph for this example and also represents the substructure minimizing the description length of the graph. Figure 3.1c shows the input example after being compressed by the substructure.

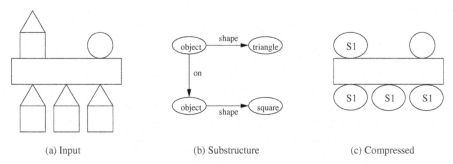

| (a) Input | (b) Substructure | (c) Compressed |

Fig. 3.1. Example of Subdue's substructure discovery capability.

3.3.2 Graph-Based Clustering

Given the ability to find a prevalent subgraph pattern in a larger graph and then compress the graph with this pattern, iterating over this process until the graph can no longer be compressed will produce a hierarchical, conceptual clustering of the input data. On the *ith* iteration, the best subgraph S_i is used to compress the input graph, introducing new vertices labeled Si in the graph input to the next iteration. Therefore, any subsequently-discovered subgraph S_j can be defined in terms of one or more S_i, where $i < j$. The result is a lattice, where each cluster can be defined in terms of more than one parent subgraph. For example, Figure 3.2 shows such a clustering done on a portion of DNA. See [13] for more information on graph-based clustering.

3.4 Supervised Learning from Graphs

Extending a graph-based discovery approach to perform supervised learning involves, of course, the need to handle negative examples (focusing on the two-class scenario). In the case of a graph the negative information can come in two forms. First, the data may be in the form of numerous small graphs, or graph transactions, each labelled either positive or negative. Second, data may be composed of two large graphs: one positive and one negative.

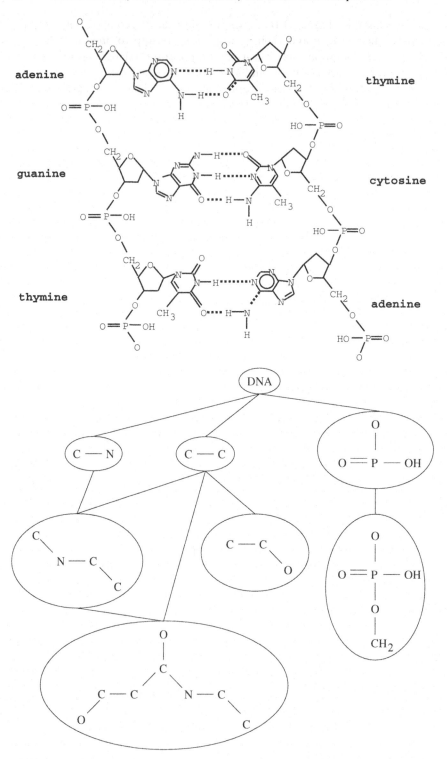

Fig. 3.2. Example of Subdue's clustering (bottom) on a portion of DNA (top).

The first scenario is closest to the standard supervised learning problem in that we have a set of clearly defined examples. Figure 3.3a depicts a simple set of positive and negative examples. Let G^+ represent the set of positive graphs, and G^- represent the set of negative graphs. Then, one approach to supervised learning is to find a subgraph that appears often in the positive graphs, but not in the negative graphs. This amounts to replacing the information-theoretic measure with an error-based measure. For example, we would find a subgraph S that minimizes

$$\frac{|\{g \in G^+ | S \not\subseteq g\}| + |g \in G^- | S \subseteq g\}|}{|G^+| + |G^-|},$$

where $S \subseteq g$ means S is isomorphic to a subgraph of g. The first term of the numerator is the number of false negatives and the second term is the number of false positives.

This approach will lead the search toward a small subgraph that discriminates well, e.g., the subgraph in Figure 3.3b. However, such a subgraph does not necessarily compress well, nor represent a characteristic description of the target concept. We can bias the search toward a more characteristic description by using the information-theoretic measure to look for a subgraph that compresses the positive examples, but not the negative examples. If $I(G)$ represents the description length (in bits) of the graph G, and $I(G|S)$ represents the description length of graph G compressed by subgraph S, then we can look for an S that minimizes $I(G^+|S) + I(S) + I(G^-) - I(G^-|S)$, where the last two terms represent the portion of the negative graph incorrectly compressed by the subgraph. This approach will lead the search toward a larger subgraph that characterizes the positive examples, but not the negative examples, e.g., the subgraph in Figure 3.3c.

Finally, this process can be iterated in a set-covering approach to learn a disjunctive hypothesis. If using the error measure, then any positive example containing the learned subgraph would be removed from subsequent iterations. If using the information-theoretic measure, then instances of the learned subgraph in both the positive and negative examples (even multiple instances per example) are compressed to a single vertex. See [9] for more information on graph-based supervised learning.

3.5 Incremental Discovery from Streaming Data

Many challenging problems require processing and assimilation of periodic increments of new data, which provides new information in addition to that which was previously processed. We introduce our first enhancement of Subdue, called Incremental-Subdue (I-Subdue), which summarizes discoveries from previous data increments so that the globally-best patterns can be computed by examining only the new data increment.

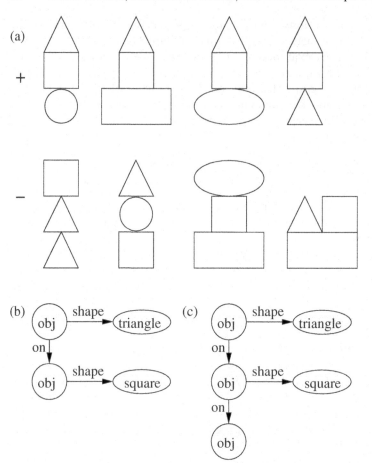

Fig. 3.3. Graph-based supervised learning example with (a) four positive and four negative examples, (b) one possible graph concept and (c) another possible graph concept.

In our work, we assume that data is received in incremental blocks, as is the case for many long-term analytical tasks. Continuously reprocessing the accumulated graph after each increment would be intractable, so instead we wish to develop methods to iteratively refine the substructure discoveries with a minimal amount of reexamination of old data so that the globally-best patterns can be identified based on previous local discoveries.

This work is related to the problem of online sequential learning in which training data is received sequentially [3, 8]. Because learning must start again with each increment, a summary must be generated of prior data to lighten the computational load in building a new model. Online approaches also deal with this incremental mining problem, but restrict the problem to itemset data and assume the data arrives in complete and independent units [1, 7, 11].

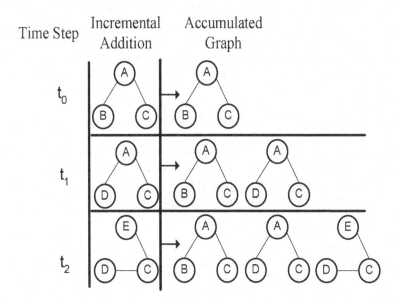

Fig. 3.4. Incremental data can be viewed as a unique extension to the accumulated graph.

In our approach, we view each new data increment as a distinct data structure. Figure 3.4 illustrates one conceptual approach to mining sequential data, where each new increment received at time step t_i is considered independently of earlier data increments so that the accumulation of these structures is viewed as one large, but disconnected, graph. The original Subdue algorithm would still work equally well if we applied it to the accumulated graph after each new data increment is received. The obstacle is the computational burden required for repeated full batch processing.

The concept depicted in Figure 3.4 can be intuitively applied to real problems. For example, a software agent deployed to assist an intelligence analyst would gradually build up a body of data as new information streams in over time. This streaming data could be viewed as independent increments from which common structures are to be derived. Although the data itself may be generated in very small increments, we would expect to accumulate some minimum amount before we mine it. Duplicating nodes and edges in the accumulated graph serves the purpose of giving more weight to frequently-repeated patterns.

3.5.1 Sequential Discovery

Storing all accumulated data and continuing to periodically repeat the entire structure discovery process is intractable both from a computational perspective and for data storage purposes. Instead, we wish to devise a method by which we can discover structures from the most recent data increment and simultaneously refine our knowledge of the globally-best substructures discovered so far. However, we can often encounter a situation where sequential applications of Subdue to individual data increments will yield a series of locally-best substructures that are not the globally-best substructures, that would be found if the data were evaluated as one aggregate block.

Figure 3.5 illustrates an example where Subdue is applied sequentially to each data increment as it is received. At each increment, Subdue discovers the best substructure for the respective data increment, which turns out to be only a local best. However, if we aggregate the same data, as depicted in Figure 3.6, and then apply the baseline Subdue algorithm we get a different best substructure, which in fact is globally best. This is illustrated in Figure 3.7. Although our simple example could easily be aggregated at each time step, realistically large data sets would be too unwieldy for this approach.

In general, sequential discovery and action brings with it a set of unique challenges, which are generally driven by the underlying system that is generating the data. One problem that is almost always a concern is how to re-evaluate the accumulated data at each time step in the light of newly-added data. There is a tradeoff between the amount of data that can be stored and re-evaluated, and the quality of the result. A summarization technique is often employed to capture salient metrics about the data. The richness of this summarization is a tradeoff between the speed of the incremental evaluation and the range of new substructures that can be considered.

3.5.2 Summarization Metrics

We need to develop a summarization metric that can be maintained from each incremental application of Subdue and will allow us to derive the globally-best substructure without reapplying Subdue when new data arrives. To accomplish this goal, we rely on a few artifacts of Subdue's discovery algorithm. First, Subdue maintains a list of the n best substructures discovered from any data set, where n is configurable by the user.

Second, we modify the Compression measure used by Subdue, as shown in Equation (3.2).

$$Compress_m(S_i) \ = \ \frac{DL(S_i) + \sum_{j=1}^{m} DL(G_j|S_i)}{\sum_{j=1}^{m} DL(G_j)} \qquad (3.2)$$

I-Subdue calculates compression achieved by a particular substructure, S_i, through the current data increment m. The $DL(S_i)$ term is the description

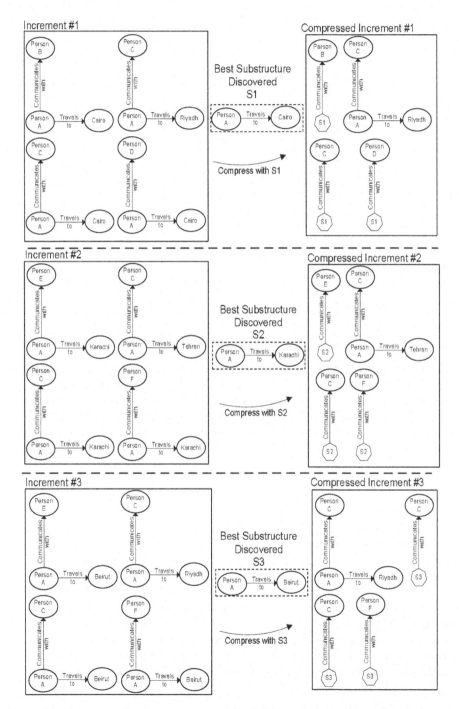

Fig. 3.5. Three data increments received serially and processed individually by Subdue. The best substructure is shown for each local increment.

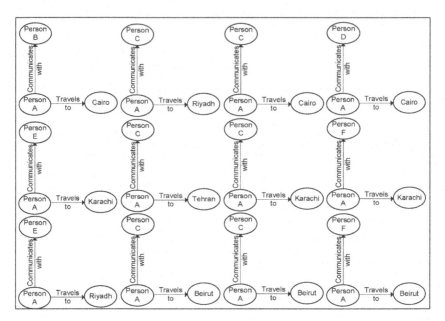

Fig. 3.6. Accumulated graph for Subdue batch processing.

length of the substructure, S_i, under consideration. The term $\sum_{j=1}^{m} DL(G_j|S_i)$ represents the description length of the accumulated graph after it is compressed by substructure S_i. Finally, the term $\sum_{j=1}^{m} DL(G_j)$ represents the full description length of the accumulated graph. I-Subdue then can re-evaluate substructures using Equation (3.3) (an inverse of Equation (3.2)), choosing the one with the lowest value as globally best.

$$argmax(i) \left[\frac{DL(S_i) + \sum_{j=1}^{m} DL(G_j|S_i)}{\sum_{j=1}^{m} DL(G_j)} \right] \qquad (3.3)$$

The process of computing the global substructure value takes place in addition to the normal operation of Subdue on the isolated data increment. We only need to store the requisite description-length metrics after each iteration for use in our global computation.

As an illustration of our approach, consider the results from the example depicted in Figure 3.6. The top $n = 3$ substructures from each iteration are shown in Figure 3.8. Table 3.1 lists the values returned by Subdue from the local top n substructures discovered in each increment. The second best substructures in increments 2 and 3 (S_{22}, S_{32}) are the same as the second best substructure in increment 1 (S_{12}), which is why the column corresponding

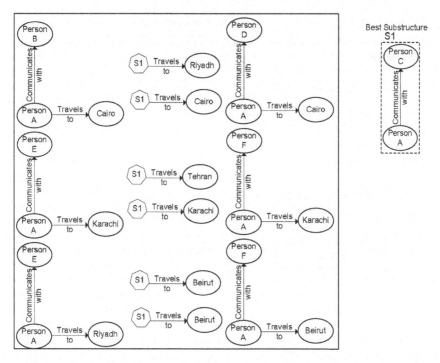

Fig. 3.7. Result from applying Subdue to the three aggregated data increments.

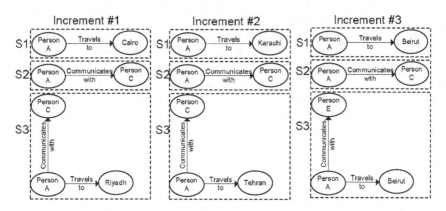

Fig. 3.8. The top n=3 substructures from each local increment.

Table 3.1. Substructure values computed independently for each iteration.

Increment	Substructures from Increment #1			Substructures from Increment #2		Substructures from Increment #3	
	S_{11}	S_{12}	S_{13}	S_{21}	S_{23}	S_{31}	S_{33}
1	**1.2182**	1.04808	0.9815				
2		1.04808		**1.21882**	0.981511		
3		1.03804				**1.15126**	0.966017

Table 3.2. Using I-Subdue to calculate the global value of each substructure.

Increment	Substructures from Increment #1			Substructures from Increment #2		Substructures from Increment #3		
	S_{11}	S_{12}	S_{13}	S_{21}	S_{23}	S_{31}	S_{33}	$DL(G_j)$
1	**1.2182**	1.04808	0.9815					117
2	1.0983	**1.1235**	0.9906	1.0986	0.9906			117
3	1.0636	**1.1474**	0.9937	1.0638	0.9937	1.0455	0.9884	116
$DL(S_i)$	15	15	25.7549	15	25.7549	15	26.5098	

to S_{12} has a value for each iteration. The values in Table 3.1 are the result of the compression evaluation metric from Equation (3.1). The locally-best substructures illustrated in Figure 3.5 have the highest values overall.

Table 3.2 depicts our application of I-Subdue to the increments from Figure 3.5. After each increment is received, we apply Equation (3.3) to select the globally-best substructure. The values in Table 3.2 are the inverse of the compression metric from Equation (3.2). As an example, the calculation of the compression metric for substructure S_{12} after iteration 3 would be $\frac{DL(S_{12})+DL(G_1|S_{12})+DL(G_2|S_{12})+DL(G_3|S_{12})}{DL(G_1)+DL(G_2)+DL(G_3)}$. Consequently the value of S_{12} would be $(117 + 117 + 116) / (15 + 96.63 + 96.63 + 96.74) = 1.1474$.

For this computation, we rely on the metrics computed by Subdue when it evaluates substructures in a graph, namely the description length of the discovered substructure, the description length of the graph compressed by the substructure, and the description length of the graph. By storing these values after each increment is processed, we can retrieve the globally-best substructure using Equation (3.3). In circumstances where a specific substructure is not present in a particular data increment, such as S_{31} in iteration 2, then $DL(G_2|S_{31}) = DL(G_2)$ and the substructure's value would be calculated as $(117 + 117 + 116) / (15 + 117 + 117 + 85.76) = 1.0455$.

3.5.3 Experimental Evaluation

To illustrate the relative value of I-Subdue with respect to performance in processing incremental data, we have conducted experiments with a synthetic data generator. This data generator takes as input a library of data labels, configuration parameters governing the size of random graph patterns and one or more specific substructures to be embedded within the random data. Connectivity can also be controlled.

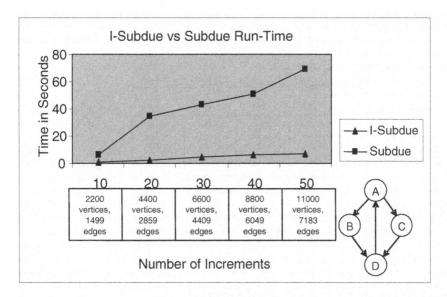

Fig. 3.9. Comparison of I-Subdue with Subdue on 10–50 increments, each with 220 new vertices and 0 or 1 outgoing edges.

For the first experiment, illustrated in Figure 3.9, we compare the performance of I-Subdue to Subdue at benchmarks ranging from 10 to 50 increments. Each increment introduced 220 new vertices, within which five instances of the four-vertex substructure pictured in Figure 3.9 were embedded. The quality of the result, in terms of the number of discovered instances, was the same.

The results from the second graph are depicted in Figure 3.10. For this experiment, we increased the increment size to 1020 vertices. Each degree value between 1 and 4 was shown with 25% probability, which means that on average there are about twice as many edges as vertices. This more densely connected graph begins to illustrate the significance of the run-time difference between I-Subdue and Subdue. Again, five instances of the four-vertex substructure shown in Figure 3.10 were embedded within each increment. The discovery results were the same for both I-Subdue and Subdue with the only qualitative difference being in the run time.

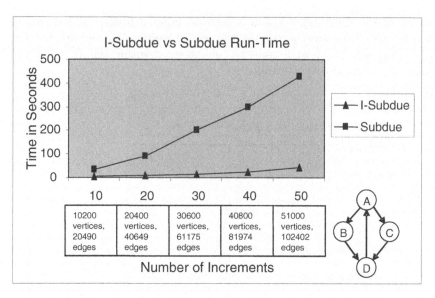

Fig. 3.10. Comparison of I-Subdue with Subdue on 10–50 increments, each with 1020 new vertices and 1 to 4 outgoing edges.

3.5.4 Learning from Supervised Graphs

In a highly relational domain, the positive and negative examples of a concept are not easily separated. We call such a graph a *supervised graph*, in that the graph as a whole contains embedded class information which may not easily be separated into individual labeled components. For example, consider a social network in which we seek to find relational patterns distinguishing various income levels. Individuals of a particular income level can appear anywhere in the graph and may be related to individuals at other income levels, so we cannot easily partition the graph into separate training cases without potentially severing the target relationships.

This scenario presents a challenge to any data mining system, but especially to a graph-based relational learning system, where clearly classified data (data labeled with a class value) may be tightly related to less clearly classified data. This is the second challenge discussed in this chapter. We are investigating two approaches to this task. We assume that the class values of certain vertices and edges are specified in the input data file. Not all vertices and edges will have such a value, as some may provide supplementary supporting information.

For the first approach, we rely upon a cost mechanism available in Subdue. A cost mechanism was added because expenses might be associated with the retrieval of portions of data. For example, adding personal details such as credit history to our social network can enhance the input data, but may be acquired at a price in terms of money, time, or other resources. To implement the cost feature, the cost of specific vertices and edges is specified in the input file. The cost for substructure S averaged over all of its instances, $Cost(S)$, is then combined with the MDL value of S using the equation $E(S) = (1 - Cost(S)) \times MDL(S)$. The evaluation measure, $E(S)$, determines the overall value of the substructure and is used to order candidate substructures.

Class membership in a supervised graph can now be treated as a cost, which varies from no cost for clearly positive members to +1 for clearly negative members. As an example, we consider the problem of learning which regions of the ocean surface can expect a temperature increase in the next time step. Our data set contains gridded sea surface temperatures (SST) derived from NASA's Pathfinder algorithm and a five-channel Advanced Very High Resolution Radiometer instrument. The data contains location, time of year, and temperature data for each region of the globe.

The portion of the data used for training is represented as a graph with vertices for each month, discretized latitude and longitude values, hemisphere, and change in temperature from one month to the next. Vertices labelled with "increase" thus represent the positive examples and "decrease" or "same" labels represent negative examples. A portion of the graph is shown in Figure 3.11. The primary substructure discovered by Subdue for this data set reports the rule that when there are two regions in the Southern hemisphere, one just north of the other, an increase in temperature can be expected for the next month in the southernmost of the two regions. Using three-fold cross validation experimentation, Subdue classified this data set with 71% accuracy.

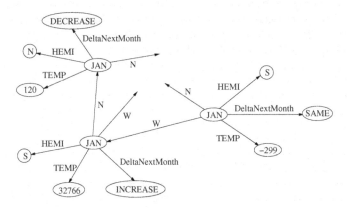

Fig. 3.11. Graph representation of a portion of NASA's SST data.

The second approach we intend to explore involves modifying the MDL encoding to take into account the amount of information necessary to describe the class membership of the compressed graph. Substructures would now be discovered that not only compress the raw data of the graph but also express class membership for vertices and edges within the graph.

3.6 Conclusions

There are several future directions for our graph-based relational learning research that will improve our ability to handle such challenging data as described in this chapter. The incremental discovery technique described in this chapter did not address data that is connected across increment boundaries. However, many domains will include event correlations that transcend multiple data iterations. For example, a terrorist suspect introduced in one data increment may be correlated to events that are introduced in later increments. As each data increment is received it may contain new edges that extend from vertices in the new data increment to vertices received in previous increments. We are investigating techniques of growing substructures across increment boundaries. We are also considering methods of detecting changes in the strengths of substructures across increment boundaries, that could represent concept shift or drift.

The handling of supervised graphs is an important direction for mining structural data. To extend our current work, we would like to handle embedded instances without a single representative instance node (the "increase" and "decrease" nodes in our NASA example) and instances that may possibly overlap.

Finally, improved scalability of graph operations is necessary to learn patterns, evaluate their accuracy on test cases and, ultimately, to use the patterns to find matches in future intelligence data. The graph and subgraph isomorphism operations are a significant bottleneck to these capabilities. We need to develop faster and approximate versions of these operations to improve the scalability of graph-based relational learning.

Acknowledgments: This research is sponsored by the Air Force Research Laboratory (AFRL) under contract F30602-01-2-0570. The views and conclusions contained in this document are those of the authors and should not be interpreted as necessarily representing the official policies, either expressed or implied, of AFRL or the United States Government.

References

[1] Agrawal, R. and G. Psaila, 1995: Active data mining. *Proceedings of the Conference on Knowledge Discovery in Databases and Data Mining.*

[2] Agrawal, R. and R. Srikant, 1994: Fast algorithms for mining association rules. *Proceedings of the Twentieth Conference on Very Large Databases,* 487–99.

[3] Blum, A., 1996: On-line algorithms in machine learning. *Proceedings of the workshop on on-line algorithms.*

[4] Cook, D. J. and L. B. Holder, 1994: Substructure discovery using minimum description length and background knowledge. *Journal of Artificial Intelligence Research*, **1**, 231–55.

[5] — 2000: Graph-based data mining. *IEEE Intelligent Systems*, **15**, 32–41.

[6] Dzeroski, S. and N. Lavrac, eds., 2001: *Relational Data Mining*. Springer.

[7] Fang, H., W. Fan, P. Yu and J. Han, 2003: Mining concept-drifting data streams using ensemble classifiers. *Proceedings of the Conference on Knowledge Discovery and Data Mining.*

[8] Friedman, N. and M. Goldszmidt, 1997: Sequential update of Bayesian network structure. *Proceedings of the Conference on Uncertainty in Artificial Intelligence.*

[9] Gonzalez, J., L. Holder and D. Cook, 2002: Graph-based relational concept learning. *Proceedings of the Nineteenth International Conference on Machine Learning.*

[10] Holder, L. B. and D. J. Cook, 2003: Graph-based relational learning: Current and future directions. *ACM SIGKDD Explorations*, **5**, 90–93.

[11] Hulten, G., L. Spencer and P. Domingos, 2001: Mining time-changing data streams. *Proceedings of the Conference on Knowledge Discovery and Data Mining.*

[12] Inokuchi, A., T. Washio and H. Motoda, 2003: Complete mining of frequent patterns from graphs: Mining graph data. *Machine Learning*, **50**, 321–54.

[13] Jonyer, I., D. Cook and L. Holder, 2001: Graph-based hierarchical conceptual clustering. *Journal of Machine Learning Research*, **2**, 19–43.

[14] Kashima, H. and A. Inokuchi, 2002: Kernels for graph classification. *Proceedings of the International Workshop on Active Mining.*

[15] Kuramochi, M. and G. Karypis, 2001: Frequent subgraph discovery. *Proceedings of the First IEEE Conference on Data Mining.*

[16] Muggleton, S., ed., 1992: *Inductive Logic Programming*. Academic Press, San Diego, CA, USA.

[17] Rissanen, J., 1989: *Stochastic Complexity in Statistical Inquiry*. World Scientific, Singapore.

[18] US Senate, 2002: Joint inquiry into intelligence community activities before and after the terrorist attacks of September 11, 2001. S. Rept.107-351.

[19] Yan, X. and J. Han, 2002: gSpan: Graph-based substructure pattern mining. *Proceedings of the International Conference on Data Mining.*

[20] Yoshida, K., H. Motoda and N. Indurkhya, 1994: Graph-based induction as a unified learning framework. *Journal of Applied Intelligence*, **4**, 297–328.

4

Predictive Graph Mining with Kernel Methods

Thomas Gärtner

Summary. Graphs are a major tool for modeling objects with complex data structures. Devising learning algorithms that are able to handle graph representations is thus a core issue in knowledge discovery with complex data. While a significant amount of recent research has been devoted to inducing functions on the vertices of the graph, we concentrate on the task of inducing a function on the set of graphs. Application areas of such learning algorithms range from computer vision to biology and beyond. Here, we present a number of results on extending kernel methods to complex data, in general, and graph representations, in particular. With the very good performance of kernel methods on data that can easily be embedded in a Euclidean space, kernel methods have the potential to overcome some of the major weaknesses of previous approaches to learning from complex data. In order to apply kernel methods to graph data, we propose two different kernel functions and compare them on a relational reinforcement learning problem and a molecule classification problem.

4.1 Introduction

Graphs are an important tool for modeling complex data in a systematic way. Technically, different types of graphs can be used to model the objects. Conceptually, different aspects of the objects can be modeled by graphs: (i) Each object is a vertex in a graph modeling the relation between the objects, and (ii) each object is modeled by a graph. While a significant amount of recent research is devoted to case i, here we are concerned with case ii. An important example for this case is the prediction of biological activity of molecules given their chemical structure graph.

Suppose we know of a function that estimates the effectiveness of chemical compounds against a particular illness. This function would be very helpful in developing new drugs. One possibility for obtaining such a function is to use in-depth chemical knowledge. A different – and for us more interesting – possibility is to try to learn from chemical compounds with known effectiveness against that illness. We will call these compounds "training instances". Supervised machine learning tries to to find a function that generalizes over these training instances, i.e., a function that is able to estimate the effectiveness of other chemical compounds against this disease. We will call this function the "hypothesis" and the set of all functions considered as possible hypotheses, the "hypothesis space".

Though chemical compounds are three-dimensional structures, the three-dimensional shape is often determined by the chemical structure graph. That is, the representation of a molecule by a set of atoms, a set of bonds connecting pairs of atoms, and a mapping from atoms to element-types (carbon, hydrogen, ...) as well as from bonds to bond-types (single, double, aromatic, ...). Standard machine learning algorithms can not be applied to such a representation.

Predictive graph mining is interested in supervised machine learning problems with graph-based representations. This is an emerging research topic at the heart of knowledge discovery from complex data. In contrast with other graph mining approaches it is not primarily concerned with finding interesting or frequent patterns in a graph database but only with supervised machine learning, i.e., with inducing a function on the set of all graphs that approximates well some unknown functional or conditional dependence. In the above mentioned application this would be effectiveness against an illness depending on the chemical structure of a compound.

Kernel methods are a class of learning algorithms that can be applied to any learning problem as long as a positive-definite kernel function has been defined on the set of instances. The hypothesis space of kernel methods is the linear hull (i.e., the set of linear combinations) of positive-definite kernel functions "centered" at some training instances. Kernel methods have shown good predictive performance on many learning problems, such as text classification. In order to apply kernel methods to instances represented by graphs, we need to define meaningful and efficiently computable positive-definite kernel functions on graphs.

In this article we describe two different kernels for labeled graphs together with applications to relational reinforcement learning and molecule classification. The first graph kernel is based on comparing the label sequences corresponding to walks occurring in each graph. Although these walks may have infinite length, for undirected graphs, such as molecules, this kernel function can be computed in polynomial time by using properties of the direct product graph and computing the limit of a power series. In the molecule classification domain that we will look at, however, exact computation of this kernel function is infeasible and we need to resort to approximations. This motivates the search for other graph kernels that can be computed more efficiently on this domain. We thus propose a graph kernel based on the decomposition of each graph into a set of simple cycles and into the set of connected components of the graph induced by the set of bridges in the graph. Each of these cycles and trees is transformed into a pattern and the cyclic-pattern kernel for graphs is the cardinality of the intersection of two pattern sets. Although cyclic-pattern kernels can not be computed in polynomial time, empirical results on a molecule classification problem show that, while walk-based graph kernels exhibit higher predictive performance, cyclic-pattern kernels can be computed much faster. Both kernels perform better than, or at least as good as, previously proposed predictive graph mining approaches over different subproblems and parameter settings.

Section 4.2 introduces kernel methods, kernels for structured instances spaces, and discusses the relation between kernels and distances for structured instances. Section 4.3 begins with the introduction of general set kernels and conceptually describes kernels for other data structures afterwards. Section 4.4 describes walk-based graph kernels and cyclic-pattern kernels for graphs. Two applications of predictive graph mining are shown in Section 4.5, before Section 4.6 concludes.

4.2 Learning with Kernels and Distances

In this section we first define what is meant by a positive-definite kernel function and briefly introduce the basics of kernel methods. We illustrate the importance of choosing the "right" kernel function on a simple example. After that, we summarise different definitions of kernel functions for instances represented by vertices in a graph. Last but not least, we discuss the relation between well known distance functions for complex data and kernel functions.

4.2.1 Kernel Methods

Kernel methods [41] are a popular class of algorithms within the machine-learning and data-mining communities. Being theoretically well founded in statistical learning theory, they have shown good empirical results in many applications. One particular aspect of kernel methods such as the support vector machine is the formation of hypotheses by linear combination of positive-definite kernel functions "centered" at individual training instances. By the restriction to positive-definite kernel functions, the regularized risk minimization problem (we will define this problem once we have defined positive-definite functions) becomes convex and every locally optimal solution is globally optimal.

Kernel Functions
Kernel methods can be applied to different kinds of (structured) data by using any positive-definite kernel function defined on the data.

A symmetric function $k : \mathcal{X} \times \mathcal{X} \to \mathbb{R}$ on a set $\mathcal{X}$ is called a *positive-definite kernel* on that set if, for all $n \in \mathbb{Z}^+$, $x_1, \ldots, x_n \in \mathcal{X}$, and $c_1, \ldots, c_n \in \mathbb{R}$, it follows that

$$\sum_{i,j\in\{1,\dots,n\}} c_i\, c_j\, k(x_i, x_j) \geq 0.$$

Kernel Machines
The usual supervised learning model [44] considers a set $\mathcal{X}$ of individuals and a set $\mathcal{Y}$ of labels, such that the relation between individuals and labels is a fixed but unknown probability measure on the set $\mathcal{X} \times \mathcal{Y}$. The common theme in many different kernel methods such as support vector machines, Gaussian processes, or regularized least squares regression is to find a hypothesis function that minimizes not just the empirical risk (the training error) but also the *regularized risk*. This gives rise to the optimization problem

$$\min_{f(\cdot)\in\mathcal{H}} \frac{C}{n} \sum_{i=1}^{n} V(y_i, f(x_i)) + \|f(\cdot)\|_{\mathcal{H}}^2$$

where C is a parameter, $\{(x_i, y_i)\}_{i=1}^{n}$ is a set of individuals with known label (the training set), $\mathcal{H}$ is a set of functions forming a Hilbert space (the hypothesis space) and V is a function that takes on small values whenever $f(x_i)$ is a good guess for y_i and large values whenever it is a bad guess (the loss function). The *representer theorem* shows that under rather general conditions on V, solutions of the above optimization problem have the form

$$f(\cdot) = \sum_{i=1}^{n} c_i k(x_i, \cdot). \tag{4.1}$$

Different kernel methods arise from using different loss functions.

Regularized Least Squares
Choosing the square loss function, i.e., $V(y_i, f(x_i)) = (y_i - f(x_i))^2$, we obtain the optimization problem of the algorithm [39, 40]:

$$\min_{f(\cdot)\in\mathcal{H}} \frac{C}{n} \sum_{i=1}^{n} (y_i - f(x_i))^2 + \|f(\cdot)\|_{\mathcal{H}}^2$$

Plugging in our knowledge about the form of solutions and taking the directional derivative with respect to the parameter vector c of Equation (4.1), we can find the analytic solution to the optimization problem as:

$$c = \left(K + \frac{n}{C}\mathbf{I}\right)^{-1} y$$

where $\mathbf{I}$ denotes the identity matrix of appropriate size.

Support Vector Machines
Support vector machines [2, 41] are a kernel method that can be applied to binary-supervised classification problems. They are derived from the above

optimization problem by choosing the so-called *hinge loss* $V(y, f(x)) = \max\{0, 1 - yf(x)\}$. The motivation for support vector machines often given in the literature is that the solution can be interpreted as a hyperplane that separates both classes (if it exists) and is maximally distant from the convex hulls of both classes. A different motivation is the computational attractiveness of sparse solutions of Equation (4.1) used for classification.

For support vector machines the problem of minimizing the regularized risk can be transformed into the so-called "primal" optimization problem of soft-margin support vector machines:

$$\min_{c \in \mathbb{R}^n} \frac{C}{n} \sum_{i=1}^{n} \xi_i + c^\top K c$$

$$\text{subject to: } y_i \sum_j c_j k(x_i, x_j) \geq 1 - \xi_i \; i = 1, \ldots n$$

$$\xi_i \geq 0 \qquad\qquad\qquad i = 1, \ldots n.$$

Gaussian Processes

Gaussian processes [35] are an incrementally learnable Bayesian regression algorithm. Rather than parameterizing some set of possible target functions and specifying a prior over these parameters, Gaussian processes directly put a (Gaussian) prior over the function space. A Gaussian process is defined by a mean function and a covariance function, implicitly specifying the prior. The choice of covariance functions is thereby only limited to positive-definite kernels. It can be seen that the mean prediction of a Gaussian process corresponds to the prediction found by a regularized least squares algorithm. This links the regularization parameter C with the variance of the Gaussian noise distribution assumed in Gaussian processes.

Illustration

To illustrate the importance of choosing the "right" kernel function, we next illustrate the hypothesis found by a Gaussian process with different kernel functions.

In Figure 4.1 the training examples are pairs of real numbers $x \in \mathcal{X} = \mathbb{R}^2$ illustrated by black discs and circles in the figure. The (unknown) target function is an XOR-type function, the target variable y takes values -1 for the black discs and $+1$ for the black circles. The probability of a test example being of class $+1$ is illustrated by the color of the corresponding pixel in the figure. The different kernels used are the linear kernel $k(x, x') = \langle x, x' \rangle$, the polynomial kernel $k(x, x') = (\langle x, x' \rangle + l)^p$, the sigmoid kernel $k(x, x') = \tanh(\gamma \langle x, x' \rangle)$, and the Gaussian kernel function $k(x, x') = \exp\left[-\|x - x'\|^2/\sigma^2\right]$.

Figure 4.2 illustrates the impact of choosing the parameter of a Gaussian kernel function on the regularization of the solution found by a Gaussian process. Training examples are single real numbers and the target value is

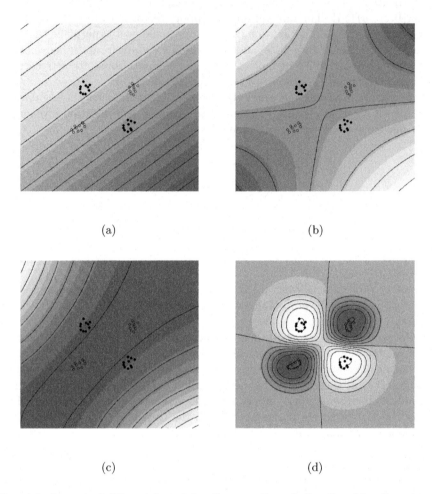

(a)   (b)

(c)   (d)

Fig. 4.1. Impact of different kernel functions on the solution found by Gaussian processes. Kernel functions are (a) linear kernel, (b) polynomial kernel of degree 2, (c) sigmoid kernel and (d) Gaussian kernel.

also a real number. The unknown target function is a sinusoid function shown by a thin line in the figure. Training examples perturbed by random noise are depicted by black circles. The color of each pixel illustrates the likeliness of a target value given a test example, with the most likely value colored white.

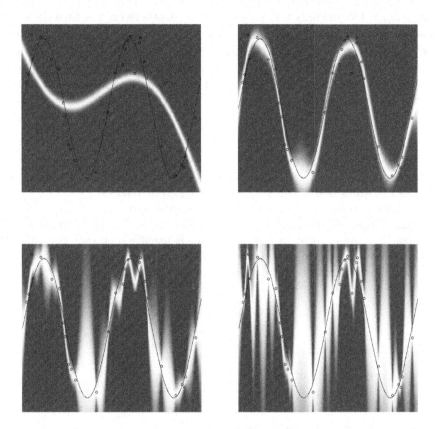

Fig. 4.2. Impact of the bandwidth of a Gaussian kernel function on the regularization of the solution found by Gaussian processes. The bandwidth is decreasing from left to right, top to bottom.

4.2.2 Kernels for Structured Instance Spaces

To model the structure of instance spaces, undirected graphs or hypergraphs are often used. While the use of hypergraphs is less common in the literature, it appears more systematic and intuitive.

A hypergraph is described by a set of vertices $\mathcal{V}$ – the instances – and a set of edges $\mathcal{E}$, where each edge corresponds to a set of vertices. Each edge of the hypergraph can be interpreted as some property that all vertices of the edge have in common. For documents, for example, the edges could correspond to words or citations that they have in common; in a metric space the hyperedge could include all vertices with distance less than a given threshold from some point.

For a hypergraph with n vertices and m edges, we define the $n \times m$ matrix B by $B_{ij} = 1$ if and only if $v_i \in e_j$ and $B_{ij} = 0$, otherwise. Let then the $n \times n$ matrix D be defined by $D_{ii} = \sum_j [B^\top B]_{ij} = \sum_j [B^\top B]_{ji}$. The matrices $B^\top B$ and $L = D - B^\top B$ are positive-definite by construction. The matrix L is known as the graph Laplacian. Often also the normalized Laplacian is used.

Conceptually, kernel matrices are then defined as the limits of matrix power series of the form

$$K = \sum_{i=0}^{\infty} \lambda_i \left(B^\top B \right)^i \qquad \text{or} \qquad K = \sum_{i=0}^{\infty} \lambda_i \left(-L \right)^i$$

with parameters λ_i. These power series can be interpreted as measuring the number of walks of different lengths between given vertices.

Limits of such power series can be computed by means of an eigenvalue decomposition of $-L$ or $B^\top B$, and a "recomposition" with modified eigenvalues. The modification of the eigenvalues is usually such that the order of eigenvalues is kept, while all eigenvalues are forced to become positive.

Examples for such kernel functions are the diffusion kernel [29]

$$K = \sum_{i=0}^{\infty} \frac{\beta^i}{i!} (-L)^i \ ,$$

the von Neumann kernel [25]

$$K = \sum_{i=1}^{\infty} \gamma^{i-1} \left(B^\top B \right)^i \ ,$$

and the regularized Laplacian kernel [42]

$$K = \sum_{i=1}^{\infty} \gamma^i (-L)^i \ .$$

For exponential power series such as the diffusion kernel, the limit can be computed by exponentiating the eigenvalues, while for geometrical power series, the limit can be computed by the formula $1/(1 - \gamma e)$, where e is an eigenvalue of $B^\top B$ or $-L$, respectively. A general framework and analysis of these kernels is given in [42].

4.2.3 Kernels versus Distances for Structured Instances

Previous approaches to predictive graph mining mostly used decision trees [20] or distance-based algorithms. Due to the close relation between kernels and distances[1] we thus investigate how distances on structured instances are defined.

---

[1] Every inner product space is a metric space.

In the literature, distances are often defined using the minima and/or maxima over a set of distances, e.g., all distances described in [12] between point sets, the string edit distance [13] between sequences, or the subgraph distance [3, 36] between graphs. It is thus interesting to investigate whether in general kernel functions can be defined as the minimum and/or maximum of a set of kernels. In this section we investigate whether certain uses of minima and/or maxima give rise to positive-definite kernels and discuss minima- and maxima-based kernels on instances represented by sets.

Minimal and Maximal Functions
We begin our discussion with two very simple uses of minima and maxima.

The function $\min\{x, x'\}$ defined on non-negative real numbers is positive-definite: Let $\theta_x(\cdot)$ be the function such that $\theta_x(z) = 1$ if $z \in [0; x]$ and $\theta_x(z) = 0$ otherwise. Then,

$$\min\{x, x'\} = \int_{\mathbb{R}} \theta_x(\cdot) * \theta_{x'}(\cdot) d\mu$$

coincides with the usual (L_2) inner product between the functions $\theta_x(\cdot)$ and $\theta_{x'}(\cdot)$. Thus it is positive-definite.

The function $\max\{x, x'\}$ defined on non-negative real numbers is not positive-definite. Setting $x = 0, x' = 1$ we obtain the indefinite matrix

$$\begin{pmatrix} 0 & 1 \\ 1 & 1 \end{pmatrix} .$$

We show next, that – in general – functions built from positive-definite kernels using the min or max function are not positive-definite.

The function $\min_i k_i(x, x')$ where each k_i is a positive-definite kernel, is not necessarily positive-definite: Setting $x = 1; x' = 2; k_1(x, x') = xx'; k_2(x, x') = (3 - x)(3 - x')$ gives rise to the indefinite matrix

$$\begin{pmatrix} 1 & 2 \\ 2 & 1 \end{pmatrix} .$$

The function $\max_i k_i(x, x')$ where again each k_i is a positive-definite kernel, is not necessarily positive-definite: If this function was positive-definite then the component wise maximum of two positive-definite matrices would also be positive-definite. Consider the matrices

$$A = \begin{pmatrix} 1 & 1 & 0 \\ 1 & 1 & 0 \\ 0 & 0 & 1 \end{pmatrix} ; \quad B = \begin{pmatrix} 1 & 0 & 0 \\ 0 & 1 & 1 \\ 0 & 1 & 1 \end{pmatrix} .$$

Here, A has the eigenvectors $(1, 1, 0)^\top$; $(0, 0, 1)^\top$; $(1, -1, 0)^\top$ with corresponding eigenvalues $2, 1, 0 \geq 0$, showing that both matrices are positive-definite. The component wise maximum of A and B

$$D = \begin{pmatrix} 1 & 1 & 0 \\ 1 & 1 & 1 \\ 0 & 1 & 1 \end{pmatrix}$$

is, however, indefinite: $(1, 0, 0)D(1, 0, 0)^\top = 1 > 0$ and $(1, -1, 1)D(1, -1, 1)^\top = -1 < 0$.

Minimal and Maximal Functions on Sets

We now proceed with two simple cases in which positive-definiteness holds for kernels on sets using minima or maxima functions.

The function $\min_{x \in X, x' \in X'} x * x'$ defined on sets of non-negative real numbers $X, X' \subset \mathbb{R}^+$ is positive-definite as

$$\min_{x \in X, x' \in X'} x * x' = \left(\min_{x \in X} x \right) * \left(\min_{x' \in X'} x' \right).$$

The function $\max_{x \in X, x' \in X'} x * x'$ defined on sets of non-negative real numbers $X, X' \subset \mathbb{R}^+$ is positive-definite as

$$\max_{x \in X, x' \in X'} x * x' = \left(\max_{x \in X} x \right) * \left(\max_{x' \in X'} x' \right).$$

Now we turn to the more general functions $\min_{x \in X, x' \in X'} k(x, x')$ and $\max_{x \in X, x' \in X'} k(x, x')$. These are strongly related to the functions $\min_i k_i(x, x')$ and $\max_i k_i(x, x')$ considered above. To see this let $X = \{x_i\}; X' = \{x'_j\}$ and $k_{ij}(X, X') = k(x_i, x'_j)$. Then

$$\min_{x \in X, x' \in X'} k(x, x') = \min_{ij} k_{ij}(X, X')$$

and

$$\max_{x \in X, x' \in X'} k(x, x') = \max_{ij} k_{ij}(X, X').$$

Though this indicates that $\min_{x \in X, x' \in X'} k(x, x')$ and $\max_{x \in X, x' \in X'} k(x, x')$ are not positive-definite, it does not prove it yet. Thus we continue with two counter-examples. For $\min_{x \in X, x' \in X'} k(x, x')$ with $X = \{(1, 2)^\top, (2, 1)^\top, (2, 0)^\top\}$, $X' = \{(2, 1)^\top\}$, and using $k(x, x') = \langle x, x' \rangle$ we obtain the indefinite matrix

$$\begin{pmatrix} 2 & 4 \\ 4 & 5 \end{pmatrix}.$$

Similarly, for $\max_{x \in X, x' \in X'} k(x, x')$ with $x_1 = \{(1, 0)^\top\}$, $x_2 = \{(1, 0)^\top, (0, 1)^\top\}$, $x_3 = \{(0, 1)^\top\}$, and again $k(x, x') = \langle x, x' \rangle$ we obtain the matrix

$$D = \begin{pmatrix} 1 & 1 & 0 \\ 1 & 1 & 1 \\ 0 & 1 & 1 \end{pmatrix}$$

which is again indefinite.

The observations made above indicate that kernels for complex data can not be made up such that they directly correspond to the previously defined distances for complex data. This motivates the search for alternative kernel functions such as the ones described below.

4.3 Sets and Beyond

An integral part of many kernels for complex data is the *decomposition* of an object into a set of its parts and the *intersection* of two sets of parts. The kernel on two objects is then defined as a measure of the intersection of the two corresponding sets of parts. In this section we first summarise some basics about kernels on sets. Then we give a brief overview of different kernel functions for complex data.

The general case of interest for set kernels is when the instances X_i are elements of a semi-ring of sets $\mathfrak{S}$ and there is a measure μ with $\mathfrak{S}$ as its domain of definition.

A natural choice of a kernel on such data is the intersection kernel defined as

$$k_\cap(X_i, X_j) = \mu(X_i \cap X_j); X_i, X_i \in \mathfrak{S} . \tag{4.2}$$

It is known [28] that for any $X_1, \ldots X_n$ belonging to $\mathfrak{S}$ there is a finite system of pairwise disjoint sets $\mathcal{A} = \{A_1, \ldots A_m\} \subseteq \mathfrak{S}$ such that every X_i is a union of some A_l. Let $\mathcal{B}_i \subseteq \mathcal{A}$ be such that $X_i = \bigcup_{B \in \mathcal{B}_i} B$. Furthermore let the characteristic function $\Gamma_X : \mathcal{A} \to \{0; 1\}$ be defined as $\Gamma_X(A) = 1 \Leftrightarrow A \subseteq X$ and $\Gamma_X(A) = 0$ otherwise. With these definitions we can write

$$\mu(X_i \cap X_j) = \sum_{B \in \mathcal{B}_i \cap \mathcal{B}_j} \mu(B) = \sum_{A \in \mathcal{A}} \Gamma_{X_i}(A)\Gamma_{X_j}(A)\mu(A) .$$

The intersection kernel is then positive-definite on $X_1, \ldots X_n$ as

$$\sum_{ij} c_i c_j \mu(X_i \cap X_j) = \sum_{ij} c_i c_j \sum_{A \in \mathcal{A}} \Gamma_{X_i}(A)\Gamma_{X_j}(A)\mu(A)$$

$$= \sum_{A \in \mathcal{A}} \left(\sum_i c_i \Gamma_{X_i}(A) \right)^2 \mu(A)$$

$$\geq 0 .$$

Note that in the simplest case (finite sets with $\mu(\cdot)$ being the set cardinality) the intersection kernel coincides with the inner product of the bitvector representations of the sets.

In the case that the sets X_i are finite or countable sets of elements on which a kernel has been defined, it is often beneficial to use set kernels other than the intersection kernel. For example the crossproduct kernel

$$k_\times(X_i, X_j) = \sum_{x_i \in X_i, x_j \in X_j} k(x_i, x_j) . \tag{4.3}$$

The crossproduct kernel with the right kernel set to the matching kernel (defined as $k_\delta(x_i, x_j) = 1 \Leftrightarrow x_i = x_j$ and 0 otherwise) coincides with the intersection kernel.

In the remainder of this section we are more interested in the case that $\mathfrak{S}$ is a Borel algebra with unit $\mathcal{X}$, and μ is countably additive with $\mu(\mathcal{X}) < \infty$. We can then extend the definition of the characteristic functions to $\mathcal{X} = \bigcup_{C \in \mathfrak{S}} C$ such that $\Gamma_X(x) = 1 \Leftrightarrow x \in X$ and $\Gamma_X(x) = 0$ otherwise. We can then write the intersection kernel as

$$k_\cap(X_i, X_j) = \mu(X \cap X') = \int_\mathcal{X} \Gamma_{X_i}(x) * \Gamma_{X_j}(x) d\mu \tag{4.4}$$

this shows the relation of the intersection kernel to the usual (L_2) inner product between the characteristic functions $\Gamma_X(\cdot), \Gamma_{X'}(\cdot)$ of the sets.

Similarly, for the crossproduct kernel in Equation (4.3) we obtain in this setting the integral equation

$$\int_{X \times X'} k(x, x') d\mu d\mu = \int_{\mathcal{X} \times \mathcal{X}} \Gamma_X(x) * k(x, x') * \Gamma_{X'}(x') d\mu d\mu$$

with any positive-definite kernel k defined on the elements.

Note, that with the matching kernel k_δ we recover the intersection kernel from Equation (4.4) albeit with different measure.

In the remainder of this section we describe kernels for complex data that have been defined in the literature. For a more complete survey of kernels for structured data we recommend [16].

4.3.1 Convolution Kernels

The best known kernel for representation spaces that are not mere attribute-value tuples is the convolution kernel proposed by Haussler [22]. The basic idea of convolution kernels is that the semantics of composite objects can often be captured by a relation R between the object and its parts. The kernel on the object is then made up from kernels defined on different parts.

Let $x, x' \in \mathcal{X}$ be the objects and $\mathbf{x}, \mathbf{x}' \in \mathcal{X}_1 \times \cdots \times \mathcal{X}_D$ be tuples of parts of these objects. Given the relation $R : (\mathcal{X}_1 \times \cdots \times \mathcal{X}_D) \times \mathcal{X}$ we can define the decomposition R^{-1} as $R^{-1}(x) = \{\mathbf{x} : R(\mathbf{x}, x)\}$. Then the convolution kernel is defined as

$$k_{conv}(x, x') = \sum_{\mathbf{x} \in R^{-1}(x), \mathbf{x}' \in R^{-1}(x')} \prod_{d=1}^{D} k_d(x_d, x'_d) .$$

The term "convolution kernel" refers to a class of kernels that can be formulated in the above way. The advantage of convolution kernels is that they are very general and can be applied in many different problems. However, because of that generality, they require a significant amount of work to adapt them to a specific problem, which makes choosing R in "real-world" applications a non-trivial task.

4.3.2 String Kernels

The idea of most string kernels [34, 47] defined in the literature is to base the similarity of two strings on the number of common subsequences. These subsequences need not occur contiguously in the strings but the more gaps in the occurrence of the subsequence, the less weight is given to it in the kernel function. For example, the string "cat" would be decomposed in the subsequences "c", "a", "t", "ca", "at", "ct", and "cat". These subsequences also occur in the string "cart", albeit with different length of the occurrence. Usually the length of the occurrence of the substring is used as a penalty. With an exponentially decaying penalty, the weight of every occurrence in "cat"/"cart" becomes: "c":$(\lambda^1\lambda^1)$, "a":$(\lambda^1\lambda^1)$, "t":$(\lambda^1\lambda^1)$, "ca":$(\lambda^2\lambda^2)$, "at":$(\lambda^2\lambda^3)$, "ct":$(\lambda^3\lambda^4)$, "cat":$(\lambda^3\lambda^4)$ and the kernel of "cat" and "cart" becomes $k(\text{"cat"}, \text{"cart"}) = 2\lambda^7 + \lambda^5 + \lambda^4 + 3\lambda^2$. Using a divide and conquer approach, computation of this kernel can be reduced to $\mathcal{O}(n|s||t|)$ [34]. In [45] and [32] other string kernels are proposed and it is shown how these can be computed efficiently by using suffix and mismatch trees, respectively.

4.3.3 Tree Kernels

A kernel function that can be applied in many natural language processing tasks is described in [4]. The instances of the learning task are considered to be labeled ordered directed trees. The key idea for capturing structural information about the trees in the kernel function is to consider all subtrees occurring in a parse tree. Here, a subtree is defined as a connected subgraph of a tree such that either all children or no child of a vertex is in the subgraph. The children of a vertex are the vertices that can be reached from the vertex by traversing one directed edge. The kernel function is the inner product in the space which describes the number of occurrences of all possible subtrees.

Recently, [45] proposed the application of string kernels to trees by representing each tree by the sequence of labels generated by a depth-first traversal of the trees, written in preorder notation. To ensure that trees only differing in the order of their children are represented in the same way, the children of each vertex are ordered according to the lexical order of their string representation.

4.3.4 Kernels for Higher-Order Terms

In [19], a framework has been been proposed that allows for the application of kernel methods to different kinds of structured data. This approach is based on the idea of having a powerful representation that allows for modeling the semantics of an object by means of the syntax of the representation. The underlying principle is that of representing individuals as (closed) terms in a typed higher-order logic [33]. The biggest difference to terms of a first-order logic is the use of types and the presence of abstractions that allow explicit modeling of sets, multisets, and so on.

The typed syntax is important for pruning search spaces and for modeling as closely as possible the semantics of the data in a human- and machine-readable form. The individuals-as-terms representation is a natural generalization of the attribute-value representation and collects all information about an individual in a single term.

Basic terms represent the individuals that are the subject of learning and fall into one of three categories: basic structures that represent individuals that are lists, trees, and so on; basic abstractions that represent sets, multisets, and so on; and basic tuples that represent tuples. Basic abstractions are almost constant mappings $\beta \to \gamma$ that can be regarded as lookup tables, where all basic terms of type β in the table are mapped to some basic term of type γ and all basic terms not in the table are mapped to one particular basic term, the default term of type γ.

Applications of this kernel are spatial clustering of demographic data, multi-instance learning for drug-activity prediction and predicting the structure of molecules from their NMR spectra.

Multi-instance learning problems [8] occur whenever example objects, individuals, can only be described by a set of which any single element could be responsible for the classification of the set. Here, it can be shown that with a particular abstraction kernel, the number of iterations needed by a kernel perceptron to converge to a consistent hypothesis is bound by a polynomial in the number of elements in the sets.

4.4 Graphs, Graphs, Graphs ...

The obvious approach to defining kernels on objects that have a natural representation as a graph is to decompose each graph into a set of subgraphs and measure the intersection of two decompositions. With such a graph kernel, one could decide whether a graph has a Hamiltonian path or not [18]. As this problem is known to be NP-hard, it is strongly believed that the obvious graph kernel can not be computed in polynomial time. This holds even if the decomposition is restricted to paths only.

In the literature different approaches are described to overcome this problem. Graepel [21] restricted the decomposition to paths up to a given size, and Deshpande et al. [6] only considers the set of connected graphs that occur frequently as subgraphs in the graph database. The approach taken there to compute the decomposition of each graph is an iterative one [31]. The algorithm starts with a frequent set of subgraphs with one or two edges only.

Then, in each step, from the set of frequent subgraphs of size l, a set of candidate graphs of size $l + 1$ is generated by joining those graphs of size l that have a subgraph of size $l - 1$ in common. Of the candidate graphs only those satisfying a frequency threshold are retained for the next step. The iteration stops when the set of frequent subgraphs of size l is empty.

Conceptually, the graph kernels presented in [15, 18, 26, 27] are based on a measure of the walks in two graphs that have some or all labels in common. In [15] walks with equal initial and terminal label are counted, in [26, 27] the probability of random walks with equal label sequences is computed, and in [18] walks with equal label sequences, possibly containing gaps, are counted. In [18] computation of these – possibly infinite – walks is made possible in polynomial time by using the direct product graph and computing the limit of matrix power series involving its adjacency matrix. The work on rational graph kernels [5] generalizes these graph kernels by applying a general transducer between weighted automata instead of forming the direct product graph. However, only walks up to a given length are considered in the kernel computation. More recently, Horvath *et al.* [23] suggested that the computational intractability of detecting all cycles in a graph can be overcome in practical applications by observing that "difficult structures" occur only infrequently in real-world databases. As a consequence of this assertion, Horvath *et al.* [23] use a cycle-detection algorithm to decompose all graphs in a molecule database into all simple cycles occurring.

In the remainder of this section we will describe walk- and cycle-based graph kernels in more detail.

4.4.1 Walk-Based Graph Kernels

A labeled directed graph G is described by a finite set of vertices $\mathcal{V}$, a finite set of edges $\mathcal{E}$, and a function ℓ. The set of edges is a subset of the Cartesian product of the set of vertices with itself ($\mathcal{E} \subseteq \mathcal{V} \times \mathcal{V}$) such that that $(\nu_i, \nu_j) \in \mathcal{E}$ if and only if there is an edge from ν_i to ν_j in graph G. The function ℓ maps each edge and/or vertex to a label. The adjacency matrix of the graph is a $|\mathcal{V}| \times |\mathcal{V}|$ matrix E where the $E_{ij} = 1$ if and only if $(\nu_i, \nu_j) \in \mathcal{E}$ and $E_{ij} = 0$ otherwise.

We concentrate now on one type of kernel introduced in [18], measuring the number of walks with common label sequence in two graphs. There, efficient computation of these – possibly infinite – walks is made possible by using the direct product graph and computing the limit of matrix power series involving its adjacency matrix.

The two graphs generating the product graph are called the factor graphs. The vertex set of the direct product of two graphs is a subset of the Cartesian product of the vertex sets of the factor graphs. The direct product graph has a vertex if and only if the labels of the corresponding vertices in the factor graphs are the same. There is an edge between two vertices in the product graph if and only if there is an edge between the corresponding vertices in both factor graphs and both edges have the same label. For unlabeled graphs, the adjacency matrix of the direct product graph corresponds to the tensor product of the adjacency matrices of its factors.

With a sequence of weights $\lambda_0, \lambda_1, \ldots$ ($\lambda_i \in \mathbb{R}; \lambda_i \geq 0$ for all $i \in \mathbb{N}$) the direct product kernel is defined as

$$k_\times(G_1, G_2) = \sum_{i,j=1}^{|\mathcal{V}_\times|} \left[\sum_{n=0}^{\infty} \lambda_n E_\times^n \right]_{ij}$$

if the limit exists.

For symmetric $E_\times$, limits of such power series can be computed by means of an eigenvalue decomposition of E, and a "recomposition" with modified eigenvalues. The modification of the eigenvalues is usually such that the order of eigenvalues is kept.

To illustrate these kernels, consider a simple graph with four vertices labeled "c", "a", "r", and "t", respectively. We also have four edges in this graph: one from the vertex labeled "c" to the vertex labeled "a", one from "a" to "r", one from "r" to "t", and one from "a" to "t". The non-zero features in the label sequence feature space are $\phi_c = \phi_a = \phi_r = \phi_t = \sqrt{\lambda_0}$, $\phi_{ca} = \phi_{ar} = \phi_{at} = \phi_{rt} = \sqrt{\lambda_1}$, $\phi_{car} = \phi_{cat} = \phi_{art} = \lambda_2$, and $\phi_{cart} = \sqrt{\lambda_3}$. The λ_i are user defined weights and the square-roots appear only to make the computation of the kernel more elegant. The above kernel function corresponds to the inner product between such feature vectors (of possibly infinite dimension).

4.4.2 Cyclic-Pattern Kernels

A labeled undirected graph can be seen as a labeled directed graph where the existence of an edge between two vertices implies the existence of an edge in the other direction and both edges are mapped to the same label. Each edge of an undirected graph is usually represented by a subset of the vertex set with cardinality two. A path in an undirected graph is a sequence $v_1, \ldots v_n$ of distinct vertices $v_i \in \mathcal{V}$ where $\{v_i, v_{i+1}\} \in \mathcal{E}$. A simple cycle in an undirected graph is a path, where also $\{v_1, v_n\} \in \mathcal{E}$. A bridge is an edge not part of any simple cycle; the graph made up by all bridges is a forest, i.e., a set of trees.

We describe now the kernel proposed in [23] for molecule classification. The key idea is to decompose every undirected graph into the set of cyclic and tree patterns in the graph. A cyclic pattern is a unique representation of the label sequence corresponding to a simple cycle in the graph. A tree pattern in the graph is a unique representation of the label sequence corresponding to a tree in the forest made up by all bridges. The cyclic-pattern kernel between two graphs is defined by the cardinality of the intersection of the pattern sets associated with each graph.

Consider a graph with vertices $1, \ldots 6$ and labels (in the order of vertices) "c", "a", "r", "t", "e", and "s". Let the edges be the set

$$\{\{1, 2\}, \{2, 3\}, \{3, 4\}, \{2, 4\}, \{1, 5\}, \{1, 6\}\}.$$

This graph has one simple cycle and the lexicographically smallest representation of the labels along this cycle is the string "art". The bridges of the graph are $\{1, 2\}, \{1, 5\}, \{1, 6\}$ and the bridges form a forest consisting of a single tree. The lexicographically smallest representation of the labels of this tree (in pre-order notation) is the string "aces".

If the cyclic-pattern kernel between any two graphs could be computed in polynomial time, the Hamiltonian cycle problem could also be solved in polynomial time. Furthermore, the set of simple cycles in a graph can not be computed in polynomial time – even worse, the number of simple cycles in a graph can be exponential in the number of vertices of the graph. Consider a graph consisting of two paths $v_0, \ldots v_n$ and $u_0, \ldots u_n$ with additional edges $\{\{v_i, u_i\} : 0 \leq i \leq n\} \cup \{\{v_i, u_{i-2}\} : 2 \leq i \leq n\}$ where the number of paths from v_0 to u_n is lower bound by 2^n. It follows directly that the number of simple cycles in the graph with the additional edge $\{u_n, v_0\}$ is also lower bound by 2^n.

The only remaining hope for a practically feasible algorithm is that the number of simple cycles in each graph can be bound by a small polynomial. Read and Tarjan [38] proposed an algorithm with polynomial delay complexity, i.e., the number of steps that the algorithm needs between finding one simple cycle and finding the next simple cycle is polynomial. This algorithm can be used to enumerate all cyclic patterns. Note that this does not imply that the number of steps the algorithm needs between two cyclic patterns is polynomial.

In the next section we will compare walk- and cycle-based graph kernels in the context of drug design and prediction of properties of molecules. It is illustrated there that indeed for the application considered, only a few molecules exist that have a large number of simple cycles. Before that we describe an application of walk-based graph kernels in a relational reinforcement learning setting.

4.5 Applications of Predictive Graph-Mining

In this section we describe two applications of graph kernels. The first application is a relational reinforcement learning task in the blocks world. The second application is a molecule classification task on a relatively large database ($> 40,000$ instances) of molecules classified according to their ability to protect human cells from the HIV virus.

4.5.1 Relational Reinforcement Learning

Reinforcement learning [43], in a nutshell, is about controlling an autonomous agent in an environment about which he has no prior knowledge. The only information the agent can get about the environment is its current state and whether it received a reward. The goal of reinforcement learning is to maximize this reward. One particular form of reinforcement learning is Q-learning [46]. It tries to learn a map from state-action-pairs to real numbers (Q-values) reflecting the quality of that action in that state.

Relational reinforcement learning [10, 11] (RRL) is a Q-learning technique that can be applied whenever the state-action space can not easily be represented by tuples of constants but has an inherently relational representation instead. In this case, explicitly representing the mapping from state-action-pairs to Q-values is usually not feasible.

The RRL-system learns through exploration of the state-space in a way that is very similar to normal Q-learning algorithms. It starts with running an episode[2] just like table-based Q-learning, but uses the encountered states, chosen actions and the received rewards to generate a set of examples that can then be used to build a Q-function generalization. These examples use a structural representation of states and actions.

To build this generalized Q-function, RRL applies an incremental relational regression engine that can exploit the structural representation of the constructed example set. The resulting Q-function is then used to decide which actions to take in the following episodes. Every new episode can be seen as a new experience and is thus used to updated the Q-function generalization.

A rather simple example of relational reinforcement learning takes place in the blocks world. The aim there is to learn how to put blocks that are in an arbitrary configuration into a given configuration.

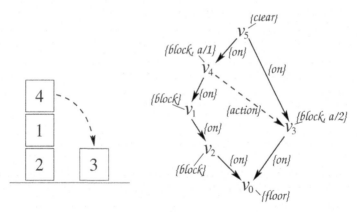

Fig. 4.3. Simple example of a blocks world state and action (left) and its representation as a graph (right).

---

[2]An "episode" is a sequence of states and actions from an initial state to a terminal state. In each state, the current Q-function is used to decide which action to take.

In this section we describe an application of Gaussian processes to learn the mapping from relational state-action spaces to Q-values in the blocks world. One advantage of using Gaussian processes in RRL is that rather than predicting a single Q-value, they actually return a probability distribution over Q-values. In order to employ Gaussian processes in a relational reinforcement learning setting, we use graph kernels as the covariance function between state-action pairs. For that we needed to extend the above described graph kernels to graphs that may have multiple edges between the same vertices. The details of this extension are described in [17].

State and Action Representation

A blocks world consists of a constant number of identical blocks. Each block is put either on the floor or on another block. On top of each block is either another block or the top of the block is clear. Figure 4.3 illustrates a (*state*, *action*)-pair in a blocks world with four blocks in two stacks. The right side of Figure 4.3 shows the graph representation of this blocks world. The vertices of the graph correspond either to a block, the floor, or "clear". This is reflected in the labels of the vertices. Each edge labeled "on" (solid arrows) denotes that the block corresponding to its initial vertex is on top of the block corresponding to its terminal vertex. The edge labeled "action" (dashed arrow) denotes the action of putting the block corresponding to its initial vertex on top of the block corresponding to its terminal vertex; in the example "put block 4 on block 3". The labels "a/1" and "a/2" denote the initial and terminal vertex of the action, respectively. Every blocks world state–action pair can be represented by a directed graph in this way.

Blocks World Kernel

In finite state–action spaces, Q-learning is guaranteed to converge if the mapping between state–action pairs and Q-values is represented explicitly. One advantage of Gaussian processes is that for particular choices of the covariance function, the representation is explicit.

A frequently used kernel function for instances that can be represented by vectors is the Gaussian radial basis function kernel (RBF). Given the bandwidth parameter σ the RBF kernel is defined as: $k_{\mathrm{rbf}}(x, x') = \exp(-||x - x'||^2/\sigma^2)$. For small enough σ the RBF kernel behaves like the matching kernel. In other words, the parameter σ can be used to regulate the amount of generalization performed in the Gaussian process algorithm: For very small σ all instances are very different and the Q-function is represented explicitly; for large enough σ all examples are considered very similar and the resulting function is very smooth.

In order to have a similar way to regulate the amount of generalization in the blocks world setting, we do not use the above proposed walk-based graph kernel directly, but use a Gaussian modifier with it. Let k be the graph kernel with exponential weights, then the kernel used in the blocks world is given by

$$k^*(x, x') = \exp[-(k(x, x) - 2k(x, x') + k(x', x'))/\sigma^2].$$

Evaluation

We evaluated RRL with Gaussian processes and walk-based graph kernels on three different goals: stacking all blocks, unstacking all blocks and putting two specific blocks on top of each other. The RRL-system was trained in worlds where the number of blocks varied between three and five, and given "guided" traces [9] in a world with 10 blocks. The Q-function and the related policy were tested at regular intervals on 100 randomly generated starting states in worlds where the number of blocks varied from 3 to 10 blocks.

In our empirical evaluation, RRL with Gaussian processes and walk-based graph kernels proved competitive or better than the previous implementations of RRL. However, this is not the only advantage of using graph kernels and Gaussian processes in RRL. The biggest advantages are the elegance and potential of our approach. Very good results could be achieved without sophisticated instance selection or averaging strategies. The generalization ability can be tuned by a single parameter. Probabilistic predictions can be used to guide exploration of the state–action space.

4.5.2 Molecule Classification

One of the most interesting application areas for predictive graph mining algorithms is the classification of molecules.

We used the HIV data set of chemical compounds to evaluate the predictive power of walk- and cycle-based graph kernels. The HIV database is maintained by the US National Cancer Institute (NCI) [37] and describes information of the compounds' capability to inhibit the HIV virus. This database has been used frequently in the empirical evaluation of graph-mining approaches (for example [1, 7, 30]). However, the only approaches to predictive graph mining on this data set are described in [6, 7]. There, a support vector machine was used with the frequent subgraph kernel mentioned at the beginning of Section 4.4.

Figure 4.4 shows the number of molecules with a given number of simple cycles. This illustrates that in the HIV domain the assumption made in the development of cyclic-pattern kernels holds.

Data set

In the NCI HIV database, each compound is described by its chemical structure and classified into one of three categories: confirmed inactive (CI), moderately active (CM), or active (CA). A compound is inactive if a test showed less than 50% protection of human CEM cells. All other compounds were re-tested. Compounds showing less than 50% protection (in the second test) are also classified inactive. The other compounds are classified active, if they

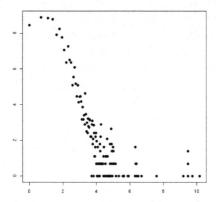

Fig. 4.4. Log-log plot of the number of molecules (y) versus the number of simple cycles (x).

provided 100% protection in both tests, and moderately active, otherwise. The NCI HIV data set we used[3] contains 42, 689 molecules, 423 of which are active, 1081 are moderately active, and 41, 185 are inactive.

Vertex coloring
Though the number of molecules and thus atoms in this data set is rather large, the number of vertex labels is limited by the number of elements occurring in natural compounds. For that, it is reasonable to not just use the element of the atom as its label. Instead, we use the pair consisting of the atom's element and the multiset of all neighbouring elements as the label. In the HIV data set, this increases the number of different labels from 62 to 1391.

More sophisticated vertex coloring algorithms are used in isomorphism tests. There, one would like two vertices to be colored differently iff they do not lie on the same orbit of the automorphism group [14]. As no efficient algorithm for the ideal case is known, one often resorts to colorings such that two differently colored vertices can not lie on the same orbit. One possibility there is to apply the above simple vertex coloring recursively. This is guaranteed to converge to a "stable coloring".

Implementation Issues
The size of this data set, in particular the size of the graphs in this data set, hinders the computation of walk-based graph kernels by means of eigen decompositions on the product graphs. The largest graph contains 214 atoms (not counting hydrogen atoms). If all had the same label, the product graph would

---
[3]http://cactus.nci.nih.gov/ncidb/download.html

have 45, 796 vertices. As different elements occur in this molecule, the product graph has fewer vertices. However, it turns out that the largest product graph (without the vertex coloring step) still has 34, 645 vertices. The vertex coloring above changes the number of vertices with the same label, thus the product graph is reduced to 12, 293 vertices. For each kernel computation, either eigendecomposition or inversion of the adjacency matrix of a product graph has to be performed. With cubic time complexity, such operations on matrices of this size are not feasible.

The only chance to compute graph kernels in this application is to approximate them. There are two choices. First we consider counting the number of walks in the product graph up to a certain depth. In our experiments it turned out that counting walks with 13 or fewer vertices is still feasible. An alternative is to explicitly construct the image of each graph in feature space. In the original data set 62 different labels occur and after the vertex coloring 1391 different labels occur. The size of the feature space of label sequences of length 13 is then $62^{13} > 10^{23}$ for the original data set and $1391^{13} > 10^{40}$ with the vertex coloring. We would also have to take into account walks with fewer than 13 vertices but at the same time not all walks will occur in at least one graph. The size of this feature space hinders explicit computation. We thus resorted to counting walks with 13 or fewer vertices in the product graph.

Experimental Methodology

We compare our approach to the results presented in [6] and [7]. The classification problems considered there were: (1) distinguish CA from CM, (2) distinguish CA and CM from CI, and (3) distinguish CA from CI. For each problem, the area under the ROC curve (AUC), averaged over a five-fold crossvalidation, is given for different misclassification cost settings.

In order to choose the parameters of the walk-based graph kernel we proceeded as follows. We split the smallest problem (1) into 10% for parameter tuning and 90% for evaluation. First we tried different parameters for the exponential weight $(10^{-3}, 10^{-2}, 10^{-1}, 1, 10)$ in a single nearest neighbor algorithm (leading to an average AUC of $0.660, 0.660, 0.674, 0.759, 0.338$) and decided to use 1 from now. Next we needed to choose the complexity (regularization) parameter of the SVM. Here we tried different parameters $(10^{-3}, 10^{-2}, 10^{-1}$ leading to an average AUC of $0.694, 0.716, 0.708)$ and found the parameter 10^{-2} to work best. Evaluating with an SVM and these parameters on the remaining 90% of the data, we achieved an average AUC of 0.820 and standard deviation of 0.024.

For cyclic-pattern kernels, only the complexity constant of the support vector machine has to be chosen. Here, the heuristic as implemented in SVM-light [24] is used. Also, we did not use any vertex coloring with cyclic pattern kernels.

Table 4.1. Area under the ROC curve for different costs and problems (•: significant loss against walk-based kernels at 10% / ••: significant loss against walk-based kernels at 1% / ∘: significant loss against cyclic-pattern kernels at 10% / ∘∘: significant loss against cyclic-pattern kernels at 1%).

problem	cost	walk-based kernels	cyclic-pattern kernels	FSG	FSG*
CA vs CM	1.0	0.818(±0.024)	0.813(±0.014)	0.774 ••∘∘	0.810
CA vs CM	2.5	0.825(±0.032)	0.827(±0.013)	0.782 • ∘∘	0.792 • ∘∘
CA vs CM+CI	1.0	0.926(±0.015)	0.908(±0.024) •	—	—
CA vs CM+CI	100.0	0.928(±0.013)	0.921(±0.026)	—	—
CA+CM vs CI	1.0	0.815(±0.015)	0.775(±0.017) ••	0.742 ••∘∘	0.765 ••
CA+CM vs CI	35.0	0.799(±0.011)	0.801(±0.017)	0.778 ••∘	0.794
CA vs CI	1.0	0.942(±0.015)	0.919(±0.011) •	0.868 ••∘∘	0.839 ••∘∘
CA vs CI	100.0	0.944(±0.015)	0.929(±0.01) •	0.914 ••∘	0.908 ••∘∘

Results of Experimental Evaluation

To compare our results to those achieved in previous work, we fixed these parameters and reran the experiments on the full data of all three problems. Table 4.1 summarises these results and the results reported in [6]. In [7] the authors of [6] describe improved results (FSG*). There, the authors report results obtained with an optimized threshold on the frequency of patterns.[4] Clearly, the graph kernels proposed here outperform FSG and FSG* over all problems and misclassification cost settings

To evaluate the significance of our results we proceeded as follows: As we did not know the variance of the area under the ROC curve for FSG, we assumed the same variance as obtained with graph kernels. Thus, to test the hypothesis that graph kernels significantly outperform FSG, we used a pooled sample variance equal to the variance exhibited by graph kernels. As FSG and graph kernels were applied in a five-fold crossvalidation, the estimated standard error of the average difference is the pooled sample variance multiplied by $\sqrt{\frac{2}{5}}$. The test statistic is then the average difference divided by its estimated standard error. This statistic follows a t distribution. The null hypothesis — graph kernels perform no better than FSG — can be rejected at the significance level α if the test statistic is greater than $t_8(\alpha)$, the corresponding percentile of the t distribution.

Table 4.1 shows the detailed results of this comparison. Walk-based graph kernels always perform better or at least not significantly worse than any other kernel. Cyclic-pattern kernels are sometimes outperformed by walk-based graph kernels but can be computed much more efficiently. For example, in the classification problem where we tried to distinguish active compounds

---

[4]In [7], including a description of the three-dimensional shape of each molecule is also considered. We do not compare our results to those obtained using the three-dimensional information. We are also considering including three-dimensional information in our future work and expect similar improvements.

from moderately active compounds and inactive compounds, five-fold cross-validation with walk-based graph kernels finished in about eight hours, while changing to cyclic-pattern kernels reduced the run time to about 20 minutes.

4.6 Concluding Remarks

In this article we described a kernel based approach to predictive graph-mining. In contrast to other graph mining problems, predictive graph mining is concerned with the predictive performance of classifiers rather than interestingness or frequency of patterns. In contrast to other predictive learning approaches, predictive graph mining is concerned with learning problems where each example has a natural graph-based representation.

We described different kernel functions on objects with complex data structures and made clear why these approaches can not easily be extended to handle graphs – the obvious way to do this would result in a kernel function that, if it could be computed in polynomial time, would allow us to solve the Hamiltonian path problem in polynomial time. We then described walk-based graph kernels and cyclic-pattern kernels for graphs in more detail.

Walk-based graph kernels circumvent the computational problems by resorting to a measure of the common walks in graphs rather than common paths. Using a few computational tricks, walk-based graph kernels can be computed in polynomial time.

Cyclic pattern kernels explicitly compute the set of cyclic and tree patterns of each graph. Although computing this set is, in general, computationally hard, for graph databases where the number of simple cycles in each graph is small, cyclic pattern kernels can be computed efficiently. This is, for example, the case in a database with more than 40,000 molecules, used in the empirical evaluation in this paper. There, using cyclic-pattern kernels instead of walk-based kernels leads to a small decrease in predictive performance but to a large improvement of the run time of support vector machines.

Acknowledgements: This research was supported in part by the DFG project (WR 40/2-1) *Hybride Methoden und Systemarchitekturen für heterogene Informationsräume.* Part of this work resulted from collaborations with Kurt Driessens, Peter Flach, Tamás Horváth, Jan Ramon and Stefan Wrobel.

References

[1] Borgelt, C. and M. R. Berthold, 2002: Mining molecular fragments: Finding relevant substructures of molecules. *Proc. of the 2002 IEEE International Conference on Data Mining*, IEEE Computer Society.

[2] Boser, B. E., I. M. Guyon and V. N. Vapnik, 1992: A training algorithm for optimal margin classifiers. *Proceedings of the 5th Annual ACM Workshop on Computational Learning Theory*, D. Haussler, ed., ACM Press, 144–52.

[3] Bunke, H. and G. Allerman, 1983: Inexact graph matching for structural pattern recognition. *Pattern Recognition Letters*, **4**.

[4] Collins, M. and N. Duffy, 2002: Convolution kernels for natural language. *Advances in Neural Information Processing Systems*, T. G. Dietterich, S. Becker and Z. Ghahramani, eds., MIT Press, **14**.

[5] Cortes, C., P. Haffner and M. Mohri, 2003: Positive definite rational kernels. *Proceedings of the 16th Annual Conference on Computational Learning Theory and the 7th Kernel Workshop*.

[6] Deshpande, M., M. Kuramochi and G. Karypis, 2002: Automated approaches for classifying structures. *Proceedings of the 2nd ACM SIGKDD Workshop on Data Mining in Bioinformatics*.

[7] — 2003: Frequent sub-structure based approaches for classifying chemical compounds. *Proc. of the 2003 IEEE International Conference on Data Mining*, IEEE Computer Society.

[8] Dietterich, T. G., R. H. Lathrop and T. Lozano-Pérez, 1997: Solving the multiple instance problem with axis-parallel rectangles. *Artificial Intelligence*, **89**, 31–71.

[9] Driessens, K. and S. Džeroski, 2002: Integrating experimentation and guidance in relational reinforcement learning. *Proceedings of the 19th International Conference on Machine Learning*, C. Sammut and A. Hoffmann, eds., Morgan Kaufmann, 115–22.
URL: www.cs.kuleuven.ac.be/cgi-bin-dtai/publ_info.pl?id=38637

[10] Driessens, K., J. Ramon and H. Blockeel, 2001: Speeding up relational reinforcement learning through the use of an incremental first order decision tree learner. *Proceedings of the 13th European Conference on Machine Learning*, L. De Raedt and P. Flach, eds., Springer-Verlag, *Lecture Notes in Artificial Intelligence*, **2167**, 97–108.

[11] Džeroski, S., L. De Raedt and H. Blockeel, 1998: Relational reinforcement learning. *Proceedings of the 15th International Conference on Machine Learning*, Morgan Kaufmann, 136–43.

[12] Eiter, T. and H. Mannila, 1997: Distance measures for point sets and their computation. *Acta Informatica*, **34**.

[13] Fischer, R. and M. Fischer, 1974: The string-to-string correction problem. *Journal of the Association for Computing Machinery*, **21**.

[14] Fürer, M., 1995: Graph isomorphism testing without numerics for graphs of bounded eigenvalue multiplicity. *Proceedings of the 6th Annual ACM-SIAM Symposium on Discrete Algorithms*.

[15] Gärtner, T., 2002: Exponential and geometric kernels for graphs. *NIPS Workshop on Unreal Data: Principles of Modeling Nonvectorial Data*.

[16] — 2003: A survey of kernels for structured data. *SIGKDD Explorations*.

[17] Gärtner, T., K. Driessens and J. Ramon, 2003: Graph kernels and Gaussian processes for relational reinforcement learning. *Proceedings of the 13th International Conference on Inductive Logic Programming.*

[18] Gärtner, T., P. A. Flach and S. Wrobel, 2003: On graph kernels: Hardness results and efficient alternatives. *Proceedings of the 16th Annual Conference on Computational Learning Theory and the 7th Kernel Workshop.*

[19] Gärtner, T., J. W. Lloyd and P. A. Flach, 2004: Kernels for structured data. *Machine Learning.*

[20] Geibel, P. and F. Wysotzki, 1996: Relational learning with decision trees. *Proceedings of the 12th European Conference on Artificial Intelligence,* W. Wahlster, ed., John Wiley, 428–32.

[21] Graepel, T., 2002: *PAC-Bayesian Pattern Classification with Kernels.* Ph.D. thesis, TU Berlin.

[22] Haussler, D., 1999: Convolution kernels on discrete structures. Technical report, Department of Computer Science, University of California at Santa Cruz.

[23] Horvath, T., T. Gärtner and S. Wrobel, 2004: Cyclic pattern kernels for predictive graph mining. *Proceedings of the International Conference on Knowledge Discovery and Data Mining.*

[24] Joachims, T., 1999: Making large-scale SVM learning practical. *Advances in Kernel Methods: Support Vector Learning,* B. Schölkopf, C. J. C. Burges and A. J. Smola, eds., MIT Press.

[25] Kandola, J., J. Shawe-Taylor and N. Christianini, 2003: Learning semantic similarity. *Advances in Neural Information Processing Systems,* S. Becker, S. Thrun and K. Obermayer, eds., MIT Press, **15**.

[26] Kashima, H., and A. Inokuchi, 2002: Kernels for graph classification. *ICDM Workshop on Active Mining.*

[27] Kashima, H., K. Tsuda and A. Inokuchi, 2003: Marginalized kernels between labeled graphs. *Proceedings of the 20th International Conference on Machine Learning.*

[28] Kolmogorov, A. N., and S. V. Fomin, 1960: *Elements of the Theory of Functions and Functional Analysis: Measure, Lebesgue Integrals, and Hilbert Space,* Academic Press, NY, USA, **2**.

[29] Kondor, R. I. and J. Lafferty, 2002: Diffusion kernels on graphs and other discrete input spaces. *Proceedings of the 19th International Conference on Machine Learning,* C. Sammut and A. Hoffmann, eds., Morgan Kaufmann, 315–22.

[30] Kramer, S., L. De Raedt and C. Helma, 2001: Molecular feature mining in HIV data. *Proceedings of the 7th ACM SIGKDD International Conference on Knowledge Discovery and Data Mining,* F. Provost and R. Srikant, eds., 136–43.

[31] Kuramochi, M. and G. Karypis, 2001: Frequent subgraph discovery. *Proceedings of the IEEE International Conference on Data Mining.*

[32] Leslie, C., E. Eskin, J. Weston and W. Noble, 2003: Mismatch string kernels for SVM protein classification. *Advances in Neural Information*

Processing Systems, S. Becker, S. Thrun and K. Obermayer, eds., MIT Press, **15**.

[33] Lloyd, J., 2003: *Logic for Learning*. Springer-Verlag.

[34] Lodhi, H., J. Shawe-Taylor, N. Christianini and C. Watkins, 2001: Text classification using string kernels. *Advances in Neural Information Processing Systems*, T. Leen, T. Dietterich and V. Tresp, eds., MIT Press, **13**.

[35] MacKay, D. J. C., 1997: Introduction to Gaussian processes, available at http://wol.ra.phy.cam.ac.uk/mackay.

[36] Messmer, B., 1995: *Graph Matching Algorithms and Applications*. Ph.D. thesis, University of Bern.

[37] NCI HIV database. URL: http://cactus.nci.nih.gov/.

[38] Read, R. C. and R. E. Tarjan, 1975: Bounds on backtrack algorithms for listing cycles, paths, and spanning trees. *Networks*, **5**, 237–52.

[39] Rifkin, R. M., 2002: *Everything Old is New Again: A fresh look at historical approaches to machine learning*. Ph.D. thesis, MIT.

[40] Saunders, C., A. Gammerman and V. Vovk, 1998: Ridge regression learning algorithm in dual variables. *Proceedings of the 15th International Conference on Machine Learning*, Morgan Kaufmann.

[41] Schölkopf, B. and A. J. Smola, 2002: *Learning with Kernels*. MIT Press.

[42] Smola, A. J. and R. Kondor, 2003: Kernels and regularization on graphs. *Proceedings of the 16th Annual Conference on Computational Learning Theory and the 7th Kernel Workshop*.

[43] Sutton, R. and A. Barto, 1998: *Reinforcement Learning: an introduction*. MIT Press, Cambridge, MA.

[44] Vapnik, V., 1995: *The Nature of Statistical Learning Theory*. Springer-Verlag.

[45] Vishwanathan, S. and A. Smola, 2003: Fast kernels for string and tree matching. *Advances in Neural Information Processing Systems*, S. Becker, S. Thrun and K. Obermayer, eds., MIT Press, **15**.

[46] Watkins, C., 1989: *Learning from Delayed Rewards*. Ph.D. thesis, King's College, Cambridge.

[47] — 1999: Kernels from matching operations. Technical report, Department of Computer Science, Royal Holloway, University of London.

5

TreeMiner: An Efficient Algorithm for Mining Embedded Ordered Frequent Trees

Mohammed J. Zaki

Summary. Mining frequent trees is very useful in domains like bioinformatics, web mining, mining semi-structured data, and so on. We formulate the problem of mining (embedded) subtrees in a forest of rooted, labeled, and ordered trees. We present TreeMiner, a novel algorithm to discover all frequent subtrees in a forest, using a new data structure called a scope-list. We contrast TreeMiner with a pattern-matching tree-mining algorithm (PatternMatcher). We conduct detailed experiments to test the performance and scalability of these methods. We find that TreeMiner outperforms the pattern matching approach by a factor of 4 to 20, and has good scale-up properties. We also present an application of tree mining to analyze real web logs for usage patterns.

5.1 Introduction

Frequent structure mining (FSM) refers to an important class of exploratory mining tasks, namely those dealing with extracting patterns in massive databases representing complex interactions between entities. FSM not only encompasses mining techniques like associations [3] and sequences [4], but it also generalizes to more complex patterns like frequent trees and graphs [17, 20]. Such patterns typically arise in applications like bioinformatics, web mining, mining semi-structured documents, and so on. As one increases the complexity of the structures to be discovered, one extracts more informative patterns; we are specifically interested in mining tree-like patterns.

As a motivating example for tree mining, consider the web usage mining [13] problem. Given a database of web access logs at a popular site, one can perform several mining tasks. The simplest is to ignore all link information from the logs, and to mine only the frequent sets of pages accessed by users. The next step can be to form for each user the sequence of links they followed and to mine the most frequent user access paths. It is also possible to look at the entire forward accesses of a user, and to mine the most frequently accessed subtrees at that site. In recent years, XML has become a popular way of storing many data sets because the semi-structured nature of XML allows the modeling of a wide variety of databases as XML documents. XML data thus forms an important data mining domain, and it is valuable to develop techniques that can extract patterns from such data. Tree-structured XML documents are the most widely occurring in real applications. Given a set of such XML documents, one would like to discover the commonly occurring subtrees that appear in the collection.

Tree patterns also arise in Bioinformatics. For example, researchers have collected vast amounts of RNA structures, which are essentially trees. To get information about a newly sequenced RNA, they compare it with known RNA structures, looking for common topological patterns, which provide important clues to the function of the RNA [28].

In this paper we introduce TREEMINER, an efficient algorithm for the problem of mining frequent subtrees in a forest (the database). The key contributions of our work are as follows:

- We introduce the problem of mining *embedded* subtrees in a collection of rooted, ordered, and labeled trees.
- We use the notion of a *scope* for a node in a tree. We show how any tree can be represented as a list of its node scopes, in a novel vertical format called a *scope-list*.
- We develop a framework for non-redundant candidate subtree generation, i.e., we propose a systematic search of the possibly frequent subtrees, such that no pattern is generated more than once.
- We show how one can efficiently compute the frequency of a candidate tree by joining the scope-lists of its subtrees.
- Our formulation allows one to discover all subtrees in a forest, as well as all subtrees in a single large tree. Furthermore, simple modifications also allow us to mine unlabeled subtrees, unordered subtrees and also frequent sub-forests (i.e., disconnected subtrees).

We contrast TREEMINER with a base tree-mining algorithm based on pattern matching, PATTERNMATCHER. Our experiments on several synthetic data sets and one real data set show that TREEMINER outperforms PATTERN-MATCHER by a factor of 4 to 20. Both algorithms exhibit linear scale up with increasing number of trees in the database. We also present an application study of tree mining in web usage mining. The input data is in the form of XML documents that represent user sessions extracted from raw web logs. We show that the mined tree patterns do indeed capture more interesting relationships than frequent sets or sequences.

5.2 Problem Statement

A *tree* is an acyclic connected graph and a *forest* is an acyclic graph. A forest is thus a collection of trees, where each tree is a connected component of the forest. A *rooted tree* is a tree in which one of the vertices is distinguished from others and called the *root*. We refer to a vertex of a rooted tree as a *node* of the tree. An *ordered tree* is a rooted tree in which the children of each node are ordered, i.e., if a node has k children, then we can designate them as the first child, second child, and so on up to the kth child. A *labeled tree* is a tree where each node of the tree is associated with a label. In this paper, all trees we consider are ordered, labeled, and rooted trees. We choose to focus on labeled rooted trees, since those are the types of data sets that are most common in a data mining setting, i.e., data sets represent relationships between items or attributes that are named, and there is a top root element (e.g., the main web page on a site). In fact, if we treat each node as having the same label, we can mine all ordered, unlabeled subtrees as well!

Ancestors and Descendants
Consider a node x in a rooted tree T with root r. Any node y on the unique path from r to x is called an *ancestor* of x, and is denoted as $y \leq_l x$, where l is the length of the path from y to x. If y is an ancestor of x, then x is a *descendant* of y. (Every node is both an ancestor and descendant of itself.) If $y \leq_1 x$ (i.e., y is an immediate ancestor), then y is called the *parent* of x and x the *child* of y. We say that nodes x and y are *siblings* if they have the same parent and we say they are *embedded siblings* if they have some common ancestor.

Node Numbers and Labels
We denote a tree as $T = (N, B)$, where N is the set of labeled nodes, and B the set of *branches*. The *size* of T, denoted $|T|$, is the number of nodes in T. Each node has a well-defined *number*, i, according to its position in a depth-first (or pre-order) traversal of the tree. We use the notation n_i to refer to the ith node according to the numbering scheme ($i = 0 \ldots |T| - 1$). The *label* (also referred to as an *item*) of each node is taken from a set of labels $L = \{0, 1, 2, 3, ..., m-1\}$, and we allow different nodes to have the same label, i.e., the label of node number i is given by a function, $l : N \rightarrow L$, which maps n_i to some label $l(n_i) = y \in L$. Each node in T is thus identified by its number and its label. Each branch, $b = (n_x, n_y) \in B$, is an ordered pair of nodes, where n_x is the parent of n_y.

Subtrees
We say that a tree $S = (N_s, B_s)$ is an *embedded subtree* of $T = (N, B)$, denoted as $S \preceq T$, provided $N_s \subseteq N$, and $b = (n_x, n_y) \in B_s$ if and only if $n_y \leq_l n_x$, i.e., n_x is an ancestor of n_y in T. In other words, we require that a branch appears in S if and only if the two vertices are on the same path from the root to a leaf in T. If $S \preceq T$, we also say that T *contains* S. A (sub)tree of size k is also called a k-(sub)tree. Note that in the traditional definition of an *induced* subtree , for each branch $b = (n_x, n_y) \in B_s$, n_x must be a parent of n_y in T. Embedded subtrees are thus a generalization of induced subtrees; they allow not only direct parent–child branches, but also ancestor–descendant branches. As such embedded subtrees are able to extract patterns

"hidden" (or embedded) deep within large trees which might be missed by the traditional definition.

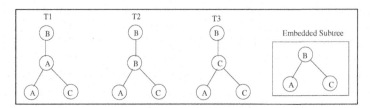

Fig. 5.1. Embedded subtree

As an example, consider Figure 5.1, which shows three trees. Let's assume we want to mine subtrees that are common to all three trees (i.e., 100% frequency). If we mine induced trees only, then there are no frequent trees of size more than one. On the other hand, if we mine embedded subtrees, then the tree shown in the box is a frequent pattern appearing in all three trees; it is obtained by skipping the "middle" node in each tree. This example shows why embedded trees are of interest. Henceforth, a reference to subtree should be taken to mean an embedded subtree, unless indicated otherwise. Also note that, by definition, a subtree must be connected. A disconnected pattern is a *sub-forest* of T. Our main focus is on mining subtrees, although a simple modification of our enumeration scheme also produces sub-forests.

Scope
Let $T(n_l)$ refer to the subtree rooted at node n_l and let n_r be the right-most leaf node in $T(n_l)$. The *scope* of node n_l is given as the interval $[l, r]$, i.e., the lower bound is the position (l) of node n_l, and the upper bound is the position (r) of node n_r. The concept of scope will play an important part in counting subtree frequency.

Tree Mining Problem
Let D denote a database of trees (i.e., a forest), and let subtree $S \preceq T$ for some $T \in D$. Each occurrence of S can be identified by its *match label*, which is given as the set of matching positions (in T) for nodes in S. More formally, let $\{t_1, t_2, \ldots, t_n\}$ be the nodes in T, with $|T| = n$, and let $\{s_1, s_2, \ldots, s_m\}$ be the nodes in S, with $|S| = m$. Then S has a match label $\{t_{i_1}, t_{i_2}, \ldots t_{i_m}\}$, if and only if: 1) $l(s_k) = l(t_{i_k})$ for all $k = 1, \ldots m$, and 2) branch $b(s_j, s_k)$ in S iff t_{i_j} is an ancestor of t_{i_k} in T. Condition 1 indicates that all node labels in S have a match in T, while Condition 2 indicates that the tree topology of the matching nodes in T is the same as S. A match label is unique for each occurrence of S in T.

Let $\delta_T(S)$ denote the number of occurrences of the subtree S in a tree T. Let $d_T(S) = 1$ if $\delta_T(S) > 0$ and $d_T(S) = 0$ if $\delta_T(S) = 0$. The *support* of a subtree S in the database is defined as $\sigma(S) = \sum_{T \in D} d_T(S)$, i.e., the number of trees in D that contain at least one occurrence of S. The *weighted support* of S is defined as $\sigma_w(S) = \sum_{T \in D} \delta_T(S)$, i.e., the total number of occurrences of S over all trees in D. Typically, support is given as a percentage of the total number of trees in D. A subtree S is *frequent* if its support is more than or equal to a user-specified *minimum support (minsup)* value. We denote by F_k the set of all frequent subtrees of size k. Given a user specified *minsup* value our goal is to efficiently enumerate all frequent subtrees in D. In some domains one might be interested in using weighted support, instead of support. Both of them are supported by our mining approach, but we focus mainly on support.

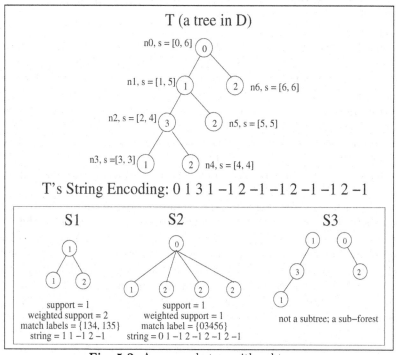

Fig. 5.2. An example tree with subtrees.

Example 1. Consider Figure 5.2, which shows an example tree T with node labels drawn from the set $L = \{0, 1, 2, 3\}$. The figure shows for each node, its label (circled), its number according to depth-first numbering, and its scope. For example, the root occurs at position $n = 0$, its label $l(n_0) = 0$, and since the right-most leaf under the root occurs at position 6, the scope of the root is $s = [0, 6]$. Tree $S1$ is a subtree of T; it has a support of 1, but its weighted support is 2, since node n_2 in $S1$ occurs at positions 4 and 5 in T, both of which support $S1$, i.e., there are two match labels for $S1$, namely 134 and 135 (we omit set notation for convenience). $S2$ is also a valid subtree. $S3$ is not a (sub)tree since it is disconnected; it is a sub-forest.

5.3 Generating Candidate Trees

There are two main steps for enumerating frequent subtrees in D. First, we need a systematic way of generating *candidate* subtrees whose frequencies are to be computed. The candidate set should be non-redundant, i.e., each subtree should be generated at most once. Second, we need efficient ways of counting the number of occurrences of each candidate in the database D, and to determine which candidates pass the *minsup* threshold. The latter step is data-structure dependent and will be treated later. Here we are concerned with the problem of non-redundant pattern generation. We describe below our tree representation and candidate generation procedure.

Representing Trees as Strings
Standard ways of representing a labeled tree are via an adjacency matrix or adjacency list. For a tree with n nodes and m branches (note, $m = n - 1$ for trees), adjacency matrix representation requires $n + fn = n(f + 1)$ space (f is the maximum fanout; n is for storing labels and fn for storing adjacency information), while adjacency lists require $2n + 2m = 4n - 2$ space ($2n$ is for storing labels and header pointers for adjacency lists and $2m$ is for storing label and next pointer per list node). Since f can possibly be large, we expect adjacency lists to be more space-efficient. If we directly store a labeled tree node as a (label, child pointer, sibling pointer) triplet, we would require $3n$ space.

For efficient subtree counting and manipulation we adopt a string representation of a tree. We use the following procedure to generate the *string encoding*, denoted $\mathcal{T}$, of a tree T. Initially we set $\mathcal{T} = \emptyset$. We then perform a depth-first preorder search starting at the root, adding the current node's label x to $\mathcal{T}$. Whenever we backtrack from a child to its parent we add a unique symbol -1 to the string (we assume that $-1 \notin L$). This format (see Figure 5.2) allows us to conveniently represent trees with an arbitrary number of children for each node. Since each branch must be traversed in both forward and backward directions, the space usage to store a tree as a string is exactly $2m + 1 = 2n - 1$. Thus our string encoding is more space-efficient than other representations. Moreover, it is simpler to manipulate strings rather than adjacency lists or trees for pattern counting. We use the notation $l(T)$ to refer to the *label sequence* of T, which consists of the node labels of T in depth-first ordering (without backtrack symbol -1), i.e., label sequence ignores tree topology.

Example 2. In Figure 5.2, we show the string encodings for the tree T as well as each of its subtrees. For example, subtree $S1$ is encoded by the string $1\ 1\ -1\ 2\ -1$. That is, we start at the root of $S1$ and add 1 to the string. The next node in preorder traversal is labeled 1, which is added to the encoding. We then backtrack to the root (adding -1) and follow down to the next node, adding 2 to the encoding. Finally we backtrack to the root adding -1 to the string. Note that the label sequence of $S1$ is given as 112.

5.3.1 Candidate Subtree Generation

We use the anti-monotone property of frequent patterns for efficient candidate generation, namely that the frequency of a super-pattern is less than or equal to the frequency of a sub-pattern. Thus, we consider only a known frequent pattern for extension. Past experience also suggests that an extension by a single item at a time is likely to be more efficient. Thus we use information from frequent k-subtrees to generate candidate $(k + 1)$-subtrees.

Equivalence Classes
We say that two k-subtrees X, Y are in the same *prefix equivalence class* iff they share a common prefix up to the $(k - 1)$th node. Formally, let $\mathcal{X}, \mathcal{Y}$ be the string encodings of two trees, and let function $p(\mathcal{X}, i)$ return the prefix up to the ith node. X, Y are in the same class iff $p(\mathcal{X}, k - 1) = p(\mathcal{Y}, k - 1)$. Thus any two members of an equivalence class differ only in the position of the last node.

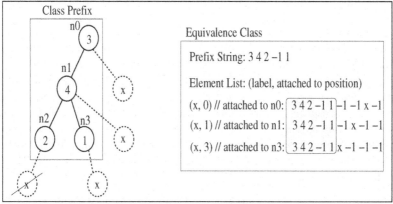

Fig. 5.3. Prefix equivalence class.

Example 3. Consider Figure 5.3, which shows a class template for subtrees of size 5 with the same prefix subtree P of size 4, with string encoding $\mathcal{P} = 3\ 4\ 2\ -1\ 1$. Here x denotes an arbitrary label from L. The valid positions where the last node with label x may be attached to the prefix are n_0, n_1 and n_3, since in each of these cases the subtree obtained by adding x to P has the same prefix. Note that a node attached to position n_2 cannot be a valid member of class $\mathcal{P}$, since it would yield a different prefix, given as $3\ 4\ 2\ x$.

The figure also shows the actual format we use to store an equivalence class; it consists of the class prefix string, and a list of elements. Each element is given as a (x, p) pair, where x is the *label* of the last node, and p specifies the depth-first position of the node in P to which x is attached. For example $(x, 1)$ refers to the case where x is attached to node n_1 at position 1. The figure shows the encoding of the subtrees corresponding to each class element. Note how each of them shares the same prefix up to the $(k-1)$th node. These subtrees are shown only for illustration purposes; we only store the element list in a class.

Let P be a prefix subtree of size $k-1$; we use the notation $[P]_{k-1}$ to refer to its class (we omit the subscript when there is no ambiguity). If (x, i) is an element of the class, we write it as $(x, i) \in [P]$. Each (x, i) pair corresponds to a subtree of size k, sharing P as the prefix, with the last node labeled x, attached to node n_i in P. We use the notation P_x to refer to the new prefix subtree formed by adding (x, i) to P.

Lemma 1. *Let P be a class prefix subtree and let n_r be the right-most leaf node in P, whose scope is given as $[r, r]$. Let $(x, i) \in [P]$. Then the set of valid node positions in P to which x can be attached is given by $\{i : n_i$ has scope $[i, r]\}$, where n_i is the ith node in P.*

This lemma states that a valid element x may be attached to only those nodes that lie on the path from the root to the right-most leaf n_r in P. It is easy to see that if x is attached to any other position the resulting prefix would be different, since x would then be before n_r in depth-first numbering.

Candidate Generation
Given an equivalence class of k-subtrees, how do we obtain candidate $(k+1)$-subtrees? First, we assume (without loss of generality) that the elements (x, p) in each class are kept sorted by node label as the primary key and position as the secondary key. Given a sorted element list, the candidate generation procedure we describe below outputs a new class list that respects that order, without explicit sorting. The main idea is to consider each ordered pair of elements in the class for extension, including self extension. There can be up to two candidates from each pair of elements to be joined. The next theorem formalizes this notion.

Theorem 1 (Class Extension). *Let P be a prefix class with encoding $\mathcal{P}$, and let (x, i) and (y, j) denote any two elements in the class. Let P_x denote the class representing extensions of element (x, i). Define a join operator $\otimes$ on the two elements, denoted $(x, i) \otimes (y, j)$, as follows:*
case I $- (i = j)$:

(a) If $\mathcal{P} \neq \emptyset$, add (y, j) and (y, n_i) to class $[P_x]$, where n_i is the depth-first number for node (x, i) in tree P_x.
(b) If $\mathcal{P} = \emptyset$, add $(y, j+1)$ to $[P_x]$.

case II $- (i > j)$: *add (y, j) to class $[P_x]$.*
case III $- (i < j)$: *no new candidate is possible in this case.*

Then all possible $(k+1)$-subtrees with the prefix P of size $k-1$ will be enumerated by applying the join operator to each ordered pair of elements (x, i) and (y, j).

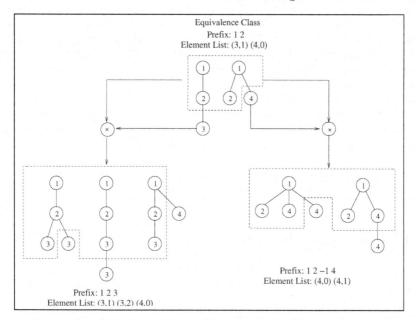

Fig. 5.4. Candidate generation

Example 4. Consider Figure 5.4, showing the prefix class $\mathcal{P} = (1\ 2)$, which contains two elements, $(3,1)$ and $(4,0)$. The first step is to perform a self join $(3,1) \otimes (3,1)$. By case I(a) this produces candidate elements $(3,1)$ and $(3,2)$ for the new class $\mathcal{P}_3 = (1\ 2\ 3)$. That is, a self join on $(3,1)$ produces two possible candidate subtrees, one where the last node is a sibling of $(3,1)$ and another where it is a child of $(3,1)$. The left-most two subtrees in the figure illustrate these cases.

When we join $(3,1) \otimes (4,0)$ case II applies, i.e., the second element is joined to some ancestor of the first one, thus $i > j$. The only possible candidate element is $(4,0)$, since 4 remains attached to node n_0 even after the join (see the third subtree in the left-most class in Figure 5.4). We thus add $(4,0)$ to class $[P_3]$. We now move to the class on the right with prefix $\mathcal{P}_4 = (1\ 2\ -1\ 4)$. When we try to join $(4,0) \otimes (3,1)$, case III applies, and no new candidate is generated. Actually, if we do merge these two subtrees, we obtain the new subtree $1\ 2\ 3\ -1\ -1\ 4$, which has a different prefix, and was already added to the class $[P_3]$. Finally we perform a self-join $(4,0) \otimes (4,0)$ adding elements $(4,0)$ and $(4,2)$ to the class $[P_4]$ shown on the right hand side.

Case I(b) applies only when we join single items to produce candidate 2-subtrees, i.e., we are given a prefix class $[\emptyset] = \{(x_i, -1), i = 1, \ldots, m\}$, where each x_i is a label, and -1 indicates that it is not attached to any node. If we join $(x_i, -1) \otimes (x_j, -1)$, since we want only (connected) 2-subtrees, we insert the element $(x_j, 0)$ into the class of x_i. This corresponds to the case where x_j is a child of x_i. If we want to generate sub-forests as well, all we have to do is to insert $(x_j, -1)$ in the class of x_i. In this case x_j would be a sibling of

x_i, but since they are not connected, they would be roots of two trees in a sub-forest. If we allow such class elements then one can show that the class extension theorem would produce all possible candidate sub-forests. However, in this paper we will focus only on subtrees.

Corollary 1 (Automatic Ordering). *Let* $[P]_{k-1}$ *be a prefix class with elements sorted according to the total ordering* $<$ *given as follows:* $(x, i) < (y, j)$ *if and only if* $x < y$ *or* $(x = y$ *and* $i < j)$. *Then the class extension method generates candidate classes* $[P]_k$ *with sorted elements.*

Corollary 2 (Correctness). *The class extension method correctly generates all possible candidate subtrees and each candidate is generated at most once.*

5.4 TREEMINER **Algorithm**

TREEMINER performs depth-first search (DFS) for frequent subtrees, using a novel tree representation called a *scope-list* for fast support counting, as discussed below.

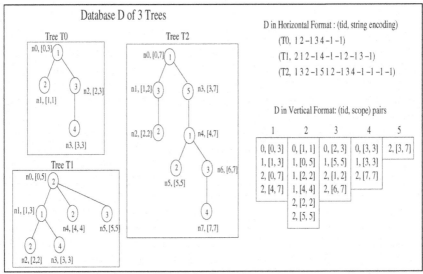

Fig. 5.5. Scope-lists.

5.4.1 Scope-List Representation

Let X be a k-subtree of a tree T. Let x_k refer to the last node of X. We use the notation $\mathcal{L}(X)$ to refer to the *scope-list* of X. Each element of the scope-list is a triple (t, m, s), where t is a tree id (tid) in which X occurs, m is a match label of the $(k-1)$ length prefix of X, and s is the scope of the last item x_k. Recall that the prefix match label gives the positions of nodes in T that match the prefix. Since a given prefix can occur multiple times in a tree, X can be associated with multiple match labels as well as multiple scopes. The initial scope-lists are created for single items (i.e., labels) i that occur in a tree T. Since a single item has an empty prefix, we don't have to store the prefix match label m for single items. We will show later how to compute pattern frequency via joins on scope-lists.

Example 5. Figure 5.5 shows a database of three trees, along with the horizontal format for each tree and the vertical scope-list format for each item. Consider item 1; since it occurs at node position 0 with scope $[0,3]$ in tree T_0, we add $(0, [0,3])$ to its scope list $\mathcal{L}(1)$. Item 1 also occurs in T_1 at position n_1 with scope $[1,3]$, so we add $(1, [1,3])$ to $\mathcal{L}(1)$. Finally, item 1 occurs with scope $[0,7]$ and $[4,7]$ in tree T_2, so we add $(2, [0,7])$ and $(2, [4,7])$ to its scope-list. In a similar manner, the scope-lists for other items are created.

5.4.2 Frequent Subtree Enumeration

Figure 5.6 shows the high-level structure of TreeMiner. The main steps include the computation of the frequent items and 2-subtrees, and the enumeration of all other frequent subtrees via DFS search within each class $[P]_1 \in F_2$. We will now describe each step in more detail.

TreeMiner (D, *minsup*):
    $F_1 = \{$ frequent 1-subtrees $\}$;
    $F_2 = \{$ classes $[P]_1$ of frequent 2-subtrees $\}$;
    for all $[P]_1 \in E$ **do** *Enumerate-Frequent-Subtrees*($[P]_1$);

Enumerate-Frequent-Subtrees($[P]$):
    for each element $(x,i) \in [P]$ **do**
        $[P_x] = \emptyset$;
        for each element $(y,j) \in [P]$ **do**
            $\mathbf{R} = \{(x,i)\otimes(y,j)\}$;
            $\mathcal{L}(\mathbf{R}) = \{\mathcal{L}(x) \cap_\otimes \mathcal{L}(y)\}$;
            if for any $R \in \mathbf{R}$, R is frequent **then**
                $[P_x] = [P_x] \cup \{R\}$;
        Enumerate-Frequent-Subtrees($[P_x]$);

Fig. 5.6. TreeMiner algorithm.

Computing F_1 and F_2: TreeMiner assumes that the initial database is in the horizontal string-encoded format. To compute F_1, for each item $i \in T$, the string encoding of tree T, we increment i's count in a one-dimensional array. This step also computes other database statistics such as the number of trees, maximum number of labels, and so on. All labels in F_1 belong to the class with empty prefix, given as $[P]_0 = [\emptyset] = \{(i, -1),\ i \in F_1\}$, and the position -1 indicates that i is not attached to any node. Total time for this step is $O(n)$ per tree, where $n = |T|$.

By Theorem 1 each candidate class $[P]_1 = [i]$ (with $i \in F_1$) consists of elements of the form $(j, 0)$, where $j \geq i$. For efficient F_2 counting we compute the supports of each candidate by using a two-dimensional integer array of size $F_1 \times F_1$, where $cnt[i][j]$ gives the count of candidate subtrees with encoding $(i\ j\ -1)$. Total time for this step is $O(n^2)$ per tree. While computing F_2 we also create the vertical scope-list representation for each frequent item $i \in F_1$.

Computing $F_k(k \geq 3)$: Figure 5.6 shows the pseudo-code for the depth-first search for frequent subtrees (ENUMERATE-FREQUENT-SUBTREES). The input to the procedure is a set of elements of a class $[P]$, along with their scope-lists. Frequent subtrees are generated by joining the scope-lists of all pairs of elements (including self-joins). Before joining the scope-lists, a pruning step can be inserted to ensure that subtrees of the resulting tree are frequent. If this is true, then we can go ahead with the scope-list join, otherwise we can avoid the join. For convenience, we use the set **R** to denote the up to two possible candidate subtrees that may result from $(x, i) \otimes (y, j)$, according to the class extension theorem, and we use $\mathcal{L}(\mathbf{R})$ to denote their respective scope-lists. The subtrees found to be frequent at the current level form the elements of classes for the next level. This recursive process is repeated until all frequent subtrees have been enumerated. If $[P]$ has n elements, the total cost is given as $O(ln^2)$, where l is the cost of a scope-list join (given later). In terms of memory management it is easy to see that we need memory to store classes along a path in the DFS search. At the very least we need to store intermediate scope-lists for two classes, i.e., the current class $[P]$ and a new candidate class $[P_x]$. Thus the memory footprint of TREEMINER is not large.

5.4.3 Scope-List Joins ($\mathcal{L}(x) \cap_\otimes \mathcal{L}(y)$)

Scope-list join for any two subtrees in a class $[P]$ is based on interval algebra on their scope lists. Let $s_x = [l_x, u_x]$ be a scope for node x, and $s_y = [l_y, u_y]$ a scope for y. We say that s_x is *strictly less* than s_y, denoted $s_x < s_y$, if and only if $u_x < l_y$, i.e., the interval s_x has no overlap with s_y, and it occurs before s_y. We say that s_x *contains* s_y, denoted $s_x \supset s_y$, if and only if $l_x \leq l_y$ and $u_x \geq u_y$, i.e., the interval s_y is a proper subset of s_x. The use of scopes allows us to compute in constant time whether y is a descendant of x or y is a embedded sibling of x. Recall from the candidate extension Theorem 1 that when we join elements $(x, i) \otimes (y, j)$ there can be at most two possible outcomes, i.e., we either add $(y, j + 1)$ or (y, j) to the class $[P_x]$.

In-Scope Test
The first candidate $(y, j + 1)$ is added to $[P_x]$ only when $i = j$, and thus refers to the candidate subtree with y as a child of node x. In other words, $(y, j + 1)$

represents the subtree with encoding $(\mathcal{P}_x \ y)$. To check if this subtree occurs in an input tree T with tid t, we search for triples $(t_y, s_y, m_y) \in \mathcal{L}(y)$ and $(t_x, s_x, m_x) \in \mathcal{L}(x)$, such that:

- $t_y = t_x = t$, i.e., the triples both occur in the same tree, with tid t.
- $m_y = m_x = m$, i.e., x and y are both extensions of the same prefix occurrence, with match label m.
- $s_y \subset s_x$, i.e., y lies within the scope of x.

If the three conditions are satisfied, we have found an instance where y is a descendant of x in some input tree T. We next extend the match label m_y of the old prefix P, to get the match label for the new prefix P_x (given as $m_y \cup l_x$), and add the triple $(t_y, s_y, \{m_y \cup l_x\})$ to the scope-list of $(y, j+1)$ in $[P_x]$. We refer to this case as an *in-scope* test.

Out-Scope Test
The second candidate (y, j) represents the case when y is a embedded sibling of x, i.e., both x and y are descendants of some node at position j in the prefix P, and the scope of x is strictly less than the scope of y. The element (y, j), when added to $[P_x]$ represents the pattern $(\mathcal{P}_x \ -1 \ldots -1 \ y)$ with the number of -1's depending on the path length from j to x. To check if (y, j) occurs in some tree T with tid t, we need to check for triples $(t_y, s_y, m_y) \in \mathcal{L}(y)$ and $(t_x, s_x, m_x) \in \mathcal{L}(x)$, such that:

- $t_y = t_x = t$, i.e., the triples both occur in the same tree, with tid t.
- $m_y = m_x = m$, i.e., x and y are both extensions of the same prefix occurrence, with match label m.
- $s_x < s_y$, i.e., x comes before y in depth-first ordering and their scopes do not overlap.

If these conditions are satisfied, we add the triple $(t_y, s_y, \{m_y \cup l_x\})$ to the scope-list of (y, j) in $[P_x]$. We refer to this case as an *out-scope* test. Note that if we just check whether s_x and s_y are disjoint (with identical tids and prefix match labels), i.e., either $s_x < s_y$ or $s_x > s_y$, then the support can be counted for unordered subtrees!

Computation Time
Each application of in-scope or out-scope test takes $O(1)$ time. Let a and b be the distinct (t, m) pairs in $\mathcal{L}(x, i)$ and $\mathcal{L}(y, j)$, respectively. Let α denote the average number of scopes with a match label. Then the time to perform scope-list joins is given as $O(\alpha^2(a + b))$, which reduces to $O(a + b)$ if α is a small constant.

Example 6. Figure 5.7 shows an example of how scope-list joins work, using the database D from Figure 5.5, with $minsup = 100\%$, i.e., we want to mine subtrees that occur in all three trees in D. The initial class with empty prefix consists of four frequent items (1, 2, 3 and 4), with their scope-lists. All

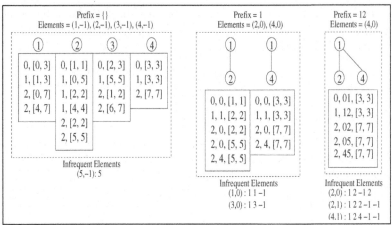

Fig. 5.7. Scope-list joins: $minsup = 100\%$.

pairs of elements are considered for extension, including self-join. Consider the extensions from item 1, which produces the new class [1] with two frequent subtrees: $(1\ 2\ -1)$ and $(1\ 4\ -1)$. The infrequent subtrees are listed at the bottom of the class.

While computing the new scope-list for the subtree $(1\ 2\ -1)$ from $\mathcal{L}(1) \cap_{\otimes} \mathcal{L}(2)$, we have to perform only in-scope tests, since we want to find those occurrences of 2 that are within some scope of 1 (i.e., under a subtree rooted at 1). Let s_i denote a scope for item i. For tree T_0 we find that $s_2 = [1,1] \subset s_1 = [0,3]$. Thus we add the triple $(0, 0, [1,1])$ to the new scope-list. In like manner, we test the other occurrences of 2 under 1 in trees T_1 and T_2. Note that for T_2 there are three instances of the candidate pattern: $s_2 = [2,2] \subset s_1 = [0,7]$, $s_2 = [5,5] \subset s_1 = [0,7]$, and $s_2 = [5,5] \subset s_1 = [4,7]$. If a new scope-list occurs in at least $minsup$ tids, the pattern is considered frequent.

Consider the result of extending class [1]. The only frequent pattern is $(1\ 2\ -1\ 4\ -1)$, whose scope-list is obtained from $\mathcal{L}(2,0) \cap_{\otimes} \mathcal{L}(4,0)$, by application of the out-scope test. We need to test for disjoint scopes, with $s_2 < s_4$, which have the same match label. For example we find that $s_2 = [1,1]$ and $s_4 = [3,3]$ satisfy these condition. Thus we add the triple $(0, 01, [1,1])$ to $\mathcal{L}(4,0)$ in class [1 2]. Notice that the new prefix match label (01) is obtained by adding to the old prefix match label (0) to the position where 2 occurs (1). The final scope list for the new candidate has three distinct tids, and is thus frequent. There are no more frequent patterns at $minsup= 100\%$.

Reducing Space Requirements

Generally speaking the most important elements of the in-scope and out-scope tests are to make sure that $s_y \subset s_x$ and $s_x < s_y$, respectively. Whenever the test is true we add $(t, s_y, \{m_y \cup l_x\})$ to the candidate's scope-list. However, the match labels are only useful for resolving the prefix context when an item occurs more than once in a tree. Using this observation it is possible to reduce the space requirements for the scope-lists. We add l_x to the match label m_y if and only if x occurs more than once in a subtree with tid t. Thus, if most items occur only once in the same tree, this optimization drastically cuts down the match label size, since the only match labels kept refer to items with more than one occurrence. In the special case that all items in a tree are distinct, the match label is always empty and each element of a scope-list reduces to a $(tid, scope)$ pair.

Example 7. Consider the scope-list of $(4, 0)$ in class [12] in Figure 5.7. Since 4 occurs only once in T_0 and T_1 we can omit the match label from the first two entries altogether, i.e., the triple $(0, 01, [3, 3])$ becomes a pair $(0, [3, 3])$, and the triple $(1, 12, [3, 3])$ becomes $(1, [3, 3])$.

Opportunistic Candidate Pruning
We mentioned above that before generating a candidate k-subtree, S, we perform a pruning test to check if its $(k - 1)$-subtrees are frequent. While this is easily done in a BFS pattern search method like PatternMatcher (see next section), in a DFS search we may not have all the information available for pruning, since some classes at level $(k - 1)$ would not have been counted yet. TreeMiner uses an opportunistic pruning scheme whereby it first determines if a $(k - 1)$-subtree would already have been counted. If it had been counted but is not found in F_{k-1}, we can safely prune S. How do we know if a subtree was counted? For this we need to impose an ordering on the candidate generation, so that we can efficiently perform the subtree pruning test. Fortunately, our candidate extension method has the automatic ordering property (see Corollary 1). Thus we know the exact order in which patterns will be enumerated. To apply the pruning test for a candidate S, we generate each subtree X, and test if $X < S$ according to the candidate ordering property. If yes, we can apply the pruning test; if not, we test the next subtree. If S is not pruned, we perform a scope-list join to get its exact frequency.

5.5 PatternMatcher **Algorithm**

PatternMatcher serves as a base pattern matching algorithm against which to compare TreeMiner. PatternMatcher employs a breadth-first iterative search for frequent subtrees. Its high-level structure, as shown in Figure 5.8, is similar to *Apriori* [3]. However, there are significant differences in how we count the number of subtree matches against an input tree T. For instance, we make use of equivalence classes throughout and we use a prefix-tree data structure to index them, as opposed to hash-trees. The details of pattern matching are also completely different. PatternMatcher assumes that each tree T in D is stored in its string encoding (horizontal) format (see Figure 5.5). F_1 and F_2 are computed as in TreeMiner. Due to lack of space we describe only the main features of PatternMatcher; see [37] for details.

PATTERNMATCHER (D, *minsup*):
1. F_1 = { frequent 1-subtrees };
2. F_2 = { classes of frequent 2-subtrees };
3. **for** $(k = 3; F_{k-1} \neq \emptyset; k = k + 1)$ **do**
4. C_k = { classes $[P]_{k-1}$ of candidate k-subtrees };
5.   **for** all trees T in D **do**
6.   Increment count of all $S \preceq T, S \in [P]_{k-1}$
7. C_k = { classes of frequent k-subtrees };
8. F_k = { hash table of frequent subtrees in C_k};
9. Set of all frequent subtrees = $\bigcup_k F_k$;

Fig. 5.8. PATTERNMATCHER algorithm.

Pattern Pruning
Before adding each candidate k-subtree to a class in C_k we make sure that all its $(k-1)$-subtrees are also frequent. To perform this step efficiently, during creation of F_{k-1} (line 8), we add each individual frequent subtree into a hash table. Thus it takes $O(1)$ time to check each subtree of a candidate, and since there can be k subtrees of length $k-1$, it takes $O(k)$ time to perform the pruning check for each candidate.

Prefix Tree Data Structure
Once a new candidate set has been generated, for each tree in D we need to find matching candidates efficiently. We use a prefix tree data structure to index the candidates (C_k) to facilitate fast support counting. Furthermore, instead of adding individual subtrees to the prefix tree, we index an entire class using the class prefix. Thus if the prefix does not match the input tree T, then none of the class elements would match either. This allows us to rapidly focus on the candidates that are likely to be contained in T. Let $[P]$ be a class in C_k. An internal node of the prefix tree at depth d refers to the dth node in P's label sequence. An internal node at depth d points to a leaf node or an internal node at depth $d+1$. A leaf node of the prefix tree consists of a list of classes with the same label sequence, thus a leaf can contain multiple classes. For example, classes with prefix encodings (1 2 −1 4 3), (1 2 4 3), (1 2 4 −1 −1 3), etc., all have the same label sequence 1243, and thus belong to the same leaf.

Storing equivalence classes in the prefix tree as opposed to individual patterns results in considerable efficiency improvements while pattern matching. For a tree T, we can ignore all classes $[P]_{k-1}$ where $P \npreceq T$. Only when the prefix has a match in T do we look at individual elements. Support counting consists of three main steps: finding a leaf containing classes that may potentially match T, checking if a given class prefix P exactly matches T, and checking which elements of $[P]$ are contained in T.

Finding Potential Matching Leaf Nodes

Let $l(T)$ be the label sequence for a tree T in the database. To locate matching leaf nodes, we traverse the prefix tree from the root, following child pointers based on the different items in $l(T)$, until we reach a leaf. This identifies classes whose prefixes have the same label sequence as a subsequence of $l(T)$. This process focuses the search to some leaf nodes of C_k, but the subtree topology for the leaf classes may be completely different. We now have to perform an exact prefix match. In the worst case there may be $\binom{n}{k} \approx n^k$ subsequences of $l(T)$ that lead to different leaf nodes. However, in practice it is much smaller, since only a small fraction of the leaf nodes match the label sequences, especially as the pattern length increases. The time to traverse from the root to a leaf is $O(k \log m)$, where m is the average number of distinct labels at an internal node. Total cost of this step is thus $O(kn^k \log m)$.

Prefix Matching

Matching the prefix P of a class in a leaf against the tree T is the main step in support counting. Let $X[i]$ denote the ith node of subtree X, and let $X[i, \ldots, j]$ denote the nodes from positions i to j, with $j \geq i$. We use a recursive routine to test prefix matching. At the rth recursive call we maintain the invariant that all nodes in $P[0, 1, ..., r]$ have been matched by nodes in $T[i_0, i_1, ..., i_r]$, i.e., prefix node $P[0]$ matches $T[i_0]$, $P[1]$ matches $T[i_1]$, and so on, and finally $P[r]$ matches $T[i_r]$. Note that while nodes in P are traversed consecutively, the matching nodes in T can be far apart. We thus have to maintain a stack of node scopes, consisting of the scope of all nodes from the root i_0 to the current right-most leaf i_r in T. If i_r occurs at depth d, then the scope stack has size $d + 1$.

Assume that we have matched all nodes up to the rth node in P. If the next node $P[r + 1]$ to be matched is the child of $P[r]$, we likewise search for $P[r + 1]$ under the subtree rooted at $T[i_r]$. If a match is found at position i_{r+1} in T, we push i_{r+1} onto the scope stack. On the other hand, if the next node $P[r + 1]$ is outside the scope of $P[r]$, and is instead attached to position l (where $0 \leq l < r$), then we pop from the scope stack all nodes i_k, where $l < k \leq r$, and search for $P[r + 1]$ under the subtree rooted at $T[i_l]$. This process is repeated until all nodes in P have been matched. This step takes $O(kn)$ time in the worst case. If each item occurs once it takes $O(k + n)$ time.

Element Matching

If $P \preceq T$, we search for a match in T for each element $(x, k) \in [P]$, by searching for x starting at the subtree $T[i_{k-1}]$. (x, k) is either a descendant or an embedded sibling of $P[k - 1]$. Either check takes $O(1)$ time. If a match is found the support of the element (x, k) is incremented by one. If we are interested in support (at least one occurrence in T), the count is incremented only once per tree; if we are interested in weighted support (all occurrences in T), we continue the recursive process until all matches have been found.

5.6 Experimental Results

All experiments were performed on a 500MHz Pentium PC with 512MB memory running RedHat Linux 6.0. Timings are based on total wall-clock time, and include preprocessing costs (such as creating scope-lists for TREEMINER).

Synthetic Data Sets
We wrote a synthetic data generation program mimicking website browsing behavior. The program first constructs a master website browsing tree, W, based on parameters supplied by the user. These parameters include the maximum fanout F of a node, the maximum depth D of the tree, the total number of nodes M in the tree, and the number of node labels N. We allow multiple nodes in the master tree to have the same label. The master tree is generated using the following recursive process. At a given node in the tree W, we decide how many children to generate. The number of children is sampled uniformly at random from the range 0 to F. Before processing child nodes, we assign random probabilities to each branch, including an option of backtracking to the node's parent. The sum of all the probabilities for a given node is 1. The probability associated with a branch $b = (x, y)$, indicates how likely is a visitor at x to follow the link to y. As long as tree depth is less than or equal to maximum depth D this process continues recursively.

Once the master tree has been created we create as many subtrees of W as specified by the parameter T. To generate a subtree we repeat the following recursive process starting at the root: generate a random number between 0 and 1 to decide which child to follow or to backtrack. If a branch has already been visited, we select one of the other unvisited branches or backtrack. We used the following default values for the parameters: the number of labels $N = 100$, the number of nodes in the master tree $M = 10,000$, the maximum depth $D = 10$, the maximum fanout $F = 10$ and total number of subtrees $T = 100,000$. We use three synthetic data sets: D10 data set had all the default values, F5 had all values set to default except for fanout $F = 5$, and for T1M we set $T = 1,000,000$, with remaining default values.

CSLOGS Data Set
This data set consists of web log files collected over one month at the CS department. The logs touched 13,361 unique web pages within our department's web site. After processing the raw logs we obtained 59,691 user browsing subtrees of the CS department website. The average string encoding length for a user-subtree was 23.3.

Figure 5.9 shows the distribution of the frequent subtrees by length for the different data sets used in our experiments; all of them exhibit a symmetric distribution. For the lowest minimum support used, the longest frequent subtrees in F5 and in T1M had 12 and 11 nodes, respectively. For cslogs and D10 data sets the longest subtrees had 18 and 19 nodes.

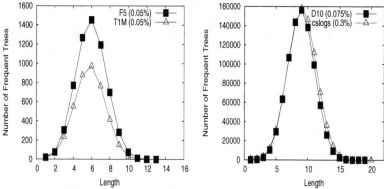

Fig. 5.9. Distribution of frequent trees by length.

Performance Comparison

Figure 5.10 shows the performance of PATTERNMATCHER versus TREE-MINER. On the real cslogs data set, we find that TREEMINER is about twice as fast as PATTERNMATCHER until support 0.5%. At 0.25% support TREE-MINER outperforms PATTERNMATCHER a factor of by more than 20! The reason is that cslogs had a maximum pattern length of 7 at 0.5% support. The level-wise pattern matching used in PATTERNMATCHER is able to easily handle such short patterns. However, at 0.25% support the maximum pattern length suddenly jumped to 19, and PATTERNMATCHER is unable to deal efficiently with such long patterns. Exactly the same thing happens for D10 as well. For supports lower than 0.5% TREEMINER outperforms PATTERN-MATCHER by a wide margin. At the lowest support the difference is a factor of 15. Both T1M and F5 have relatively short frequent subtrees. Here too TREEMINER outperforms PATTERNMATCHER but, for the lowest support shown, the difference is only a factor of four. These experiments clearly indicate the superiority of the scope-list-based method over the pattern-matching method, especially as patterns become long.

Scaleup Comparison

Figure 5.11 shows how the algorithms scale with increasing number of trees in the database D, from 10,000 to 1 million trees. At a given level of support, we find a linear increase in the running time with increasing number of transactions for both algorithms, though TREEMINER continues to be four times as fast as PATTERNMATCHER.

Effect of Pruning

In Figure 5.12 we evaluated the effect of candidate pruning on the performance of PATTERNMATCHER and TREEMINER. We find that PATTERNMATCHER (denoted PM in the graph) always benefits from pruning, since the fewer the number of candidates, the lesser the cost of support counting via pattern matching. On the other hand TREEMINER (labeled TM in the graph)

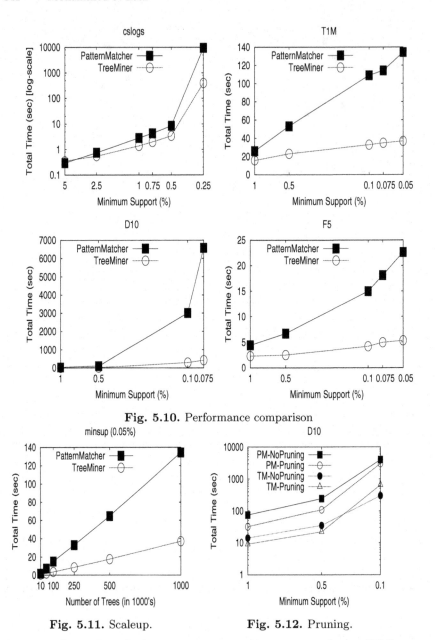

Fig. 5.10. Performance comparison

Fig. 5.11. Scaleup.   **Fig. 5.12.** Pruning.

does not always benefit from its opportunistic pruning scheme. While pruning tends to benefit it at higher supports, for lower supports its performance actually degrades by using candidate pruning. TREEMINER with pruning at 0.1% support on D10 is twice as slow as TREEMINER with no pruning. There are two main reasons for this. First, to perform pruning, we need to store F_k in a hash table, and we need to pay the cost of generating the $(k-1)$

subtrees of each new k-pattern. This adds significant overhead, especially for lower supports when there are many frequent patterns. Second, the vertical representation is extremely efficient; it is actually faster to perform scope-list joins than to perform a pruning test.

Table 5.1. Full vs opportunistic pruning.

$minsup$	No Pruning	Full Pruning	Opportunistic
1%	14595	2775	3505
0.5%	70250	10673	13736
0.1%	3555612	481234	536496

Table 5.1 shows the number of candidates generated on the D10 data set with no pruning, with full pruning (in PATTERNMATCHER), and with opportunistic pruning (in TREEMINER). Both full pruning and opportunistic pruning are extremely effective in reducing the number of candidate patterns, and opportunistic pruning is almost as good as full pruning (within a factor of 1.3). Full pruning cuts down the number of candidates by a factor of 5 to 7! Pruning is thus essential for pattern-matching methods, and may benefit scope-list methods in some cases (for high support).

5.7 Application: Web/XML Mining

To demonstrate the usefulness of mining complex patterns, we present below a detailed application study on mining usage patterns in web logs. Mining data that has been collected from web server log files, is not only useful for studying customer choices, but also helps to better organize web pages. This is accomplished by knowing which web pages are most frequently accessed by the web surfers.

We use LOGML [25], a publicly available XML application, to describe log reports of web servers. LOGML provides an XML vocabulary to structurally express the contents of the log file information in a compact manner. LOGML documents have three parts: a web graph induced by the source–target page pairs in the raw logs, a summary of statistics (such as top hosts, domains, keywords, number of bytes accessed, etc.), and a list of user-sessions (subgraphs of the web graph) extracted from the logs.

There are two inputs to our web mining system: the website to be analyzed and raw log files spanning many days, or extended periods of time. The website is used to populate a web graph with the help of a web crawler. The raw logs are processed by the LOGML generator and turned into a LOGML document that contains all the information we need to perform various mining tasks. We use the web graph to obtain the page URLs and their node identifiers.

For enabling web mining we make use of user sessions within the LOGML document. User sessions are expressed as subgraphs of the web graph and contain a complete history of the user clicks. Each user session has a session id (IP or host name) and a list of edges (**uedges**) giving source and target node pairs and the time (**utime**) when a link is traversed. An example user session is shown below:

```
<userSession name="ppp0-69.ank2.isbank.net.tr" ...>
<uedge source="5938" target="16470" utime="7:53:46"/>
<uedge source="16470" target="24754" utime="7:56:13"/>
<uedge source="16470" target="24755" utime="7:56:36"/>
<uedge source="24755" target="47387" utime="7:57:14"/>
<uedge source="24755" target="47397" utime="7:57:28"/>
<uedge source="16470" target="24756" utime="7:58:30"/>
```

Itemset Mining

To discover frequent sets of pages accessed we ignore all link information and note down the unique nodes visited in a user session. The user session above produces a user "transaction" containing the user name, and the node set, as follows: (ppp0-69.ank2.isbank.net.tr, 5938 16470 24754 24755 47387 47397 24756).

After creating transactions for all user sessions we obtain a database that is ready to be used for frequent set mining. We applied an association mining algorithm to a real LOGML document from the CS website (one day's logs). There were 200 user sessions with an average of 56 distinct nodes in each session. An example frequent set found is shown below. The pattern refers to a popular Turkish poetry site maintained by one of our department members. The user appears to be interested in the poet Akgun Akova.

```
Let Path=http://www.cs.rpi.edu/~name/poetry
FREQUENCY=16, NODE IDS = 16395 38699 38700 38698 5938
        Path/poems/akgun_akova/index.html
        Path/poems/akgun_akova/picture.html
        Path/poems/akgun_akova/biyografi.html
        Path/poems/akgun_akova/contents.html
        Path/sair_listesi.html
```

Sequence Mining

If our task is to perform sequence mining, we look for the longest forward links [7] in a user session, and generate a new sequence each time a back edge is traversed. We applied sequence mining to the LOGML document from the CS website. From the 200 user sessions, we obtain 8208 maximal forward sequences, with an average sequence size of 2.8. An example frequent sequence (shown below) indicates in what sequence the user accessed some of the pages related to Akgun Akova. The starting page **sair_listesi** contains a list of poets.

```
Let Path=http://www.cs.rpi.edu/~name/poetry
FREQUENCY = 20, NODE IDS =   5938 -> 16395 -> 38698
    Path/sair_listesi.html ->
```

```
Path/poems/akgun_akova/index.html ->
Path/poems/akgun_akova/contents.html
```

Tree Mining

For frequent tree mining, we can easily extract the forward edges from the user session (avoiding cycles or multiple parents) to obtain the subtree corresponding to each user. For our example user-session we get the tree: (ppp0-69.ank2.isbank.net.tr, 5938 16470 24754 -1 24755 47387 -1 47397 -1 -1 24756 -1 -1).

We applied the TREEMINER algorithm to the CS logs. From the 200 user sessions, we obtain 1009 subtrees (a single user session can lead to multiple trees if there are multiple roots in the user graph), with an average record length of 84.3 (including the back edges, -1). An example frequent subtree found is shown below. Notice how the subtree encompasses all the partial information of the sequence and the unordered information of the itemset relating to Akgun Akova. The mined subtree is clearly more informative, highlighting the usefulness of mining complex patterns.

```
Let Path=http://www.cs.rpi.edu/~name/poetry
Let Akova = Path/poems/akgun_akova
FREQUENCY=59, NODES = 5938 16395 38699 -1 38698 -1 38700
                    Path/sair_listesi.html
                              |
                Path/poems/akgun_akova/index.html
             /                |                   \
Akova/picture.html Akova/contents.html Akova/biyografi.html
```

We also ran detailed experiments on log files collected over one month at the CS department, which touched a total of 27,343 web pages. After processing, the LOGML database had 34,838 user graphs. We do not have space to show the results here (we refer the reader to [25] for details), but these results lead to interesting observations that support the mining of complex patterns from web logs. For example, itemset mining discovers many long patterns. Sequence mining takes a longer time but the patterns are more useful, since they contain path information. Tree mining, though it takes more time than sequence mining, produces very informative patterns beyond those obtained from item-set and sequence mining.

5.8 Related Work

Tree mining, being an instance of frequent structure mining, has an obvious relationship to association [3] and sequence [4] mining. Frequent tree mining is also related to tree isomorphism [27] and tree pattern matching [11]. Given a pattern tree P and a target tree T, with $|P| \leq |T|$, the subtree isomorphism problem is to decide whether P is isomorphic to any subtree of T, i.e., there is a one-to-one mapping from P to a subtree of T, that preserves the node adjacency relations. In tree pattern-matching, the pattern and target trees are labeled and ordered. We say that P matches T at node v if there exists a one-to-one mapping from nodes of P to nodes of T such that: a) the root of P maps to v, b) if x maps to y, then x and y have the same labels, and c) if x maps to y and x is not a leaf, then the ith child of x maps to the ith child of y. Both subtree isomorphism and pattern matching deal with induced subtrees, while we mine embedded subtrees. Further we are interested in enumerating all common subtrees in a collection of trees. The tree inclusion problem was studied in [19], i.e., given labeled trees P and T, can P be obtained from T by deleting nodes? This problem is equivalent to checking if P is embedded in T. The paper presents a dynamic programming algorithm for solving ordered tree inclusion, which could potentially be substituted for the pattern matching step in PATTERNMATCHER. However, PATTERNMATCHER utilizes prefix information for fast subtree checking, and its three-step pattern matching is very efficient over a sequence of such operations.

Recently tree mining has attracted a lot of attention. We developed TREEMINER [37, 38] to mine labeled, embedded and ordered subtrees. The notions of scope-lists and rightmost extension were introduced in that work. TREEMINER was also used in building a structural classifier for XML data [39]. Asai *et al.* [5] presented FreqT, an *Apriori*-like algorithm for mining labeled ordered trees; they independently proposed the rightmost candidate generation scheme. Wang and Liu [32] developed an algorithm to mine frequently occurring subtrees in XML documents. Their algorithm is also reminiscent of the level-wise *Apriori* [3] approach, and they mine induced subtrees only. There are several other recent algorithms that mine different types of tree patterns, including FreeTreeMiner [9] which mines induced, unordered, free trees (i.e., there is no distinct root); FreeTreeMiner for graphs [26] for extracting free trees in a graph database; and PathJoin [33], uFreqt [23], uNot [6], and HybridTreeMiner [10] which mine induced, unordered trees. TreeFinder [30] uses an Inductive Logic Programming approach to mine unordered, embedded subtrees, but it is not a complete method, i.e, it can miss many frequent subtrees, especially as support is lowered or when the different trees in the database have common node labels. SingleTreeMining [29] is another algorithm for mining rooted, unordered trees, with application to phylogenetic tree pattern mining. Recently, XSpanner [31], a pattern-growth-based method has been proposed for mining embedded ordered subtrees. They report that XSpanner outperforms TREEMINER, however, note that TREEMINER mines all embeddings, whereas XSpanner counts only the distinct trees.

There has been active work in indexing and querying XML documents [2, 15, 22, 40], which are mainly tree (or graph) structured. To efficiently answer ancestor–descendant queries, various node numbering schemes similar to ours have been proposed [1, 22, 40]. Other work has looked at path query evaluation that uses local knowledge within data graphs based on path constraints [2] or graph schemas [15]. The major difference between these works and ours is that instead of answering user-specified queries based on regular path expressions, we are interested in finding all frequent tree patterns among the documents. A related problem of accurately estimating the number of matches of a small node-labeled tree in a large labeled tree, in the context of querying XML data, was presented in [8]. They compute a summary data structure and then give frequency estimates based on this summary, rather than using the database for exact answers. In contrast, we are interested in the exact frequency of subtrees. Furthermore, their work deals with traditional (induced) subtrees, while we mine embedded subtrees.

There has also been recent work in mining frequent graph patterns. The AGM algorithm [18] discovers induced (possibly disconnected) subgraphs. The FSG algorithm [21] improves upon AGM and mines only the connected subgraphs. Both methods follow an *Apriori*-style level-wise approach. Recent methods to mining graphs using a depth-first tree based extension have been proposed in [34, 35]. Another method uses a candidate generation approach based on Canonical Adjacency Matrices [16]. The GASTON method [24] adopts an interesting step-wise approach using a combination of path, free tree and finally graph mining to discover all frequent subgraphs. There are important differences in graph mining and tree mining. Our trees are rooted and thus have a unique ordering of the nodes based on depth-first traversal. In contrast, graphs do not have a root and allow cycles. For mining graphs the methods above first apply an expensive *canonization* step to transform graphs into a uniform representation. This step is unnecessary for tree mining. Graph mining algorithms are likely to be overly general (thus not efficient) for tree mining. Our approach utilizes the tree structure for efficient enumeration.

The work by Dehaspe *et al.* [14] describes a level-wise Inductive Logic Programming technique to mine frequent substructures (subgraphs) describing the carcinogenesis of chemical compounds. They reported that mining beyond six predicates was infeasible due to the complexity of the subgraph patterns. The SUBDUE system [12] also discovers graph patterns using the Minimum Description Length principle. An approach termed Graph-Based Induction (GBI), which uses beam search for mining subgraphs, was proposed in [36]. However, both SUBDUE and GBI may miss some significant patterns, since they perform a heuristic search. We perform a complete (but not exhaustive) search, which guarantees that all patterns are found. In contrast to these approaches, we are interested in developing efficient algorithms for tree patterns.

5.9 Conclusions

In this paper we introduced the notion of mining embedded subtrees in a (forest) database of trees. Among our novel contributions is the procedure for systematic candidate subtree generation, i.e., no subtree is generated more than once. We utilize a string encoding of the tree that is space-efficient to store the horizontal data set, and we use the notion of a node's scope to develop a novel vertical representation of a tree, called a scope-list. Our formalization of the problem is flexible enough to handle several variations. For instance, if we assume the label on each node to be the same, our approach mines all unlabeled trees. A simple change in the candidate tree extension procedure allows us to discover sub-forests (disconnected patterns). Our formulation can find frequent trees in a forest of many trees or all the frequent subtrees in a single large tree. Finally, it is relatively easy to extend our techniques to find unordered trees (by modifying the out-scope test) or to use the traditional definition of a subtree. To summarize, this paper proposes a framework for tree mining which can easily encompass most variants of the problem that may arise in different domains.

We introduced a novel algorithm, TREEMINER, for tree mining. TREEM-INER uses depth-first search; it also uses the novel scope-list vertical representation of trees to quickly compute the candidate tree frequencies via scope-list joins based on interval algebra. We compared its performance against a base algorithm, PATTERNMATCHER. Experiments on real and synthetic data confirmed that TREEMINER outperforms PATTERNMATCHER by a factor of 4 to 20, and scales linearly in the number of trees in the forest. We studied an application of TREEMINER in web usage mining.

For future work we plan to extend our tree mining framework to incorporate user-specified constraints. Given that tree mining, though able to extract informative patterns, is an expensive task, performing general unconstrained mining can be too expensive and is also likely to produce many patterns that may not be relevant to a given user. Incorporating constraints is one way to focus the search and to allow interactivity. We also plan to develop efficient algorithms to mine maximal frequent subtrees from dense data sets which may have very large subtrees. Finally, we plan to apply our tree mining techniques to other compelling applications, such as finding common tree patterns in RNA structures within bioinformatics, as well as the extraction of structure from XML documents and their use in classification, clustering, and so on.

Acknowledgments: This work was supported in part by NSF Career Award IIS-0092978, DOE Career Award DE-FG02-02ER25538 and NSF grants CCF-0432098 and EIA-0103708.

References

[1] Abiteboul, S., H. Kaplan and T. Milo, 2001: Compact labeling schemes for ancestor queries. *ACM Symp. on Discrete Algorithms*.

[2] Abiteboul, S., and V. Vianu, 1997: Regular path expressions with constraints. *ACM Int'l Conf. on Principles of Database Systems*.

[3] Agrawal, R., H. Mannila, R. Srikant, H. Toivonen and A. I. Verkamo, 1996: Fast discovery of association rules. *Advances in Knowledge Discov-*

ery and Data Mining, U. Fayyad *et al.*, eds., AAAI Press, Menlo Park, CA, 307–28.

[4] Agrawal, R., and R. Srikant, 1995: Mining sequential patterns. *11th Intl. Conf. on Data Engineering*.

[5] Asai, T., K. Abe, S. Kawasoe, H. Arimura, H. Satamoto and S. Arikawa, 2002: Efficient substructure discovery from large semi-structured data. *2nd SIAM Int'l Conference on Data Mining*.

[6] Asai, T., H. Arimura, T. Uno and S. Nakano, 2003: Discovering frequent substructures in large unordered trees. *6th Int'l Conf. on Discovery Science*.

[7] Chen, M., J. Park and P. Yu, 1996: Data mining for path traversal patterns in a web environment. *International Conference on Distributed Computing Systems*.

[8] Chen, Z., H. Jagadish, F. Korn, N. Koudas, S. Muthukrishnan, R. Ng and D. Srivastava, 2001: Counting twig matches in a tree. *17th Intl. Conf. on Data Engineering*.

[9] Chi, Y., Y. Yang and R. R. Muntz, 2003: Indexing and mining free trees. *3rd IEEE International Conference on Data Mining*.

[10] — 2004: Hybridtreeminer: An efficient algorihtm for mining frequent rooted trees and free trees using canonical forms. *16th International Conference on Scientific and Statistical Database Management*.

[11] Cole, R., R. Hariharan and P. Indyk, 1999: Tree pattern matching and subset matching in deterministic $o(n \log^3 n)$-time. *10th Symposium on Discrete Algorithms*.

[12] Cook, D., and L. Holder, 1994: Substructure discovery using minimal description length and background knowledge. *Journal of Artificial Intelligence Research*, **1**, 231–55.

[13] Cooley, R., B. Mobasher and J. Srivastava, 1997: Web mining: Information and pattern discovery on the world wide web. *8th IEEE Intl. Conf. on Tools with AI*.

[14] Dehaspe, L., H. Toivonen and R. King, 1998: Finding frequent substructures in chemical compounds. *4th Intl. Conf. Knowledge Discovery and Data Mining*.

[15] Fernandez, M., and D. Suciu, 1998: Optimizing regular path expressions using graph schemas. *IEEE Int'l Conf. on Data Engineering*.

[16] Huan, J., W. Wang and J. Prins, 2003: Efficient mining of frequent subgraphs in the presence of isomorphism. *IEEE Int'l Conf. on Data Mining*.

[17] Inokuchi, A., T. Washio and H. Motoda, 2000: An *Apriori*-based algorithm for mining frequent substructures from graph data. *4th European Conference on Principles of Knowledge Discovery and Data Mining*.

[18] — 2003: Complete mining of frequent patterns from graphs: Mining graph data. *Machine Learning*, **50**, 321–54.

[19] Kilpelainen, P., and H. Mannila, 1995: Ordered and unordered tree inclusion. *SIAM J. of Computing*, **24**, 340–56.

[20] Kuramochi, M., and G. Karypis, 2001: Frequent subgraph discovery. *1st IEEE Int'l Conf. on Data Mining.*

[21] — 2004: An efficient algorithm for discovering frequent subgraphs. *IEEE Transactions on Knowledge and Data Engineering*, **16**, 1038–51.

[22] Li, Q., and B. Moon, 2001: Indexing and querying XML data for regular path expressions. *27th Int'l Conf. on Very Large Databases.*

[23] Nijssen, S., and J. N. Kok, 2003: Efficient discovery of frequent unordered trees. *1st Int'l Workshop on Mining Graphs, Trees and Sequences.*

[24] — 2004: A quickstart in frequent structure mining can make a difference. *ACM SIGKDD Int'l Conf. on KDD.*

[25] Punin, J., M. Krishnamoorthy and M. J. Zaki, 2001: LOGML: Log markup language for web usage mining. *ACM SIGKDD Workshop on Mining Log Data Across All Customer TouchPoints.*

[26] Ruckert, U., and S. Kramer, 2004: Frequent free tree discovery in graph data. *Special Track on Data Mining, ACM Symposium on Applied Computing.*

[27] Shamir, R., and D. Tsur, 1999: Faster subtree isomorphism. *Journal of Algorithms*, **33**, 267–80.

[28] Shapiro, B., and K. Zhang, 1990: Comparing multiple RNA secondary structures using tree comparisons. *Computer Applications in Biosciences*, **6(4)**, 309–18.

[29] Shasha, D., J. Wang and S. Zhang, 2004: Unordered tree mining with applications to phylogeny. *International Conference on Data Engineering.*

[30] Termier, A., M.-C. Rousset and M. Sebag, 2002: Treefinder: a first step towards XML data mining. *IEEE Int'l Conf. on Data Mining.*

[31] Wang, C., M. Hong, J. Pei, H. Zhou, W. Wang and B. Shi, 2004: Efficient pattern-growth methods for frequent tree pattern mining. *Pacific-Asia Conference on KDD.*

[32] Wang, K., and H. Liu, 1998: Discovering typical structures of documents: A road map approach. *ACM SIGIR Conference on Information Retrieval.*

[33] Xiao, Y., J.-F. Yao, Z. Li and M. H. Dunham, 2003: Efficient data mining for maximal frequent subtrees. *International Conference on Data Mining.*

[34] Yan, X., and J. Han, 2002: gSpan: Graph-based substructure pattern mining. *IEEE Int'l Conf. on Data Mining.*

[35] — 2003: Closegraph: Mining closed frequent graph patterns. *ACM SIGKDD Int. Conf. on Knowledge Discovery and Data Mining.*

[36] Yoshida, K., and H. Motoda, 1995: CLIP: Concept learning from inference patterns. *Artificial Intelligence*, **75**, 63–92.

[37] Zaki, M. J., 2001: Efficiently mining trees in a forest. Technical Report 01-7, Computer Science Dept., Rensselaer Polytechnic Institute.

[38] — 2002: Efficiently mining frequent trees in a forest. *8th ACM SIGKDD Int'l Conf. Knowledge Discovery and Data Mining.*

[39] Zaki, M. J. and C. Aggarwal, 2003: Xrules: An effective structural classifier for XML data. *9th ACM SIGKDD Int'l Conf. Knowledge Discovery and Data Mining.*

[40] Zhang, C., J. Naughton, D. DeWitt, Q. Luo and G. Lohman, 2001: On supporting containment queries in relational database managment systems. *ACM Int'l Conf. on Management of Data.*

6

Sequence Data Mining

Sunita Sarawagi

Summary. Many interesting real-life mining applications rely on modeling data as sequences of discrete multi-attribute records. Existing literature on sequence mining is partitioned on application-specific boundaries. In this article we distill the basic operations and techniques that are common to these applications. These include conventional mining operations, such as classification and clustering, and sequence specific operations, such as tagging and segmentation. We review state-of-the-art techniques for sequential labeling and show how these apply in two real-life applications arising in address cleaning and information extraction from websites.

6.1 Introduction

Sequences are fundamental to modeling the three primary media of human communication: speech, handwriting and language. They are the primary data types in several sensor and monitoring applications. Mining models for network-intrusion detection view data as sequences of TCP/IP packets. Text information-extraction systems model the input text as a sequence of words and delimiters. Customer data-mining applications profile buying habits of customers as a sequence of items purchased. In computational biology, DNA, RNA and protein data are all best modeled as sequences.

A sequence is an ordered set of pairs $(t_1\ x_1)\ldots(t_n\ x_n)$ where t_i denotes an ordered attribute like time $(t_{i-1} \le t_i)$ and x_i is an element value. The length n of sequences in a database is typically variable. Often the first attribute is not explicitly specified and the order of the elements is implicit in the position of the element. Thus, a sequence **x** can be written as $x_1 \ldots x_n$. The elements of a sequence are allowed to be of many different types. When x_i is a real number, we get a time series. Examples of such sequences abound – stock prices over time, temperature measurements obtained from a monitoring instrument in a plant or day to day carbon monoxide levels in the atmosphere. When s_i is of discrete or symbolic type we have a categorical sequence. Examples of such sequences are protein sequences where each element is an amino acid that can take one of 20 possible values, or a gene sequence where each element can take one of four possible values, or a program trace consisting of a sequence of system calls [18]. In the general case, the element could be any multi-attribute record.

We will study the basic operations used for analyzing sequence data. These include conventional mining operations like classification (Section 6.2) and clustering (Section 6.3) and sequence specific operations like tagging (Section 6.4) and segmentation (Section 6.6). In Section 6.5 we present two applications of sequence tagging. These operators bring out interesting issues in feature engineering, probabilistic modeling and distance function design. Lack of space prevents us from covering a few other popular sequence mining primitives including frequent subsequence discovery, periodicity detection, and trend analysis.

We will use bold-faced symbols to denote vectors or sequences and non-bold-faced symbols to denote scalars.

6.2 Sequence Classification

Given a set of classes C and a number of example sequences in each class, the goal during classification is to train a model so that for an unseen sequence we can predict to which class it belongs. This arises in several real-life applications:

- Given a set of protein families, find the family of a new protein.
- Given a sequence of packets, label a session as intrusion or normal.
- Given several utterances of a set of words, classify a new utterance to the right word.
- Given a set of acoustic and seismic signals generated from sensors below a road surface, recognize the category of the moving vehicle as truck, car or scooter.

Classification is an extensively researched topic in data mining and machine learning. The main hurdle to leveraging the existing classification methods is that these assume record data with a fixed number of attributes. In contrast, sequences are of variable length with a special notion of order that seems important to capture. To see how the wide variety of existing methods of classification can be made to handle sequence data, it is best to categorize them into the following three types: generative classifiers, boundary-based classifiers and distance/kernel-based classifiers.

6.2.1 Boundary-based Classifiers

Many popular classification methods like decision trees, neural networks, and linear discriminants like Fisher's fall in this class. These differ a lot in what kind of model they produce and how they train such models but they all require the data to have a fixed set of attributes so that each data instance can be treated as a point in a multidimensional space. The training process partitions the space into regions for each class. When predicting the class label of an instance $\mathbf{x}$, we use the defined region boundaries to find the region to which $\mathbf{x}$ belongs and predict the associated class.

A number of methods have been applied for embedding sequences in a fixed-dimensional space in the context of various applications.

The simplest of these ignore the order of attributes and aggregate the elements over the sequence. For example, in text-classification tasks a document that is logically a sequence of words is commonly cast as a vector where each word is a dimension and its coordinate value is the aggregated count or the TF-IDF score of the word in the document [9].

Another set of techniques are the sliding window techniques where for a fixed parameter, called the window size k, we create dimensions corresponding to k-grams of elements. Thus, if the domain size of elements is m, the number of possible coordinates is m^k. The a-th coordinate is the number of times the k-gram a appears in the sequence. In Figure 6.1 we present an example of these alternatives. The first table shows the coordinate representation of the sequence on the left with the simplest method of assuming no order. The second table shows the coordinates corresponding to a size 3 sliding window method. The sliding window approach has been applied to classify sequences of system calls as intrusions or not [29, 48].

The main shortcoming of the sliding window method is that it creates an extremely sparse embedded space. A clever idea to get around this problem is proposed in [30] where the a-th coordinate is the number of k-grams in the sequence with at most b mismatches where $b < k$ is another parameter. The third table of Figure 6.1 shows an example of this method with mismatch score $b = 1$. Accordingly, the coordinate value of the first 3-gram "ioe" is 2 since in the sequence we have two 3-grams "ioe" and "ime" within a distance of one of this coordinate. Methods based on k-grams have been applied to classify system call sequences as intrusion or not [29].

The next option is to respect the global order in determining a fixed set of properties of the sequence. For categorical elements, an example of such order-sensitive derived features is the number of symbol changes or the average length of segments with the same element. For real-valued elements, examples are properties like Fourier coefficients, Wavelet coefficients, and Autoregressive coefficients. In an example application, Deng *et al.* [14] show how the parameters of the Auto Regression Moving Average (ARMA) model can help distinguish between sober and drunk drivers. The experiments reported in [14] showed that sober drivers have large values of the second and third coefficients, indicating steadiness. In contrast, drunk drivers exhibit close to zero values of the second and third coefficients, indicating erratic behavior. In the area of sensor networks, a common application of time series classification is target recognition. For example, [31] deploys Fast Fourier Transform-based coefficients and Autoregressive coefficients on seismic and acoustic sensor outputs to discriminate between tracked and wheeled vehicles on a road.

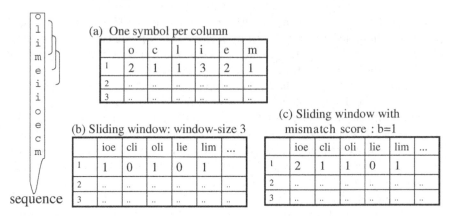

Fig. 6.1. Three different coordinate representations for a categorical sequence.

6.2.2 Generative Classifiers

As the name suggests, generative classifiers require a generative model of the data in each class. For each class i, the training process constructs a generative model M_i to maximize the likelihood over all training instances in the class i. Thus, M_i models the probability $\Pr(\mathbf{x}|c_i)$ of generating any instance $\mathbf{x}$ in class i. Also, we estimate the prior or background probability of a class $\Pr(c_i)$ as the fraction of training instances in class i.

For predicting the class of an instance $\mathbf{x}$, we apply Bayes rule to find the posterior probability $\Pr(c_i|\mathbf{x})$ of each class as follows:

$$\Pr(c_i|\mathbf{x}) = \frac{\Pr(\mathbf{x}|c_i)\,\Pr(c_i)}{\sum_j \Pr(\mathbf{x}|c_j)\,\Pr(c_j)}$$

The class with the highest posterior probability is chosen as the winner.

This method has been extensively applied to classification tasks. We can apply it to sequence classification provided we can design a distribution that can adequately model the probability of generating a sequence while being trainable with realistic amounts of training data. We discuss models for doing so next.

Denote a sequence $\mathbf{x}$ of n elements as $x_1, \ldots, x_n$. Applying the chain rule we can express the probability of generating a sequence $\Pr(\mathbf{x})$ as a product of n terms as follows:

$$\Pr(x_1, \ldots, x_n) = \Pr(x_1)\Pr(x_2|x_1)\Pr(x_3|x_1x_2)\ldots Pr(x_n|x_1\ldots x_{n-1})$$
$$= \prod_{i=1}^n \Pr(x_i|x_1\ldots x_{i-1})$$

This general form, where the probability of generating the i-th element depends on all previous elements, is too complex to train and too expensive to compute. In practice, simpler forms with limited amounts of dependency suffice. We list them in increasing order of complexity below.

For ease of explanation we will assume sequences with m categorical elements $v_1 \ldots v_m$. We will illustrate each model with an example sequence comprising of one of two possible elements "A" and "C", thus $m = 2$. Assume the training set T is a collection of N sequences $\mathbf{x}_1 \ldots \mathbf{x}_N$. An example sequence "AACA" will be used to explain the computation of the probability of generating a sequence from each model.

The Independent Model
The simplest is the independent model where we assume that the probability distribution of an element at position i is independent of all elements before it, i.e., $\Pr(x_i | x_1 \ldots x_{i-1}) = \Pr(x_i)$. If x_i is categorical with m possible values in the domain $v_1 \ldots v_m$, then $\Pr(x_i)$ can be modeled as a multinomial distribution with m possible parameters of the form $p(v_j)$ and $\sum_{j=1}^n p(v_j) = 1$. The number of parameters to train are then $m - 1$. Given a set T of training sequences, the parameter $p(v_j)$ can be easily estimated as the fraction of sequence positions over T where the element value is equal to v_j. For example, a sequence that is generated by the outcomes of an m-faced die rolled n times, is modeled perfectly by this independent model.

Figure 6.2(a) shows an example trained independent model with two possible elements. In this example, the probability of a sequence $AACA$ is calculated as $\Pr(AACA) = \Pr(A)^3 \Pr(C) = 0.1^3 \times 0.9$.

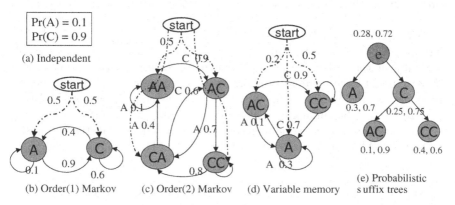

(a) Independent

(b) Order(1) Markov   (c) Order(2) Markov   (d) Variable memory   (e) Probabilistic suffix trees

Fig. 6.2. Models of increasing complexity for a sequence data set with two categorical elements "A" and "C".

First-order Markov Model
In a first-order Markov model, the probability of generating the i-th element is assumed to depend on the element immediately preceding it. Thus, $\Pr(x_i | x_1 \ldots x_{i-1}) = \Pr(x_i | x_{i-1})$. This gives rise to m^2 parameters of the form $\Pr(v_j | v_k)$ plus m parameters that denote the probability of starting a sequence with each of the m possible values denoted by π_j.

Figure 6.2(b) shows an example trained Markov model with two possible elements. In this example, the probability of a sequence $AACA$ is calculated as $\Pr(AACA) = \Pr(A)\Pr(A|A)\Pr(C|A)\Pr(A|C) = 0.5 \times 0.1 \times 0.9 \times 0.4$.

During training the maximum likelihood value of the parameter $\Pr(v_j|v_k)$ is estimated as the ratio of $v_k v_j$ occurrences in T over the number of v_k occurrences. The value of π_j is the fraction of sequences in T that start with value v_j.

Higher-order Markov Model

In general the probability of generating an element at position i could depend on a fixed length ℓ of symbols before it. Thus, $\Pr(x_i|x_1 \ldots x_{i-1}) = \Pr(x_i|x_{i-\ell} \ldots x_{i-1})$. The number of parameters in the model then becomes $m^{\ell+1}$ for the conditional probabilities and m^ℓ for the starting probabilities.

Figure 6.2c shows an example Markov model with two possible elements and $\ell = 2$. In this example, the probability of a sequence $AACA$ is calculated as $\Pr(AACA) = \Pr(AA)\Pr(C|AA)\Pr(A|AC) = 0.5 \times 0.9 \times 0.7$.

During training the maximum likelihood value of the parameter

$$\Pr(v_j|v_{k_\ell} \ldots v_{k_1})$$

is estimated as the ratio of $v_{k_\ell} \ldots v_{k_1} v_j$ occurrences in T over the number of $v_{k_\ell} \ldots v_{k_1}$ occurrences. For each l-gram $v_{k_\ell} \ldots v_{k_1}$, the value of the starting probability is the fraction of sequences in T that start with that l-gram.

Variable-Memory Markov Model

The number of parameters in higher-order Markov models increases exponentially in the order of the model. In many cases, it may not be necessary to model large memories uniformly for all elements. This motivated the need for variable-memory models where each element value v_j is assumed to have a variable number of elements on which it depends. An important special class of variable-memory models is a Probabilistic Suffix Automata (PSA) introduced in [41]. A PSA is a Markov model where each state comprises symbol sequences of length no more than ℓ (the maximum memory length) and the state labels are such that no label is a suffix of another. Figure 6.2d shows an example PSA for maximum memory $\ell = 2$. The probability of a sequence $AACA$ here is calculated as $\Pr(AACA) = \Pr(A)\Pr(A|A)\Pr(C|A)\Pr(A|AC) = 0.5 \times 0.3 \times 0.7 \times 0.1$.

The training process for these models is not as for straightforward as the previous models because we need to simultaneously discover a subset of states that capture all significant dependencies in the model. A closely related structure to PSA that enables efficient discovery of such states is the probabilistic suffix tree (PST). A PST is a suffix tree with emission probabilities of observation attached with each tree node. In Figure 6.2e we show the PST that is roughly equivalent to the PSA to its left. The j-th emission probability attached to each node denotes the probability of generating v_j provided the label of the node is the largest match that can be achieved with the suffix of the sequence immediately before v_j. The probability of an example sequence $\Pr(AACA)$ is evaluated as $0.28 \times 0.3 \times 0.7 \times 0.1$. The first 0.28 is for the first "A" in "AACA" obtained from the root node with an empty history. The second 0.3 denotes the probability of generating "A" from the node labeled "A". The third "0.7" denotes the probability of generating a "C" from the same node. The fourth multiplicand "0.1" is the probability of generating "A" from the node labeled "AC". The "AC"-labeled node has the largest suffix match with the part of the sequence before the last "A". This example, shows that calculating the probability of generating a sequence is more expensive with a PST than with a PSA. However, PSTs are amenable to more efficient training. Linear time algorithms exist for constructing such PSTs from training data in one single pass [2]. Simple procedures exist to convert a PST to the equivalent PSA after the training [41].

PSTs/PSAs have been generalized to even sparser Markov models and applied to protein classification in [17] and for classifying sequences of system calls as intrusions or not [18].

Hidden Markov Model
In the previous models, the probability distribution of an element in the sequence depended just on symbols before some distance but on no other factor. Often in real-life it is necessary to allow for more general distributions where an element's distribution also depends on some external cause. Consider the example of the dice sequence captured by an independent model. Suppose instead of rolling a single die to generate the sequence, we probabilistically pick any one of a set of s dice each with a different probability distribution and roll that for a while before switching to another. Then, none of the models presented earlier can capture this distribution. However a set of s independent distributions with some probability of switching between them models this perfectly. Such distributions are generalized elegantly by hidden Markov hodels (HMMs). In HMMs, states do not correspond to observed sequence elements hence the name "hidden". The basic HMM model consists of:

- a set of s states,
- a dictionary of m output symbols,
- an $s \times s$ transition matrix $\mathbf{A}$ where the ij^{th} element a_{ij} is the probability of making a transition from state i to state j,
- an $s \times m$ emission matrix $\mathbf{B}$ where entry $b_{jk} = b_j(v_k)$ denotes the probability of emitting the k-th element v_k in state j and
- an s-vector π where the j-th entry denotes the probability of starting in state j.

HMMs have been extensively used for modeling various kinds of sequence data. HMMs are popularly used for word recognition in speech processing [39]. [48] reports much higher classification accuracy with HMMs when used for detecting intrusions compared to previous k-grams approach. A lot of work

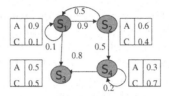

Fig. 6.3. A hidden Markov model with four states, transition and emission probabilities as shown and starting probability $\pi = [1\ 0\ 0\ 0]$.

has been done on building specialized hidden Markov models for capturing the distribution of protein sequences within a family [16].

The probability of generating a sequence

The probability of generating a sequence $\mathbf{x} = x_1, x_2, \ldots, x_n$ from a trained HMM model is not as straightforward to find as in the previous models where a sequence could be generated only from a single path through the states of the model. In the case of an HMM, a sequence in general could have been generated from an exponential number of paths. For example, for $AACA$ and the HMM in Figure 6.3 each element of the sequence can be generated from any of the four states giving rise to 4^4 possible state sequences over which the sum has to be computed. Thus, the total probability of generating $AACA$ from the HMM in Figure 6.3 is given by

$$\Pr(AACA) = \sum_{ijkl} \Pr(AACA, S_i S_j S_k S_l)$$
$$= \sum_{ijkl} \Pr(S_i) \Pr(A|S_i) \Pr(S_j|S_i) .. \Pr(A|S_l).$$

Given a state sequence $S_1 S_2 S_4 S_4$, the probability of generating $AACA$ through this sequence is

$$\Pr(AACA, S_1 S_2 S_4 S_4) = 1 \times 0.9 \times 0.9 \times 0.6 \times 0.5 \times 0.7 \times 0.2 \times 0.3.$$

We can exploit the Markov property of the model to design an efficient dynamic programming algorithm to avoid enumerating the exponential number of paths. Let $\alpha(i, q)$ be the value of $\sum_{\mathbf{q}' \in \mathbf{q}_{i:q}} \Pr(\mathbf{x}_{1..i}, \mathbf{q}')$ where $\mathbf{q}_{i:q}$ denotes all state sequences from 1 to i with the i-th state q and $\mathbf{x}_{1..i}$ denotes the part of the sequence from 1 to i, that is $x_1 \ldots x_i$. $\alpha()$ can be expressed recursively as

$$\alpha(i, q) = \begin{cases} \sum_{q' \in S} \alpha(i-1, q') a_{q'q} b_q(x_i) & \text{if } i > 1 \\ \pi_q b_q(x_i) & \text{if } i = 1 \end{cases}$$

The value of $\Pr(\mathbf{x})$ can then be written as $\Pr(\mathbf{x}) = \sum_q \alpha(|\mathbf{x}|, q)$.

The running time of this algorithm is $O(ns)$ where n is the sequence length and s is the number of states.

Training an HMM

The parameters of the HMM comprising of the number of states s, the set of symbols in the dictionary m, the edge transition matrix $\mathbf{A}$, the emission probability matrix $\mathbf{B}$, and starting probability π are learnt from training data. The training of an HMM has two phases. In the first phase we choose the structure of the HMM, that is, the number of states s and the edges amongst states. This is often decided manually based on domain knowledge. A number of algorithms have also been proposed for learning the structure automatically from the training data [42, 45]. We will not go into a discussion of these algorithms. In the second phase we learn the probabilities, assuming a fixed structure of the HMM.

Learning transition and emission probabilities

The goal of the training process is to learn the model parameters $\boldsymbol{\Theta} = (A, B, \pi)$ such that the probability of the HMM generating the training sequences $\mathbf{x}_1 \ldots \mathbf{x}_N$ is maximized. We write the training objective function as

$$\text{argmax}_{\boldsymbol{\Theta}} L(\boldsymbol{\Theta}) = \text{argmax}_{\boldsymbol{\Theta}} \prod_{\ell=1}^{N} \Pr(\mathbf{x}_\ell | \boldsymbol{\Theta}). \tag{6.1}$$

Since a given sequence can take multiple paths, direct estimates of the maximum likelihood parameters is not possible. An expectation maximization (EM) algorithm is used to estimate these parameters. For HMMs the EM algorithm is popularly called the Baum-Welch algorithm. It starts with initial guesses of the parameter values and then makes multiple passes over the training sequence to iteratively refine the estimates. In each pass, first in the E-step the previous values of parameters are used to assign the *expected* probability of each transition and each emission for each training sequence. Then, in the M-step the *maximum-likelihood* values of the parameters are recalculated by a straight aggregation of the weighted assignments of the E-step. Exact formulas can be found elsewhere [38, 39]. The above algorithm is guaranteed to converge to the locally optimum value of the likelihood of the training data.

6.2.3 Kernel-based Classifiers

Kernel-based classification is a powerful classification technique that includes well-known classifiers like Support Vector Machines, Radial Basis functions, and Nearest Neighbor classifiers.

Kernel classifiers require a function $K(\mathbf{x}_i, \mathbf{x}_j)$ that intuitively defines the similarity between two instances and satisfies two properties: K is symmetric i.e., $K(\mathbf{x}_i, \mathbf{x}_j) = K(\mathbf{x}_j, \mathbf{x}_i)$, and, K is positive definite, i.e., the kernel matrix defined on training instance pairs is positive definite [7]. Each class c is associated with a set of weight values w_i^c over each training sequence $\mathbf{x}_i$ and a bias term b^c. These parameters are learnt during training via classifier-specific methods [7]. The predicted class of a sequence $\mathbf{x}$ is found by computing for each class c, $f(\mathbf{x}, c) = \sum_i w_i^c K(\mathbf{x}_i, \mathbf{x}) + b^c$ and choosing the class with the highest value of $f(\mathbf{x}, c)$.

We can exploit kernel classifiers like SVMs for sequence classification, provided we can design appropriate kernel functions that take as input two data points and output a real value that roughly denotes their similarity. For nearest neighbor classifiers it is not necessary for the function to satisfy the above two kernel properties but the basic structure of the similarity functions is often shared. We now discuss examples of similarity/kernel functions proposed for sequence data.

A common approach is to first embed the sequence in a fixed dimensional space using methods discussed in Section 6.2.1 and then compute similarity using well-known functions like Euclidean, or any of the other L_p norms, or a dot-product. For time series data, [31] deploys a degree three polynomial over a fixed number of Fourier coefficients computed as $K(\mathbf{x}, \mathbf{x}') = (FFT(\mathbf{x}).FFT(\mathbf{x}')+1)^3$. The mismatch coefficients for categorical data described in Section 6.2.1 were used in [30] with a dot-product kernel function to perform protein classification using SVMs.

Another interesting technique is to define a fixed set of dimensions from intermediate computations of a structural generative model and then superimpose a suitable distance function on these dimensions. **Fisher's kernel** is an example of such a kernel [23] which has been applied to the task of protein family classification. A lot of work has been done on building specialized hidden Markov models for capturing the distribution of protein sequences within a family [16]. The Fisher's kernel provides a mechanism of exploiting these models for building kernels to be used in powerful discriminative classifiers like SVMs. First we train the parameters Θ_p of an HMM using all positive example sequences in a family. Now, for any given sequence $\mathbf{x}$ the Fisher's co-ordinate is derived from the HMM as the derivative of the generative probability $\Pr(\mathbf{x}|\Theta_p)$ with respect to each parameter of the model. Thus $\mathbf{x}$ is expressed as a vector $\nabla_\Theta \Pr(\mathbf{x}|\Theta)$ of size equal to the number of parameters of the HMM. This intuitively captures the influence of each of the model parameters on the sequence $\mathbf{x}$ and thus captures the key characteristics of the sequence as far as the classification problem is concerned. Now, given any two sequences $\mathbf{x}$ and $\mathbf{x}'$ the distance between them can be measured using either a scaled Euclidean or a general scaled similarity computation based on a co-variance matrix. [23] deployed such a distance computation on a Gaussian kernel and obtained accuracies that are significantly higher than with applying the Bayes rule on generative models as discussed in Section 6.2.2.

Finally, a number of sequence-specific similarity measures have also been proposed. For real-valued elements these include measures such as the Dynamic Time Warping method [39] and for categorical data these include measures such as the edit distance, the more general Levenstein distance [3], and sequence alignment distances like BLAST and PSI-BLAST protein data.

6.3 Sequence Clustering

Given a set of sequences, during clustering the goal is to create groups such that similar sequences are in the same group and sequences in different groups are dissimilar. Like classification, clustering is also an extensively researched topic with several formulations and algorithms. With the goal of mapping the problem of clustering sequences to clustering normal record data, we partition the clustering algorithms into three main types.

6.3.1 Distance-based Clustering

This is the most popular clustering method and includes the famous K-means and K-medoid clustering algorithms and the various hierarchical algorithms [21]. The primary requirement for these algorithms is to be able to design a similarity measure over a pair of sequences. We have already discussed sequence similarity measures in Section 6.2.3.

6.3.2 Model-based Algorithms

Model-based clustering assumes that data is generated from a mixture of K underlying distributions in which each distribution represents a group or a cluster. Each group k is associated with a mixing parameter called τ_k ($\sum_{k=1}^{K} \tau_k = 1$) in addition to the parameters Θ_k of the distribution function of that group. The goal during clustering is to recover the K sets of parameters of the distributions and the mixing value τ_k such that the probability of generating the data is maximized. This clustering method is better known in terms of the expectation maximization (EM) algorithm used to discover these clusters.

The only primitive needed to adapt the algorithms of model-based clustering to sequence data is designing a suitable generative model. We have already presented sequence-specific generative models in Section 6.2.2 and these apply directly to sequence data clustering.

6.3.3 Density-based Algorithms

In density-based clustering [21], the goal is to define clusters such that regions of high point density in a multidimensional space are grouped together into a connected region. The primary requirement to be able to deploy these algorithms is to be able to embed the variable-length sequence data into a fixed dimensional space. Techniques for creating such embeddings are discussed in Section 6.2.1.

6.4 Sequence Tagging

The sequence tagging problem is defined as follows: We are given a set of tags L and several training examples of sequences showing the breakup of the sequence into the set of tags. During training we learn to assign tags to elements of the sequence so that given a sequence $\mathbf{x} = x_1 \ldots x_n$ we can classify each of its elements into one of L tags giving rise to a tag sequence $\mathbf{y} = y_1 \ldots y_n$. Tagging is often referred as *sequential labeling*.

This operation has several applications. Information extraction or Named Entity Recognition (NER) is a tagging problem. Well-studied cases of NER are identifying personal names and company names in newswire text (e.g., [5]), identifying gene and protein names in biomedical publications (e.g., [6, 22]), identifying titles and authors in on-line publications (e.g., [28, 35]), breaking an address record into tag labels like Road, City name, etc.[4]. In continuous speech recognition, the tagging problem arises in trying to identify the boundary of individual words from continuous speech. In bio-informatics, the problem of identifying coding regions from gene sequences is a tagging problem. Figure 6.4 shows a sequence of nine words forming an address record tagged using six label elements.

A number of solutions have been proposed for the tagging problem particularly in the context of information extraction.

House number	Building	Road	City	State	Zip
4089	Whispering Pines	Nobel Drive	San Diego	CA	92122

Fig. 6.4. An example showing the tagging of a sequence of nine words with six labels.

6.4.1 Reduce to Per-element Tagging

As for whole sequence classification, one set of methods for the sequence tagging problems is based on reduction to existing classification methods. The simplest approach is to independently assign for each element x_i of a sequence $\mathbf{x}$ a label y_i using features derived from the element x_i. This ignores the context in which x_i is placed. The context can be captured by taking a window of w elements around x_i. Thus, for getting predictions for x_i we would use as input features derived from the record $(x_{i-w} \ldots x_{i-1} x_i x_{i+1} \ldots x_{i+w})$. Any existing classifier like SVM or decision trees can be applied on such fixed-dimensional record data to get a predicted value for y_i. However, in several applications the tags assigned to adjacent elements of a sequence depend on each other and assigning independent labels may not be a good idea. A popular method of capturing such dependency is to assign tags to the sequence elements in a fixed left to right or right to left order. The predicted labels of the previous h positions are added as features in addition to the usual x context features. During training, the features corresponding to each position consist of the x-window features and the true labels of the previous h positions. This method has been applied for named-entity recognition by [46] and for English pronunciation prediction by [15]. In Section 6.4.3 we will consider extensions where instead of using a fixed prediction from the previous labels, we could exploit multiple predictions each attached with a probability value to assign a globally optimum assignment.

6.4.2 Probabilistic Generative Models

A more unified approach is to build a joint global probability distribution relating the $\mathbf{x}$ and $\mathbf{y}$ sequences with varying amounts of memory/dependency information as discussed in Section 6.2.2. Hidden Markov models provide a ready solution where each state is associated with a label from the set L and the distribution of the elements x_i is modeled via the emission probabilities attached with a dictionary. Each state of the HMM is marked with exactly one of the L elements, although more than one state could be marked with the same element. The training data consists of a sequence of element-symbol pairs. This imposes the restriction that for each pair $\langle e, x \rangle$ the symbol x can only be emitted from a state marked with element e.

In Section 6.5.1 we present an application where HMMs are used for text segmentation.

After training such a model, predicting the $\mathbf{y}$ sequence for a given $\mathbf{x}$ sequence reduces to the problem of finding the best path through the model, such that the ith symbol x_i is emitted by the ith state in the path. The label associated with this state is the predicted label of x_i. Given s states and a sequence of length n, there can be $O(n^s)$ possible paths that the sequence can go through. This exponential complexity is cut down to $O(ns^2)$ by the famous dynamic programming-based *Viterbi Algorithm* [39].

The Viterbi algorithm for HMMs

Given a sequence $\mathbf{x} = x_1, x_2, \ldots, x_n$ of length n, we want to find out the most probable state sequence $\mathbf{y} = y_1 \ldots y_n$ such that $\Pr(\mathbf{x}, \mathbf{y})$ is maximized.

Let $\delta(i, y)$ be the value of $\max_{\mathbf{y}' \in \mathbf{y}_{i:y}} \Pr(\mathbf{x}_{1..i}, \mathbf{y}')$ where $\mathbf{y}_{i:y}$ denotes all state sequences from 1 to i with the i-th state y and $\mathbf{x}_{1..i}$ denotes the part of the sequence from 1 to i, that is $x_1 \ldots x_i$. $\delta()$ can be expressed recursively as

$$\delta(i, y) = \begin{cases} \max_{y' \in \mathcal{L}} \; \delta(i-1, y') a_{y'y} b_y(x_i) & \text{if } i > 1 \\ \pi_y b_y(x_i) & \text{if } i = 1 \end{cases}$$

The value of the highest probability path corresponds to $\max_y \delta(|\mathbf{x}|, y)$.

6.4.3 Probabilistic Conditional Models

A major shortcoming of generative models like HMMs is that they maximize the joint probability of sequence **x** and labels **y**. This does not necessarily maximize accuracy. During testing, **x** is already known and we are only interesting in finding the best **y** corresponding to this **x**. Hence, a number of models have been proposed to directly capture the distribution of $\Pr(\mathbf{y}|\mathbf{x})$ through discriminative methods. There are two categories of models in this space.

Local Models
A common variant is to define the conditional distribution of **y** given **x** as

$$P(\mathbf{y}|\mathbf{x}) = \prod_{i=1}^{n} P(y_i|y_{i-1}, x_i)$$

This is the formalism used in maximum-entropy taggers [40] and it has been variously called a maximum- entropy Markov model (MEMM) [34] and a conditional Markov model (CMM) [24].

Given training data in the form of pairs $(\mathbf{x}, \mathbf{y})$, the "local" conditional distribution $P(y_i|y_{i-1}, x_i)$ can be learned from derived triples (y_i, y_{i-1}, x_i), for example by using maximum- entropy methods. For maximum-entropy taggers the value of $P(y_i|y_{i-1}, x_i)$ is expressed as an exponential function of the form:

$$P(y_i|y_{i-1}, x_i) = \frac{1}{Z(x_i)} e^{W.\mathbf{f}(y_i, x_i, y_{i-1})} \tag{6.2}$$

where $\mathbf{f}(y_i, x_i, y_{i-1})$ is the set of local features at position x_i, current label y_i and previous label y_{i-1}. The normalization term $Z(x_i) = \sum_{y'} e^{W.\mathbf{f}(y', x_i, y_{i-1})}$.

Inferencing in these models is discussed along with the global models of the next section.

Global Conditional Models: Conditional Random Fields
Conditionally-structured models like the CMM have been improved recently by algorithms that learn a single global conditional model for $P(\mathbf{y}|\mathbf{x})$[26]. A CRF models $\Pr(\mathbf{y}|\mathbf{x})$ a Markov random field, with nodes corresponding to elements of the structured object **y** and potential functions that are conditional on (features of) **x**. For sequential learning tasks, NP chunking [43] and POS tagging [26] the Markov field is a chain, and **y** is a linear sequence of labels from a fixed set $\mathcal{Y}$ and the label at position i depends only on its previous label. For instance, in the NER application, **x** might be a sequence of words, and **y** might be a sequence in $\{I, O\}^{|\mathbf{x}|}$, where $y_i = I$ indicates "word x_i is inside a name" and $y_i = O$ indicates the opposite.

Assume a vector **f** of *local feature functions* $\mathbf{f} = \langle f^1, \ldots, f^K \rangle$, each of which maps a pair $(\mathbf{x}, \mathbf{y})$ and a position i in the vector **x** to a measurement $f^k(i, \mathbf{x}, \mathbf{y}) \in R$. Let $\mathbf{f}(i, \mathbf{x}, \mathbf{y})$ be the vector of these measurements, and let

$$\mathbf{F}(\mathbf{x}, \mathbf{y}) = \sum_{i}^{|\mathbf{x}|} \mathbf{f}(i, \mathbf{x}, \mathbf{y}).\tag{6.3}$$

For the case of NER, the components of $\mathbf{f}$ might include the measurement $f^{13}(i, \mathbf{x}, \mathbf{y}) = [\![x_i \text{ is capitalized}]\!] \cdot [\![y_i = I]\!]$, where the indicator function $[\![c]\!] = 1$ if c if true and zero otherwise; this implies that $F^{13}(\mathbf{x}, \mathbf{y})$ would be the number of capitalized words x_i paired with the label I.

For sequence learning, any feature $f^k(i, \mathbf{x}, \mathbf{y})$ is **local** in the sense that the feature at a position i will depend only on the previous labels. With a slight abuse of notation, we claim that a local feature $f^k(i, \mathbf{x}, \mathbf{y})$ can be expressed as $f^k(y_i, y_{i-1}, \mathbf{x}, i)$. Some subset of these features can be simplified further to depend only on the current state and are independent of the previous state. We will refer to these as **state features** and denote them by $f^k(y_i, \mathbf{x}, i)$ when we want to make the distinction explicit. The term **transition features** refers to the remaining features that are not independent of the previous state.

A conditional random field (CRF) [26, 43] is an estimator of the form

$$\Pr(\mathbf{y}|\mathbf{x}, \mathbf{W}) = \frac{1}{Z(\mathbf{x})} e^{\mathbf{W} \cdot \mathbf{F}(\mathbf{x}, \mathbf{y})}\tag{6.4}$$

where $\mathbf{W}$ is a weight vector over the components of $\mathbf{F}$, and the normalizing term $Z(\mathbf{x}) = \sum_{\mathbf{y}'} e^{\mathbf{W} \cdot \mathbf{F}(\mathbf{x}, \mathbf{y}')}$.

The only difference between the CRF equation above and the maximum-entropy (Maxent) Equation (6.2) is in the normalization term. The normalization for Maxent models is local to each position i causing all positions to have the same normalized weight equal to 1. Thus, even if there is a particular x_i which is not too sure about discriminating between two possible labels it will still have to contribute a weight of 0.5 at least to the objective function (assuming $|L| = 2$). This leads to a problem, termed *label bias* in [26]. A CRF through global optimization and normalization can more effectively suppress the weight of such weak predictors and avoid the label bias.

An efficient inference algorithm

The *inference problem* for a CRF and the Maxent classifier of Equation (6.2) is identical and is defined as follows: given $\mathbf{W}$ and $\mathbf{x}$, find the best label sequence, $argmax_{\mathbf{y}} \Pr(\mathbf{y}|\mathbf{x}, \mathbf{W})$, where $\Pr(\mathbf{y}|\mathbf{x}, \mathbf{W})$ is defined by Equation (6.4).

$$argmax_{\mathbf{y}} \Pr(\mathbf{y}|\mathbf{x}, \mathbf{W}) = argmax_{\mathbf{y}} \mathbf{W} \cdot \mathbf{F}(\mathbf{x}, \mathbf{y})$$
$$= argmax_{\mathbf{y}} \mathbf{W} \cdot \sum_{j} \mathbf{f}(y_j, y_{j-1}, \mathbf{x}, j)$$

An efficient inference algorithm is possible because all features are assumed to be local. Let $\mathbf{y}_{i:l}$ denote the set of all partial labels starting from 1 (the first index of the sequence) to i, such that the i-th label is y. Let $\delta(i, y)$ denote the largest value of $W \cdot \mathbf{F}(\mathbf{x}, \mathbf{y}')$ for any $\mathbf{y}' \in \mathbf{y}_{i:l}$. The following recursive calculation implements the usual Viterbi algorithm:

$$\delta(i, y) = \begin{cases} \max_{y'} \ \delta(i - 1, y') + \mathbf{W} \cdot \mathbf{f}(y, y', \mathbf{x}, i) & \text{if } i > 0 \\ 0 & \text{if } i = 0 \end{cases} \quad (6.5)$$

The best label then corresponds to the path traced by $\max_y \delta(|\mathbf{x}|, y)$.

Training algorithm

Learning is performed by setting parameters to maximize the likelihood of a training set $T = \{(\mathbf{x}_\ell, \mathbf{y}_\ell)\}_{\ell=1}^N$ expressed as

$$L(\mathbf{W}) = \sum_\ell \log \Pr(\mathbf{y}_\ell | \mathbf{x}_\ell, \mathbf{W}) = \sum_\ell (\mathbf{W} \cdot \mathbf{F}(\mathbf{x}_\ell, \mathbf{y}_\ell) - \log Z_{\mathbf{W}}(\mathbf{x}_\ell))$$

We wish to find a $\mathbf{W}$ that maximizes $L(\mathbf{W})$. The above equation is convex, and can thus be maximized by gradient ascent, or one of many related methods like a limited-memory quasi-Newton method [32, 33]. The gradient of $L(\mathbf{W})$ is the following:

$$\nabla L(\mathbf{W}) = \sum_\ell \mathbf{F}(\mathbf{x}_\ell, \mathbf{y}_\ell) - \frac{\sum_{\mathbf{y}'} \mathbf{F}(\mathbf{y}', \mathbf{x}_\ell) e^{\mathbf{W} \cdot \mathbf{F}(\mathbf{x}_\ell, \mathbf{y}')}}{Z_{\mathbf{W}}(\mathbf{x}_\ell)}$$

$$= \sum_\ell \mathbf{F}(\mathbf{x}_\ell, \mathbf{y}_\ell) - E_{\Pr(\mathbf{y}'|\mathbf{W})} \mathbf{F}(\mathbf{x}_\ell, \mathbf{y}')$$

The first set of terms is easy to compute. However, we must use the Markov property of $\mathbf{F}$ and a dynamic programming step to compute the normalizer, $Z_{\mathbf{W}}(\mathbf{x}_\ell)$, and the expected value of the features under the current weight vector, $E_{\Pr(\mathbf{y}'|\mathbf{W})} \mathbf{F}(\mathbf{x}_\ell, \mathbf{y}')$. We thus define $\alpha(i, y)$ as the value of $\sum_{\mathbf{y}' \in \mathbf{y}_{i:y}} e^{\mathbf{W} \cdot \mathbf{F}(\mathbf{y}', \mathbf{x})}$ where again $\mathbf{y}_{i:y}$ denotes all label sequences from 1 to i with i-th position labeled y. For $i > 0$, this can be expressed recursively as

$$\alpha(i, y) = \sum_{y' \in \mathcal{L}} \alpha(i - 1, y') e^{\mathbf{W} \cdot \mathbf{f}(y, y', \mathbf{x}, i)}$$

with the base cases defined as $\alpha(0, y) = 1$. The value of $Z_{\mathbf{W}}(\mathbf{x})$ can then be written as $Z_{\mathbf{W}}(\mathbf{x}) = \sum_y \alpha(|\mathbf{x}|, y)$.

A similar approach can be used to compute the expectation

$$\sum_{\mathbf{y}'} \mathbf{F}(\mathbf{x}_\ell, \mathbf{y}') e^{\mathbf{W} \cdot \mathbf{F}(\mathbf{x}_\ell, \mathbf{y}')}.$$

For the k-th component of $\mathbf{F}$, let $\eta^k(i, y)$ be the value of the sum

$$\sum_{\mathbf{y}' \in \mathbf{y}_{i:y}} F^k(\mathbf{y}', \mathbf{x}_\ell) e^{\mathbf{W} \cdot \mathbf{F}(\mathbf{x}_\ell, \mathbf{y}')},$$

restricted to the part of the label ending at position i. The following recursion can then be used to compute $\eta^k(i, y)$:

$$\eta^k(i, y) = \sum_{y' \in \mathcal{L}} (\eta^k(i - 1, y') + \alpha(i - 1, y')f^k(y, y', \mathbf{x}, i))e^{\mathbf{W} \cdot \mathbf{f}(y, y', \mathbf{x}, i)}$$

Finally we let $E_{\Pr(\mathbf{y}'|\mathbf{W})}F^k(\mathbf{y}', \mathbf{x}) = \frac{1}{Z_{\mathbf{W}}(\mathbf{x})} \sum_y \eta^k(|\mathbf{x}|, y)$.

As in the forward-backward algorithm for chain CRFs [43], space requirements here can be reduced from $K|\mathcal{L}| + |\mathcal{L}|n$ to $K + |\mathcal{L}|n$, where K is the number of features, by pre-computing an appropriate set of β values.

6.4.4 Perceptron-based Models

Another interesting mechanism for sequence tagging, is based on an extension of the perceptron model for discriminative classification [12]. The structure of the model is similar to the global CRF model involving the feature vector $\mathbf{F}(\mathbf{x}, \mathbf{y})$ defined as in Equation (6.3) and corresponding weight parameters $\mathbf{W}$. Inferencing is done by picking the $\mathbf{y}$ corresponding to which $\mathbf{WF}(\mathbf{x}, \mathbf{y})$ is maximum. The predicted label sequence can be efficiently found using the same Viterbi procedure as for CRFs. The goal during training is to learn the value of $\mathbf{W}$ so as to minimize the error between the correct labels and the predicted Viterbi labels. This "best" W is found by repeatedly updating W to improve the quality of the Viterbi decoding on a particular example $(\mathbf{x}_t, \mathbf{y}_t)$. Specifically, Collin's algorithm starts with $W_0 = \mathbf{0}$. After the t-th example $\mathbf{x}_t, \mathbf{y}_t$, the Viterbi sequence $\hat{\mathbf{y}}_t$ is computed, and W_t is replaced with

$$W_{t+1} = W_t + \mathbf{F}(\mathbf{x}_t, \mathbf{y}_t) - \mathbf{F}(\mathbf{x}_t, \hat{\mathbf{y}}_t)$$
$$= W_t + \sum_{i=1}^{M} \mathbf{f}(i, \mathbf{x}_t, \mathbf{y}_t) - \mathbf{f}(i, \mathbf{x}_t, \hat{\mathbf{y}}_t) \tag{6.6}$$

After training, one takes as the final learned weight vector W the average value of W_t over all time steps t.

This simple perceptron-like training algorithm has been shown to perform surprisingly well for sequence learning tasks in [12].

6.4.5 Boundary-based Models

Boundary-based models learn to identify start and end boundaries of each label by building two classifiers for accepting its two boundaries along with the classifiers that identify the content part of the tag. Such an approach is useful in applications like NER where we need to identify a multi-word entity name (like person or company) from a long word sequence where most of the words are not part of the entity. Although any classifier could be used to identify the boundaries, the rule-based method has been most popular [8, 44]. Rapier [8] is one such rule-learning approach where a bottom-up algorithm is used to learn the pattern marking the beginning, the ending and the content part of each entity type.

6.5 Applications of Sequence Tagging

In this section we present two applications of the sequence-tagging operation. The first is an example of text segmentation where noisy text strings like addresses are segmented based on a fixed set of labels using hidden Markov models [4]. The second is an example of learning paths leading to informative pages in a website using conditional random fields [47].

6.5.1 Address Segmentation using Hidden Markov Models

Large customer-oriented organizations like banks, telephone companies, and universities store millions of addresses. In the original form, these addresses have little explicit structure. Often for the same person, there are different address records stored in different databases. During warehouse construction, it is necessary to put all these addresses in a standard canonical format where the different structured fields like names of street, city and state comprising an address are identified and duplicates removed. An address record broken into its structured fields not only enables better querying, it also provides a more robust way of doing deduplication and householding — a process that identifies all addresses belonging to the same household.

Existing commercial approaches rely on hand-coded rule-based methods coupled with a database of cities, states and zipcodes. This solution is not practical and general because postal addresses in different parts of the world have drastically different structures. In some countries, zip codes are five-digit numbers whereas in others they are allowed to have letters. The problem is more challenging in older countries like India because most street names do not follow a uniform building numbering scheme, the reliance on ad hoc descriptive landmarks is common, city names keep changing, state abbreviations are not standardized, spelling mistakes are rampant and zip codes optional. Further each region has evolved its own style of writing addresses that differs significantly from those of the other regions. Consider for instance the following two valid addresses from two different Indian cities:

`7D-Brijdham 16-B Bangur Nagar Goregaon (West) Bombay 400 090`

`13 Shopping Center Kota (Raj) 324 007`

The first address consists of seven elements: house number: `''7D''`, building name: `''Brijdham''`, building number: `''16-B''`, colony name: `''Bangur Nagar''`, area: `''Goregaon (West)''`, city: `''Bombay''` and zip code: `''400 090''`. The second address consists of the following five elements: house number: `''13''`, Colony name: `''Shopping center''`, city: `''Kota''`, State: `''(Raj)''` and zip code: `''324 007''`. In the first address, "West" was enclosed in parentheses and depicted direction while in the second the string "Raj" within parentheses is the name of a geographical State. This element is missing in the first address. In the second address building name, colony name and area elements are missing.

We propose an automated method for elementizing addresses based on hidden Markov models. An HMM combines information about multiple different aspects of the record in segmenting it. One source is the characteristic words in each elements, for example the word "street" appears in road-names. A second source is the limited partial ordering between its element. Often the first element is a house number, then a possible building name and so on and the last few elements are zipcode and state name. A third source is the typical number of words in each element. For example, state names usually have one or two words whereas road names are longer. Finally, the HMM simultaneously extracts each element from the address to optimize some global objective function. This is in contrast to existing rule learners used in traditional information tasks [1, 13, 25, 36, 37] that treat each element in isolation.

Structure of the HMM for Address Elementization
An easy way to exploit HMMs for address segmentation is to associate a state for each label or tag as described in Section 6.4.2. In Figure 6.5 we show an example HMM for address segmentation. The number of states s is 10 and the edge labels depict the state transition probabilities (A Matrix). For example, the probability of an address beginning with House Number is 0.92 and that of seeing a City after Road is 0.22. The dictionary and the emission probabilities are not shown for compactness. The dictionary would comprise of words that appeared in the training sequences.

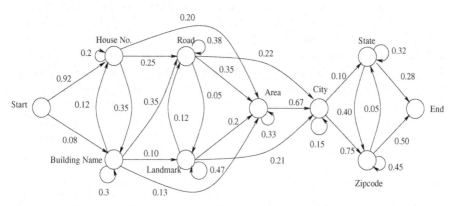

Fig. 6.5. Structure of an HMM used for tagging addresses.

However, the above model does not provide a sufficiently detailed model of the text within each tag. We therefore associate each tag with another inner HMM embedded within the outer HMM that captures inter-tag transitions. We found a parallel-path HMM as shown in Figure 6.6 to provide the best accuracy while requiring little or no tuning over different tag types. In the figure, the start and end states are dummy nodes to mark the two end points of a tag. They do not output any token. All records of length one will pass through the first path, length two will go through the second path and so on. The last path captures all records with four or more tokens. Different elements would have different numbers of such parallel paths depending on the element lengths observed during training.

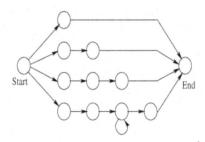

Fig. 6.6. A four-length parallel path structure.

Estimating Parameters during Training

During training, we get examples of addresses where structured elements have been identified. Each training token maps to exactly one state of the HMM even with the above multi-state nested structure for each tag. Therefore, we can deploy straight maximum likelihood estimates for the transition and emission probabilities.

An important issue in practice is dealing with zero probability estimates arising when the training data is insufficient. The traditional smoothing method is Laplace smoothing [27] according to an unseen symbol k, state j will be assigned probability $\frac{1}{T_j+m}$ where T_j is the number of training symbols in state j and m is the number of distinct symbols. We found this smoothing method unsuitable in our case. An element like "road name", that during training has seen more distinct words than an element like "country", is expected to also encounter unseen symbols more frequently during testing. Laplace smoothing does not capture this intuition. We use a method called absolute discounting. In this method we subtract a small value, say ϵ from the probability of all known m_j distinct words seen in state j. We then distribute the accumulated probability equally amongst all unknown values. Thus, the probability of an unknown symbol is $\frac{m_j\epsilon}{m-m_j}$. The choice of ϵ depends on whether the unknown symbol is unseen over all states of the HMM or just a subset of the sets. We want ϵ to be lower in the second case, which we arbitrarily fix to be a factor of 1000 lower. The value of ϵ is then chosen empirically.

We experimented with a number of more principled methods of smoothing including cross-validation but we found them not to perform as well as the above ad hoc method.

Experimental Evaluation

We report evaluation results on the following three real-life address data sets:

- US address: The US address data set consisted of 740 addresses down-loaded from an Internet directory.[1] The addresses were segmented into six elements: House No, Box No. Road Name, City, State, Zip.
- Student address: This data set consisted of 2388 home addresses of students in the author's university. These addresses were partitioned into 16 elements based on the postal format of the country. The addresses in this set do not have the kind of regularity found in US addresses.
- Company address: This data set consisted of 769 addresses of customers of a major national bank in a large Asian metropolis. The address was segmented into six elements: Care Of, House Name, Road Name, Area, City, Zipcode.

For the experiments all the data instances were first manually segmented into their constituent elements. In each set, one-third of the data set was used for training and the remaining two-thirds used for testing as summarized in Table 6.1.

Table 6.1. Data sets used for the experiments.

Data set	Number of elements (E)	Number of training instances	Number of test instances
US address	6	250	490
Student address	16	650	1738
Company address	6	250	519

All tokens were converted to lower case. Each word, digit and delimiter in the address formed a separate token to the HMM. Each record was prepro-cessed where all numbers were represented by a special symbol "digit" and all delimiters where represented with a special "delimit" symbol.

We obtained accuracy of 99%, 88.9% and 83.7% on the US, Student and Company data sets respectively. The Asian addresses have a much higher complexity compared to the US addresses. The company data set had lower accuracy because of several errors in the segmentation of data that was handed to us.

We compare the performance of the proposed nested HMM with the following three automated approaches.

---

[1] www.superpages.com

Naive HMM

This is the HMM model with just one state per element. The purpose here is to evaluate the benefit of the nested HMM model.

Independent HMM

In this approach, for each element we train a separate HMM to extract just its part from a text record, independent of all other elements. Each independent HMM has a prefix and suffix state to absorb the text before and after its own segment. Otherwise the structure of the HMM is similar to what we used in the inner HMMs. Unlike the nested-model there is no outer HMM to capture the dependency amongst elements. The independent HMMs learn the relative location in the address where their element appears through the self-loop transition probabilities of the prefix and suffix states. This is similar to the approach used in [19] for extracting location and timings from talk announcements.

The main idea here is to evaluate the benefit of simultaneously tagging all the elements of a record exploiting the sequential relationship amongst the elements using the outer HMM.

Rule learner

We compare HMM-based approaches with a rule learner, Rapier [8], a bottom-up inductive learning system for finding information extraction rules to mark the beginning, content and end of an entity. Like the independent HMM approach it also extracts each tag in isolation from the rest.

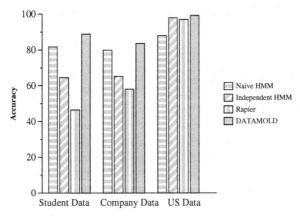

Fig. 6.7. Comparison of four different methods of text segmentation

Figure 6.7 shows a comparison of the accuracy of the four methods naive HMM, independent HMM, rule learner and nested HMM. We can make the following observations:

- The independent HMM approach is significantly worse than the nested model because of the loss of valuable sequence information. For example, in the former case there is no restriction that tags cannot overlap – thus the same part of the address could be tagged as being part of two different elements. With a single HMM the different tags corroborate each other's finding to pick the segmentation that is globally optimal.
- Naive HMM gives 3% to 10% lower accuracy than the nested HMM. This shows the benefit of a detailed HMM for learning the finer structure of each element.
- The accuracy of Rapier is considerably lower. Rapier leaves many tokens untagged by not assigning them to any of the elements. Thus it has low recall. However, the precision of Rapier was found to be competitive to our method – 89.2%, 88%, and 98.3% for Student, Company and US data sets respectively. The overall accuracy is acceptable only for US addresses where the address format is regular enough to be amenable to rule-based processing. For the complicated sixteen-element Student data set such rule-based processing could not successfully tag all elements.

6.5.2 Learning Paths in Websites using Conditional Random Fields

Another interesting application of sequential tagging models is in learning the sequence of links that lead to a specific goal page on a large website. Often websites within a domain are structurally similar to each other. Humans are good at navigating these websites to reach specific information within large domain-specific websites. Our goal is to learn the navigation path by observing the user's clicks on as few example websites as possible. Next, when presented with a list of new websites, we use the learnt model to automatically crawl the desired pages using as few redundant page fetches as possible.

We present a scenario where such a capability would be useful. Citation portals, such as Citeseer, need to gather publications on a particular discipline from home pages of faculty starting from lists of universities easily obtained from web directories such as Dmoz. This requires following a path starting from the root page of the university, to the home pages of departments relevant to the discipline, from there visiting the home pages of faculty members, and then searching for links such as "Papers", "Publications", or "Research Interests" that lead to the publications page, if it exists. Several universities follow this template website, although there is lot of variation in the exact words used on pages and around links and the placement of links. We expect such a learning-based approach to capture the main structure in a few examples so as to automatically gather all faculty publications from any given list of universities without fetching too many superflous pages.

There are two phases to this task: first is the training phase, where the user teaches the system by clicking through pages and labeling a subset with a dynamically defined set of classes, one of them being the goal class. The classes assigned on intermittent pages along the path can be thought of as "milestones" that capture the structural similarity across websites. At the end of this process, we have a set of classes L, and a set of training paths where a subset of the pages in the path are labeled with a class from L. All unlabeled pages before a labeled page are represented with a special prefix state for that label. The system trains a model using the example paths, modeling each class in L as a milestone state. The second phase is the foraging phase where the given list of websites is automatically navigated to find all goal pages.

The ratio of relevant pages visited to the total number of pages visited during the execution is called the **harvest rate**. The objective function is to maximize the harvest rate.

We treat this as a sequence-tagging problem where the path is a sequence of pages ending in a goal page. We first train a CRF to recognize such paths. We then superimpose ideas from reinforcement learning to prioritize the order in which pages should be fetched to reach the goal page. This provides an elegant and unified mechanism of modeling the path learning and foraging problem. Also, as we will see in the experimental results section, it provides very high accuracy.

Model Training

During training, we are given examples of several paths of labeled pages where some of the paths end in goal pages and others end with a special "fail" label. We can treat each path as a sequence of pages denoted by the vector $\mathbf{x}$ and their corresponding labels denoted by $\mathbf{y}$. Each x_i is a web page represented suitably in terms of features derived from the words in the page, its URL, and anchor text in the link pointing to x_i.

A number of design decisions about the label space and feature space need to be made in constructing a CRF to recognize characteristics of valid paths. One option is to assign a state to each possible label in the set L which consists of the milestone labels and two special labels "goal" and "fail". An example of such a model for the publications scenario is given in Figure 6.8(a) where each circle represents a label.

State features are defined on the words or other properties comprising a page. For example, state features derived from words are of the form $f^k(i, \mathbf{x}, y_i) = [\![x_i \text{ is "computer" and } y_i = \text{faculty}]\!]$. The URL of a page also yields valuable features. For example, a "tilda" in the URL is strongly associated with a personal home page and a link name with the word "contact" is strongly associated with an address page. We tokenize each URL on delimiters and add a feature corresponding to each feature.

Transition features capture the soft precedence order amongst labels. One set of transition features is of the form:
$f^k(i, \mathbf{x}, y_i, y_{i-1}) = [\![y_i \text{ is "faculty" and } y_{i-1} \text{ is "department"}]\!]$. They are independent of x_i and are called **edge features** since they capture dependency amongst adjacent labels. In this model, transition features are also derived from the words in and around the anchor text surrounding the link leading to

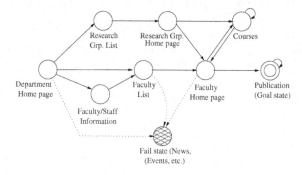

(a) One state per label with links as transitions

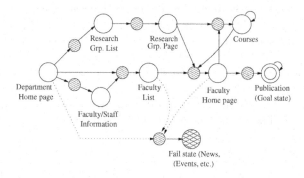

(b) A state for each label and each link

Fig. 6.8. State transition diagram for the Publications domain.

the next state. Thus, a transition feature could be of the form $f^k(i, \mathbf{x}, y_i, y_{i-1})$ = $[\![x_i$ is an anchor word "advisor", y_i is "faculty", and y_{i-1} is "student"$]\!]$.

A second option is to model each given label as a dual-state — one for the characteristics of the page itself (**page-states**) and the other for the information around links that lead to such a page (**link-states**). Hence, every path alternates between a page-state and a link-state.

In Figure 6.8(b), we show the state space corresponding to this option for the publications domain. There are two advantages of this labeling. First, it reduces the sparcity of parameters by making the anchor word features be independent of the label of the source page. In practice, it is often found that the anchor text pointing to the same page are highly similar and this is captured by allowing multiple source labels to point to the same link state of label. Second for the foraging phase, it allows one to easily reason about intermediate probability of a path prefix where only the link is known and the page leading to it has not been fetched.

In this model, the state features of the page states are the same as in the previous model and the state features of the link states are derived from the anchor text. Thus, the anchor-text transition features of the previous model, become state features of the link state. Thus the only transition features in this model are the edge features that capture the precedence order between labels.

Path Foraging

Given the trained sequential model M and a list of starting pages of websites, our goal is to find all paths from the list that lead to the "goal" state in M while fetching as few unrelated pages.

The key issue in solving this is to be able to score from a prefix of a path already fetched, all the set of outgoing links with a value that is inversely proportional to the expected work involved in reaching the goal pages. Consider a path prefix of the form $P_1 L_2 P_3 \ldots L_i$ where L_{i-1} is a link to page P_i in the path. We need to find for link L_i a score value that would indicate the desirability of fetching the page pointed to by L_i. This score is computed in two parts. First, we estimate for each state y, the proximity of the state to the goal state. We call this the reward associated with the state. Then we compute for the link L_i the probability of its being in state y.

Reward of a state

We apply techniques from reinforcement learning to compute the reward score that captures the probability of a partially-observed sequence to end up in a goal state of the CRF model M. Reinforcement learning is a machine learning paradigm that helps in choosing the optimal action at each state to reach the goal states. The goal states are associated with rewards that start to depreciate as the goal states get farther from the current state. The actions are chosen so as to maximize the cumulative discounted reward. We estimate this probability based on the training data by learning a reward function $\mathcal{R}$ for each state. For each position i of a given sequence $\mathbf{x}$ we estimate the expected proximity to the goal state from a state y $\mathcal{R}_i^{\mathbf{x}}(y)$ recursively as follows:

$$\mathcal{R}_i^{\mathbf{x}}(y) = \begin{cases} \sum_{y'} e^{\mathbf{W} \cdot \mathbf{f}(y', y, \mathbf{x}, i+1)} \mathcal{R}_{i+1}^{\mathbf{x}}(y') & 1 \le i < n \\ [\![y == goal]\!] & i = n \end{cases} \tag{6.7}$$

When $i = n$, the reward is 1 for the goal state and 0 for every other label. Otherwise the values are computed recursively from the proximity of the next state and the probability of transition to the next state from the current state.

We then compute a weighted sum of these positioned reward values to get position-independent reward values. The weights are controlled via γ, a discount factor that captures the desirability of preferring states that are closer to the goal state as follows:

$$\mathcal{R}^{\mathbf{x}} = \frac{\sum_{k=1}^{n} \gamma^k \cdot \mathcal{R}^{\mathbf{x}}_{n-k}}{\sum_{k=1}^{n} \gamma^k} \qquad (6.8)$$

where n is the length of the sequence.

The final reward value of a state is computed by averaging over all training sequences $\mathbf{x}_1 \ldots \mathbf{x}_N$ as

$$\mathcal{R} = \frac{\sum_{\ell=1}^{N} \mathcal{R}^{\mathbf{x}_\ell}}{N}. \qquad (6.9)$$

Probability of being in a state

Consider a path prefix of the form $P_1 L_2 P_3 \ldots L_i$ where L_{i-1} is a link to page P_i in the path. We need to find for link L_i the probability of its being in any one of the link states. We provide a method for computing this. Let $\alpha_i(y)$ denote the total weight of ending in state y after i states. We thus define $\alpha_i(y)$ as the value of $\sum_{\mathbf{y}' \in \mathbf{y}_{i:y}} e^{\mathbf{W} \cdot \mathbf{F}(\mathbf{y}', \mathbf{x})}$ where $\mathbf{y}_{i:y}$ denotes all label sequences from 1 to i with i-th position labeled y. For $i > 0$, this can be expressed recursively as

$$\alpha_i(y) = \sum_{y' \in \mathcal{Y}} \alpha_{i-1}(y') e^{\mathbf{W} \cdot \mathbf{f}(y,y',\mathbf{x},i)} \qquad (6.10)$$

with the base cases defined as $\alpha_0(y) = 1$.

The probability of L_i being in the link state y is then $\frac{\alpha_i(y)}{\sum_{y' \in \mathcal{Y}_\mathcal{L}} \alpha_i(y')}$ where $\mathcal{Y}_\mathcal{L}$ denotes the link states.

Score of a link

Finally, the score of a link L_i, after i steps, is calculated as the sum of the product of reaching a state y and the static reward at state y.

$$\text{Score}(L_i) = \sum_{y} \frac{\alpha_i(y)}{\sum_{y' \in \mathcal{Y}_\mathcal{L}} \alpha_i(y')} \mathcal{R}(y) \qquad (6.11)$$

If a link appears in multiple paths, we sum over its score from each path.

Thus, at any give snapshot of the crawl we have a set of unfetched links whose scores we compute and maintain in a priority queue. We pick the link with the highest score to fetch next. The links in the newly fetched page are added to the queue. We stop when no more unfetched links have a score above a threshold value.

Experimental Results

We present a summary of experiments over two applications — a task of fetching publication pages starting from university pages and a task of reaching company contact addresses starting from a root company web page. The results are compared with generic focused crawlers [10] that are not designed to exploit the commonality of the structure of groups such as university websites. More details of the experiment can be found in [47].

Publications data set

The data sets were built manually by navigating sample websites and enlisting the sequence of web pages from the entry page to a goal page. Sequences that led to irrelevant pages were identified as negative examples. The Publications model was trained on 44 sequences (of which 28 were positive paths) from seven university domains and computer science departments of US universities chosen randomly from an online list.[2]

We show the percentage of relevant pages as a function of pages fetched for two different websites where we applied the above trained model for finding publications:

- www.cs.cmu.edu/, henceforth referred to as the **CMU** domain.
- www.cs.utexas.edu/, henceforth referred to as the **UTX** domain.

Performance is measured in terms of harvest rates. The **harvest rate** is defined as the ratio of relevant pages (goal pages, in our case) found to the total number of pages visited.

Figure 6.9 shows a comparison of how our model performs against the simplified model of the accelerated focused crawler (AFC). We observe that the performance of our model is significantly better than the AFC model. The relevant pages fetched by the CRF model increases rapidly at the beginning before stabilizing at over 60%, when the Crawler model barely reaches 40%.

Address data set

The Address data set was trained on 32 sequences out of which 17 sequences were positive. There was a single milestone state "About-us" in addition to the start, goal and fail states.

The foraging experimentation on the address data set differs slightly from the one on the Publications data set. In the Publications data set, we have multiple goal pages with a website. During the foraging experiment, the model aims at reaching as many goal pages as possible quickly. In effect, the model tries to reach a hub — i.e. a page that links many desired pages directly such that the outlink probability from the page to goal state is maximum.

In the Address data set, there is only one (or a countable few) goal pages. Hence, following an approach similar to that of the Publications data set would lead to declining harvest rates once the address page is fetched. Hence we modify the foraging run to stop when a goal page is reached. We proceed

---

[2]www.clas.ufl.edu/CLAS/american-universities.html

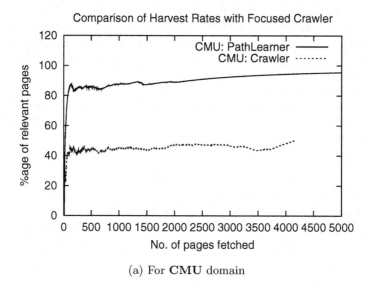

(a) For **CMU** domain

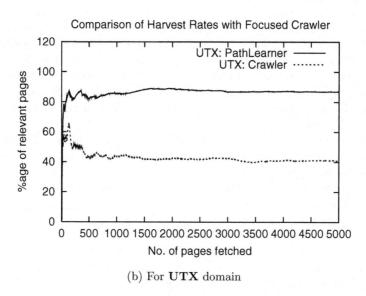

(b) For **UTX** domain

Fig. 6.9. Comparison with simplified accelerated focused crawler. The graphs labeled PathLearner show the performance of our model.

with the crawling only when we have a link with a higher score of reaching the goal state than the current page score.

The experiment was run on 108 domains of company addresses taken randomly from the list of companies available at www.hoovers.com. We calculate the average number of pages required to reach the goal page from the company home page.

The average length of path from home page to goal page was observed to be 3.426, with the median and mode value being 2. This agrees with the usual practice of having a "Contact Us" link on the company home page that leads in one link access to the contact address.

Summary

This study showed that conditional random fields provide an elegant, unified and high-performance method of solving the information foraging task from large domain-specific websites. The proposed model performs significantly better than a generic focused crawler and is easy to train and deploy.

6.6 Sequence Segmentation

In sequence segmentation we need to break up a sequence along boundaries where the sequence appears to be transitioning to a different distribution. This is unlike the tagging problem above in that there is no fixed labeled set to be assigned to each tag. The basic premise behind this operation is that the given sequence was generated from multiple models one after another and the goal during segmentation is to identify the point of switching from one model to the next.

The segmentation operation has applications in bioinformatics and in exploratory mining to detect shifts in measures like the buying rate of a product. For example, [20] discusses a bioinformatics application where a DNA sequence needs to be segmented to detect viral or microbial inserts. [11] discusses an application in market basket analysis where 0/1 buying patterns of products over time are segmented to detect surprising changes in co-occurrence patterns of groups of products.

We first consider a simpler formulation of the segmentation problem where our goal is to recover the segments of a sequence under the simplifying assumption that the segments are independent of each other. This problem has been studied by a number of researchers and for a variety of scoring functions, dynamic programming can be used to find the segments in time proportional to $O(n^2k)$ where n is the length of the segment and k is the number of segments.

In the previous formulation each segment is assumed to be independent of every other, requiring a user to fit as many model parameters as the number of segments. [20] addresses a more general formulation called the (k, h)

segmentation problem where a fixed number h of models is to be used for segmenting into k parts an n-element sequence $(k > h)$. Unfortunately, this new formulation is NP-hard for the general case. A number of approximation algorithms are proposed in [20]. We present one of these here. The first step is to get a (k, k) segmentation that is solvable using the dynamic programming algorithm of independent segments. The second step is to solve (n, h) to get h models: that is to find the best h models to describe the n unordered sequence elements. Finally, assign each of the k segments of the first step to the best of the h models found in the second step. The second step can be replaced with a variant where for each of the k segments we find the best fit model, cluster these k models into h groups and choose a representative of the h clusters as the h chosen model.

6.7 Conclusions

In this article we reviewed various techniques for analyzing sequence data. We first studied two conventional mining operations, classification and clustering, that work on whole sequences. We were able to exploit the wealth of existing formalisms and algorithms developed for fixed attribute record data by defining three primitive operations on sequence data. The first primitive was to map variable length sequences to a fixed-dimensional space using a wealth of techniques ranging from aggregation after collapsing order, k-grams, to capturing limited order and mismatching scores on k-grams. The second primitive was defining generative models for sequences where we considered models starting from simple independent models to variable- length Markov models to the popular hidden Markov models. The third primitive was designing kernels or similarity functions between sequence pairs where amongst standard sequence similarity functions we discussed the interesting Fisher's kernels that allow a powerful integration of generative and discriminative models such as SVMs.

We studied two sequence specific operations, tagging and segmentation, that operate on parts of the sequence and can be thought of as the equivalent of classification and clustering respectively for whole sequences. Sequence tagging is an extremely useful operation that has seen extensive applications in the field of information extraction. We explored generative approaches like hidden Markov models and conditional approaches like conditional random fields (CRFs) for sequence tagging.

The field of sequence mining is still being actively explored, spurred by emerging applications in information extraction, bio-informatics and sensor networks. We can hope to witness more exciting research in the techniques and application of sequence mining in the coming years.

References

[1] Aldelberg, B., 1998: Nodose: A tool for semi-automatically extracting structured and semistructured data from text documents. *SIGMOD*.

[2] Apostolico, A., and G. Bejerano, 2000: Optimal amnesic probabilistic automata or how to learn and classify proteins in linear time and space. *Proceedings of RECOMB2000*.

[3] Bilenko, M., R. Mooney, W. Cohen, P. Ravikumar and S. Fienberg, 2003: Adaptive name-matching in information integration. *IEEE Intelligent Systems*.

[4] Borkar, V. R., K. Deshmukh and S. Sarawagi, 2001: Automatic text segmentation for extracting structured records. *Proc. ACM SIGMOD International Conf. on Management of Data*, Santa Barbara, USA.

[5] Borthwick, A., J. Sterling, E. Agichtein and R. Grishman, 1998: Exploiting diverse knowledge sources via maximum entropy in named entity recognition. *Sixth Workshop on Very Large Corpora, New Brunswick, New Jersey. Association for Computational Linguistics*.

[6] Bunescu, R., R. Ge, R. J. Mooney, E. Marcotte and A. K. Ramani, 2002: Extracting gene and protein names from biomedical abstracts, unpublished Technical Note. Available from
URL: www.cs.utexas.edu/users/ml/publication/ie.html.

[7] Burges, C. J. C., 1998: A tutorial on support vector machines for pattern recognition. *Data Mining and Knowledge Discovery*, **2**, 121–67.

[8] Califf, M. E., and R. J. Mooney, 1999: Relational learning of pattern-match rules for information extraction. *Proceedings of the Sixteenth National Conference on Artificial Intelligence (AAAI-99)*, 328–34.

[9] Chakrabarti, S., 2002: *Mining the Web: Discovering Knowledge from Hypertext Data*. Morgan Kauffman.
URL: www.cse.iitb.ac.in/∼ soumen/mining-the-web/

[10] Chakrabarti, S., K. Punera and M. Subramanyam, 2002: Accelerated focused crawling through online relevance feedback. *WWW, Hawaii*, ACM.

[11] Chakrabarti, S., S. Sarawagi and B. Dom, 1998: Mining surprising temporal patterns. *Proc. of the Twentyfourth Int'l Conf. on Very Large Databases (VLDB)*, New York, USA.

[12] Collins, M., 2002: Discriminative training methods for hidden Markov models: Theory and experiments with perceptron algorithms. *Empirical Methods in Natural Language Processing (EMNLP)*.

[13] Crespo, A., J. Jannink, E. Neuhold, M. Rys and R. Studer, 2002: A survey of semi-automatic extraction and transformation.
URL: www-db.stanford.edu/∼ crespo/publications/.

[14] Deng, K., A. Moore and M. Nechyba, 1997: Learning to recognize time series: Combining ARMA models with memory-based learning. *IEEE Int. Symp. on Computational Intelligence in Robotics and Automation*, **1**, 246–50.

[15] Dietterich, T., 2002: Machine learning for sequential data: A review. *Structural, Syntactic, and Statistical Pattern Recognition; Lecture Notes in Computer Science*, T. Caelli, ed., Springer-Verlag, **2396**, 15–30.

[16] Durbin, R., S. Eddy, A. Krogh and G. Mitchison, 1998: *Biological sequence analysis: probabilistic models of proteins and nucleic acids.* Cambridge University Press.

[17] Eskin, E., W. N. Grundy and Y. Singer, 2000: Protein family classification using sparse Markov transducers. *Proceedings of the Eighth International Conference on Intelligent Systems for Molecular Biology (ISMB-2000). San Diego, CA.*

[18] Eskin, E., W. Lee and S. J. Stolfo, 2001: Modeling system calls for intrusion detection with dynamic window sizes. *Proceedings of DISCEX II.*

[19] Freitag, D., and A. McCallum, 1999: Information extraction using HMMs and shrinkage. *Papers from the AAAI-99 Workshop on Machine Learning for Information Extraction*, 31–6.

[20] Gionis, A., and H. Mannila, 2003: Finding recurrent sources in sequences. *In Proceedings of the 7th annual conference on Computational Molecular Biology.* Berlin, Germany.

[21] Han, J., and M. Kamber, 2000: *Data Mining: Concepts and Techniques.* Morgan Kaufmann.

[22] Humphreys, K., G. Demetriou and R. Gaizauskas, 2000: Two applications of information extraction to biological science journal articles: Enzyme interactions and protein structures. *Proceedings of the 2000 Pacific Symposium on Biocomputing (PSB-2000)*, 502–13.

[23] Jaakkola, T., M. Diekhans and D. Haussler, 1999: Using the Fisher kernel method to detect remote protein homologies. *ISMB*, 149–58.

[24] Klein, D., and C. D. Manning, 2002: Conditional structure versus conditional estimation in NLP models. *Workshop on Empirical Methods in Natural Language Processing (EMNLP).*

[25] Kushmerick, N., D. Weld and R. Doorenbos, 1997: Wrapper induction for information extraction. *Proceedings of IJCAI.*

[26] Lafferty, J., A. McCallum and F. Pereira, 2001: Conditional random fields: Probabilistic models for segmenting and labeling sequence data. *Proceedings of the International Conference on Machine Learning (ICML-2001)*, Williams, MA.

[27] Laplace, P.-S., 1995: *Philosophical Essays on Probabilities.* Springer-Verlag, New York, translated by A. I. Dale from the 5th French edition of 1825.

[28] Lawrence, S., C. L. Giles and K. Bollacker, 1999: Digital libraries and autonomous citation indexing. *IEEE Computer*, **32**, 67–71.

[29] Lee, W., and S. Stolfo, 1998: Data mining approaches for intrusion detection. *Proceedings of the Seventh USENIX Security Symposium (SECURITY '98), San Antonio, TX.*

[30] Leslie, C., E. Eskin, J. Weston, and W. S. Noble, 2004: Mismatch string kernels for discriminative protein classification. *Bioinformatics*, **20**, 467–76.

[31] Li, D., K. Wong, Y. H. Hu and A. Sayeed., 2002: Detection, classification and tracking of targets in distributed sensor networks. *IEEE Signal Processing Magazine*, **19**.

[32] Liu, D. C., and J. Nocedal, 1989: On the limited memory BFGS method for large-scale optimization. *Mathematic Programming*, **45**, 503–28.

[33] Malouf, R., 2002: A comparison of algorithms for maximum entropy parameter estimation. *Proceedings of The Sixth Conference on Natural Language Learning (CoNLL-2002)*, 49–55.

[34] McCallum, A., D. Freitag and F. Pereira, 2000: Maximum entropy Markov models for information extraction and segmentation. *Proceedings of the International Conference on Machine Learning (ICML-2000)*, Palo Alto, CA, 591–8.

[35] McCallum, A. K., K. Nigam, J. Rennie, and K. Seymore, 2000: Automating the construction of Internet portals with machine learning. *Information Retrieval Journal*, **3**, 127–63.

[36] Muslea, I., 1999: Extraction patterns for information extraction tasks: A survey. *The AAAI-99 Workshop on Machine Learning for Information Extraction*.

[37] Muslea, I., S. Minton and C. A. Knoblock, 1999: A hierarchical approach to wrapper induction. *Proceedings of the Third International Conference on Autonomous Agents*, Seattle, WA.

[38] Rabiner, L., 1989: A tutorial on Hidden Markov Models and selected applications in speech recognition. *Proceedings of the IEEE, 77(2)*.

[39] Rabiner, L., and B.-H. Juang, 1993: *Fundamentals of Speech Recognition*, Prentice-Hall, Chapter 6.

[40] Ratnaparkhi, A., 1999: Learning to parse natural language with maximum entropy models. *Machine Learning*, **34**.

[41] Ron, D., Y. Singer and N. Tishby, 1996: The power of amnesia: learning probabilistic automata with variable memory length. *Machine Learning*, **25**, 117–49.

[42] Seymore, K., A. McCallum and R. Rosenfeld, 1999: Learning Hidden Markov Model structure for information extraction. *Papers from the AAAI-99 Workshop on Machine Learning for Information Extraction*, 37–42.

[43] Sha, F., and F. Pereira, 2003: Shallow parsing with conditional random fields. In*Proceedings of HLT-NAACL*.

[44] Soderland, S., 1999: Learning information extraction rules for semi-structured and free text. *Machine Learning*, **34**.

[45] Stolcke, A., 1994: *Bayesian Learning of Probabilistic Language Models*. Ph.D. thesis, UC Berkeley.

[46] Takeuchi, K., and N. Collier, 2002: Use of support vector machines in extended named entity recognition. *The 6th Conference on Natural Language Learning (CoNLL)*.

[47] Vydiswaran, V., and S. Sarawagi, 2005: Learning to extract information from large websites using sequential models. *COMAD*.

[48] Warrender, C., S. Forrest and B. Pearlmutter, 1999: Detecting intrusions using system calls: Alternative data models. *IEEE Symposium on Security and Privacy*.

7

Link-based Classification

Lise Getoor

Summary. A key challenge for machine learning is the problem of mining richly structured data sets, where the objects are linked in some way due to either an explicit or implicit relationship that exists between the objects. Links among the objects demonstrate certain patterns, which can be helpful for many machine learning tasks and are usually hard to capture with traditional statistical models. Recently there has been a surge of interest in this area, fuelled largely by interest in web and hypertext mining, but also by interest in mining social networks, bibliographic citation data, epidemiological data and other domains best described using a linked or graph structure. In this chapter we propose a framework for modeling link distributions, a link-based model that supports discriminative models describing both the link distributions and the attributes of linked objects. We use a structured logistic regression model, capturing both content and links. We systematically evaluate several variants of our link-based model on a range of data sets including both web and citation collections. In all cases, the use of the link distribution improves classification performance.

7.1 Introduction

Traditional data mining tasks such as association rule mining, market basket analysis and cluster analysis commonly attempt to find patterns in a data set characterized by a collection of independent instances of a single relation. This is consistent with the classical statistical inference problem of trying to identify a model given a random sample from a common underlying distribution.

A key challenge for machine learning is to tackle the problem of mining more richly structured data sets, for example multi-relational data sets in which there are record linkages. In this case, the instances in the data set are linked in some way, either by an explicit link, such as a URL, or a constructed link, such as join between tables stored in a database. Naively applying traditional statistical inference procedures, which assume that instances are independent, can lead to inappropriate conclusions [15]. Care must be taken that potential correlations due to links are handled appropriately. Clearly, this is information that should be exploited to improve the predictive accuracy of the learned models.

Link mining is a newly emerging research area that is at the intersection of the work in link analysis [10, 16], hypertext and web mining [3], relational learning and inductive logic programming [9] and graph mining [5]. Link mining is potentially useful in a wide range of application areas including bioinformatics, bibliographic citations, financial analysis, national security, and the Internet. Link mining includes tasks such as predicting the strength of links, predicting the existence of links, and clustering objects based on similar link patterns.

The link mining task that we focus on in this chapter is *link-based classification*. Link-based classification is the problem of labeling, or classifying, objects in a graph, based in part on properties of the objects, and based in part on the properties of neighboring objects. Examples of link-based classification include web-page classification based both on content of the web page and also on the categories of linked web pages, and document classification based both on the content of a document and also the properties of cited, citing and co-cited documents.

Three elements fundamental to link-based classification are:

- **link-based feature construction** – how do we represent and make use of properties of the neighborhood of an object to help with prediction?
- **collective classification** – the classifications of linked objects are usually correlated, in other words the classification of an object depends on the classification of neighboring objects. This means we cannot optimize each classification independently, rather we must find a globally optimal classification.
- **use of labeled and unlabeled data** – The use of labeled and unlabeled data is especially important to link-based classification. A principled approach to collective classification easily supports the use of labeled and unlabeled data.

In this chapter we examine each of these elements and propose a statistical framework for modeling link distributions and study its properties in detail. Rather than an ad hoc collection of methods, the proposed framework extends classical statistical approaches to more complex and richly structured domains than commonly studied.

The framework we propose stems from our earlier work on link uncertainty in probabilistic relational models [12]. However in this work, we *do not* construct explicit models for link existence. Instead we model link distributions, which describe the neighborhood of links around an object, and can capture the correlations among links. With these link distributions, we propose algorithms for link-based classification. In order to capture the joint distributions of the links, we use a logistic regression model for both the content and the links. A key challenge is structuring the model appropriately; simply throwing both links and content attributes into a "flat" logistic regression model does not perform as well as a structured logistic regression model that combines one logistic regression model built over content with a separate logistic regression model built over links.

Having learned a model, the next challenge is classification using the learned model. A learned link-based model specifies a distribution over link and content attributes and, unlike traditional statistical models, these attributes may be correlated. Intuitively, for linked objects, updating the category of one object can influence our inference about the categories of its linked neighbors. This requires a more complex classification algorithm. Iterative classification and inference algorithms have been proposed for hypertext categorization [4, 28] and for relational learning [17, 25, 31, 32]. Here, we also use an iterative classification algorithm. One novel aspect is that unlike approaches that make assumptions about the influence of the neighbor's categories (such as that linked objects have similar categories), we explicitly learn how the link distribution affects the category. We also examine a range of ordering strategies for the inference and evaluate their impact on overall classification accuracy.

7.2 Background

There has been a growing interest in learning from structured data. By structured data, we simply mean data best described by a graph where the nodes in the graph are objects and the edges/hyper-edges in the graph are links or relations between objects. Tasks include hypertext classification, segmentation, information extraction, searching and information retrieval, discovery of authorities and link discovery. Domains include the world-wide web, bibliographic citations, criminology, bio-informatics to name just a few. Learning tasks range from predictive tasks, such as classification, to descriptive tasks, such as the discovery of frequently occurring sub-patterns.

Here, we describe some of the most closely related work to ours, however because of the surge of interest in recent years, and the wide range of venues where research is reported (including the International World Wide Web Conference (WWW), the Conference on Neural Information Processing (NIPS), the International Conference on Machine Learning (ICML), the International ACM conference on Information Retrieval (SIGIR), the International Conference of Management of Data (SIGMOD) and the International Conference on Very Large Databases (VLDB)), our list is sure to be incomplete.

Probably the most famous example of exploiting link structure is the use of links to improve information retrieval results. Both the well-known page rank [29] and hubs and authority scores [19] are based on the link-structure of the web. These algorithms work using in-links and out-links of the web pages to evaluated the importance or relevance of a web-page. Other work, such Dean and Henzinger [8] propose an algorithm based on co-citation to find related web pages. Our work is not directly related to this class of link-based algorithms.

One line of work more closely related to link-based classification is the work on hypertext and web page classification. This work has its roots in the information retrieval community. A hypertext collection has a rich structure beyond that of a collection of text documents. In addition to words, hypertext has both incoming and outgoing links. Traditional bag-of-words models discard this rich structure of hypertext and do not make full use of the link structure of hypertext.

Beyond making use of links, another important aspect of link-based classification is the use of unlabeled data. In supervised learning, it is expensive and labor-intensive to construct a large, labeled set of examples. However in many domains it is relatively inexpensive to collect unlabeled examples. Recently several algorithms have been developed to learn a model from both labeled and unlabeled examples [1, 27, 34]. Successful applications in a number of areas, especially text classification, have been reported. Interestingly, a number of results show that while careful use of unlabeled data is helpful, it is not always the case that more unlabeled data improves performance [26].

Blum and Mitchell [2] propose a co-training algorithm to make use of unlabeled data to boost the performance of a learning algorithm. They assume that the data can be described by two separate feature sets which are not completely correlated, and each of which is predictive enough for a weak predictor. The co-training procedure works to augment the labeled sample with data from unlabeled data using these two weak predictors. Their experiments show positive results on the use of unlabeled examples to improve the performance of the learned model. In [24], the author states that many natural learning problems fit the problem class where the features describing the examples are redundantly sufficient for classifying the examples. In this case, the unlabeled data can significantly improve learning accuracy. There are many problems falling into this category: web page classification; semantic classification of noun phrases; learning to select word sense and object recognition in multimedia data.

Nigam *et al.* [27] introduce an EM algorithm for learning a naive Bayes classifier from labeled and unlabeled examples. The algorithm first trains a classifier based on labeled documents and then probabilistically classifies the unlabeled documents. Then both labeled and unlabeled documents participate in the learning procedure. This process repeats until it converges. The ideas of using co-training and EM algorithms for learning from labeled and unlabeled data are fully investigated in [13].

Joachims *et al.* [18] proposes a transductive support vector machine (TSVM) for text classification. A TSVM takes into account a particular test set and tries to optimize the classification accuracy for that particular test set. This also is an important means of using labeled and unlabeled examples for learning.

In other recent work on link mining [12, 25, 31], models are learned from fully labeled training examples and evaluated on a disjoint test set. In some cases, the separation occurs naturally, for example in the WebKB data set [6]. This data set describes the web pages at four different universities, and one can naturally split the data into a collection of training schools and a test school, and there are no links from the test school web pages to the training school pages. But in other cases, the data sets are either manipulated to extract disconnected components, or the links between the training and test sets are simply ignored. One major disadvantage of this approach is that it discards links between labeled and unlabeled data which may be very helpful for making predictions or may artificially create skewed training and test sets.

Chakrabarti *et al.* [4] proposed an iterative relaxation labeling algorithm to classify a patent database and a small web collection. They examine using text, neighboring text and neighbor class labels for classification in a rather realistic setting wherein some portion of the neighbor class labels are known. In the start of their iteration, a bootstrap mechanism is introduced to classify unlabeled documents. After that, classes from labeled and unlabeled documents participate in the relaxation labeling iteration. They showed that naively incorporating words from neighboring pages reduces performance, while incorporating category information, such has hierarchical category prefixes, improves performance.

Oh *et al.* [28] also suggest an incremental categorization method, where the classified documents can take part in the categorization of other documents in the neighborhood. In contrast to the approach used in Chakrabarti *et al.*, they do not introduce a bootstrap stage to classify all unlabeled documents. Instead they incrementally classify documents and take into account the classes of unlabeled documents as they become available in the categorization process. They report similar results on a collection of encyclopedia articles: merely incorporating words from neighboring documents was not helpful, while making use of the predicted class of neighboring documents was helpful.

Popescul *et al.* [30] study the use of inductive logic programming (ILP) to combine text and link features for classification. In contrast to Chakrabarti *et al.* and Oh *et al.*, where class labels are used as features, they incorporate the unique document IDs of the neighborhood as features. Their results also demonstrate that the combination of text and link features often improves performance.

These results indicate that simply assuming that link documents are on the same topic and incorporating the features of linked neighbors is not generally effective. One approach is to identify certain types of hypertext regularities such as encyclopedic regularity (linked objects typically have the same class) and co-citation regularity (linked objects do not share the same class, but objects that are cited by the same object tend to have the same class). Yang *et al.* [33] compare several well-known categorization learning algorithms: naive Bayes [22], kNN [7], and FOIL on three data sets. They find that adding words from linked neighbors is sometimes helpful for categorization and sometimes harmful. They define five hypertext regularities for hypertext categorization. Their experiments indicate that application of this knowledge to classifier design is crucial for real-world categorization. However, the issue of discovering the regularity is still an open issue.

Here, we propose a probabilistic method that can learn a variety of different regularities among the categories of linked objects using labeled and unlabeled examples. Our method differs from the previous work in several ways. First, instead of assuming a naive Bayes model [4] for the class labels in the neighborhood, we adopt a logistic regression model to capture the conditional probability of the class labels given the object attributes and link descriptions. In this way our method is able to learn a variety of different regularities and is not limited to a self-reinforcing encyclopedic regularity. We examine a number of different types of links and methods for representing the link neighborhood of an object. We propose an algorithm to make predictions using both labeled and unlabeled data. Our approach makes use of the description of unlabeled data and all of the links between unlabeled and labeled data in an iterative algorithm for finding the collective labeling which maximizes the posterior probability for the class labels of all of the unlabeled data given the observed labeled data and links.

7.3 Link-based Models

Here we propose a general notion of a link-based model that supports rich probabilistic models based on the distribution of links and based on attributes of linked objects.

7.3.1 Definitions

The generic link-based data we consider is essentially a directed graph, in which the nodes are objects and edges are links between objects.

- $\mathcal{O}$ – The collection of objects, $\mathcal{O} = \{X_1, \ldots, X_N\}$ where X_i is an object, or node in the graph. $\mathcal{O}$ is the set of nodes in the graph.
- $\mathcal{L}$ – The collections of links between objects. $L_{i \to j}$ is a link between object X_i and object X_j. $\mathcal{L}$ is the set of edges in the graph.
- $\mathcal{G}(\mathcal{O}, \mathcal{L})$ – The directed graph defined over $\mathcal{O}$ by $\mathcal{L}$.

Our model supports classification of objects based both on features of the object *and* on properties of its links. The object classifications are a finite set of categories $\{c_1, \ldots, c_k\}$ where $c(X)$ is the category c of object X. We will consider the neighbors of an object X_i via the following relations:

- $In(X_i)$ – the set of incoming neighbors of object X_i, $\{X_j \mid L_{j \to i} \in \mathcal{L}\}$.
- $Out(X_i)$ – the set of outgoing neighbors of object X_i, $\{X_j \mid L_{i \to j} \in \mathcal{L}\}$.

- $Co\text{-}In(X_i)$ – The set of objects co-cited with object X_i, $\{X_j \mid X_j \neq X_i$ and there is a third object X_k that links to both X_i and $X_j\}$. We can think of these as the co-citation in-links (Co-In), because there is an object X_k with in-links to both X_i and X_j.
- $Co\text{-}Out(X_i)$ – The set of objects co-cited by object X_i, $\{X_j \mid X_j \neq X_i$ and there is a third object X_k to which both X_i and X_j link$\}$. We can think of these as the co-citation out-links (Co-Out), because both X_i and X_j have out links to some object X_k.

7.3.2 Object Features

The attributes of an object provide a basic description of the object. Traditional classification algorithms are based on object attributes. In a linked-based approach, it may also make sense to use attributes of *linked* objects. Furthermore, if the links themselves have attributes, these may also be used.[1] However, in this paper, we simply use object attributes, and we use the notation $OA(X)$ for the attributes of object X. As an example, in the scientific literature domain, the object features might consist of a variety of text information such as title, abstract, authorship and content. In the domains we examined, the objects are text documents and the object features we use are word occurrences.

7.3.3 Link Features

To capture the link patterns, we introduce the notion of link features as a way of capturing the salient characteristics of the objects' links. We examine a variety of simple mechanisms for doing this. All are based on statistics computed from the linked objects rather than the *identity* of the linked objects. Describing only the limited collection of statistics computed from the links can be significantly more compact than storing the link incidence matrix. In addition, these models can accommodate the introduction of new objects, and thus are applicable in a wider range of situations.

We examine several ways of constructing link features. All are constructed from the collection of the categories of the linked objects. We use $LD(X)$ to denote the link description.

The simplest statistic to compute is a single feature, the mode, from each set of linked objects from the in-links, out-links and both in and out co-citation links. We call this the *mode-link* model.

We can use the frequency of the categories of the linked objects; we refer to this as the *count-link* model. In this case, while we have lost the information

---

[1]Essentially this is a propositionalization [11, 20] of the aspects of the neighborhood of an object in the graph. This is a technique that has been proposed in the inductive logic programming community and is applicable here.

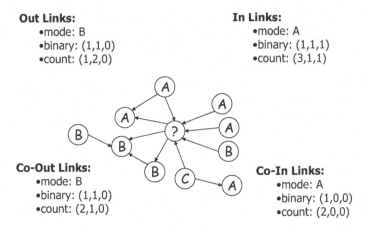

Out Links:
- mode: B
- binary: (1,1,0)
- count: (1,2,0)

In Links:
- mode: A
- binary: (1,1,1)
- count: (3,1,1)

Co-Out Links:
- mode: B
- binary: (1,1,0)
- count: (2,1,0)

Co-In Links:
- mode: A
- binary: (1,0,0)
- count: (2,0,0)

Fig. 7.1. Assuming there are three possible categories for objects, A, B and C, the figure shows examples of the mode, binary and count link features constructed for the object labeled with ?.

about the individual entity to which the object is connected, we maintain the frequencies of the different categories.

A middle ground between these two is a simple binary feature vector; for each category, if a link to an object of that category occurs at least once, the corresponding feature is 1; the feature is 0 if there are no links to this category. In this case, we use the term *binary-link* model. Figure 7.1 shows examples of the three types of link features computed for an object for each category of links (In links, Out links, Co-In links and Co-Out links).

7.4 Predictive Model for Object Classification

Clearly we may make use of the object and link features in a variety of models such as naive Bayes classifiers, SVMs and logistic regression models. For the domains that we have examined, logistic regression models have outperformed naive Bayes models, so these are the models we have focused on.

For our predictive model, we used a regularized logistic regression model. Given a training set of labeled data (x_i, c_i), where $i = 1, 2, \ldots, n$ and $c_i \in \{-1, +1\}$, to compute the conditional probability $P(c \mid w, x)$ is to find the optimal w for the discriminative function, which is equivalent to the following regularized logistic regression formulation [35]:

$$\hat{w} = \mathrm{arginf}_w \frac{1}{n} \sum_{i=1}^{n} \ln(1 + exp(-w^T x_i c_i)) + \lambda w^2$$

where we use a zero-mean independent Gaussian prior for the parameter w: $P(w) = exp(\lambda w^2)$.

The simplest model is a flat model, which uses a single logistic regression model over both the object attributes and link features. We found that this model did not perform well, and instead we found that a structured logistic regression model, which uses separate logistic regression models (with different regularization parameters) for the object features and the link features, outperformed the flat model. Now the MAP estimation for categorization becomes

$$\hat{C}(X) = \text{argmax}_{c \in C} \frac{P(c \mid OA(X)) \prod_{t \in \{In, Out, Co\text{-}In, Co\text{-}Out\}} P(c \mid LD_t(X))}{P(c)}$$

where OA(X) are the object features and $LD_t(X)$ are the link features for each of the different types of links t and we make the (probably incorrect) assumption that they are independent. $P(c \mid OA(X))$ and $P(c \mid LD_t(X))$ are defined as

$$P(c \mid OA(X)) = \frac{1}{exp(-w_o^T OA(X)c) + 1}$$

$$P(c \mid LD_t(X)) = \frac{1}{exp(-w_l^T LD_t(X)c) + 1}$$

where w_o and w_l are the parameters for the regularized logistic regression models for $P(c \mid OA(X))$ and the $P(c \mid LD_t(X))$ respectively.

7.5 Link-based Classification using Labeled and Unlabeled Data

Given data D consisting of labeled data D^l and unlabeled data D^u, we define a posterior probability over D^u as

$$P(c(X) : X \in D^u \mid D) =$$
$$\prod_{X \in D^u} P(c(X) \mid OA(X), LD_{In}(X), LD_{Out}(X), LD_{Co\text{-}In}(X), LD_{Co\text{-}Out}(X))$$

We use an EM-like iterative algorithm to make use of both labeled data $D^l = \{(x_i, c(x_i) : i = 1, .., n\}$ and unlabeled data $D^u = \{(x_j^*, c(x_j^*) : j = 1, ..., m\}$ to learn our model. Initally a structured logistic regression model is built using labeled data D^l. First, we categorize data in D^u

$$c(x_j^*) = \text{argmax}_{c \in C} \frac{P(c \mid OA(x_j^*)) \prod_t P(c \mid LD_t(x_j^*))}{P(c)}$$

where $j = 1, ..., m$. Next this categorized D^u and labeled data D^l are used to build a new model.

Step 1: (Initialization) Build an initial structured logistic regression classifier using content and link features using only the labeled training data.

Step 2: (Iteration) Loop while the posterior probability over the unlabeled test data increases:
1. Classify unlabeled data using the current model.
2. Recompute the link features of each object. Re-estimate the parameters of the logistic regression models.

In our above iterative algorithm, after we categorize the unlabeled data, the link descriptions for all labeled and unlabeled data will change due to the links between labeled and unlabeled data. The first step is to recompute the link descriptions for all data based on the results from the current estimates and the link graph over labeled and unlabeled data.

In the iterative step there are many possible orderings for objects. One approach is based simply on the number of links; Oh et al. [28] report no significant improvement using this method. Neville and Jensen [25] propose an iterative classification algorithm where the ordering is based on the inference posterior probability of the categories. They report an improvement in classification accuracy. We explore several alternate orderings based on the estimated link statistics. We propose a range of link-based adaptive strategies which we call *Link Diversity*. Link diversity measures the number of different categories to which an object is linked. The idea is that, in some domains at least, we may be more confident of categorizations of objects with low link – diversity in essence, the object's neighbors are all in agreement. So we may wish to make these assignments first, and then move on to the rest of the pages. In our experiments, we evaluate the effectiveness of different ordering schemes based on link diversity.

7.6 Results

We evaluated our link-based classification algorithm on two variants of the Cora data set [23], a data set that we constructed from CiteSeer entries [14] and WebKB [6].

The first Cora data set, CoraI, contains 4187 machine learning papers, each categorized into one of seven possible topics. We consider only the 3181 papers that are cited or cite other papers. There are 6185 citations in the data set. After stemming and removing stop words and rare words, the dictionary contains 1400 words.

The second Cora data set, CoraII,[2] contains 30,000 papers, each categorized into one of ten possible topics: information retrieval, databases, artificial intelligence, encryption and compression, operating systems, networking, hardware and architecture, data structure algorithms and theory, programming and human–computer interaction. We consider only the 3352 documents that are cited or cite other papers. There are 8594 citations in the data set.

---

[2] www.cs.umass.edu/~mccallum/code-data.html

After stemming and removing stop words and rare words, the dictionary contains 3174 words.

The CiteSeer data set has 3312 papers from six categories: Agents, Artificial Intelligence, Database, Human Computer Interaction, Machine Learning and Information Retrieval. There are 7522 citations in the data set. After stemming and removing stop words and rare words, the dictionary for CiteSeer contains 3703 words.

The WebKB data set contains web pages from four computer science departments, categorized into topics such as faculty, student, project, course and a catch-all category, other. In our experiments we discard pages in the "other" category, which generates a data set with 700 pages. After stemming and removing stop words, the dictionary contains 2338 words. For WebKB, we train on three schools, plus 2/3 of the fourth school, and test on the last 1/3.

On Cora and CiteSeer, for each experiment, we take one split as a test set, and the remaining two splits are used to train our model: one for training and the other for a validation set used to find the appropriate regularization parameter λ. Common values of λ were 10^{-4} or 10^{-5}. On WebKB, we learned models for a variety of λ; here we show the best result.

In our experiments, we compared a baseline classifier (Content) with our link-based classifiers (Mode, Binary, Count). We compared the classifiers:

- **Content**: Uses only object attributes.
- **Mode**: Combines a logistic regression classifier over the object attributes with separate logistic regression classifiers over the mode of the In Links, Out Links, Co-In Links, and Co-Out Links.
- **Binary**: Combines a logistic regression classifier over the object attributes with a separate logistic regression classifier over the binary link statistics for all of the links.
- **Count-Link**: Combines a logistic regression classifier over the object attributes with a separate logistic regression classifier over the counts link statistics for all of the links.

7.6.1 Link Model Comparison

Table 7.1 shows details of our results using four different metrics (accuracy, precision, recall and F1 measure)[3] on the four data sets. Figure 7.2 shows a summary of the results for the F1 measure.

---

[3] A true positive is a document that is correctly labeled. Let TP be the number of true positives, FP be the number of false positive, TN be the number of true negatives, FP be the number of false negatives. Accuracy is the percentage of correctly labeled documents, $\frac{TP+TN}{TP+FP+TN+FN}$. Precision, recall and the F1 measure are macro-averaged over each of the categories. Precision is the percentage of documents that are predicted to be of a category, that actually are of that category $\frac{TP}{TP+FP}$. Recall is the percentage of documents that are predicted to be of a category, out of all the documents of the category $\frac{TP}{TP+FN}$. The F1 measure is $\frac{2PR}{R+P}$.

Table 7.1. Results with **Content, Mode, Binary** and **Count** models on CoraI, CoraII, CiteSeer and WebKB. Statistically significant results (at or above 90% confidence level) for each row are shown in bold.

CoraI				
	Content	Mode	Binary	Count
avg accuracy	68.14	82.35	77.53	**83.14**
avg precision	67.47	81.01	77.35	81.74
avg recall	63.08	80.08	76.34	81.20
avg F1 measure	64.17	80.0	75.69	**81.14**

CoraII				
	Content	Mode	Binary	Count
avg accuracy	67.55	83.03	81.46	**83.66**
avg precision	65.87	78.62	74.54	80.62
avg recall	47.51	75.27	75.69	76.15
avg F1 measure	52.11	76.52	74.62	**77.77**

CiteSeer				
	Content	Mode	Binary	Count
avg accuracy	60.59	71.01	69.83	**71.52**
avg precision	55.48	64.61	62.6	65.22
avg recall	55.33	60.09	60.3	61.22
avg F1 measure	53.08	60.68	60.28	**61.87**

WebKB				
	Content	Mode	Binary	Count
avg accuracy	87.45	88.52	78.91	87.93
avg precision	78.67	77.27	70.48	77.71
avg recall	72.82	73.43	71.32	73.33
avg F1 measure	71.77	73.03	66.41	72.83

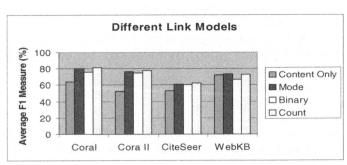

Fig. 7.2. Average F1 measure for different models (**Content, Mode, Binary** and **Count**) on four data sets (CoraI, CoraII, CiteSeer and WebKB).

In this set of experiments, all of the links (In Links, Out Links, Co-In Links, Co-Out Links) are used and we use a fixed ordering for the iterative classification algorithm.

For all four data sets, the link-based models outperform the content only models. For three of the four data sets, the difference is statistically significant at the 99% significance level. For three of the four data sets, **count** outperforms **mode** at the 90% significance level or higher, for both accuracy and F1 measure. Both **mode** and **count** outperform **binary**; the difference is most dramatic for CoraI and WebKB.

Clearly, the **mode**, **binary** and **count** link-based models are using information from the description of the link neighborhood of an object to improve classification performance. **Mode** and **count** seem to make the best use of the information; one explanation is that while **binary** contains more information in terms of which categories of links exist, it loses the information about which link category is most frequent. In many domains one might think that **mode** should be enough information, particulary bibliographic domains. So it is somewhat surprising that the **count** model is the best for our three citation data sets.

Our results on WebKB were less reliable. Small changes to the ways that we structured the classifiers resulted in different outcomes. Overall, we felt there were problems because the link distributions were quite different among the different schools. Also, after removing the other pages, the data set is rather small.

7.6.2 Effect of Link Types

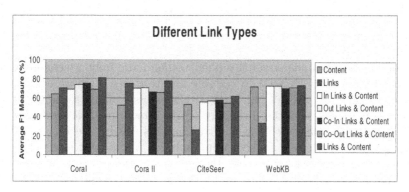

Fig. 7.3. Average F1 measure for **Count** on four data sets (CoraI, CoraII, CiteSeer and WebKB) for varying content and links (Content, Links, In Links & Content, Out Links & Content, Co-In Links & Content, Co-Out links & Content and Links & Content).

Next we examined the individual effect of the different categories of links: **In Links**, **Out Links**, **Co-In Links** and **Co-Out links**. Using the **count** model, we included in the comparision **Content**, with a model which used all the links, but no content (**Links**),[4] and **Link & Content** (which gave us the best results in the previous section). Figure 7.3 shows the average F1 accuracy for the four of the data sets using different link types.

Clearly using all of the links performs best. Individually, the **Out Links** and **Co-In Links** seem to add the most information, although again, the results for WebKB are less definitive.

More interesting is the difference in results when using *only* **Links** versus **Links & Content**. For Coral and Citeseer, **Links** only performs reasonably well, while for the other two cases, CoraII and WebKB, it performs horribly. Recall that the content helps give us an initial starting point for the iterative classification algorithm. Our theory is that, for some data sets, especially those with fewer links, getting a good initial starting point is very important. In others, there is enough information in the links to overcome a bad starting point for the iterative classification algorithm. This is an area that requires further investigation.

7.6.3 Prediction with Links Between Training and Test Sets

Next we were interested in investigating the issue of exploiting the links between test and training data for predictions. In other work, Neville and Jensen [25], Getoor *et al.* [12] and Taskar *et al.* [31] used link distributions for categorization; the experimental data set are split into training set and test set, and any links across training and test sets are ignored.

In reality, in domains such as web and scientific literature, document collections are constantly expanding. There are new papers published and new web sites created. New objects and edges are being added to the existing graph. A more realistic evaluation, such as that done in Chakrabarti *et al.* [4], exploits the links between test and training.

In an effort to understand this phenomenon more fully, we examined the effect of ignoring links between training and test sets. Here we compared a method which discards all link information across training set and test set, which is denoted as "Test Links Only", with a more realistic method which keeps all the links between test and training sets which is denoted as "Complete Links". The results are shown in Table 7.2. With "Test Links Only", in our iterative classification process, the link descriptions of test data are constructed based only on the link graph over test data, while with "Complete Links" link descriptions of test data are formulated over the link graph using both training and test data. These results demonstrate that the complete link structure is informative and can be used to improve overall performance.

7.6.4 Link-based Classification using Labeled and Unlabeled Data

In the previous section we experimented with making use of labeled data from the training set during testing. Next we explore the more general setting

---

[4]This model was inspired by results in [21].

Table 7.2. Avg F1 results using "Test Links Only" and "Complete Links" on CoraI, CoraII, CiteSeer and WebKB.

	Test Links Only			Complete Links		
	Mode	Binary	Count	Mode	Binary	Count
CoraI	75.85	71.57	79.16	80.00	75.69	81.14
CoraII	58.70	58.19	61.50	76.52	74.62	77.77
CiteSeer	59.06	60.03	60.74	60.68	60.28	61.87
WebKB	73.02	67.29	71.79	73.03	66.41	72.83

of learning with labeled and unlabeled data using the iterative algorithm proposed in Section 7.5. To better understand the effects of unlabeled data, we compared the performance of our algorithm with varying amounts of labeled and unlabeled data.

For two of the domains, CoraII and CiteSeer, we randomly choose 20% of the data as test data. We compared the performance of the algorithms when different percentages (20%, 40%, 60%, 80%) of the remaining data is labeled. We compared the accuracy when only the labeled data is used for training (**Labeled only**) with the case where both labeled and the remaining unlabeled data is used for training (**Labeled and Unlabeled**).

- **Content**: Uses only object attributes.
- **Labeled Only**: The link model is learned on labeled data only. The only unlabeled data used is the test set.
- **Labeled and Unlabeled**: The link model is learned on both labeled and all of the unlabeled data.

Figure 7.4 shows the results averaged over five different runs. The algorithm which makes use of all of the unlabeled data gives better performance than the model which uses only the labeled data.

For both data sets, the algorithm which uses both labeled and unlabeled data outperforms the algorithm which uses Labeled Only data; even with 80% of the data labeled and only 20% of the data unlabeled, the improvement in error on the test set using unlabeled data is statistically significant at the 95% confidence level for both Cora and Citeseer.

7.6.5 Ordering Strategies

In the last set of experiments, we examined various ICA ordering strategies. Our experiments indicate that final test errors with different ordering strategy have a standard deviation around 0.001. There is no significant difference with various link diversity to order the predictions. We also compared with an ordering based on the posterior probability of the categories as done in Neville and Jensen [25], denoted PP.

While the different iteration schemes converge to about the same accuracy, their convergence rate varies. To understand the effect of the ordering scheme

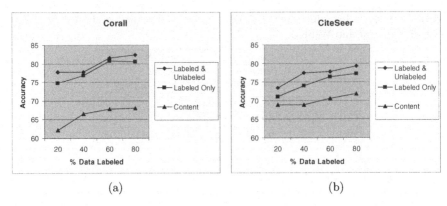

Fig. 7.4. (a) Results varying the amount of labeled and unlabeled data used for training on CoraII (b) and on CiteSeer. The results are averages of five runs.

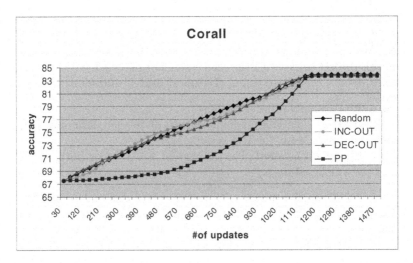

Fig. 7.5. The convergence rates of different iteration methods on the CoraII data set.

at a finer level of detail, Figure 7.5 shows an example of the accuracy of the different iteration schemes for the CoraII data set (to make the graph readable, we show only ordering by increasing diversity of out links (INC-Out) and decreasing diversity of out-links (DEC-Out); the results for in links, co-in links and co-out links are similar). Our experiments indicate that ordering by increasing link diversity converges faster than ordering by decreasing link diversity, and the RAND ordering converges the most quickly at the start.

7.7 Conclusions

Many real-world data sets have rich structures, where the objects are linked in some way. Link mining targets data-mining tasks on this richly-structured data. One major task of link mining is to model and exploit the link distributions among objects. Here we focus on using the link structure to help improve classification accuracy.

In this chapter we have proposed a simple framework for modeling link distributions, based on link statistics. We have seen that for the domains we examined, a combined logistic classifier built over the object attributes and link statistics outperforms a simple content-only classifier. We found the effect of different link types is significant. More surprisingly, the mode of the link statistics is not always enough to capture the dependence. Avoiding the assumption of homogeneity of labels and modeling the distribution of the link categories at a finer grain is useful.

Acknowledgments: I'd like to thank Prithviraj Sen and Qing Lu for their work on the implementation of the link-based classification system. This study was supported by NSF Grant 0308030 and the Advanced Research and Development Activity (ARDA) under Award Number NMA401-02-1-2018. The views, opinions, and findings contained in this report are those of the author and should not be construed as an official Department of Defense position, policy, or decision unless so designated by other official documentation.

References

[1] Blum, A., and S. Chawla, 2001: Learning from labeled and unlabeled data using graph mincuts. *Proc. 18th International Conf. on Machine Learning.* Morgan Kaufmann, San Francisco, CA, 19–26.

[2] Blum, A. and T. Mitchell, 1998: Combining labeled and unlabeled data with co-training. *COLT: Proceedings of the Workshop on Computational Learning Theory.* Morgan Kaufmann.

[3] Chakrabarti, S., 2002: *Mining the Web.* Morgan Kaufman.

[4] Chakrabarti, S., B. Dom and P. Indyk, 1998: Enhanced hypertext categorization using hyperlinks. *Proc of SIGMOD-98.*

[5] Cook, D., and L. Holder, 2000: Graph-based data mining. *IEEE Intelligent Systems*, **15**, 32–41.

[6] Craven, M., D. DiPasquo, D. Freitag, A. McCallum, T. Mitchell, K. Nigam and S. Slattery, 1998: Learning to extract symbolic knowledge from the world wide web. *Proc. of AAAI-98.*

[7] Dasarathy, B. V., 1991: *Nearest neighbor norms: NN pattern classification techniques.* IEEE Computer Society Press, Los Alamitos, CA.

[8] Dean, J., and M. Henzinger, 1999: Finding related pages in the World Wide Web. *Computer Networks*, **31**, 1467–79.

[9] Dzeroski, S., and N. Lavrac, eds., 2001: *Relational Data Mining*. Kluwer, Berlin.

[10] Feldman, R., 2002: Link analysis: Current state of the art. *Tutorial at the KDD-02*.

[11] Flach, P., and N. Lavrac, 2000: The role of feature construction in inductive rule learning. *Proc. of the ICML2000 workshop on Attribute-Value and Relational Learning: crossing the boundaries*.

[12] Getoor, L., N. Friedman, D. Koller and B. Taskar, 2002: Learning probabilistic models with link uncertainty. *Journal of Machine Learning Research*.

[13] Ghani, R., 2001: Combining labeled and unlabeled data for text classification with a large number of categories. *Proceedings of the IEEE International Conference on Data Mining*, N. Cercone, T. Y. Lin and X. Wu, eds., IEEE Computer Society, San Jose, US, 597–8.

[14] Giles, C., K. Bollacker, and S. Lawrence, 1998: CiteSeer: An automatic citation indexing system. *ACM Digital Libraries 98*.

[15] Jensen, D., 1999: Statistical challenges to inductive inference in linked data. *Seventh International Workshop on Artificial Intelligence and Statistics*.

[16] Jensen, D., and H. Goldberg, 1998: *AAAI Fall Symposium on AI and Link Analysis*. AAAI Press.

[17] Jensen, D, J. Neville. and B. Gallagher, 2004: Why collective inference improves relational classification. *Proceedings of the 10th ACM SIGKDD International Conference on Knowledge Discovery and Data Mining*.

[18] Joachims, T., 1999: Transductive inference for text classification using support vector machines. *Proceedings of ICML-99, 16th International Conference on Machine Learning*, I. Bratko and S. Dzeroski, eds., Morgan Kaufmann, San Francisco, US, 200–9.

[19] Kleinberg, J., 1999: Authoritative sources in a hyperlinked environment. *Journal of the ACM*, **46**, 604–32.

[20] Kramer, S., N. Lavrac and P. Flach, 2001: Propositionalization approaches to relational data mining. *Relational Data Mining*, S. Dzeroski and N. Lavrac, eds., Kluwer, 262–91.

[21] Macskassy, S., and F. Provost, 2003: A simple relational classifier. *KDD Workshop on Multi-Relational Data Mining*.

[22] McCallum, A., and K. Nigam, 1998: A comparison of event models for naive Bayes text classification. *AAAI-98 Workshop on Learning for Text Categorization*.

[23] McCallum, A., K. Nigam, J. Rennie and K. Seymore, 2000: Automating the construction of Internet portals with machine learning. *Information Retrieval*, **3**, 127–63.

[24] Mitchell, T., 1999: The role of unlabeled data in supervised learning. *Proceedings of the Sixth International Colloquium on Cognitive Science*.

[25] Neville, J., and D. Jensen, 2000: Iterative classification in relational data. *Proc. AAAI-2000 Workshop on Learning Statistical Models from Relational Data*, AAAI Press.

[26] Nigam, K., 2001: *Using Unlabeled Data to Improve Text Classification*. Ph.D. thesis, Carnegie Mellon University.

[27] Nigam, K., A. McCallum, S. Thrun, and T. Mitchell, 2000: Text classification from labeled and unlabeled documents using EM. *Machine Learning*, **39**, 103–34.

[28] Oh, H., S. Myaeng, and M. Lee, 2000: A practical hypertext categorization method using links and incrementally available class information. *Proc. of SIGIR-00*.

[29] Page, L., S. Brin, R. Motwani and T. Winograd, 1998: The page rank citation ranking: Bringing order to the web. Technical report, Stanford University.

[30] Popescul, A., L. Ungar, S. Lawrence and D. Pennock, 2002: Towards structural logistic regression: Combining relational and statistical learning. *KDD Workshop on Multi-Relational Data Mining*.

[31] Taskar, B., P. Abbeel and D. Koller, 2002: Discriminative probabilistic models for relational data. *Proc. of UAI-02*, Edmonton, Canada, 485–92.

[32] Taskar, B., E. Segal and D. Koller, 2001: Probabilistic classification and clustering in relational data. *Proc. of IJCAI-01*.

[33] Yang, Y., S. Slattery and R. Ghani, 2002: A study of approaches to hypertext categorization. *Journal of Intelligent Information Systems*, **18**, 219–41.

[34] Zhang, T., and F. J. Oles, 2000: A probability analysis on the value of unlabeled data for classification problems. *Proc. 17th International Conf. on Machine Learning*, Morgan Kaufmann, San Francisco, CA, 1191–8.

[35] — 2001: Text categorization based on regularized linear classification methods. *IEEE Transactions on Pattern Analysis and Machine Intelligence*, 5–31.

Part II

Applications

8

Knowledge Discovery from Evolutionary Trees

Sen Zhang and Jason T. L. Wang

Summary. In this chapter we present new techniques for discovering knowledge from evolutionary trees. An evolutionary tree is a rooted unordered labeled tree in which there is a root and the order among siblings is unimportant. The knowledge to be discovered from these trees refers to "cousin pairs" in the trees. A cousin pair is a pair of nodes sharing the same parent, the same grandparent, or the same great-grandparent, etc. Given a tree T, our algorithm finds all interesting cousin pairs of T in $O(|T|^2)$ time where $|T|$ is the number of nodes in T. We also extend this algorithm to find interesting cousin pairs in multiple trees. Experimental results on synthetic data and real trees demonstrate the scalability and effectiveness of the proposed algorithms. To show the usefulness of these techniques, we discuss an application of the cousin pairs to evaluate the consensus of equally parsimonious trees and compare them with the widely used clusters in the trees. We also report the implementation status of the system built based on the proposed algorithms, which is fully operational and available on the world-wide web.

8.1 Introduction

Data mining, or knowledge discovery from data, refers to the process of extracting interesting, non-trivial, implicit, previously unknown and potentially useful information or patterns from data [13]. In life sciences, this process could refer to detecting patterns in evolutionary trees, extracting clustering rules for gene expressions, summarizing classification rules for proteins, inferring associations between metabolic pathways and predicting genes in genomic DNA sequences [25, 26, 28, 29], among others. This chapter presents knowledge discovery algorithms for extracting patterns from evolutionary trees.

Scientists model the evolutionary history of a set of taxa (organisms or species) that have a common ancestor using rooted unordered labeled trees, also known as phylogenetic trees (phylogenies) or evolutionary trees [20]. The internal nodes within a particular tree represent older organisms from which their child nodes descend. The children represent divergences in the genetic composition in the parent organism. Since these divergences cause new organisms to evolve, these organisms are shown as children of the previous organism. Evolutionary trees are usually constructed from molecular data [20]. They can provide guidance in aligning multiple molecular sequences [24] and in analyzing genome sequences [6].

The patterns we want to find from evolutionary trees contain "cousin pairs." For example, consider the three hypothetical evolutionary trees in Figure 8.1. In the figure, a and y are cousins with distance 0 in T_1; e and f are cousins with distance 0.5 in T_2; b and f are cousins with distance 1 in all the three trees.

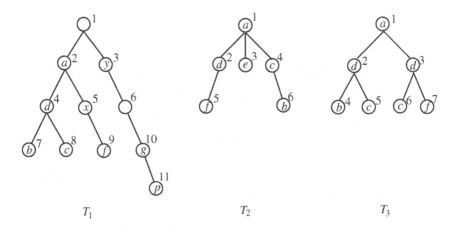

Fig. 8.1. Three trees T_1, T_2 and T_3. Each node in a tree may or may not have a label, and is associated with a unique identification number (represented by the integer outside the node).

The measure "distance" represents kinship of two nodes; two cousins with distance 0 are siblings, sharing the same parent node. Cousins of distance 1 share the same grandparent. Cousins of distance 0.5 represent aunt–niece relationships. Our algorithms can find cousin pairs of varying distances in a single tree or multiple trees. The cousin pairs in the trees represent evolutionary relationships between species that share a common ancestor. Finding the cousin pairs helps one to better understand the evolutionary history of the species [22], and to produce better results in multiple sequence alignment [24].

The rest of the chapter is organized as follows. Section 8.2 introduces notation and terminology. Section 8.3 presents algorithms for finding frequent cousin pairs in trees. Section 8.4 reports experimental results on both synthetic data and real trees, showing the scalability and effectiveness of the proposed approach. Section 8.5 reports implementation efforts and discusses several applications where we use cousin pairs to define new similarity measures for trees and to evaluate the quality of consensuses of equally parsimonious trees.

Section 8.6 compares our work with existing methods. Section 8.7 concludes the chapter and points out some future work.

8.2 Preliminaries

We model evolutionary trees by rooted unordered labeled trees. Let Σ be a finite set of labels. A rooted unordered labeled tree of size $k > 0$ on Σ is a quadruple $T = (V, N, L, E)$, where

- V is the set of nodes of T in which a node $r(T) \in V$ is designated as the root of T and $|V| = k$;
- $N : V \mapsto \{1 \ldots, k\}$ is a numbering function that assigns a unique identification number $N(v)$ to each node $v \in V$;
- $L : V' \mapsto \Sigma$, $V' \subseteq V$, is a labeling function that assigns a label $L(v)$ to each node $v \in V'$; the nodes in $V - V'$ do not have a label;
- $E \subset N(V) \times N(V)$ contains all parent–child pairs in T.

For example, refer to the trees in Figure 8.1. The node numbered 6 in T_1 does not have a label. The nodes numbered 2, 3 in T_3 have the same label d and the nodes numbered 5, 6 in T_3 have the same label c. We now introduce a series of definitions that will be used in our algorithms.

Cousin Distance
Given two labeled nodes u, v of tree T where neither node is the parent of the other, we represent the least common ancestor, w, of u and v as $lca(u, v)$, and represent the height of u, v respectively, in the subtree rooted at w as $H(u, w)$, $H(v, w)$ respectively. We define the *cousin distance* of u and v, denoted $c\_dist(u, v)$, as shown in Equation (8.1).

$$c\_dist(u, v) = \begin{cases} H(u, w) - 1 & \text{if } H(u, w) = H(v, w) \\ \max\{H(u, w), H(v, w)\} - 1.5 & \text{if } |H(u, w) - H(v, w)| = 1 \end{cases}$$
(8.1)

The cousin distance $c\_dist(u, v)$ is undefined if $|H(u, w) - H(v, w)|$ is greater than 1, or one of the nodes u, v is unlabeled. (The cutoff of 1 is a heuristic choice that works well for phylogeny. In general there could be no cutoff, or the cutoff could be much greater.)

Our cousin distance definition is inspired by genealogy [12]. Node u is a first cousin of v, or $c\_dist(u, v) = 1$, if u and v share the same grandparent. In other words, v is a child of u's aunts or vice versa. Node u is a second cousin of v, or $c\_dist(u, v) = 2$, if u and v have the same great-grandparent, but not the same grandparent. For two nodes u, v that are siblings, i.e. they share the same parent, $c\_dist(u, v) = 0$.

We use the number "0.5" to represent the "once removed" relationship. When the word "removed" is used to describe a relationship between two nodes, it indicates that the two nodes are from different generations. The words "once removed" mean that there is a difference of one generation. For any two labeled nodes u and v, if u is v's parent's first cousin, then u is v's first cousin once removed [12], and $c\_dist(u, v) = 1.5$. "Twice removed" means that there is a two-generation difference. Our cousin distance definition requires $|H(u, w) - H(v, w)| \leq 1$ and excludes the twice removed relationship. As mentioned above, this is a heuristic rather than a fundamental restriction.

For example, consider again T_1 in Figure 8.1. There is a one-generation difference between the aunt–niece pair y, x and $c\_dist(y, x) = 0.5$. Node b is node f's first cousin and $c\_dist(b, f) = 1$. Node d is node g's first cousin once removed, and $c\_dist(d, g) = 1.5$. Node f is node g's second cousin, and $c\_dist(f, g) = 2$. Node f is node p's second cousin once removed, and $c\_dist(f, p) = 2.5$.

Notice that parent–child relationships are not included in our work because the internal nodes of evolutionary trees usually have no labels. (Each leaf in these trees has a label, which is a taxon name.) So, we do not treat parent–child pairs at all. This heuristic works well in phylogenetic applications, but could be generalized. We proposed one such generalization using the UpDown distance [27]. Another approach would be to use one upper limit parameter for inter-generational (vertical) distance and another upper limit parameter for horizontal distance.

Cousin Pair Item

Let u, v be cousins in tree T. A *cousin pair item* of T is a quadruple $(L(u), L(v), c\_dist(u, v), occur(u, v))$ where $L(u)$ and $L(v)$ are labels of u, v, respectively, $c\_dist(u, v)$ is the cousin distance of u, v and $occur(u, v) > 0$ is the number of occurrences of the cousin pair in T with the specified cousin distance. Table 8.1 lists all the cousin pair items of tree T_3 in Figure 8.1. Consider, for example, the cousin pair item $(d, c, 0.5, 2)$ in the second row of Table 8.1. Nodes 2 and 6, and nodes 3 and 5 are an aunt–niece pairs with cousin distance 0.5. When taking into account labels of these nodes, we see that the cousin pair (d, c) with distance 0.5 occurs 2 times totally in tree T_3, and hence $(d, c, 0.5, 2)$ is a valid cousin pair item in T_3.

Table 8.1. Cousin pair items of T_3 in Figure 8.1.

Cousin Distance	Cousin Pair Items
0	$(b, c, 0, 1), (c, f, 0, 1), (d, d, 0, 1)$
0.5	$(d, b, 0.5, 1), (d, c, 0.5, 2), (d, f, 0.5, 1)$
1	$(b, f, 1, 1), (b, c, 1, 1), (c, c, 1, 1), (c, f, 1, 1)$

We may also consider the total number of occurrences of the cousins u and v regardless of their distance, for which case we use λ in place of $c\_dist(u, v)$ in the cousin pair item. For example, in Table 8.1, T_3 has $(b, c, 0, 1)$ and $(b, c, 1, 1)$, and hence we obtain $(b, c, \lambda, 2)$. Here, the cousin pair (b, c) occurs once with distance 0 and occurs once with distance 1. Therefore, when ignoring the distance, the total number of occurrences of (b, c) is 2. Likewise we can ignore the number of occurrences of a cousin pair (u, v) by using λ in place of $occur(u, v)$ in the cousin pair item. For example, in Table 8.1, T_3 has $(b, c, 0, \lambda)$ and $(b, c, 1, \lambda)$. We may ignore both the cousin distance and the number of occurrences and focus on the cousin labels only. For example, T_3 has (b, c, λ, λ), which simply indicates that b, c are cousins in T_3.

Frequent Cousin Pair

Let $\mathcal{S} = \{T_1, T_2, \ldots, T_n\}$ be a set of n trees and let d be a given distance value. We define $\delta_{u,v,i}$ to be 1 if T_i has the cousin pair item $(L(u), L(v), d, occur(u, v))$, $occur(u, v) > 0$; otherwise $\delta_{u,v,i}$ is 0. We define the *support* of the cousin pair (u, v) with respect to the distance value d as $\Sigma_{1 \leq i \leq n} \delta_{u,v,i}$. Thus the support value represents the number of trees in the set $\mathcal{S}$ that contain *at least* one occurrence of the cousin pair (u, v) having the specified distance value d. A cousin pair is *frequent* if its support value is greater than or equal to a user-specified threshold, *minsup*.

For example, consider Figure 8.1 again. T_1 has the cousin pair item $(c, f, 1, 1)$, T_2 has the cousin pair item $(c, f, 0.5, 1)$ and T_3 has the cousin pair item $(c, f, 1, 1)$ and $(c, f, 0, 1)$. The support of (c, f) w.r.t. distance 1 is 2 because both T_1 and T_3 have this cousin pair with the specified distance. One can also ignore cousin distances when finding frequent cousin pairs. For example, the support of (c, f) is 3 when the cousin distances are ignored.

Given a set $\mathcal{S}$ of evolutionary trees, our approach offers the user several alternative kinds of frequent cousin pairs in these trees. For example, the algorithm can find, in a tree T of $\mathcal{S}$, all cousin pairs in T whose distances are less than or equal to *maxdist* and whose occurrence numbers are greater than or equal to *minoccur*, where *maxdist* and *minoccur* are user-specified parameters. The algorithm can also find all frequent cousin pairs in $\mathcal{S}$ whose distance values are at most *maxdist* and whose support values are at least *minsup* for a user-specified *minsup* value. In the following section, we will describe the techniques used in finding these frequent cousin pairs in a single tree or in multiple trees.

8.3 Tree-Mining Algorithms

Given a tree T and a node u of T, let *children_set(u)* contain all children of u. Our algorithm preprocesses T to obtain *children_set(u)* for every node u in T. We also preprocess T to be able to locate a list of all ancestors of any node u in $O(1)$ time using a conventional hash table.

Now, given a user-specified value *maxdist*, we consider all valid distance values 0, 0.5, 1, 1.5, ..., *maxdist*. For each valid distance value d, we define *my_level(d)* and *mycousin_level(d)* as follows:

$$my\_level(d) = 1 + \lfloor d \rfloor \tag{8.2}$$
$$mycousin\_level(d) = my\_level(d) + R \tag{8.3}$$

where

$$R = 2 \times (d - \lfloor d \rfloor) \tag{8.4}$$

Let $m = my\_level(d)$ and $n = mycousin\_level(d)$. Intuitively, given a node u and the distance value d, beginning with u, we can go m levels up to reach an ancestor w of u. Then, from w, we can go n levels down to reach a descendant v of w. Referring to the cousin distance definition in Equation (8.1), $c\_dist(u, v)$ must be equal to the distance value d. Furthermore, all the siblings of u must also be cousins of the siblings of v with the same distance value d. These nodes are identified by their unique identification numbers. To obtain cousin pair items having the form $(L(u), L(v), c\_dist(u, v), occur(u, v))$, we check the node labels of u, v and add up the occurrence numbers for cousin pairs whose corresponding node labels are the same and whose cousin distances are the same. Figure 8.2 summarizes the algorithm.

Notice that within the loop (Steps 3 to 10) of the algorithm in Figure 8.2, we find cousin pairs with cousin distance d where d is incremented from 0 to *maxdist*. In Step 8 where a cousin pair with the current distance value d is formed, we check, through node identification numbers, to make sure this cousin pair is not identical to any cousin pair with less distance found in a previous iteration in the loop. This guarantees that only cousin pairs with exact distance d are formed in the current iteration in the loop.

Lemma 1. Algorithm Single_Tree_Mining correctly finds all cousin pair items of T where the cousin pairs have a distance less than or equal to *maxdist* and an occurrence number greater than or equal to *minoccur*.
Proof. The correctness of the algorithm follows directly from two observations: (i) every cousin pair with distance d where $0 \leq d \leq maxdist$ is found by the algorithm; (ii) because Step 9 eliminates duplicate cousin pairs from consideration, no cousin pair with the same identification numbers is counted twice.

Lemma 2. The time complexity of algorithm Single_Tree_Mining is $O(|T|^2)$.
Proof. The algorithm visits each children set of T. For each visited node, it takes at most $O(|T|)$ time to go up and down to locate its cousins. Thus, the time spent in finding all cousin pairs identified by their unique identification numbers is $O(|T|^2)$. There are at most $O(|T|^2)$ such cousin pairs. Through the table lookup, we get their node labels and add up the occurrence numbers of cousin pairs whose distances and corresponding node labels are the same in $O(|T|^2)$ time.

Procedure: Single_Tree_Mining
Input: A tree T and a maximum distance value allowed, *maxdist*, and a minimum
    occurrence number allowed, *minoccur*.
Output: All cousin pair items of T where the cousin pairs have a distance less
    than or equal to *maxdist* and an occurrence number greater than or
    equal to *minoccur*.

1. **for** each node p where *children_set*$(p) \neq \emptyset$ **do**
2.   **begin**
3.   **for** each valid distance value $d \leq maxdist$ **do**
4.   **begin**
5.   let u be a node in *children_set*(p);
6.   calculate $m = my\_level(d)$ and $n = mycousin\_level(d)$ as defined
                    in Equations (8.2), (8.3);
7.   beginning with u, go m levels up to reach an ancestor w and
                    then from w, go n levels down to reach a descendant v of w;
8.   combine all siblings of u and all siblings of v to form cousin pairs
                    with the distance value d;
9.   if a specific pair of nodes with the distance d has been found
                    previously, don't double-count them;
10.   **end**;
11.   **end**;
12. add up the occurrence numbers of cousin pairs whose corresponding node
    labels are the same and whose cousin distances are the same to get
    qualified cousin pair items of T.

Fig. 8.2. Algorithm for finding frequent cousin pair items in a single tree.

To find all frequent cousin pairs in a set of trees $\{T_1, \ldots, T_k\}$ whose distance is at most *maxdist* and whose support is at least *minsup* for a user-specified *minsup* value, we first find all cousin pair items in each of the trees that satisfy the distance requirement. Then we locate all frequent cousin pairs by counting the number of trees in which a qualified cousin pair item occurs. This procedure will be referred to as Multiple_Tree_Mining and its time complexity is clearly $O(kn^2)$ where $n = \max\{|T_1|, \ldots, |T_k|\}$.

8.4 Experiments and Results

We conducted a series of experiments to evaluate the performance of the proposed tree-mining algorithms, on both synthetic data and real trees, run under the Solaris operating system on a SUN Ultra 60 workstation. The synthetic data was produced by a C++ program based on the algorithm developed in [15]. This program is able to generate a large number of random trees from the whole tree space. The real trees were obtained from TreeBASE, available at www.treebase.org [21].

Table 8.2 summarizes the parameters of our algorithms and their default values used in the experiments. The value of 4 was used for minimum support because the evolutionary trees in TreeBASE differ substantially and using this support value allowed us to find interesting patterns in the trees. Table 8.3 lists the parameters and their default values related to the synthetic trees. The *fanout* of a tree is the number of children of each node in the tree. The *alphabet_size* is the total number of distinct node labels these synthetic trees have.

Table 8.2. Parameters and their default values used in the algorithms.

Name	Meaning	Value
minoccur	minimum occurrence number of an interesting cousin pair in a tree	1
maxdist	maximum distance allowed for an interesting cousin pair	1.5
minsup	minimum number of trees in the database that contain an interesting cousin pair	4

Table 8.3. Parameters and their default values related to synthetic trees.

Name	Meaning	Value
tree_size	number of nodes in a tree	200
database_size	number of trees in the database	1000
fanout	number of children of each node in a tree	5
alphabet_size	size of the node label alphabet	200

Figure 8.3 shows how changing the *fanout* of synthetic trees affects the running time of the algorithm Single_Tree_Mining. 1000 trees were tested and the average was plotted. The other parameter values are as shown in Table 8.2 and Table 8.3. Given a fixed *tree_size* value, a large fanout value will result in a small number of children sets, which will consequently reduce the times of executing the outer for-loop of the algorithm, see Step 1 in Figure 8.2. Therefore, one may expect that the running time of Single_Tree_Mining drops as *fanout* increases. To our surprise, however, Figure 8.3 shows that the running time of Single_Tree_Mining increases as a tree becomes bushy, i.e. its *fanout* becomes large. This happens mainly because for bushy trees, each node has many siblings and hence more qualified cousin pairs could be generated, see Step 8 in Figure 8.2. As a result, it takes more time in the postprocessing stage to aggregate those cousin pairs, see Step 12 in Figure 8.2.

Figure 8.4 shows the running times of Single_Tree_Mining with different *maxdist* values for varying node numbers of trees. 1000 synthetic trees were

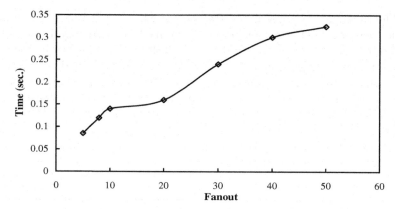

Fig. 8.3. Effect of *fanout*.

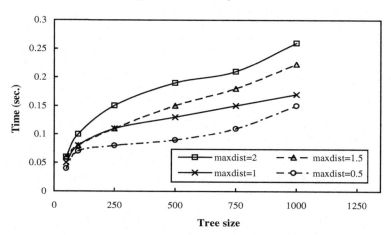

Fig. 8.4. Effect of *maxdist* and *tree_size*.

tested and the average was plotted. The other parameter values are as shown in Table 8.2 and Table 8.3. It can be seen from the figure that as *maxdist* increases, the running time becomes large, because more time will be spent in the inner for-loop of the algorithm for generating cousin pairs, Steps 3 to 10 in Figure 8.2. We also observed that a lot of time needs to be spent in aggregating qualified cousin pairs in the postprocessing stage of the algorithm, Step 12 in Figure 8.2. This extra time, though not explicitly described by the asymptotic time complexity $O(|T|^2)$ in Lemma 2, is reflected by the graphs in Figure 8.4.

The running times of Multiple_Tree_Mining when applied to 1 million synthetic trees and 1,500 evolutionary trees obtained from TreeBASE are shown in Figures 8.5 and 8.6, respectively. Each evolutionary tree has between 50 and 200 nodes and each node has between two and nine children (most internal nodes have two children). The size of the node label alphabet for the evolutionary trees is 18,870. The other parameter values are as shown in Table 8.2 and Table 8.3. We see from Figure 8.6 that Multiple_Tree_Mining can find all frequent cousin pair items in the 1,500 evolutionary trees in less than 150 seconds. The algorithm scales up well – its running time increases linearly with increasing number of trees (Figure 8.5).

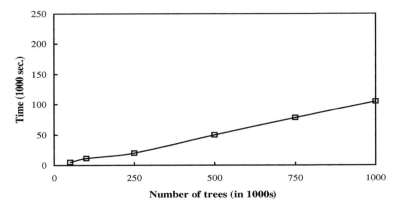

Fig. 8.5. Effect of *database_size* for synthetic trees.

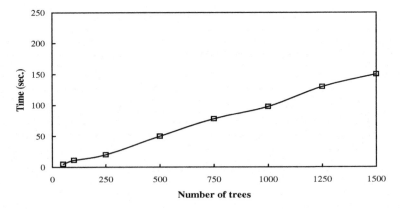

Fig. 8.6. Effect of *database_size* for evolutionary trees.

8.5 Implementation and Applications

8.5.1 Evolutionary Tree Miner

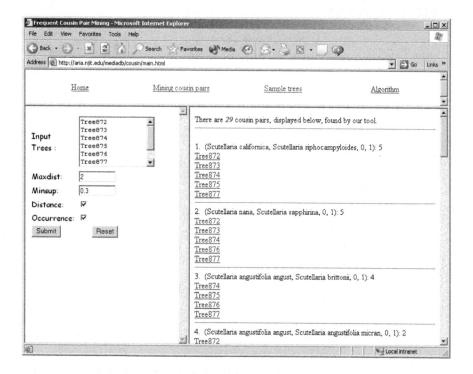

Fig. 8.7. Interface of the proposed evolutionary tree miner.

We have implemented the proposed algorithms into a system, called evolutionary tree miner, that runs on a collection of phylogenies obtained from TreeBASE. Figure 8.7 shows the interface of the evolutionary tree miner. The user can input a set of tree IDs as described in TreeBASE and specify appropriate parameter values through the interface shown in the left window of the system. The data mining result is shown in the right window of the system. Each discovered cousin pair has the format (label$_1$, label$_2$, c_dist, occurrence): k, where k is the number of input trees in which the cousin pair occurs. For example, (Scutellaria californica, Scutellaria siphocampyloides, 0, 1): 5 indicates that Scutellaria californica and Scutellaria siphocampyloides is a cousin pair of distance 0 that occurs in five input trees, with the occurrence number in each tree being one. The cousin pairs in the output list shown in the right window are sorted and displayed based on cousin distances and support values. By clicking on a tree ID (e.g. Tree873), the user can see a graphical display of the tree via a pop-up window, as shown in Figure 8.8. In this figure, the found cousin pair (Scutellaria californica and Scutellaria siphocampyloides) is highlighted with a pair of bullets.

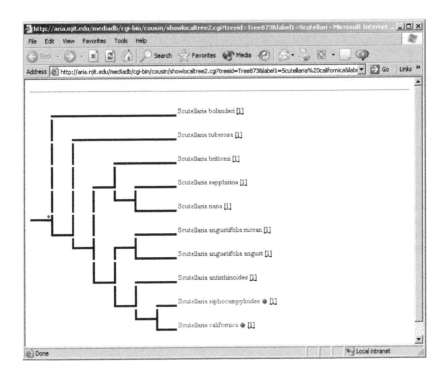

Fig. 8.8. A discovered cousin pair highlighted with bullets.

8.5.2 New Similarity Measures for Trees

We develop new similarity measures for comparing evolutionary trees based on the cousin pairs found in the trees. Specifically, let T_1 and T_2 be two trees. Let $cpi(T_1)$ contain all the cousin pair items of T_1 and let $cpi(T_2)$ contain all the cousin pair items generated from T_2. We define the similarity of T_1 and T_2, denoted $t\_sim(T_1, T_2)$, as

$$t\_sim(T_1, T_2) = \frac{|cpi(T_1) \cap cpi(T_2)|}{|cpi(T_1) \cup cpi(T_2)|} \tag{8.5}$$

Depending on whether the cousin distance and the number of occurrences of a cousin pair in a tree are considered, we have four different types of cousin pair items in the tree. Consequently we obtain four different tree similarity measures. We represent them by $t\_sim_{null}(T_1, T_2)$ (considering neither the cousin distance nor the occurrence number in each tree), $t\_sim_{cdist}(T_1, T_2)$ (considering the cousin distance only in each tree), $t\_sim_{occ}(T_1, T_2)$ (considering the occurrence number only in each tree), and $t\_sim_{occ\_cdist}(T_1, T_2)$ (considering both the cousin distance and the occurrence number in each tree), respectively.

For example, referring to the trees T_2 and T_3 in Figure 8.1, we have t_sim_{null} $(T_2, T_3) = \frac{4}{12} = 0.33$, $t\_sim_{cdist}(T_2, T_3) = \frac{2}{16} = 0.125$, $t\_sim_{occ}(T_2,$ $T_3) = \frac{4}{12} = 0.33$, $t\_sim_{occ\_cdist}(T_2, T_3) = \frac{2}{16} = 0.125$. The intersection and union of two sets of cousin pair items take into account the occurrence numbers in them. For example, suppose $cpi(T_1) = \{(a, b, m, occur1)\}$ and $cpi(T_2) = \{(a, b, m, occur2)\}$. Then $cpi(T_1) \cap cpi(T_2) = \{(a, b, m, \min(occur1, occur2))\}$ and $cpi(T_1) \cup cpi(T_2) = \{(a, b, m, \max(occur1, occur2))\}$. These similarity measures can be used to find kernel trees in a set of phylogenies [22].

8.5.3 Evaluating the Quality of Consensus Trees

One important topic in phylogeny is to automatically infer or reconstruct evolutionary trees from a set of molecular sequences or species. The most commonly used method for tree reconstruction is based on the maximum parsimony principle [11]. This method often generates multiple trees rather than a single tree for the input sequences or species. When the number of equally parsimonious trees is too large to suggest an informative evolution hypothesis, a consensus tree is sought to summarize the set of parsimonious trees. Sometimes the set is divided into several clusters and a consensus tree for each cluster is derived [23].

There are five most popular methods for generating consensus trees: Adams [1], strict [8], majority [17], semi-strict [2], and Nelson [18]. We develop a method to evaluate the quality of these consensus trees based on a similarity measure defined in the previous subsection.

Specifically, let C be a consensus tree and let S be the set of original parsimonious trees from which the consensus tree C is generated. Let T be a tree in S. We define the similarity score, based on cousins, between C and T, denoted $\delta_{cus}(C, T)$, as

$$\delta_{cus}(C, T) = t\_sim_{cdist}(C, T) \tag{8.6}$$

where the similarity measure t_sim_{cdist} is as defined in the previous subsection.

The average similarity score, based on cousins, of the consensus tree C with respect to the set S, denoted $\Delta_{cus}(C, S)$, is

$$\Delta_{cus}(C, S) = \frac{\sum_{T \in S} \delta_{cus}(C, T)}{|S|} \tag{8.7}$$

where $|S|$ is the total number of trees in the set S. The higher the average similarity score $\Delta_{cus}(C, S)$ is, the better consensus tree C is.

Figure 8.9 compares average similarity scores of the consensus trees generated by the five methods mentioned above for varying number of parsimonious trees. The parameter values used by our algorithms for finding the cousin pairs are as shown in Table 8.2. The parsimonious trees were generated by the PHYLIP tool [10] using the first 500 nucleotides extracted from six genes representing paternally, maternally, and biparentally inherited regions of the genome among 16 species of Mus [16]. There are 33 trees in total. We randomly choose 10, 15, 20, 25, 30 or 33 trees for each test. In each test, five different individual runs of the algorithms are performed and the average is plotted. It can be seen from Figure 8.9 that the majority consensus method and Nelson consensus method are better than the other three consensus methods – they yield consensus trees with higher average similarity scores.

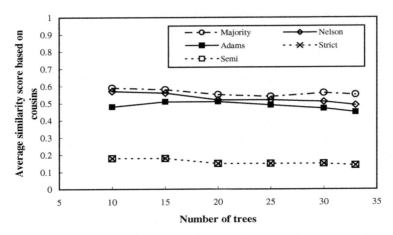

Fig. 8.9. Comparing the quality of consensus trees using cousin pairs.

In addition to cousin patterns, we have also considered another type of patterns, namely clusters, for evaluating the quality of consensus trees. Given an evolutionary tree T and a non-leaf node n of T, the cluster in T with respect to n is defined to be the set of all leaves in the subtree rooted at n [19]. The cluster set of T, denoted $cluster\_set(T)$, is the set of clusters with respect to all non-leaf nodes in T. For example, consider T_3 in Figure 8.1. The cluster set of T_3 is $\{\{4, 5\}, \{6, 7\}, \{4, 5, 6, 7\}\}$ where each integer represents a node identification number in T_3.

Now, let C be a consensus tree and let S be the set of original parsimonious trees from which the consensus tree C is generated. Let T be a tree in S. We define the similarity score, based on clusters, between C and T, denoted $\delta_{clu}(C,T)$, as

$$\delta_{clu}(C,T) = \frac{|cluster\_set(C) \cap cluster\_set(T)|}{|cluster\_set(C) \cup cluster\_set(T)|} \tag{8.8}$$

The average similarity score, based on clusters, of the consensus tree C with respect to the set S, denoted $\Delta_{clu}(C,S)$, is

$$\Delta_{clu}(C,S) = \frac{\sum_{T \in S} \delta_{clu}(C,T)}{|S|} \qquad (8.9)$$

For example, let us assume the cluster set of tree C, $cluster\_set(C)$, is $\{\{a, b, c\},\{d, e\}\}$. Assume the cluster set of tree T, $cluster\_set(T)$, is $\{\{a, b\},\{a, b, c\}, \{a, b, c, d\}\}$. Since only $\{a, b, c\}$ appears in both sets, $\delta_{clu}(C,T)$ is

$$\delta_{clu}(C,T) = \frac{|cluster\_set(C) \cap cluster\_set(T)|}{|cluster\_set(C) \cup cluster\_set(T)|}$$

$$= 1/4$$

$$= 0.25$$

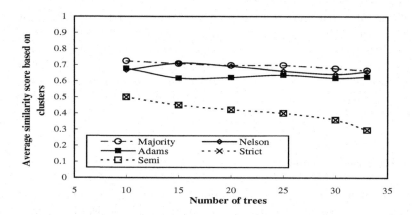

Fig. 8.10. Comparing the quality of consensus trees using clusters.

Figure 8.10 shows the experimental results in which clusters are used to evaluate the quality of consensus trees. The data used here are the same as the data for cousin pairs. In comparing the graphs in Figure 8.9 and Figure 8.10, we observe that majority consensus and Nelson consensus trees are the best consensus trees, yielding the highest average similarity scores between the consensus trees and the original parsimonious trees. A close look at the data reveals why this happens. All the original parsimonious trees are fully resolved; i.e. the resolution rate [23] of these trees is 100%. This means every node in an original parsimonious tree has two children, i.e. the tree is a binary tree. Furthermore the average depth of these trees is eight. When considering 10 out of 33 parsimonious trees, the average resolution rate and the depth of the obtained majority consensus trees are 73% and 7 respectively. The average resolution rate and the depth of the obtained Nelson consensus trees are 66% and 7 respectively. The average resolution rate and the depth of Adams consensus trees are 60% and 6 respectively. The average resolution rate and the depth of the strict consensus trees are only 33% and 4 respectively. This shows that the majority consensus trees and Nelson consensus trees are closest to the original parsimonious trees. On average, the majority consensus trees differ from the Nelson consensus trees by only two clusters and five cousin pairs. These small differences indicate that these two kinds of consensus trees are close to each other. Similar results were observed for the other input data.

Notice that, in Figure 8.10 where clusters are used, the average similarity scores for strict consensus trees decrease monotonously as the number of equally parsimonious trees increases. This happens because when the number of equally parsimonious trees is large, the number of common clusters shared by all the parsimonious trees becomes small. Thus, the obtained strict consensus trees become less resolved; i.e., they are shallow and bushy. As a result, the similarity scores between the strict consensus trees and each fully resolved parsimonious tree become small.

Notice also that, in both Figure 8.9 and Figure 8.10, the average similarity scores of semi-strict consensus trees and strict consensus trees are almost the same. This happens because the parsimonious trees used in the experiments are all generated by the PHYLIP tool, which produces fully resolved binary trees. It is well known that a semi-strict consensus tree and a strict consensus tree are exactly the same when the original equally parsimonious trees are binary trees [2].

8.6 Related Work

In this section, we compare the proposed cousin-finding method and similarity measures with existing approaches. Computational biologists have developed several metrics for analyzing phylogenetic trees. The best known tree metrics include the quartet metric, triplet metric, partition metric, nearest neighbor interchange (NNI) metric and maximum agreement subtree metric. All of these metrics have been implemented in Page's COMPONENT toolbox [19].

The quartet metric, designed mainly for unrooted trees, is to check whether two given trees have similar "quartets", which are obtained based on adjacency relationships among all possible subsets of four leaves (species or taxa). The similarity between the two trees is then computed as the proportion of quartets that are shared in the two trees. A naive algorithm for calculating the quartet metric between two trees has the time complexity of $O(n^4)$ where n is the number of nodes in the trees. Douchette [9] proposed an efficient algorithm with the time complexity of $O(n^3)$, which is implemented in COMPONENT. More recently, Bryant et al. [5] proposed a method to compute the quartet metric between two trees in time $O(n^2)$. Brodal et al. [3] presented an algorithm that runs in time $O(n \log n)$ with the constraint that the trees have to be fully resolved. When using COMPONENT to calculate the quartet metric for rooted trees, these trees are treated as unrooted trees.

The triplet metric is similar to the quartet metric except that we enumerate triplets (three leaves) as opposed to quartets (four leaves). In other words, the triplet metric counts the number of subtrees with three taxa that are different in two trees. This metric is useful for rooted trees while the quartet metric is useful for unrooted trees. The algorithm for calculating the triplet metric of two trees runs in time $O(n^2)$.

The partition metric treats each phylogenetic tree as an unrooted tree and analyzes the partitions of species resulting from removing one edge at a time from the tree. By removing one edge from a tree, we are able to partition that tree. The distance between two trees is defined as the number of edges for which there is no equivalent (in the sense of creating the same partitions) edge in the other tree. The algorithm implemented in COMPONENT for computing the partition metric runs in time $O(n)$.

An agreement subtree between two trees T_1 and T_2 is a substructure of T_1 and T_2 on which the two trees are the same. Commonly such a subtree will have fewer leaves than either T_1 or T_2. A maximum agreement subtree (MAS) between T_1 and T_2 is an agreement subtree of T_1 and T_2. Furthermore there is no other agreement subtree of T_1 and T_2 that has more leaves (species or taxa) than MAS. The MAS metric is defined as the number of leaves removed from T_1 and T_2 to obtain an MAS of T_1 and T_2. In COMPONENT, programs have been written to find the MAS for two (rooted or unrooted) fully resolved binary trees.

Given two unrooted, unordered trees with the same set of labeled leaves, the NNI metric is defined to be the number of NNI operations needed to transform one tree to the other. DasGupta *et al.* [7] showed that calculating the NNI metric is NP-hard, for both labeled and unlabeled unrooted trees. Brown and Day [4] developed approximation algorithms, which were implemented in COMPONENT. The time complexities of the algorithms are $O(n log n)$ and $O(n^2 log n)$, respectively, for rooted trees and unrooted trees, respectively.

Another widely used metric for trees is the edit distance, defined through three edit operations, *change node label*, *insert a node* and *delete a node*, on trees. Finding the edit distance between two unordered trees is NP-hard, and hence a constrained edit distance, known as the degree-2 edit distance, was developed [30]. In contrast to the above tree metrics, the similarity measures between two trees proposed in this chapter are defined in terms of the cousin pairs found in the two trees. The definition of cousin pairs is different from the definitions for quartets, triplets, partitions, maximum agreement subtrees, NNI operations and edit operations, and consequently the proposed similarity measures are different from the existing tree metrics. These measures provide complementary information when applied to real-world data.

8.7 Conclusion

We presented new algorithms for finding and extracting frequent cousin pairs with varying distances from a single evolutionary tree or multiple evolutionary trees. A system built based on these algorithms can be accessed at `http://aria.njit.edu/mediadb/cousin/main.html`. The proposed single tree mining method, described in Section 8.3, is a quadratic-time algorithm. We suspect the best-case time complexity for finding all frequent cousin pairs in a tree is also quadratic. We have also presented some applications of the proposed techniques, including the development of new similarity measures for evolutionary trees and new methods to evaluate the quality of consensus trees through a quantitative measure. Future work includes (i) extending the proposed techniques to trees whose edges have weights, and (ii) finding different types of patterns in the trees and using them in phylogenetic data clustering as well as other applications (e.g. the analysis of metabolic pathways [14]).

Acknowledgments: We thank Professor Dennis Shasha for providing the software used in the chapter and for helpful comments while preparing this chapter. We also thank Professor William Piel for useful discussions on Tree-BASE. The anonymous reviewers provided very useful suggestions that helped to improve the quality and presentation of this work.

References

[1] Adams, E. N., 1972: Consensus techniques and the comparison of taxonomic trees. *Systematic Zoology*, **21**, 390–97.

[2] Bremer, K., 1990: Combinable component consensus. *Cladistics*, **6**, 369–72.

[3] Brodal, G. S., R. Fagerberg and C. N. S. Pedersen, 2003: Computing the quartet distance between evolutionary trees in time $O(n \log n)$. *Algorithmica*, **38(2)**, 377–95.

[4] Brown, E. K., and W. H. E. Day, 1984: A computationally efficient approximation to the nearest neighbor interchange metric. *Journal of Classification*, **1**, 93–124.

[5] Bryant, D., J. Tsang, P. E. Kearney and M. Li, 2000: Computing the quartet distance between evolutionary trees. In *Proceedings of the 11th Annual ACM-SIAM Symposium on Discrete Algorithms*, 285–6.

[6] Bustamante, C. D., R. Nielsen and D. L. Hartl, 2002: Maximum likelihood method for analyzing pseudogene evolution: Implications for silent site evolution in humans and rodents. *Molecular Biology and Evolution*, **19(1)**, 110–17.

[7] DasGupta, B., X. He, T. Jiang, M. Li, J. Tromp and L. Zhang, 1997: On distances between phylogenetic trees. In *Proceedings of the 8th Annual ACM-SIAM Symposium on Discrete Algorithms*, 427–36.

[8] Day W. H. E., 1985: Optimal algorithms for comparing trees with labeled leaves. *Journal of Classification*, **1**, 7–28.

[9] Douchette, C. R., 1985: An efficient algorithm to compute quartet dissimilarity measures. Unpublished BSc (Hons) dissertation, Memorial University of Newfoundland.

[10] Felsenstein, J., 1989: PHYLIP: Phylogeny inference package (version 3.2). *Cladistics*, **5**, 164–6.

[11] Fitch, W., 1971: Toward the defining the course of evolution: Minimum change for a specific tree topology. *Systematic Zoology*, **20**, 406–16.

[12] Genealogy.com, *What is a first cousin, twice removed?* Available at URL: `www.genealogy.com/16_cousn.html`.

[13] Han, J., and M. Kamber, 2000: *Data Mining: Concepts and Techniques*. Morgan Kaufmann, San Francisco, California.

[14] Heymans, M., and A. K. Singh, 2003: Deriving phylogenetic trees from the similarity analysis of metabolic pathways. In *Proceedings of the 11th International Conference on Intelligent Systems for Molecular Biology*, 138–46.

[15] Holmes, S., and P. Diaconis, 2002: Random walks on trees and matchings. *Electronic Journal of Probability*, **7**.

[16] Lundrigan, B. L., S. Jansa and P. K. Tucker, 2002: Phylogenetic relationships in the genus mus, based on paternally, maternally, and biparentally inherited characters. *Systematic Biology*, **51**, 23–53.

[17] Margush, T., and F. R. McMorris, 1981: Consensus n-trees. *Bull. Math. Biol.*, **43**, 239–44.

[18] Nelson, G., 1979: Cladistic analysis and synthesis: Principles and definitions, with a historical note on Adanson's Famille des Plantes (1763–4). *Systematic Zoology*, **28**, 1–21.

[19] Page, R. D. M., 1989: COMPONENT user's manual (release 1.5). University of Auckland, Auckland.

[20] Pearson, W. R., G. Robins and T. Zhang, 1999: Generalized neighbor-joining: More reliable phylogenetic tree reconstruction. *Molecular Biology and Evolution*, **16(6)**, 806–16.

[21] Sanderson, M. J., M. J. Donoghue, W. H. Piel and T. Erikson, 1994: Treebase: A prototype database of phylogenetic analyses and an interactive tool for browsing the phylogeny of life. *American Journal of Botany*, **81(6)**, 183.

[22] Shasha, D., J. T. L. Wang, and S. Zhang, 2004: Unordered tree mining with applications to phylogeny. In *Proceedings of the 20th International Conference on Data Engineering*, 708–19.

[23] Stockham, C., L. Wang and T. Warnow, 2002: Statistically based postprocessing of phylogenetic analysis by clustering. In *Proceedings of the 10th International Conference on Intelligent Systems for Molecular Biology*, 285–93.

[24] Tao, J., E. L. Lawler and L. Wang, 1994: Aligning sequences via an evolutionary tree: Complexity and approximation. In *Proceedings of the 26th Annual ACM Symposium on Theory of Computing*, 760–9.

[25] Wang, J. T. L., T. G. Marr, D. Shasha, B. A. Shapiro, G. W. Chirn and T. Y. Lee, 1996: Complementary classification approaches for protein sequences. *Protein Engineering,* **9(5)**, 381–6.

[26] Wang, J. T. L., S. Rozen, B. A. Shapiro, D. Shasha, Z. Wang and M. Yin, 1999: New techniques for DNA sequence classification. *Journal of Computational Biology,* **6(2)**, 209–218.

[27] Wang, J. T. L., H. Shan, D. Shasha and W. H. Piel, 2003: Tree–Rank: A similarity measure for nearest neighbor searching in phylogenetic databases. In *Proceedings of the 15th International Conference on Scientific and Statistical Database Management,* 171–80.

[28] Wang, J. T. L, B. A. Shapiro and D. Shasha, eds., 1999: *Pattern Discovery in Biomolecular Data: Tools, Techniques and Applications.* Oxford University Press, New York, New York.

[29] Wang, J. T. L., C. H. Wu and P. P. Wang, eds., 2003: *Computational Biology and Genome Informatics.* World Scientific, Singapore.

[30] Zhang, K., J. T. L. Wang and D. Shasha, 1996: On the editing distance between undirected acyclic graphs. *International Journal of Foundations of Computer Science,* **7(1)**, 43–58.

9

Ontology-Assisted Mining of RDF Documents

Tao Jiang and Ah-Hwee Tan

Summary. Resource description framework (RDF) is becoming a popular encoding language for describing and interchanging metadata of web resources. In this paper, we propose an *Apriori*-based algorithm for mining association rules (AR) from RDF documents. We treat relations (RDF statements) as items in traditional AR mining to mine associations among relations. The algorithm further makes use of a domain ontology to provide generalization of relations. To obtain compact rule sets, we present a generalized pruning method for removing uninteresting rules. We illustrate a potential usage of AR mining on RDF documents for detecting patterns of terrorist activities. Experiments conducted based on a synthetic set of terrorist events have shown that the proposed methods were able to derive a reasonably small set of association rules capturing the key underlying associations.

9.1 Introduction

Resource description framework (RDF) [19, 20] is a data modeling language proposed by the World Wide Web Consortium (W3C) for describing and interchanging metadata about web resources. The basic element of RDF is *statements*, each consisting of a subject, an attribute (or predicate), and an object. A sample RDF statement based on the XML syntax is depicted in Figure 9.1. At the semantic level, an RDF statement could be interpreted as "the subject has an attribute whose value is given by the object" or "the subject has a relation with the object". For example, the statement in Figure 9.1 represents the relation: "Samudra participates in a car bombing event". For simplicity, we use a triplet of the form <subject, predicate, object> to express an RDF statement. The components in the triplets are typically described using an ontology [15], which provides the set of commonly approved vocabularies for concepts of a specific domain. In general, the ontology also defines the taxonomic relations between concepts in the form of a concept hierarchy.

Due to the continual popularity of the semantic web, in a foreseeable future there will be a sizeable amount of RDF-based content available on the web.

```
<rdf:Description about="http://localhost:8080/TerroristOntoEx.rdfs#Samudra ">
<TerroristOntoEx: participate
    rdf:resource = "http://localhost:8080/TerroristOntoEx.rdfs#CarBombing"/>
</rdf:Description>
```

Fig. 9.1. A sample RDF statement based on the XML syntax. "Samudra" denotes the subject, "participate" denotes the attribute (predicate), and "CarBombing" denotes the object.

A new challenge thus arises as to how we can efficiently manage and tap the information represented in RDF documents.

In this paper, we propose a method, known as *Apriori*-based RDF Association Rule Mining (ARARM), for discovering association rules from RDF documents. The method is based on the *Apriori* algorithm [2], whose simplistic underlying principles enable it to be adapted for a new data model. Our work is motivated by the fact that humans could learn useful patterns from a set of similar events or evidences. As an event is typically decomposed into a set of relations, we treat a relation as an item to discover associations among relations. For example, many terrorist attack events may include the scenario that the terrorists carried out a robbery before the terrorist attacks. Though the robberies may be carried out by different terrorist groups and may have different types of targets, we can still derive useful rules from those events, such as "<Terrorist, participate, TerroristAttack> → <Terrorist, rob, CommercialEntity>".

The flow of the proposed knowledge discovery process is summarized in Figure 9.2. First, the raw information content of a domain is encoded using the vocabularies defined in the domain ontology to produce a set of RDF documents. The RDF documents, each containing a set of relations, are used as the input of the association rule mining process. For RDF association rule mining, RDF documents and RDF statements correspond to transactions and items in the traditional AR mining context respectively. Using the ontology, the ARARM algorithm is used to discover generalized associations between relations in RDF documents. To derive compact rule sets, we further present a generalized pruning method for removing uninteresting rules.

The rest of this chapter is organized as follows. Section 9.2 provides a review of the related work. Section 9.3 discusses the key issues of mining association rules from RDF documents. Section 9.4 formulates the problem statement for RDF association rule mining. Section 9.5 presents the proposed ARARM algorithm. An illustration of how the ARARM algorithm works is provided in Section 9.6. Section 9.7 discusses the rule redundancy issue and presents a new algorithm for pruning uninteresting rules. Section 9.8 reports our experimental results by evaluating the proposed algorithms on an RDF

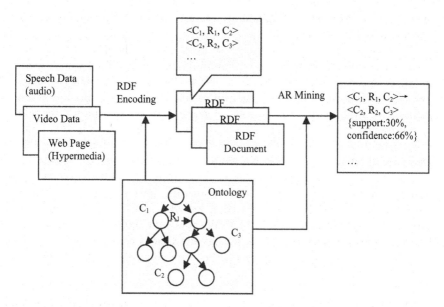

Fig. 9.2. The flow of the proposed RDF association rule mining process.

document set in the Terrorist domain. Section 9.9 concludes and highlights the future work.

9.2 Related Work

Association rule (AR) mining [1] is one of the most important tasks in the field of data mining. It was originally designed for well-structured data in transaction and relational databases. The formalism of typical AR mining was presented by Agrawal and Srikant [2]. Many efficient algorithms, such as *Apriori* [2], Close [16], and FP-growth [10], have been developed. A general survey of AR mining algorithms was given in [12]. Among those algorithms, *Apriori* is the most popular one because of its simplicity.

In addition to typical association mining, variants of the *Apriori* algorithm for mining generalized association rules have been proposed by Srikant and Agrawal [17] to find associations between items located in any level of a taxonomy (*is-a* concept hierarchy). For example, a supermarket may want to find not only specific associations, such as "users who buy the Brand A milk usually tend to buy the Brand B bread", but also generalized associations, such as "users who buy milk tend to buy bread". For generalized rule mining, several optimization strategies have been proposed to speed up support counting. An innovative rule pruning method based on taxonomic information was also provided. Han and Fu [9] addressed a similar problem and presented an approach to generate frequent itemsets in a top-down manner using an *Apriori*-based algorithm.

In recent years, AR mining has also been used in the field of text mining. Some basic differences between text mining and data mining were described in [8]. Whereas data mining handles relational or tabular data with relatively low dimensions, text mining generally deals with unstructured text documents with high feature dimensions. A framework of text mining techniques was presented in [18]. According to [13], text mining involves two kinds of tasks, namely deductive text mining (DTM) and inductive text mining (ITM). Deductive text mining (or information extraction) involves the extraction of useful information using predefined patterns from a set of text. Inductive text mining, on the other hand, detects interesting patterns or rules from text data. In [5], an AR mining algorithm, known as the Close algorithm, was proposed to extract explicit formal concepts and implicit association rules between concepts with the use of a taxonomy. However, the method was designed to discover *statistical* relations between concepts. It therefore can not be used to extract *semantic* relations among concepts from unstructured text data.

Recently, some interesting work on mining semi-structured XML data has been reported [3, 4, 6, 7, 14]. A general discussion of the potential issues in applying data mining to XML was presented in [4]. XML is a data markup language that provides users with a syntax specification to freely define elements, to describe their data and to facilitate data exchange on the web. However, the flexibility has resulted in a heterogeneous problem for knowledge discovery on XML. Specifically, XML documents that describe similar data content may have very different structures and element definitions. In [14], this problem was discussed and a method for determining the similarity between XML documents was proposed. In contrast to relational and transaction databases, XML data have a tree structure. Therefore, the context for knowledge discovery in XML documents should be redefined. Two approaches for mining association rules from XML documents have been introduced [3, 7]. In general, both approaches aimed to find similar nested element structures among the branches of the XML Document Object Model (DOM) trees [21]. At the semantic level, the detected association rules represent the correlation among attributes (nested elements) of a certain kind of elements. In [6], an approach was presented that used association rule mining methods for detecting patterns among RDF queries. The detected association rules were then used to improve the performance of RDF storage and query engines. However, the method was designed for mining association rules among subjects and attributes, but not among RDF statements.

9.3 Mining Association Rules from RDF

RDF/RDFS data consist of a set of RDF statements in the form of triplets. The RDF triplets form a directed graph (RDF Graph) with labels (attributes or predicates) on its edges. For the purpose of data exchange, RDF/RDFS uses an XML-based syntax. Mining association rules from RDF/RDFS data presents a number of unique challenges, described as follows.

First, each RDF statement is composed of a subject, an attribute (or predicate), and an object, that are described using the vocabularies from a predefined domain ontology. Suppose the ontology includes 100 concepts and an average of three predicates between each pair of concepts, the number of possible RDF statements is already 30,000. In real applications, the number of concepts defined in domain ontology could far exceed 100. Therefore, the number of distinct statements may be so large that each single RDF statement only appears a very small number of times, far below the typical minimum support threshold. This motivates our approach in mining generalized association rules.

Second, RDF statements with the same attributes can be generalized, if both their subjects and objects share common super-concepts. Recursively generalizing a set of statements creates a relation lattice. The information in the relation lattices can be used to improve the performance of itemset candidate generation and frequency counting (see Section 9.5).

Third, in contrast to items in relational databases, statements in RDF documents may be semantically related. Intuitively, semantically related statements should be statistically correlated as well. This motivates us to define a new interestingness measure for pruning uninteresting rules.

Furthermore, RDF statements express a rich set of explicit semantic relations between concepts. This makes the association rules discovered from RDF documents more understandable for humans.

9.4 Problem Statement

The problem formulation of association rule mining on RDF documents is given as follows. As we are interested in mining the associations among RDF statements, i.e., relations, we will use the term "relationset" instead of "itemset" in our description.

Let $O = <E, S, H>$ be an ontology, in which $E=\{e_1, e_2, \ldots, e_m\}$ is a set of literals called entities; $S=\{s_1, s_2, \ldots, s_n\}$ is a set of literals called predicates (or attributes); and H is a tree whose nodes are entities. An edge in H represents an *is-a* relationship between two entities. If there is an edge from e_1 to e_2, we say e_1 is a parent of e_2, denoted by $e_1 > e_2$; and e_2 is a child of e_1, denoted by $e_2 < e_1$. We call e+ an **ancestor** of e, if there is a path from e+ to e in H, denoted by $e+ >> e$. If $e >> e_1, e >> e_2 \ldots e >> e_k$, we call e a **common ancestor** of $e_1, e_2, \ldots, e_k$, denoted by $e >> e_1, e_2, \ldots, e_k$. For a set of entities

$e_1, e_2, \ldots e_k$, if $e' \in \{ e \mid e >> e_1, e_2, \ldots e_k \}$ and not exists $e'' \in \{ e \mid e >> e_1, e_2, \ldots e_k \}$ such that $e' >> e''$, e' is called the **least common ancestor** of $e_1, e_2, \ldots e_k$, denoted by $e' = \mathrm{lca}(e_1, e_2, \ldots e_k)$.

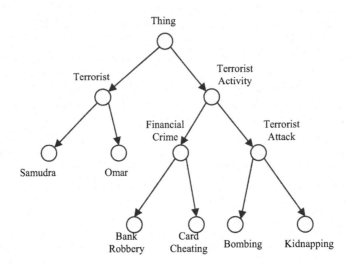

Fig. 9.3. A simple concept hierarchy for the Terrorist domain ontology.

Table 9.1. A sample RDF knowledge base **SD** in the terrorist domain.

Transaction	Relation
1	<Samudra, raiseFundBy, BankRobbery > < Samudra, participate, Bombing>
2	<Omar, raiseFundBy, CardCheating> <Omar, participate, Kidnapping>
3	<Omar, participate, Bombing>

Typically, there is a top-most entity in the ontology, called **thing**, which is the ancestor of all other entities in **E**. Thus, **E** and **H** define a concept hierarchy. A sample concept hierarchy for the Terrorist domain is shown in Figure 9.3. The ontology **O** defines a set of vocabularies for describing knowledge in a specific domain.

Let **D** be a set of *transactions*, called a **knowledge base**. Each **transaction** T is a set of *relations* (RDF statements), where each **relation** r is a triplet in the form of <x, s, y>, in which x, y∈**E**, and s∈**S**. We call x the **subject** of the relation r, denoted by sub(r)=x; we call s the **predicate** of the relation r, denoted by pred(r)=s; we call y the **object** of the relation r, denoted by obj(r) = y.

A sample knowledge base **SD** in the terrorist domain is shown in Table 9.1. There are three transactions in the knowledge base, each of which contains a set of relations describing a terrorist event.

A set of relations $R = \{r_1, r_2, \ldots, r_d\}$ (where $r_i = < x_i, s_i, y_i >$ for $i = 1, \ldots, d$) is called an **abstract relation** of $r_1, r_2, \ldots, r_d$ in **D**, if and only if $s_1 = s_2 = \ldots = s_d$ and there exist e' and $e'' \in E$, such that $e'=lca\{x_1, x_2, \ldots, x_d\}$, $e'' = lca\{y_1, y_2, \ldots, y_d\}$, $e' \neq thing$, and $e'' \neq thing$, and not exist $r' = < x', s', y' >$ in transactions of **D** where $r' \notin R$, $s' = s_1 = \ldots = s_d, e' >> x'$ and $e'' >> y'$. We also define the subject of R as $sub(R) = e' = lca\{x_1, x_2, \ldots, x_d\}$; the predicate of R as $pred(R) = s'$, where $s' = s_1 = s_2 \ldots = s_d$; and the object of R as $obj(R) = e'' = lca\{y_1, y_2, \ldots, y_d\}$. For simplicity, we use the triplet $< e', s', e'' >$, similar to that for denoting relations, to represent abstract relations. We call an abstract relation R a **sub-relation** of an abstract relation R', if $R \subset R'$ hold. An abstract relation R is the **most abstract relation**, if and only if there does not exist another abstract relation R' in **D** where $R \subset R'$.

We say a transaction T supports a relation r if $r \in T$. We say a transaction T supports an abstract relation R if $R \cap T \neq \emptyset$. We assume that each transaction T has an id, denoted by tid. We use $r.tids = \{tid_1, tid_2, \ldots, tid_n\}$ to denote the set of ids of the transactions in **D** that support the relation r. We define the **support** of r, denoted by $support(r) = |r.tids|$. Similarly, for an abstract relation R, we define $R.tids = \cup r.tids$, for all $r \in R$. We further define the **support** of R, denoted by $support(R) = |R.tids|$. In this paper, we use A, B, or C to represent a set of abstract relations $\{R_1, R_2 \ldots R_n\}$, named **relationset**. We define the **support** of a relationset A, denoted by $support(A) = |\cap R_i.tids|, i = 1, 2, \ldots n$. We call a relationset A a **frequent relationset**, if $support(A)$ is greater than a user-defined minimum support (minSup). An **association rule** in **D** is of the form A→B, where A, B, and A∪B are frequent relationsets and its **confidence**, denoted by $confidence(A \rightarrow B) = support(A \cup B)/support(A)$, is greater than a user-defined minimum confidence (minConf).

9.5 The ARARM Algorithm

Following the method presented in [2], our *Apriori*-based approach for mining association rules can be decomposed into the following steps.

1. Find all 1-frequent relationsets. Each 1-frequent relationset contains only one abstract relation R, which may contain one or more relations $r_1 \ldots r_n$ ($n \geq 1$).
2. Repeatedly generate k-frequent ($k \geq 2$) relationsets based on $k-1$-frequent relationsets, until no new frequent relationsets could be generated.
3. Generate association rules and prune uninteresting rules.

9.5.1 Generation of 1-Frequent Relationsets

For generating 1-frequent relationsets, we use a top-down strategy. We first find all the most abstract relations by scanning the RDF knowledge base **D** and merging similar relations that have common abstract relations. Next, we repeatedly split the frequent abstract relations into their sub-relations until all abstract relations are not frequent. We then keep all the frequent abstract relations as the 1-frequent relationsets. The procedure of identifying most abstract relations is summarized in Figure 9.4.

Algorithm 1: Find Most Abstract Relations
Input: A set of transactions **D**
Output: A set of most abstract relations
(1)   Rlist:=Φ
(2)   **for each** transaction $T \in D$ do
(3)   **for each** relation r in T do
(4)   **if** (exist an abstract relation R in Rlist **AND**
(5)   (r ∈ R **OR** (pred(r) == pred(R) **AND** lca(sub(R), sub(r)) != ***thing*** **AND**
(6)   lca(obj(R), obj(r)) != ***thing***)))
(7)   R := {r} ∪ R   //For the set of transactions **D'** scanned, R is an abstract relation.
(8)   R.r.tids := R.r.tids ∪ {T.tid}   //In R, R.r.tids represents the set of ids of the
transactions that have been scanned and support r. If r doesn't exist in R before, R.r.tids represents Φ.
(9)   **else**
(10)   R' :={r}   //if r could not be merged into an existing abstract relation, create a
new abstract relation R' for r.
(11)   R'.r.tids := {T.tid}
(12)   Rlist :={R'} ∪ Rlist
(13)   Output Rlist

Fig. 9.4. The algorithm for identifying most abstract relations.

Through the algorithm defined in Figure 9.4, we obtain a set of most abstract relations (*Rlist*). Each abstract relation and its sub-relations form a relation lattice. An example of a relation lattice is shown in Figure 9.5. In this lattice, <Terrorist, participate, TerroristAttack> is the most abstract relation subsuming the eight relations at the bottom levels. The middle-level nodes in the lattice represent sub-abstract-relations. For example, <Samudra, participate, Bombing> represents a sub-abstract-relation composed of two relations, namely <Samudra, participate, CarBombing> and <Samudra, participate, SuicideBombing>.

The algorithm for finding all 1-frequent relationsets is given in Figure 9.6. For each most abstract relation R in Rlist, if R is frequent, we add R into 1-frequent relationsets L_1 and we traverse the relation lattice whose top vertex is R to find all 1-frequent sub-relations of R (Figure 9.6a).

Figures 9.6b and 9.6c define the procedures of searching the abstract relation lattice. First, we recursively search the right children of the top relation to find 1-frequent relationsets and add them into L_1. Then, we look at each

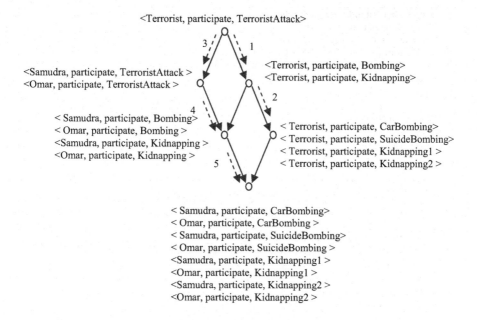

Fig. 9.5. The flow of searching in a sample relation lattice.

left child of the top abstract relation. If it is frequent, we add it into L_1 and recursively search the sub-lattice using this left child as the new top relation. In Figure 9.5, the dashed arrows and the order numbers of the arrows illustrate the process of searching the lattice for 1-frequent relationsets.

Here, we define the notions of right/left children, right/left sibling, and left/right parent of an abstract relation in a relation lattice. In Figure 9.5, <Terrorist, participate, Bombing> and <Terrorist, participate, Kidnapping> are sub-relations of <Terrorist, participate, TerroristAttack>. They are derived from their parent by drilling down its object based on the domain concept hierarchy. We call them the **right children** of <Terrorist, participate, TerroristAttack> and call <Terrorist, participate, TerroristAttack> the **left parent** of <Terrorist,participate, Bombing> and <Terrorist, participate, Kidnapping>. Similarly, if some sub-relations are derived from their parent by drilling down its subject, we call them the **left children** of their parent and call their parent the **right parent** of these sub-relations. If there exists an abstract relation that has a left child A and a right child B, A is called a **left sibling** of B and B is called a **right sibling** of A.

Lemma 1. (Abstract Relation Lattice) *Given an abstract relation $R = <x, s, y>$ with a right parent $R_{rp} = <x+, s, y>$ (or left parent $R_{lp} = <x, s, y+>$), if $support(R_{rp}) < minSup$ (or $support(R_{lp}) < minSup$), it can be derived that $support(R) < minSup$.*

Algorithm 2: Find 1-frequent relationsets
Input: A set of transactions D
Output: A set of 1-frequent relationsets
(1)   marList := getMostAbsRelations(D)
(2)   **for each** most abstract relation R in marList do
(3)   **if** (support(R) $\geq$ minSup)
(4) $L_1 := \{R\} \cup L_1$
(5) $L_1' :=$searchAbsRelationLattice(R, NULL); //NULL means that most abstract relations
don't have right siblings.
(6) $L_1 := L_1 \cup L_1'$
(7)   Output L_1

(a)

Procedure searchAbsRelationLattice
Input: Abstract relation **R**; hash table that stores right siblings of R, **rSiblings**
Output: 1-frequent relationsets in the relation lattice of R (excluding R)
(1) $L_1' := \Phi$
(2) $L_1' :=$searchRightChildren(R, rSiblings)
(3)   **for each** left children R_{lc} of R do //get left child by drilling down the subject of R
(4)   **if** support(R_{lc}) $\geq$ minSup
(5) $L_1' := \{ R_{lc} \} \cup L_1'$
(6) R_{lc}.rightParent := R
(7)   R.leftChildren.insert(R_{lc})
(8) $L_1'' :=$searchAbsRelationLattice(R_{lc}, R.rightChildren)
(9) $L_1' := L_1' \cup L_1''$
(10) Output L_1'

(b)

Procedure searchRightChildren
Input: Abstract relation **R**; hash table that stores right siblings of R, **rSiblings**
Output: 1-frequent relationsets among the right descendants of R
(1) $L_1^R := \Phi$
(2)   **for each** right children R_{rc} of R do
(3)   rParent := getRParent(R_{rc}, rSiblings)   //get the right parent of R_{rc} by finding the right
sibling of R that has the same object with R_{rc}.
(4)   **if** support(rParent) < minSup
(5)   **continue**; //Optimization 1.
(6)   **if** support(R_{rc}) $\geq$ minSup
(7)   **if** rParent != NULL
(8)   rParent.leftChildren.insert(R_{rc});
(9) R_{rc}.rightParent := rParent
(10)   R.rightChildren.insert(R_{rc})
(11) R_{rc}.leftParent := R
(12) $L_1^R := \{ R_{rc} \} \cup L_1^R$
(13) $L_1^{R'} :=$searchRightChildren(R_{rc},
                   rParent.rightChildren)
(14) $L_1^R := L_1^R \cup L_1^{R'}$
(15) Output L_1^R

(c)

Fig. 9.6. The algorithm for generating 1-frequent relationsets.

Proof. We only need to prove support(R) ≤ support(R_{rp}) (and support(R) ≤ support(R_{lp})). Since R is a sub-relation of R_{rp} (or R_{lp}), for each relation r∈R, r∈R_{rp}(or r∈R_{lp}) holds. Therefore, ∪r.tids (r∈R) is a subset of ∪r′.tids (r′ ∈R_{rp} or r′ ∈R_{lp}). Then the cardinality of ∪r.tids is smaller than or equals to the cardinality of ∪r′.tids, i.e. support(R) ≤ support(R_{rp}) (support(R) ≤ support(R_{lp})).

According to Lemma 1, once we find that the left parent or right parent of an abstract relation is not frequent, we do not need to calculate the support of this abstract relation and can simply prune it away. This forms our *Optimization Strategy 1*.

9.5.2 Generation of *k*-Frequent Relationsets

Observation 1. Given two abstract relations R_1 and R_2, if $R_1 \cap R_2 \neq \emptyset$ and $|R_1| \geq |R_2|$, either R_2 is a sub-abstract-relation of R_1 (i.e. $R_1 \cap R_2 = R_2$), or R_1 and R_2 have a common sub-abstract-relation R_3 in the relation lattice (i.e. $R_1 \cap R_2 = R_3$). For example, in Figure 9.5, two abstract relations <Samudra, participate, TerroristAttack> and <Terrorist, participate, Kidnapping> have a common sub-abstract-relation <Samudra, participate, Kidnapping> = {<Samudra, participate, Kidnapping1>, <Samudra, participate, Kidnapping2>}.

Lemma 2. *Given a k-relationset A={R_1,R_2, ...,R_k}, if there are two abstract relations R_i and R_j (1≤i, j≤k and i≠j), such that $|R_i| \geq |R_j|$ and $R_i \cap R_j \neq \emptyset$, there exists a k−1-relationset B with support(B) = support(A).*

Proof. According to Observation 1, there exists an abstract relation R', where either $R'=R_j$ or R' is a common sub-abstract-relation of R_i and R_j ($R_i \cap R_j=R'$). Therefore, there exists a $k-1$-relationset B = A∪{R'} <minus> {R_i, R_j} and support(B) = support(A).

According to Lemma 2, a *k*-relationset that includes two intersecting abstract relations is redundant and should be discarded. This is the basis of our *Optimization Strategy 2*.

Observation 2. Given two 2-frequent relationsets A={R_1, R_2} and B={R_1, R_2+}, where R_1, R_2, and R_2+ are frequent abstract relations and R_2+ is an ancestor of R_2, if the support of the relationset {R_1, R_2} equals the support of the relationset {R_1, R_2+}, the relationset B is redundant because A and B are supported by the same set of transactions. As {R_1, R_2} provides a more precise semantics than {R_1, R_2+}, the latter is redundant and should be discarded. This is *Optimization Strategy 3*.

The procedure of generating *k*-frequent relationsets L_k is described in Figure 9.7. To generate L_k, we need to first generate *k*-candidate relationsets based on $k-1$-frequent relationsets. We search the $k-1$-frequent relationset

```
Algorithm 3: Find k-frequent relationsets
Input: 1-frequent relationset list L₁

Output: k-frequent relationsets(k ≥ 2)
 (1)  k:=2
 (2)  L:= Φ
 (3)  while |Lₖ₋₁| ≥ k do
 (4)      Cₖ:= generateCandidate(Lₖ₋₁)
 (5)      for each candidate relationset A ∈ Cₖ do
 (6)          if support(A) ≥ minSup
 (7)              Lₖ={A} U Lₖ
 (8)          prune(Lₖ)          //Optimization 3
 (9)      L := L ∪ Lₖ
(10)      k := k+1
(11) Output L
```

Fig. 9.7. The algorithm for identifying k-frequent relationsets.

pair (A, B), where A, B ∈ L_{k-1}, A={$R_1,R_2,\ldots,R_{k-1}$}, B={$R'_1,R'_2,\ldots,R'_{k-1}$}, $R_i = R'_i$ (i=1,2,..., $k-2$), and $R_{k-1} \cap R'_{k-1} = \emptyset$ (*Optimization Strategy 2*). For each such pair of k-1-frequent relationsets (A, B), we generate a k-candidate relationset A∪B={$R_1,R_2,\ldots,R_{k-1},R'_{k-1}$}. We use C_k to denote the entire set of k-candidate relationsets. We further generate L_k by pruning the k-candidate relationsets whose supports are below minSup. In L_k, some redundant k-frequent relationsets also need to be removed according to *Optimization Strategy 3*.

9.5.3 Generation of Association Rules

For each frequent relationset A, the algorithm finds each possible sub-relationset B and calculates the confidence of the association rule B → A < minus > B, where A < minus > B denotes the set of relations in A but not in B. If confidence(B→A<minus>B) is larger than minConf, B→A<minus>B is generated as a rule.

9.6 Illustration

In this section, we illustrate our ARARM algorithm by mining associations from the sample knowledge base **SD** depicted in Table 9.1. Suppose that the minimum support is 2 and the minimum confidence is 66%. The relations (RDF statements) in the knowledge base are constructed using the ontology as shown in Figure 9.3. The predicate set is defined as **S** = {raiseFundBy, participate}.

First, we aggregate all relations in **SD** (as described in Figure 9.4) and obtain two most-abstract relations (Table 9.2). Because the supports of those two abstract relations are all greater than or equal to minimum support of 2, they will be used in the next step to generate 1-frequent relationsets.

Table 9.2. The most-abstract relations obtained from the knowledge base *SD*.

Most-Abstract Relations	Support
<Terrorist, raiseFundBy, FinancialCrime>	2
<Terrorist, participate, TerroristAttack>	3

<Terrorist, raiseFundBy, FinancialCrime> , support 2

<Samudra, raiseFundBy,
FinancialCrime>, support 1
<Omar, raiseFundBy,
FinancialCrime >, support 1

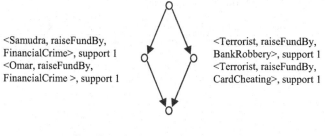

<Terrorist, raiseFundBy,
BankRobbery>, support 1
<Terrorist, raiseFundBy,
CardCheating>, support 1

< Samudra, raiseFundBy, BankRobbery>, support 1
< Omar, raiseFundBy, BankRobbery >, support 0
<Samudra, raiseFundBy, CardCheating >, support 0
<Omar, raiseFundBy, CardCheating >, support 1

(a)

<Terrorist, participate, TerroristAttack> , support 3

<Samudra, participate,
TerroristAttack >, support 1
**<Omar, participate,
TerroristAttack >, support 2**

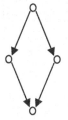

**<Terrorist, participate,
Bombing>, support 2**
<Terrorist, participate,
Kidnapping>, support 1

< Samudra, participate, Bombing>, support 1
< Omar, participate, Bombing >, support 1
<Samudra, participate, Kidnapping >, support 0
<Omar, participate, Kidnapping >, support 1

(b)

Fig. 9.8. The relation lattices of the two most-abstract relations.

Next, we search the relation lattices to find 1-frequent relationsets. The relation lattices of the two most-abstract relations are shown in Figure 9.8.

In Figure 9.8a, because all of the relations in the second level are below the minimum support, the relations at the bottom of the lattice will not be considered. In Figure 9.8b, because the relations <Omar, participate, TerroristAttack> and <Terrorist, participate, Bombing> are frequent, their child relation <Omar, participate, Bombing> at the bottom of the lattice will still be considered. Other relations will be directly pruned because either the support of their left parent or right parent is below the minimum support.

Table 9.3. The 1-frequent relationsets identified from the sample knowledge base *SD*.

1-Frequent Relationsets	Support
{<Terrorist, raiseFundBy, FinancialCrime>}	2 {1,2}
{<Terrorist, participate, TerroristAttack>}	3 {1,2,3}
{<Omar, participate, TerroristAttack >}	2 {2,3}
{<Terrorist, participate, Bombing>}	2 {1,3}

Table 9.4. The k-frequent relationsets ($k \geq 2$) identified from the sample knowledge base *SD*.

k-Frequent Relationsets	Support
{<Terrorist, raiseFundBy, FinancialCrime>, <Terrorist, participate, TerroristAttack> }	2{1,2}

Table 9.5. The association rules discovered from the sample knowledge base *SD*.

Association rules	Support/ Confidence
<Terrorist, raiseFundBy, FinancialCrime> →<Terrorist, participate, TerroristAttack>	2/66.6%
<Terrorist, participate, TerroristAttack> →<Terrorist, raiseFundBy, FinancialCrime>	2/100%

After traversing the relation lattices, we obtain the 1-frequent relationsets as shown in Table 9.3. Using the k-frequent relationset generation algorithm, we obtain the k-frequent relationsets $(k \geq 2)$, depicted in Table 9.4. The association rule generation algorithm then derives the two association rules as shown in Table 9.5.

9.7 Pruning Uninteresting Rules

Association rule mining algorithms typically produce a large number of rules. Therefore, efficient methods for detecting and pruning uninteresting rules are usually needed. A general survey on rule interestingness measures was presented in [11]. In [13], a set of commonly used properties for defining the interestingness of the associations were introduced. The issues of pruning redundant rules with the use of a concept hierarchy were discussed in [9] and [17]. Srikant and Agrawal presented a method for calculating the expected support and confidence of a rule according to its "ancestors" in a concept hierarchy. A rule is considered as "redundant" if its support and confidence can be estimated from those of its "ancestors". The method however assumes that the items appearing in an association are independent.

For mining association rules among the relations in RDF documents, the problem of measuring interestingness becomes more complex on two accounts. First, generalization and specialization of RDF relations are more complicated. For example, a relation may have two direct parents in the relation lattice. Second, the relations may be semantically related. For example, the relations <Samudra, raiseFundBy, BankRobbery> and <Samudra, participate, Bombing> refer to the same subject *Samudra*. They are thus more likely to appear together than two unrelated relations. To improve upon Srikant's method [17], we develop a generalized solution for calculating the expected support and confidence of a rule based on its ancestors.

We call a relationset A+ an *ancestor* of relationset A if A+ and A have the same number of relations and A+ can be derived from A by replacing one or more concepts in A with their ancestors in a concept hierarchy. Given an association rule A→B, we call the association rules A+→B, A+→B+, and A→B+, the *ancestors* of A→B. We call A+→B+ a close ancestor of A→B, if there does not exist a rule $A' \rightarrow B'$ such that $A' \rightarrow B'$ is an ancestor of A→B and A+→B+ is an ancestor of $A' \rightarrow B'$. A similar definition applies to both A+→B and A→B+.

For calculating the expected support and confidence of an association rule based on its close ancestors' support and confidence, the contribution of the concept replacement could be estimated according to the three cases described below.

- Concept replacement in both the left- and right-hand sides. For example, an association rule AR1: <a, rel1, b> → <c, rel2, a> could be derived from an association rule AR2: <a+, rel1, b> → <c, rel2, a+> by replacing concept "a+" with its sub-concept "a". This kind of concept replacement only influences the support of the association rule. The expected support and confidence of AR1 is given by

$$support_E(AR1) = support(AR2) \cdot P(a|a+) \qquad (9.1)$$

and

$$confidence_E(AR1) = confidence(AR2) \qquad (9.2)$$

where P(a|a+) is the conditional probability of a, given a+.

- Concept replacement in the left-hand side only. For example, an association rule AR1: <a, rel1, b> → <c, rel2, d> could be generated from an association rule AR2: <a+, rel1, b> → <c, rel2, d> by replacing the concept "a+" with its sub concept "a". This kind of concept replacement influences only the support of the association rule. We can calculate the support and confidence of AR1 by using Eqns. (9.1) and (9.2).
- Concept replacement in the right-hand side only. For example, an association rule AR1: <c, rel1, d> → <a, rel2, b> could be generated from an association rule AR2: <c, rel1, d> → <a+, rel2, b> by replacing concept "a+" with its sub concept "a". This kind of concept replacement influences both the support and the confidence of the association rule. We can calculate the expected support and confidence of AR1 by

$$support_E(AR1) = support(AR2) \cdot P(a|a+) \qquad (9.3)$$

and

$$confidence_E(AR1) = confidence(AR2) \cdot P(a|a+) \qquad (9.4)$$

respectively.

Note that the above three cases may be combined to calculate the overall expected support and confidence of an association rule. The conditional probability P(a|a+) can be estimated by the ratio of the number of the leaf sub-concepts of "a" and the number of the leaf sub-concepts of "a+" in the domain concept hierarchy. For example, in Figure 9.3, the number of the leaf sub-concepts of "Financial Crime" is two and the number of the leaf sub-concepts of "Terrorist Activity" is four. The conditional probability P(Financial Crime |Terrorist Activity) is thus estimated as 0.5.

Following the idea of Srikant and Agrawal [17], we define the interestingness of a rule as follows. Given a set of rules S and a minimum interest factor F, a rule A→B is *interesting*, if there is no ancestor of A→B in S or both the support and confidence of A→B are at least F times the expected support and confidence of its close ancestors respectively. We name the above interestingness measure *expectation measure with semantic relationships* (EMSR). EMSR may be used in conjunction with other pruning methods, such as those described in [13].

9.8 Experiments

Experiments were conducted to evaluate the performance of the proposed association rule mining and pruning algorithms both quantitatively and qualitatively. Our experiments were performed on an IBM T40 (1.5GHz Pentium Mobile CPU, 512MB RAM) running Windows XP. The RDF storage system was Sesame (release 1.0RC1) running on MySQL database (release 4.0.17). The ARARM algorithm was implemented using Java (JDK 1.4.2).

---

(1) Every event includes an RDF relation <Terrorist, participate, TerroristActivity>.

(2) 90% of the events, which include an RDF relation <Terrorist, participate, Bombing> also include an RDF relation <Terrorist, participate, Robbery>.

(3) 85% of the events include an RDF relation <Terrorist, takeVehicle, Vehicle>.

(4) For any event containing an RDF relation <Terrorist, participate, SuicideBombing >, if it also includes (probability of 85%) <Terrorist, takeVehicle, Vehicle>, there is a probability of 80% that <Terrorist, takeVehicle, Vehicle> is in specialized form <Terrorist, takeVehicle, Truck>.

(5) 85% of the events include an RDF relation <Terrorist, useWeapon, Weapon>.

(6) For any event containing <Terrorist, participate, Bombing>, if it also includes (probability of 85%) <Terrorist, useWeapon, Weapon>, there is a probability of 100% that <Terrorist, useWeapon, Weapon> is in specialized form <Terrorist, useWeapon, Bomb>, and there is a probability of 70% that <Terrorist, useWeapon, Weapon> is in specialized form <Terrorist, useWeapon, PlasticBomb>.

(7) For any event containing an RDF relation <Terrorist, participate, Kidnapping >, if it also includes (probability of 85%) <Terrorist, useWeapon, Weapon>, there is a probability of 100% that <Terrorist, useWeapon, Weapon> is in specialized form <Terrorist, useWeapon, NormalWeapon>, and there is a probability of 90% that <Terrorist, useWeapon, Weapon> is in specialized form <Terrorist, useWeapon, AK-47>.

Fig. 9.9. The seven domain axioms for generating the terrorist events.

Due to a lack of large RDF document sets, we created a synthetic data set, which contained a large number of RDF statements related to the terrorist domain. The data set has enabled us to conduct empirically extensive experiments of the various algorithms. The ontology for encoding terrorist events contained a total of 44 concepts (including classes and instances) and four predicates (attributes). Among the four predicates, three were used for describing the relationships between concepts in the terrorist events and one was used to provide additional information, such as the start time of terrorist events. To perform empirical evaluation, 1000 RDF documents were generated using a set of domain axioms (Figure 9.9). The maximum number of RDF statements in a single RDF document was four. We then performed association rule mining according to the ARARM algorithm and evaluated if the extracted rules captured the underlying associations specified by the domain axioms. With a 5% minimum support and a 50% minimum confidence, the ARARM algorithm generated 76 1-frequent and 524 k-frequent ($k \geq 2$) relationsets, based on which 1061 association rules were extracted. With a 10% minimum support and a 60% minimum confidence, the algorithm produced 42 1-frequent relationsets, 261 k-frequent relationsets, and 516 association rules.

We observed that although the events were generated based on only seven domain axioms, a much larger number of rules were extracted. For example, axiom 2 may cause the association rule "<Terrorist, participate, Bombing> → <Terrorist, participate, Robbery>" to be generated. Axiom 2 may also result in the association rule "<Terrorist, participate, Robbery> → <Terrorist, participate, Bombing>", as <Terrorist, participate, Bombing> tended to co-occur with <Terrorist, participate, Robbery>. In addition, axioms can be combined to generate new rules. For example, axioms 1, 3, and 5 can combine to generate association rules, such as "<Terrorist, participate, TerroristActivity> → <Terrorist, takeVehicle, Vehicle>, <Terrorist, useWeapon, Weapon>". As the association rule sets generated using the ARARM algorithm may still be quite large, pruning methods were further applied to derive more compact rule sets.

We experimented with a revised version of Srikant's interestingness measure method [17] and the EMSR method for pruning the rules. The experimental results are summarized in Table 9.6 and Table 9.7. We further experimented with two simple statistical interestingness measure methods [13] described below:

- *Statistical correlations measure (SC):* Given a rule R1→R2, where R1 and R2 are relationsets, if the conjunctive probability $P(R1,R2) \neq P(R1) \cdot P(R2)$, R1 and R2 are correlated and the rule R1→R2 is considered as interesting.
- *Conditional independency measure (CI):* Given two rules R1→R2 and R1, R3→R2 where R1, R2 and R3 are relationsets, if the conditional probability $P(R2|R1) = P(R2|R1,R3)$, we say R2 and R3 are conditionally independent and the rule R1, R3→R2 is considered as redundant and uninteresting.

Table 9.6. The experimental results using Srikant's method.

minSup/ minConf	Number of rules before pruning	Number of rules after applying Srikant's method	Number of rules after combining with SC and CI
5%/50%	1061	297	148
10%/60%	516	162	72

Table 9.7. The experimental results using the EMSR interestingness measure method.

minSup/ minConf	Number of rules before pruning	Number of rules after applying EMSR	Number of rules after combining with SC and CI
5%/50%	1061	277	91
10%/60%	516	177	46

When pruning association rules, we first applied Srikant's and the EMSR methods on the rule sets produced by the ARARM algorithm and derived association rule sets considered as interesting for each strategy. Then we combined Srikant's method and the EMSR method individually with the SC and CI interestingness measures to derive even smaller rule sets.

We observed that there was no significant difference between the numbers of rules obtained using the EMSR method and Srikant's method. However, by combining with other pruning methods, the resultant rule sets of EMSR were about 40% smaller than those produced by Srikant's method. The reason was that the rule sets produced by Srikant's method contained more rules similar to those produced using the SC and CI measures. In other words, Srikant's method failed to remove those uninteresting rules that could not be detected by the SC and CI measures.

For evaluating the quality of the rule sets produced by the EMSR method, we analyzed the association rule set obtained using a 5% minimum support and a 50% minimum confidence. We found that the heuristics of all seven axioms were represented in the rules discovered. In addition, most of the association rules can be traced to one or more of the domain axioms. A representative set of the association rules is shown in Table 9.8.

9.9 Conclusions

We have presented an *Apriori*-based algorithm for discovering association rules from RDF documents. We have also described how uninteresting rules can be detected and pruned in the RDF AR mining context.

Our experiments so far have made use of a synthetic data set, created based on a set of predefined domain axioms. The data set has allowed us to evaluate the performance of our algorithms in a quantitative manner. We are in the process of building a real Terrorist data set by annotating web pages.

Our ARARM algorithm assumes that all the RDF relations of interest could fit into the main memory. In fact, the maximum memory usage of our algorithm is proportional to the number of relations. When the number of

Table 9.8. Sample association rules obtained by ARARM and EMSR.

Examples of association rules discovered	Explanation	Domain axioms
<Terrorist, participate, Kidnapping>→ <Terrorist, useWeapon, AK-47> {support:0.166; confidence:0.817}	The rule reflects the heuristics of a domain axiom directly.	7
<Terrorist, useWeapon, AK-47>→ <Terrorist, participate, Kidnapping> {support:0.166; confidence:0.790}	The rule reflects the heuristics of a domain axiom indirectly.	7
<Terrorist, participate, Kidnapping>→ <Terrorist, useWeapon, Gun> {support:0.168; confidence:0.827}	The rule is a generalized form of a domain axiom.	7
<Terrorist, useWeapon, PlasticBomb>→ <Terrorist, participate, Robbery> {support:0.251; confidence:0.916}	The rule reflects the interaction of two or more domain axioms.	2, 6
<terroristA, participate,TerroristActivity>→ <terroristA, useWeapon, Weapon>{support:0.051; confidence:0.809}	The rule is generated due to spurious events. The support for this type of rule is usually very low.	

relations is extremely large, an optimization strategy should be developed to maintain the efficiency of the AR mining process.

For simplicity, we assume that the subjects and objects of the RDF statements in the document sets are in the form of RDF Unified Resource Identifier (URI), each referring to a term defined in a domain ontology. According to the RDF/RDFS specification [19, 20], an RDF statement could also include RDF literals and blank nodes. We will address these issues in our future work.

References

[1] Agrawal, R., T. Imielinski and A. Swami, 1993: Mining association rules between sets of items in large databases. *Proceedings of the ACM SIG-MOD International Conference on Management of Data*, 207–16.

[2] Agrawal, R., and R. Srikant, 1994: Fast algorithms for mining association rules. *Proceedings of the 20th International Conference in Very Large Databases*, 487–99.

[3] Braga, D., A. Campi, S. Ceri, M. Klemettinen and P.L. Lanzi, 2003: Discovering interesting information in XML data with association rules. *Proceedings of ACM Symposium on Applied Computing*, 450–4.

[4] Buchner, A. G., M. Baumgarten, M. D. Mulvenna, R. Bohm and S. S. Anand, 2000: Data mining and XML: Current and future issues. *Proceedings of International Conference on Web Information Systems Engineering 2000 IEEE,* **II**, 131–5.

[5] Cherif Latiri, Ch. and S. Ben Yahia, 2001: Generating implicit association rules from textual data. *Proceedings of ACS/IEEE International Conference on Computer Systems and Applications,* 137–43.

[6] Ding, L., K. Wilkinson, C. Sayer and H. Kuno, 2003: Application-specific schema design for storing large RDF datasets. *First International Workshop on Practical and Scalable Semantic Systems.*

[7] Ding, Q., K. Ricords and J. Lumpkin, 2003: Deriving general association rules from XML data. *Proceedings of International Conference on Software Engineering, Artificial Intelligence, Networking, and Parallel/Distributed Computing,* 348–52.

[8] Dorre, J., P. Gerstl and R. Seiffert, 1999: Text mining: Finding nuggets in mountains of textual data. *Proceedings of ACM SIGKDD International Conference on Knowledge Discovery and Data Mining,* 398-401.

[9] Han, J., and Y. Fu, 1995: Discovery of multi-level association rules from large databases. *Proceedings of the 21st International Conference in Very Large Databases,* 420–31.

[10] Han, J., J. Pei and Y. Yin, 2000: Mining frequent patterns without candidate generation. *Proceedings of the 2000 ACM-SIGMOD International Conference on Management of Data,* 1–12.

[11] Hilderman, R., J., and H. J. Hamilton, 1999: Knowledge discovery and interestingness measures: A survey. *Technical Report CS 99-04*, Department of Computer Science, University of Regina.

[12] Hipp, J., U. Guntzer and G. Nakaeizadeh, 2000: Algorithms for association rule mining: A general survey and comparison. *ACM SIGKDD Explorations,* **2(1)**, 58–64.

[13] Kodratoff, Y., 2001: Rating the interest of rules induced from data and within texts. *Proceedings of Database and Expert Systems Applications 12th International Conference,* 265–9.

[14] Lee, J.-W., K. Lee and W. Kim, 2001: Preparations for semantics-based XML mining. *Proceedings of 1st IEEE International Conference on Data Mining,* 345–52.

[15] Maedche, A., and V. Zacharias, 2002: Clustering ontology-based metadata in the semantic web. *Proceedings of the 6th European Conference on Principles and Practice of Knowledge Discovery in Databases,* 342–60.

[16] Pasquier, N., Y. Bastide, R. Taouil and L. Lakhal, 1998: Pruning closed itemset lattices for association rules. *Proceedings of the BDA French Conference on Advanced Databases,* 177–96.

[17] Srikant, R., and R. Agrawal, 1995: Mining generalized association rules. *Proceedings of the 21st International Conference in Very Large Databases,* 407–19.

[18] Tan, A.-H., 1999: Text mining: The state of the art and the challenges. *Proceedings of the Pacific Asia Conference on Knowledge Discovery and Data Mining PAKDD'99 workshop on Knowledge Discovery from Advanced Databases*, 65–70.

[19] W3C, RDF Specification. URL: `www.w3.org/RDF/`.

[20] W3C, RDF Schema Specification. URL: `www.w3.org/TR/rdf-schema/`.

[21] XML DOM Tutorial. URL: `www.w3schools.com/dom/default.asp`.

Image Retrieval using Visual Features and Relevance Feedback

Sanjoy Kumar Saha, Amit Kumar Das and Bhabatosh Chanda

Summary. The present paper describes the design and implementation of a novel CBIR system using a set of complex data that comes from completely different kinds of low-level visual features such as shape, texture and color. In the proposed system, a petal projection technique is used to extract the shape information of an object. To represent the texture of an image, a co-occurrence matrix of a texture pattern over a 2×2 block is proposed. A fuzzy index of color is suggested to measure the closeness of the image color to six major colors. Finally, a human-perception-based similarity measure is employed to retrieve images and its performance is established through rigorous experimentation. Performance of the system is enhanced through a novel relevance feedback scheme as evident from the experimental results. Performance of the system is compared with that of the others.

10.1 Introduction

Image search and retrieval has been a field of very active research since the 1970s and this field has observed an exponential growth in recent years as a result of unparalleled increase in the volume of digital images. This has led to the development and flourishing of *Content-based Image Retrieval* (CBIR) systems [12, 18, 34]. There are, in general, two fundamental modules in a CBIR system, visual feature extraction and retrieval engine. An image may be considered as the integrated representation of a large volume of complex information. Spatial and spectral distribution of image data or pixel values together carry some complex visual information. Thus visual feature extraction is crucial to any CBIR scheme, since it annotates the image automatically using its contents. Secondly, these visual features may be completely different from one another suggesting complex relations among them inherent in the image. So the retrieval engine handles all such complex data and retrieves the images using some sort of similarity measure. Quality of retrieval can be improved deploying the relevance feedback scheme. Proper indexing improves efficiency of the system considerably.

Visual features may be classified into two broad categories: *high-level features* and *low-level features*. High-level features mostly involve semantics of the region(s) as well as that of the entire image. On the other hand, low-level features are more elementary and general and are computed from pixel values. In this work, we confine ourselves to extraction of low-level features only. *Shape, texture* and *color* are three main independent groups of low-level features that are used in CBIR systems.

Most of the CBIR systems measure shape features either by *geometric moments* or by *Fourier descriptor* [4, 38] methods. Hu [14] suggested seven moment invariants by combining raw geometric moments. Teh and Chin [53] studied various types of moments and their capabilities for characterizing visual patterns. Fourier descriptor methods use as shape features the coefficients obtained by Fourier transformation of object boundaries [35]. Other methods proposed for shape matching include features like *area, perimeter, convexity, aspect ratio, circularity* and *elongatedness* [4, 38]. Elastic deformation of templates [3], comparison of directional histograms of edges [17], skeletal representation [20] and polygonal approximation [42] of shapes are also used.

Texture is another feature that has been extensively explored by various research groups. Texture features are measured using either a signal processing or statistical model [28] or a human perception model [52]. In [13], Haralick *et al.* proposed the *co-occurrence matrix* representation of texture features. Many researchers have used wavelets [2, 27] and their variants to extract appropriate texture features. Gabor Filters [9] and fractal dimensions [19] are also used as a measure of the texture property.

Another widely used visual feature for CBIR is color. The main advantage of this feature is its invariance to size, position, orientation and arrangements of the objects. On the other hand, the disadvantage is its immense variation within a single image. In CBIR systems, a color histogram is most commonly used for representing color features. Various color similarity measures based on histogram intersection have been reported [50, 51]. Other than color histogram, color layout vectors [24], color correlograms [16], color coherence vectors [7], color sets [47] and color moments [22, 56] are also commonly used.

The retrieval engine is responsible for finding the set of similar images from the database against a query on the basis of certain similarity measures on the feature set. It is evident from the literature that various distance/similarity measures have been adopted by CBIR systems. Mukherjee *et al.* [31] have used template matching for shape-based retrieval. A number of systems [29, 33, 49] have used Euclidean distance (weighted or unweighted) for matching. Other schemes include the Minkowski metric [9], self-organizing maps [22], proportional transportation distance [55], the CSS matching algorithm [30], etc. For matching multivalued features such as a color histogram or texture matrix, a variety of distance measures are deployed by different systems. They include schemes like quadratic form distance [33], Jaccard's co-efficient [23], L1 distance [2, 7, 21], histogram intersection [11], etc. The details on combining the distance of various types of features is not available. But, it is clear that Euclidean distance is the most widely used similarity measure.

The quality of retrieved images can be improved through a relevance feedback mechanism. As the importance of the features varies for different queries and applications, to achieve better performance, different emphases have to be given to different features and the concept of relevance feedback (RF) comes into the picture. Relevance feedback, originally developed in [54], is a learning mechanism to improve the effectiveness of information retrieval systems. For a given query, the CBIR system retrieves a set of images according to a predefined similarity measure. Then, the user provides feedback by marking the retrieved images as relevant to the query or not. Based on the feedback, the system takes action and retrieves a new set. The classical RF schemes can be classified into two categories: query point movement (query refinement) and re-weighting (similarity measure refinement) [37, 41]. The query point movement method tries to improve the estimate of the ideal query point by moving it towards the relevant examples and away from bad ones. Rocchio's formula [37] is frequently used to improve the estimation iteratively. In [15], a composite query is created based on relevant and irrelevant images. Various systems like WebSEEk [46], Quicklook [5], iPURE [1] and Drawsearch [44] have adopted the query refinement principle. In the re-weighting method, the weight of the feature that helps in retrieving the relevant images is enhanced and the importance of the feature that hinders this process is reduced. Rui *et al.* [39] and Squire *et al.* [48] have proposed weight adjustment techniques based on the variance of the feature values. Systems like ImageRover [45] and RETIN [9] use a re-weighting technique.

Here in this paper we have given emphasis to the extraction of shape, texture and color features which together form a complex data set as they bear diverse kinds of information. A human-perception-based similarity measure and a novel relevance feedback scheme are designed and implemented to achieve the goal. This paper is organised as follows. Section 10.2 deals with the computation of features. Section 10.3 describes a new similarity measure based on human perception. A relevance feedback scheme based on the Mann-Whitney test has been elaborated in Section 10.4. Results and discussions are given in Section 10.5 followed by the concluding remarks in Section 10.6.

10.2 Computation of Features

The images we usually deal with may be classified into two groups: one consists of photos of our friends, relatives, leaders, monuments, articles of interest, etc. and the other group consists of landscape, outdoor scenery, pictures of crowds, etc. Our present system works on the images of the first group where images consist of only one dominant object, and other objects are less emphasized in the shot. We apply a fast and automatic segmentation method to extract the

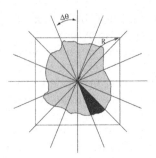

Fig. 10.1. Petal projection.

desired object [40]. All the visual features are then computed on the segmented region of interest.

10.2.1 Shape Features

Fourier descriptors and moment invariants are the two widely used shape features. In the case of Fourier descriptors, data is transformed to a completely different domain where co-coefficients may not have direct correlation with the shape perception except whether the boundary is smooth or rough, etc. They do not, in general, straightaway indicate properties like symmetry or concavity. This is also true for higher-order moments. Moreover, moments of different order vary so widely that it becomes difficult to balance their effects on distance measures. These observations have led us to look for different shape descriptors.

It is known that projection signatures retain the shape information, which is confirmed by the existence of image reconstruction algorithms from projection data [38]. Horizontal and vertical projection of image gray levels are already used in image retrieval [36]. In this work we propose petal projection which explicitly reveals the symmetricity, circularity, concavity and aspect ratio.

Petal Projection
After segmentation the object is divided into a number of petals where a petal is an angular strip originating from the center of gravity as shown in Figure 10.1. The area of the object lying within a petal is taken as the projection along it. Thus, S_{θ_i}, the projection on the ith petal can be represented as:

$$S_{\theta_i} = \int_{\theta_i}^{\theta_i + \triangle \theta} \int_{r=0}^{R} f(r, \theta) dr d\theta \qquad (10.1)$$

where, $f(r, \theta)$ represents the segmented object, R is greater than or equal to the radius of the minimum bounding circle, $\triangle \theta = \theta_{i+1} - \theta_i$ is the angular width of the petal and the ith petal lies within the angle θ_i to $\theta_i + \triangle \theta$.

In order to make the projection size invariant we consider the normalised values of S_{θ_i} so that $\sum_i S_{\theta_i}$ becomes 1. Thus, an n-dimensional vector $(S_{\theta_0}, S_{\theta_1}, \ldots S_{\theta_{n-1}})$ is obtained by taking the projection on n petals (note that n should be even). As the projections are taken from the center of gravity, the dimension of the vector can be reduced to $n/2$ and it becomes $(s_{\theta_0}, s_{\theta_1}, \ldots s_{\theta_{n/2-1}})$, where $s_{\theta_i} = (S_{\theta_i} + S_{\theta_i+180})/2$.

The vector thus obtained is scale and translation invariant. To make it rotation invariant, a cyclic shift on the data set is applied. Through successive cyclic shifts $n/2$ different cases are obtained. For each case, a plot of s_{θ_i} versus i is made (conceptually). The set of discrete points in each plot is approximated by a straight line using the least square regression technique. To make it flip invariant, projection data are considered in reverse order too. The case for which the slope of the line takes maximum value is considered and the corresponding data set forms the actual $n/2$ dimensional petal projection vector. Along with the vector, the slope and error which indicate *bulging* and *smoothness of boundary*, respectively are also used as two features. Now, using the petal projection, symmetricity, circularity, aspect ratio and concavity can be measured based on $S_{\theta_m} = max\{S_{\theta_i}\}$ as follows.

Linear symmetricity: It can be measured from the projection vector $(S_{\theta_0}, S_{\theta_1}, \ldots S_{\theta_{n-1}})$ and expressed as:

$$Symmetry = \frac{1}{n} \sum_{k=1}^{n/2} \mid S_{\theta_{(m+n-k) \bmod n}} - S_{\theta_{(m+k-1) \bmod n}} \mid \qquad (10.2)$$

For a perfectly symmetric object, the value is zero and it gives a positive value for an asymmetric one.

Circularity: It can be expressed as:

$$Circularity = \frac{1}{n} \sum_{i=0}^{n/2-1} \mid s_{\theta_m} - s_{\theta_i} \mid \qquad (10.3)$$

For a perfectly circular object it gives zero and a positive value otherwise.

Aspect ratio: In order to compute the aspect ratio, s_{θ_m} is obtained first. Then p_{θ_i}, the projection of s_{θ_i} along the direction orthogonal to θ_m is computed for all s_{θ_i} other than s_{θ_m}. Finally, the aspect ratio can be represented as:

$$Asp.Ratio = \frac{s_{\theta_m}}{max\{p_{\theta_i}\}} \qquad (10.4)$$

Concavity: Consider the the triangle BOA as shown in Figure 10.2. Suppose OC of length r is the angular bisector of $\angle BOA$. The point c is said to be a concave point with respect to $\overline{AB}$ if

$$r < \frac{r_a.r_b}{(r_a + r_b)2cos2\alpha}$$

Hence, C_i, the concavity due to the ith petal zone can be obtained as

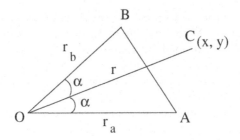

Fig. 10.2. Concavity measure.

$$C_i = \begin{cases} 0; & \text{if } s_{\theta_i} \geq \frac{s_{\theta_{i+1}} \times s_{\theta_{i-1}}}{(s_{\theta_{i+1}}+s_{\theta_{i-1}}) \times 2cos2\triangle\theta} \\ \frac{s_{\theta_{i+1}} \times s_{\theta_{i-1}}}{(s_{\theta_{i+1}}+s_{\theta_{i-1}}) \times 2cos2\triangle\theta} - s_{\theta_i}; & \text{otherwise} \end{cases}$$

Thus

$$Concavity = \sum_{i=0}^{n/2-1} C_i \qquad (10.5)$$

can act as the measure for concavity.

Supplementary Features

Petal-projection-based measures of shape features are very effective when $\triangle\theta$ is sufficiently small. However, since the mathematical formulation for measuring the shape features available in the literature, including the proposed ones, are based on intuition and heuristics, it is observed that more features usually improves performance of the system particularly for a wide variety of images. For this reason, similar types of shape features may also be computed in a different manner as described next. These supplementary features improve the performance by about 2 to 3% and do not call for much extra computation.

Three different measures for circularity, C_i, (see Figure 10.3a) are defined and computed as follows:

$$C_1 = (object\ area)/(\pi\ D^2/4)$$
$$C_2 = \frac{Length\ of\ the\ object\ boundary}{\pi D + length\ of\ the\ object\ boundary}$$
$$C_3 = (2 \times min\{r_i\})/D$$

where D is the diameter of the smallest circle enclosing the object and r_i is same as S_{θ_i} for very small $\triangle\theta$. D can be determined by taking projections of r_is along θ_m.

To compute the aspect ratio the principal axis (PA) and the axis orthogonal to it (OA) are obtained first [38] using r_i. Two different aspect ratio, AR_i features (see Figure 10.3b) are computed as

$$AR_1 = OA\ length/PA\ length$$
$$AR_2 = Median\ of\{OL_i\}/median\ of\{PL_i\}$$

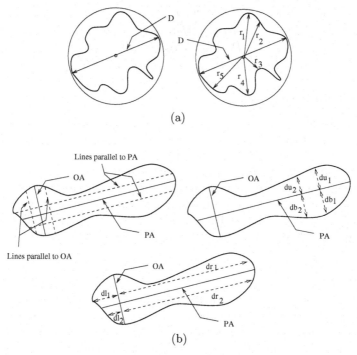

(a)

(b)

Fig. 10.3. Computing (a) circularity and (b) aspect ratio.

where the length of the lines parallel to PA (or OA) forms $\{PL_i\}$ ($\{OL_i\}$).

Symmetricity (see Figure 10.3b) about various axes are measured in the following way.

$$Symmetricity\ about\ PA = \frac{1}{n}\sum_{i=1}^{n}\frac{du_i - db_i}{du_i + db_i}$$

where n denotes the number of pixels on PA. Similarly;

$$Symmetricity\ about\ OA = \frac{1}{m}\sum_{i=1}^{m}\frac{dl_i - dr_i}{dl_i + dr_i}$$

where m denotes the number of pixels on OA. Note that du_i and db_i are the lengths of line segments parallel to OA drawn on either side of PA from the ith pixel on PA. dl_i and dr_i can be defined in a similar way. Here again, du_i (or db_i) and dl_i (dr_i) may be obtained by taking projections of S_{θ_i} along OA and PA respectively for very small $\Delta\theta$. However, we have implemented it by pixel counting along the lines.

The convex hull of the object is obtained first and then the concavity features (Con_i) are computed as follows:

$$Con_1 = \frac{Object\ area}{Area\ of\ the\ convex\ hull}$$
$$Con_2 = \frac{Perimeter\ of\ the\ convex\ hull}{Perimeter\ of\ the\ object}$$

10.2.2 Texture Feature

By the term "texture" we mean, in general, roughness or coarseness of the object surface. Texture is an innate property of virtually all object surfaces, including fabric, bark, water ripple, brick, skin, etc. In satellite images texture of a region can distinguish among grassland, beach, water body, urban area, etc. In an intensity image, texture puts its signature as the variation in intensity from pixel to pixel. Usually a small patch is required to feel or measure a local texture value. The smallest region for such a purpose could be a 2×2 block. Based on this idea, we propose a texture co-occurrence matrix for texture representation.

Texture Co-occurrence Matrix
Computation of the texture co-occurrence matrix is carried on with the intensity of image. As mentioned above, an image is divided into blocks of size 2×2 pixels. Then the gray-level pattern of the block is converted to a binary pattern by thresholding at the average value of the intensities. This operation is same as the method of obtaining the binary pattern in the case of block truncation coding [8]. The 2×2 binary pattern obtained this way provides an idea of distribution of high and low intensities or, in other words, the kind of local texture within the block.

By arranging this pattern in raster order, a binary string is formed. It is considered as the gray code and the corresponding decimal equivalent is its texture value. Thus, by virtue of the gray code, blocks with similar texture are expected to have closer values.

	(a)	(b)	(c)	(d)	(e)
Intensity Block	20 22 8 7	9 19 11 20	17 11 18 9	20 7 6 23	8 7 6 8
Binary Pattern	1 1 0 0	0 1 0 1	1 0 1 0	1 0 0 1	1 0 0 1
Gray Code	1100	0101	1010	1001	1001
Texture value	8	6	12	14	14

Fig. 10.4. Blocks and texture values.

Some examples of blocks and corresponding texture values are shown in Figure 10.4. Thus we get 15 such texture values since a block of all 1s does

Fig. 10.5. An image and corresponding texture image.

not occur. A problem of this approach is that a smooth intensity block (see Figure 10.4e) and a coarse textured block (see Figure 10.4d) may produce same binary pattern and, hence, the same texture value. To surmount this problem we define a smooth block as having an intensity variance less than a small threshold. In our experiment, the threshold is 0.0025 of the average intensity variance computed over all the blocks. All such smooth blocks have texture value 0. Thus we get the scaled (both in space and value) image whose height and width are half of that of the original image and the pixel values range from 0 to 15 except 10 (all 1 combination). This new image may be considered as the image representing the texture of the original image (see Figure 10.5).

Finally, considering left-to-right and top-to-bottom directions, the co-occurence matrix of size 15 × 15 is computed from this texture image. To make this matrix translation invariant the 2 × 2 block frames are shifted by one pixel horizontally and vertically. For each case, the co-occurence matrix is computed. To make the measure flip invariant, co-occurence matrices are also computed for the mirrored image. Thus, we have sixteen such matrices. Then, we take the element-wise average of all the matrices and normalize them to obtain the final one. In the case of landscape, this is computed over the whole image; while in the case of an image containing dominant object(s) the texture feature is computed over the segmented region(s) of interest only.

The texture co-occurrence matrix provides the detailed description of the image texture, but handling of such multivalued features is always difficult, particularly in the context of indexing and comparison cost. Hence, to obtain more perceivable features, statistical measures like entropy, energy and texture moments [13] are computed based on this matrix. We have considered moments up to order 4 as the higher orders are not perceivable. The use of gray code has enabled us to measure homogeneity and variation in texture.

10.2.3 Color Feature

It is quite common to use a 3-D color histogram of an image as its color feature. However, one important issue is to decide about the color space to use. Lim and Lu [25] have suggested that among various color models, the HSV (Hue, Saturation, Value) model is most effective for CBIR applications and is less sensitive to quantization. Hence, in our system, the color feature is computed based on the HSV model. As, H controls the luminance, it has more impact on the perception of color and we have used a fuzzy index of color based on hue histogram to improve the performance of the system.

Color is represented using the HSV model. A hue histogram is formed. The hue histogram thus obtained can not be used directly to search for similar images. As an example, a red image and an almost red image (with similar contents) are visually similar but their hue histogram may differ. Hence, to compute the color features the hue histogram is first smoothed with a Gaussian kernel and normalized. Then, for each of the six major colors (red, yellow, green, blue, cyan and magenta), an index of fuzziness is computed as follows.

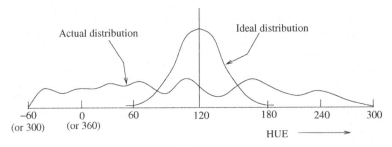

Fig. 10.6. Computation of Bhattacharya distance.

It is assumed that in the ideal case for an image with one dominant color of hue h, the hue histogram would follow the Gaussian distribution $p(i)$ with mean h and standard deviation, say, σ. In our experiment we have chosen $\sigma = 20$ so that 99% of the population falls within $h-60$ to $h+60$. Figure 10.6 shows the ideal distribution for $h = 120$ and actual hue distribution of an image. The Bhattacharya distance [10], d_h, between the actual distribution $p_a(i)$ and this ideal one $p(i)$ indicates the closeness of the image color to hue h, where $d_h = \sum_i \sqrt{p(i)p_a(i)}$. Therefore, d_h gives a measure of similarity between two distributions. Finally, an S-function [26] maps d_h to fuzzy membership $F(h)$ where

$$F(h) = \frac{1}{1 + e^{-\theta(d_h - 0.5)}}$$

For $h = 0, 60, 120, \ldots$ membership values corresponding to red, yellow, green etc. are obtained. In our experiment θ is taken as 15.

10.3 Human-Perception-Based Similarity Measure

In the previous section we have suggested some formulae to compute visual features from pixel values. The collection of features (often referred to as the feature vector) thus formed conveys, to some extent, the visual appearance of the image in quantitative terms. Image retrieval engines compare the feature vector of the query image with those of the database images and presents to the users the images of highest similarity (i.e., least distance) in order as the retrieved images. However, it must be noted that this collection is highly complex as its elements carry different kinds of information, shape, texture and color, which are mutually independent. Hence, they should be handled differently as suited to their nature. In other words, if there are n features altogether, one should not consider the collection as a point in n-dimensional space and apply a single distance measure to find similarity between two such collections. For example, in the set of shape features, circularity indicates a particular appearance of the object. If the object in the query image is circular, then objects present in the retrieved images must be circular. If those objects are not circular the images are rejected; it does not matter whether the objects of those rejected images are triangular or oblong or something else. Simply speaking, two images are considered to be similar in terms of circularity, if their circularity feature exceeds a predefined threshold. It may be observed that almost every shape feature presented in this work, as well as in the literature, usually carries some information about the appearance of the object independently. On the other hand, texture features as mentioned in the previous section together represent the type of texture of the object surface, and none of them can represent the coarseness or periodicity independently. Hence, a distance function comprising all the texture features can be used to determine the similarity between two images. Color features like redness, greenness etc. convey, in some sense, the amount of a particular color and its associated color present in the image. However, they are not as independent as the shape features (circularity, convexity etc.). Secondly, these features are represented in terms of a fuzzy index which are compared (a logical operation) to find similarity between two images. Thus, it is understandable that though these features together annotate an image, they are not in the same scale of unit nor they are evenly interpretable. Moreover, it is very difficult to find out the correlations hidden among the various features, color and texture features especially. On the other hand, there are strong implications in the retrieval of similar images against a query. As the similarity (distance) measure establishes the association between the query image and the corresponding retrieved images based on these features only, it becomes the major issue.

The early work shows that most of the schemes deal with Euclidean distance, which has a number of disadvantages. One pertinent question is how to combine the distance of multiple features. Berman and Shapiro [2] proposed the following operations to deal with the problem:

$$Addition : \ distance \ = \ \sum_i d_i \qquad (10.6)$$

where d_i is the Euclidean distance of the ith features of the images being compared. This operation may declare visually similar images as dissimilar due to the mismatch of only a few features. The effect will be further pronounced if the mismatched features are sensitive enough even for a minor dissimilarity. The situation may be improved by using

$$Weighted\ Sum: \ distance \ = \ \sum_i c_i d_i \qquad (10.7)$$

where c_i is the weight for the Euclidean distance of ith feature. The problem with this measure is that selection of the proper weight is again a difficult proposition. One plausible solution could be taking c_i as some sort of reciprocal of the variance of the ith feature. An alternative measure could be

$$Max: \ distance \ = \ Max(d_1, d_2, \ldots, d_n) \qquad (10.8)$$

It indicates that similar images will have all their features lying within a range. It suffers from similar problems as the addition method. On the other hand, the following measure

$$Min: \ distance \ = \ Min(d_1, d_2, \ldots, d_n) \qquad (10.9)$$

helps in finding images which have at least one feature within a specified threshold. The effect of all other features are thereby ignored and the measure becomes heavily biased. Hence, it is clear that for high-dimensional data, Euclidean distance-based neighbor searching can not do justice to the problem. This observation motivates us to develop a new distance-measuring scheme.

A careful investigation of a large group of perceptually similar images reveals that similarity between two images is not usually judged by all possible attributes. Which means visually similar images may be dissimilar in terms of some features as shown in Figures 10.7, 10.8 and 10.9.

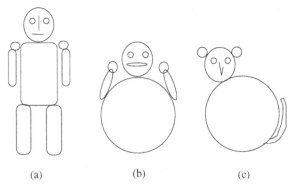

(a)   (b)   (c)

Fig. 10.7. Figure shows similar images: (a) and (b) are symmetric but differ in circularity; whereas (b) and (c) are similar in circularity but differ in symmetricity.

Fig. 10.8. Figures show similar textured objects with different shapes.

Fig. 10.9. Figures show similar shapes with different textures.

It leads us to propose that if k out of n features of two images match then they are considered similar. A low value of k will make the measurement too liberal and a high value may make the decision very conservative. Depending on the composition of the database, the value of k can be tuned.

Distance or range-based search basically looks into a region for similar images. In the case of Euclidean distance as defined in Equation (10.6) the region is a hypersphere. Weighted Euclidean distance as given by Equation (10.7) results in a hyperellipsoid. Equation (10.8) suggests a hypercube. While in range, the search region is hypercuboid. Our proposed similarity measure, i.e., matching k features out of n features leads to a star-shaped region. Figure 10.10 shows some examples of such regions. When $k = n$ we arrive at the region defined by Equation (10.8), and that defined by Equation (10.9) if $k = 1$. Hence, our similarity measure is much more generalized and flexible.

Now, the question is how to measure whether a feature of two images matches or not. If the Euclidean distance of features is considered, then sensitivity of the different features poses a problem. The same distance corresponding to a different set of features may not reflect the same quantity of

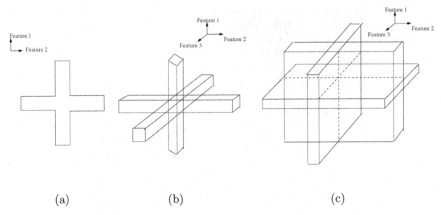

(a)   (b)   (c)

Fig. 10.10. Search regions for (a) 1 out of 2; (b) 2 out of 3; (c) 1 out of 3.

dissimilarity. Secondly, in the beginning of the section we mentioned that the collection of the features is of complex nature as they carry different kinds of information and are to be treated differently, appropriate to their characteristics. To cope with this problem, we propose the following scheme to map real feature values to character-based tag. The mapping algorithm is as follows:

Assume n is the number of features, N is the number of images in the database and D is the number of divisions into which each feature range will be divided.

for i $= 1$ to n do
begin
Divide the entire range of i-th feature values into D divisions.
Sort the i-th feature values in ascending order.
For all the feature values belonging to the topmost division, set the i-th
    feature tag $=$ "A", for the feature values belonging to next division the
    corresponding value is "B" and so on.
end

The divisions may be imposed based on absolute values, percentiles or some other criterion. Thus the n dimensional feature vector is converted into a tag consisting of n characters. For example, if $n = 8$ and $D = 10$, then a tag may look like ADGACBIH. The same division thresholds are used to generate a tag for the query image.

When we perform a query on the database on the basis of Euclidean distance, nearest neighbors are searched in the hypercube/hypersphere domain. Basically, for each feature, images within a value range participate. When characters representing the feature values are compared to check their proximity in our scheme, it also deals with a range. The differences are that there is no floating point operation and that the sensitivity factor of different features are also reduced as their ordered grades are considered instead of their absolute values. To avoid the boundary problem, at the time of comparing neighboring groups may be considered by setting a tolerance range t. As the tags represent the ordered grades based on the actual numerical values, these can be used to implement range search, comparison of linguistic terms, and thresholded comparison straightaway.

Thus in the proposed scheme, similarity between two images is measured by matching corresponding features or subsets of features based on the criteria suitable to them rather than using a single distance measure considering all the features. A counter, initially set to zero, is increased if a feature is matched and similarity is declared by comparing the count with k. The retrieved images may be ordered based on this count for top-order retrieval.

10.4 Relevance Feedback Scheme

In the previous section, the difficulty in finding the correlation among the features has been mentioned. To cope with this problem, the concept of relevance feedback can be used. Once a set of images is retrieved, they may be marked as relevant or irrelevant. This information can be used for discovering the relations and for refining the association of the features with the query as well as the retrieved images. Accordingly, the similarity measure can be refined for better performance.

In the proposed relevance feedback (RF) scheme, the distance (similarity) measure is refined by updating the emphasis of the useful features. The term *useful feature* means features capable of discriminating relevant and irrelevant images within the retrieved set. The most crucial issue is to identify the useful features. Once, it is done then the question arises how to adjust the emphasis.

10.4.1 Identification of Useful Features

A close study of past work indicates that a re-weighting technique is widely used for relevance feedback. But most of the systems address how to update the weight without identifying the good features. In this paper, we present an RF scheme that first identifies the useful features following a non-parametric statistical approach and then updates their weights.

Useful features are identified using the Mann-Whitney test. In a two-sample situation where two samples are taken from different populations, the Mann-Whitney test is used to determine whether the null hypothesis that the two populations are identical can be rejected or not.

Let, $X_1, X_2, \ldots, X_n$ be random samples of size n from population-1 and $Y_1, Y_2, \ldots, Y_m$ be random samples of size m from population-2. The Mann-Whitney test determines whether X and Y come from the same population or not. It proceeds as follows [6]. X and Y are combined to form a single ordered sample set and ranks 1 to $n+m$ are assigned to the observations from smallest to largest. In case of a tie (i.e. if the sample values are equal), the average of the ranks that would have been assigned in the case of no ties, are assigned. Based on the ranks, a test statistic is generated to check the null hypothesis. If the value of the test statistic falls within the critical region then the null hypothesis is rejected. Otherwise, it is accepted.

In CBIR systems, a set of images are retrieved according to a similarity measure. Then feedback is taken from the user to identify the relevant and irrelevant outcomes. For the time being, let us consider only the jth feature and $X_i = dist(Q_j, f_{ij})$, where Q_j is the jth feature of the query image and f_{ij} is the jth feature of the ith relevant image retrieved by the process. Similarly, $Y_i = dist(Q_j, f'_{ij})$ where f'_{ij} is the jth feature of ith irrelevant image. Thus, X_i and Y_i form the different random samples. Then, the Mann-Whitney test is applied to judge the discriminating power of the jth feature. Let $F(x)$ and $G(x)$ be the distribution functions corresponding to X and Y respectively. The null hypothesis, H_0, and alternate hypothesis, H_1, may be stated as follows: H_0: The jth feature cannot discriminate X and Y (X and Y come from same population) i.e.,
$$F(x) = G(x) \text{ for all x.}$$
H_1: The jth feature can discriminate X and Y (X and Y come from different population) i.e.,
$$F(x) \neq G(x) \text{ for some x.}$$
It becomes a two-tailed test Because, H_0 is rejected for any of the two cases: $F(x) < G(x)$ and $F(x) > G(x)$.

It can be understood that a useful feature can separate the two sets and X may be followed by Y or Y may be followed by X in the combined ordered list. Thus, if H_0 is rejected then the jth feature is taken to be a useful feature. The steps are as follows:

1. Combine X and Y to form a single sample of size N, where $N = n + m$.
2. Arrange them in ascending order
3. Assign a rank starting from 1. If required, resolve ties.
4. Compute the test statistic, T, as follows.

$$T = \frac{\sum_{i=1}^{n} R(X_i) - n \times \frac{N+1}{2}}{\sqrt{\frac{nm}{N(N-1)} \sum_{i=1}^{N} R_i^2 - \frac{nm(N+1)^2}{4(N-1)}}}$$

where $R(X_i)$ denotes the rank assigned to X_i and $\sum R_i^2$ denotes the sum of the squares of the ranks of all X and Y.

5. If the value of T falls within the critical region then H_0 is rejected and the jth feature is considered useful otherwise it is not.

The critical region depends on the level of significance α which denotes the maximum probability of rejecting a true H_0. If T is less than its $\alpha/2$ quantile or greater than its $1 - \alpha/2$ quantile then H_0 is rejected. In our experiment, the distribution of T is assumed to be normal and α is taken as 0.1. If the concerned feature discriminates and places the relevant images at the beginning of the combined ordered list, then T will fall within the lower critical region. On the other hand, if the concerned feature discriminates and places the relevant images at the end of the same list then T will fall within the upper critical region.

It may be noted that, the proposed work proceeds only if the retrieved set contains both relevant and irrelevant images. Otherwise, samples from two different populations will not be available and no feedback mechanism can be adopted.

10.4.2 Adjustment of the Emphasis of Features

Adjustment of the emphasis of features is closely related with the distance/similarity measure adopted by the system. In the current work we have adopted a human-perception-based similarity measure. However, for easy understanding we first present an emphasis adjustment scheme for Euclidean distance. Subsequently we will transfer the idea to the perception-based similarity measure.

Euclidean distance is a widely used metric for CBIR systems. If an image is described by M features, the distance between two images can be expressed as $\sum_{j=1}^{M} w_j d_j$ where d_j denotes the Euclidean distance between them with respect to the jth feature and w_j is the weight assigned to the feature.

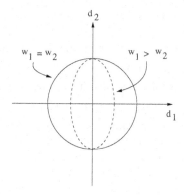

Fig. 10.11. Variation of search space with the weights of the features.

In the proposed scheme, w_j is adjusted only if the jth feature is useful. To explain the strategy for adjustment of the weights of the features, let us consider a system that relies on two features only, say, f_1 and f_2. The difference in feature values between the query image and the database image are d_1 and d_2. With $w_1 = w_2$, the search space corresponding to Euclidean distance is a circle (as shown in Figure 10.11 by the solid line). Now suppose f_1 is a useful feature such that the test statistic of d_1 lies in the lower critical region. That means f_1 can discriminate between relevant and irrelevant images and the d_1 of a relevant image is, in general, less than the d_1 of an irrelevant image. By making $w_1 > w_2$, the search space is changed to an ellipse (as shown in Figure 10.11 by the dashed line) and thereby discarding irrelevant images as much as possible from the retrieved set. Similarly, if f_1 is a useful feature and the test statistic of d_1 lies in the upper critical region then the d_1 of relevant images are, in general, greater than ithe d_1 of irrelevant images. Hence, by making $w_1 < w_2$, more relevant images can be included in the retrieved set. Thus by increasing the weight of the useful feature with the lower test statistic, we try to exclude the irrelevant images from the retrieved set. On the other hand, by decreasing the weight of the useful feature with the higher test statistic, we try to include the relevant images in the retrieved set.

Once images are retrieved, feedback is taken from the user and useful features are identified. Finally, weight adjustment is done according to the following steps:

1. Initialize all w_j to 1.
2. For each jth useful feature where the test statistic falls within the lower critical region, set w_j as follows:

$$w_j = w_j + \sigma_x^2$$

where σ_x^2 is the variance of X.
3. For each jth useful feature where the test statistic falls within the upper critical region, set w_j as follows:

$$\text{if } w_j > \sigma_x^2 \text{ then } w_j = w_j - \sigma_x^2$$

where σ_x^2 is the variance of X.
4. Repeat steps 2 and 3 for successive iterations.

In the case of the human-perception-based similarity measure, features are identified following the same technique. But the adjustment of emphasis of a feature is addressed in a slightly different manner. In this method, whether or not an image would be retrieved is decided by the count of matched features with the query image. Hence, updating the emphasis of a feature must have a direct impact on feature matching, so that irrelevant images are excluded and relevant ones are included by deploying the user feedback. It can be achieved by changing the match tolerance or threshold for the useful features. The basic principle is similar to the Euclidean distance-based search. When similar images lie in the close vicinity of the query image in terms of the useful features i.e. the test statistic falls within the lower critical region, in that case tolerance is reduced to restrict the inclusion of irrelevant images. The situation is reversed for useful features with the test statistic falling in the upper critical region. In that case, the similar images are lying in the distant buckets. Thus, to increase the possibility of inclusion of similar images, the match tolerance is increased. The steps are as follows:

1. Initialize the tolerance for all features to t.

2. For all jth useful features with the test statistic in the lower critical region set, $tolerance_j = tolerance_j - 1$.
If $tolerance_j <$ MIN then $tolerance_j =$ MIN.
3. For all jth useful features with the test statistic in the upper critical region set, $tolerance_j = tolerance_j + 1$.
If $tolerance_j >$ MAX then $tolerance_j =$ MAX.
4. Repeat steps 2 and 3 for successive iterations.

MIN and MAX denote the minimum and maximum possible tolerance values. In our experiment, we have considered t as 2, MIN as 0 and MAX as $B - 1$ where B is the number of buckets in the feature space.

10.5 Results and Discussion

In our experiment, we used two databases. The first one, referred to as our database, consists of around 2000 images. Each of these images has only one dominant object. The database was prepared by taking some images from the Corel database and downloading some thumbnails from the Internet. The database was "groundtruthed" manually. It consists of five distinct categories of images (car, airplane, flower, animal and fish) and for each category there is a large variety of examples. So we use this database for controlled experiments. The second database is the well-known COIL-100 database from Columbia University which consists of 7200 images of 100 different objects. For each object, 72 images are taken by rotating it at an interval of 5 degrees. A retrieved image is considered relevant if it is an instances of the same category of object as the query image.

Table 10.1. Comparison of precision (in %) using shape features.

No. of retrieved images	using shape features				using shape and texture features			
	Our database		COIL-100 database		Our database		COIL-100 database	
	Our system	Prasad system	Our system	Prasad system	Our system	Sciascio system	Our system	Sciascio system
10	64.74	56.63	58.14	36.62	73.62	70.24	66.84	60.72
20	59.49	53.78	48.77	32.32	68.26	64.81	57.01	50.68
50	52.98	49.10	36.54	25.58	64.10	60.96	43.46	36.76

Each image is described by 47 features of which 23 are the shape features, 18 denote texture and remaining six are fuzzy indexes of six major colors. To measure the retrieval performance, all the database images have been used as query images. As Euclidean distance is the most widely used similarity measure for CBIR systems, we used it to study the performance of the proposed

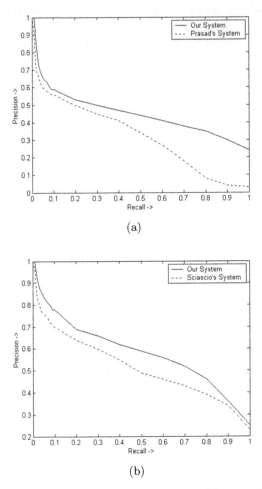

(a)

(b)

Fig. 10.12. Recall–precision graphs for our database (a) using shape features and (b) using shape and texture features.

features. Finally, we carried out our experiment using the perception-based similarity measure. An exhaustive search was made on the entire database. To compare the performance of the proposed shape features, we implemented the shape feature proposed by Prasad *et al.* [36]. We also implemented the Hough-transform based features, proposed by Sciascio and Celentano, [43], which take care of shape and texture. In the experiment using our database, the recall–precision graphs in Figure 10.12 and Table 10.1 show that the performance of the proposed features is better. The same result is also established when the experiments are carried out on the COIL-100 database. It is evident in the recall–precision graphs in Figure 10.13 and in Table 10.1. Table 10.2 and the recall–precision graphs of Figure 10.14 show the performance of the proposed system for various types of features using the two databases. Some sample results are shown in Figures 10.15 and 10.16 for our database and the COIL-100 database respectively.

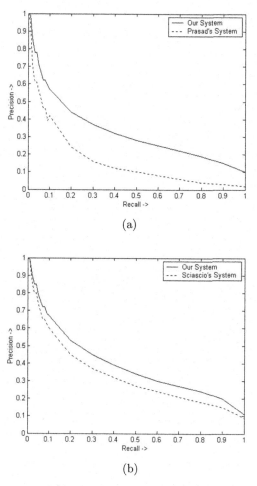

(a)

(b)

Fig. 10.13. Recall–precision graphs for the COIL-100 database (a) using shape features and (b) using shape and texture features.

In order to check the capability of the proposed human-perception-based similarity measure, the experiment is carried on using both the databases. In order to deal with our database, each feature space is divided into 10 buckets and k is taken as 35. For the COIL-100 database, the corresponding values are 20 and 30 respectively. In both the cases, t, the tolerance for matching the character tag is taken as 2. In the case of retrieval using the perception-based-

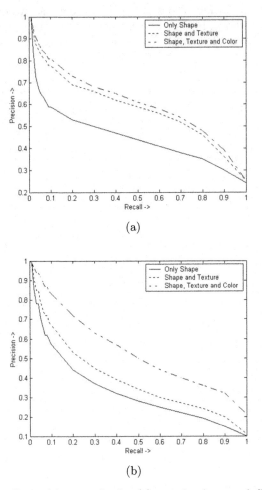

(a)

(b)

Fig. 10.14. Recall–precision graphs for (a) our database and (b) the COIL-100 database.

Table 10.2. Precision (in %) of the proposed system.

No. of retrieved images	Our database				COIL-100 database		
	Only Shape Petal	Shape & Petal & suppl.	Shape & Texture	Shape, Texture & Color	Only Shape	Shape & Texture	Shape, Texture & Color
10	61.89	64.74	73.62	76.16	58.14	66.84	82.46
20	57.25	59.49	68.26	70.87	48.77	57.01	73.59
50	51.03	52.98	64.10	66.05	36.54	43.46	58.54

similarity measure, as it is quite likely that similar images may spread over multiple divisions of a feature space, achievement of high recall is quite difficult. Hence, performance is studied based on top order retrievals. Moreover, Muller *et al.* [32] have mentioned that, from the perspective of a user, top order retrievals are of major interest. Table 10.3 shows that retrieval precision is higher in the case of the human-perception-based similarity measure and it proves the retrieval capability of the proposed similarity measure.

The proposed relevance feedback scheme is also applied to improve the retrieval performance. It has been checked for both the databases and using both Euclidean distance and the proposed human-perception-based measure. Tables 10.4 and 10.5 along with the recall–precision graphs in Figures 10.17 and 10.18 reflect the improvement achieved through the proposed scheme for the measures.

Table 10.3. Precision (in %) of retrieval using different similarity measures.

	Our database		COIL-100 database	
Number of re-trieved images	Euclidean distance based	Proposed similarity measure	Euclidean distance based	Proposed similarity measure
10	76.16	81.10	82.46	88.52
20	70.87	76.39	73.59	79.25
30	68.05	73.15	67.31	72.25

Table 10.4. Precision (in %) using relevance feedback for our database.

	Euclidean distance				Proposed similarity measure			
No. of retrieved images	No relevance feedback	Relevance feedback			No relevance feedback	Relevance feedback		
		Iter1	Iter2	Iter3		Iter1	Iter2	Iter3
10	76.16	77.91	79.61	81.40	81.10	87.39	89.32	91.17
20	70.87	74.50	76.03	78.48	76.39	82.39	84.85	86.63
30	68.05	69.89	71.38	72.63	73.15	78.61	81.34	83.20

10.6 Conclusions

In this paper we have established the capability of petal projection and other types of shape features for content-based retrieval. The use of the texture co-occurrence matrix and fuzzy indexes of color based on a hue histogram

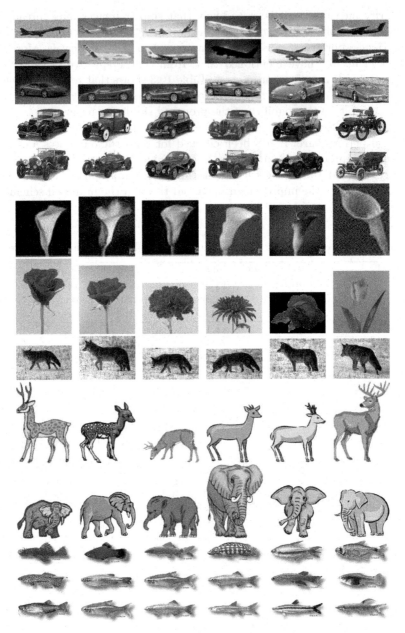

Fig. 10.15. Retrieval results (using our database): first image of each row is the query image and the others are the top five images matched.

Fig. 10.16. Retrieval results (using the COIL-100 database): first image of each row is the query image and the others are the top five images matched.

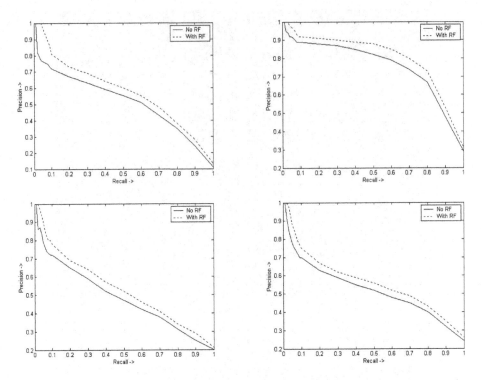

Fig. 10.17. Recall–precision graphs for different classes; they are (in raster order) Airplane, Car, Fish and Overall database.

Table 10.5. Precision (in %) using relevance feedback for COIL-100 database.

	Euclidean distance		Proposed similarity measure	
No. of retrieved images	No relevance feedback	Relevance feedback (after iteration 3)	No relevance feedback	Relevance feedback (after iteration 3)
10	82.46	84.74	88.52	91.07
20	73.59	76.47	79.25	83.91
30	67.31	70.40	72.25	79.57

further improves the performance. Comparison with similar systems was also made, as a benchmark. A new measure of similarity based on human perception was presented and its capability has been established. To improve the retrieval performance, a novel feedback mechanism was described and experiment shows that the enhancement is substantial. Hence, our proposed retrieval scheme in conjunction with the proposed relevance feedback strategy are able to discover knowledge about the image content by assigning various emphases to the annotating features.

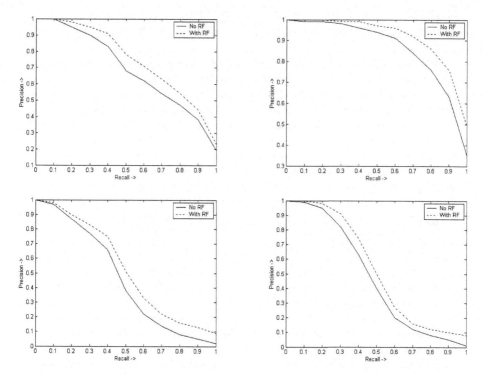

Fig. 10.18. Recall–precision graphs for different objects from the COIL-100 database; they are (in raster order) objects 17, 28, 43 and 52.

A proper multidimensional indexing scheme may be adopted in future for faster response times.

Acknowledgments: In this work, we have used databases available with Corel DRAW software from Corel Corporation and the COIL-100 database from Columbia University.

References

[1] Aggarwal, G., P. Dubey, S. Ghosal, A. Kulshreshtha and A. Sarkar, July 2000: IPURE: Perceptual and user-friendly retrieval of images. *Proceedings of IEEE Conference on Multimedia and Exposition (ICME 2000)*, New York, USA, volume 2, 693–6.

[2] Berman, A. P., and L. G. Shapiro, 1999: A flexible image database system for content-based retrieval. *Computer Vision and Image Understanding*, **75**, 175–95.

[3] Bimbo, A. D., P. Pala and S. Santini, 1996: Image retrieval by elastic matching of shapes and image patterns. *Proceedings of Multimedia'96*, 215–18.

[4] Chanda, B., and D. D. Majumdar, 2000: *Digital Image Processing and Analysis*. Prentice Halla, New Delhi, India.

[5] Ciocca, G., I. Gagliardi and R. Schettini, 2001: Quicklook2: An integrated multimedia system. *International Journal of Visual Languages and Computing, Special issue on Querying Multiple Data Sources Vol 12 (SCI 5417)*, 81–103.

[6] Conover, W. J., 1999: *Practical nonparametric statistics, 3rd edition*. John Wiley and Sons, New York.

[7] Cox, I. J., M. L. Miller, T. P. Minka, T. Papathomas and P. N. Yianilos, 2000: The Bayesian image retrieval system, pichunter: Theory, implementation and psychophysical experiments. *IEEE Transactions on Image Processing*, **9(1)**, 20–37.

[8] Delp, E. J., and O. R. Mitchell, 1979: Image compression using block truncation coding. *IEEE Trans. on Comm.*, **27**, 1335–42.

[9] Fournier, J., M. Cord and S. Philipp-Foliguet, 2001: RETIN: A content-based image indexing and retrieval system. *Pattern Analysis and Applications*, **4**, 153–73.

[10] Fukunaga, K., 1972: *Introduction to Statistical Pattern Recognition*. Academic Press, NY, USA.

[11] Gevers, T., and A. Smeulders, 2000: Pictoseek: Combining color and shape invariant features for shape retrieval. *IEEE Transactions on Image Processing*, **9(1)**, 102–19.

[12] Gudivada, V. N., and V. V. Raghavan, 1995: Content-based image retrieval systems. *IEEE Computer*, **28(9)**, 18–22.

[13] Haralick, R. M., K. Shanmugam and I. Dinstein, 1973: Texture features for image classification. *IEEE Trans. on SMC*, **3(11)**, 610–22.

[14] Hu, M. K., 1962: Visual pattern recognition by moment invariants. *IRE Trans. on Info. Theory*, **IT-8**, 179–87.

[15] Huang, J., S. R. Kumar, and M. Mitra, 1997: Combining supervised learning with color correlogram for content-based retrieval. *5th ACM Intl. Multimedia Confernce*, 325–34.

[16] Huang, J., S. R. Kumar, M. Mitra, W. J. Zhu and R. Zabih, 1997: Image indexing using color correlogram. *IEEE Conference on Computer Vision and Pattern Recognition*, 762–8.

[17] Jain, A. K., and A. Vailaya, 1998: Shape-based retrieval: A case study with trademark image database. *Pattern Recognition*, **31(9)**, 1369–90.

[18] Jain, R., ed., 1997: Special issue on visual information management. *Comm. ACM*.

[19] Kaplan, L. M., 1998: Fast texture database retrieval using extended fractal features. *SPIE 3312*, **SRIVD VI**, 162–73.

[20] Kimia, B., J. Chan, D. Bertrand, S. Coe, Z. Roadhouse and H. Tek, 1997: A shock-based approach for indexing of image databases using shape. *SPIE 3229*, **MSAS II**, 288–302.

[21] Ko, B., J. Peng and H. Byun, 2001: Region-based image retrieval using probabilistic feature relevance learning. *Pattern Analysis and Applications*, **4**, 174–84.

[22] Laaksonen, J., M. Koskela, S. Laakso and E. Oja, 2000: Picsom: content-based image retrieval with self-organizing maps. *PRL*, **21**, 1199–1207.

[23] Lai, T.-S., January 2000: *CHROMA: a Photographic Image Retrieval System*. Ph.D. thesis, School of Computing, Engineering and Technology, University of Sunderland, UK.

[24] Li, Z. N., D. R. Zaiane and Z. Tauber, 1999: Illumination invariance and object model in content-based image and video retrieval. *Journal of Visual Communication and Image Representation*, **10(3)**, 219–44.

[25] Lim, S. and G. Lu, 2003: Effectiveness and efficiency of six colour spaces for content based image retrieval. *CBMI 2003*, France, 215–21.

[26] Lin, C., and C. S. G. Lee, 1996: *Neural Fuzzy Systems*. Prentice-Hall, NJ.

[27] Ma, W. Y., and B. S. Manjunath, 1995: A comparison of wavelet transform features for texture image annotation. *IEEE Intl. Conf. on Image Processing*, 256–9.

[28] Manjunath, B. S., and W. Y. Ma, 1996: Texture features for browsing and retrieval of image data. *IEEE Trans. on PAMI*, **18**, 837–42.

[29] Mills, T. J., D. Pye, D. Sinclair and K. R. Wood, 2000: Shoebox: A digital photo management system. technical report 2000.10.

[30] Mokhtarian, F., S. Abbasi and J. Kittler, August 1996: Efficient and robust retrieval by shape content through curvature scale space. *Image Database and Multi-Media Search, Proceedings of the First International Workshop IDB-MMS'96*, Amsterdam, The Netherlands. Amsterdam University Press, 35–42.

[31] Mukherjee, S., K. Hirata and Y. Hara, 1999: A world wide web image retrieval engine. *The WWW journal*, **2(3)**, 115–32.

[32] Muller, H., W. Muller, S. Marchand-Mallet, T. Pun and D. M. Squire, 2001: Automated benchmarking in content-based image retrieval. *ICME 2001*, Tokyo, Japan, 22–5.

[33] Niblack, W., 1993: The QBIC project: Querying images by content using color, texture and shape. *SPIE*, **SRIVD**.

[34] Pentland, A., and R. Picard, 1996: Introduction to special section on the digital libraries: Representation and retrieval. *IEEE Trans. on PAMI*, **18**, 769–70.

[35] Persoon, E., and K. S. Fu, 1977: Shape discrimination using Fourier descriptors. *IEEE Trans. on SMC*, **7**, 170–9.

[36] Prasad, B. G., S. K. Gupta and K. K. Biswas, 2001: Color and shape index for region-based image retrieval. *IWVF4*, volume LNCS 2059, 716–25.

[37] Rocchio, J. J., 1971: Relevance feedback in information retrieval. *The SMART Retrieval System: Experiments in Automatic Document Processing*, G. Salton, ed., Prentice Hall, 313–23.

[38] Rosenfeld, A., and A. C. Kak, 1982: *Digital Picture Processing*, volume II. Academic Press, N.Y.

[39] Rui, Y., T. S. Haung, S. Mehrotra and M. Ortega, 1998: Relevance feedback: A power tool in interactive cotent-based image retrieval. *IEEE Tran. on Circuits and Systems for Video Technology, Special issue on interactive Multimedia Systems for the Internet*, **8(5)**, 644–55.

[40] Saha, S. K., A. K. Das and B. Chanda, 2003: Graytone image retrieval using shape feature based on petal projection. *ICAPR 2003*, India, 252–6.

[41] Salton, G., and M. J. McGill, 1983: *Introduction to Modern Information Retrieval for Image and Video Databases*. McGraw-Hill.

[42] Schettini, R., 1994: Multicolored object recognition and location. *PRL*, **15**, 1089–97.

[43] Sciascio, E. D., and A. Celentano, 1997: Similarity evaluation in image retrieval using simple features. *SPIE*, **3022**, 467–77.

[44] Sciascio, E. D., G. Mingolla and M. Mongiello, 1999: Content-based image retrieval over the web using query by sketch and relevance feedback. *Visual Information and Information Systems, Proceedings of the Third International Conference VISUAL '99*, Amsterdam, The Netherlands, June 1999, Lecture Notes in Computer Science 1614, Springer, 123–30.

[45] Sclaroff, S., L. Taycher and M. L. Cascia, 1997: ImageRover: A content-based image browser for the world wide web. *IEEE Workshop on content-based Access of Image and Video Libraries*, San Juan, Puerto Rico, 2–9.

[46] Smith, J. R., February 1997: *Integrated Spatial and Feature Image Systems: Retrieval, Compression and Analysis*. Ph.D. thesis, Graduate School of Arts and Sciences, Columbia University.

[47] Smith, J. R., and S. F. Chang, 1995: Tools and techniques for color image retrieval. *SPIE 2420*, **SRIVD III**.

[48] Squire, D. M., W. Muller, H. Muller and T. Pun, 2000: Content-based query of image databases: inspirations from text retrieval. *PRL*, **21**, 1193–98.

[49] Srihari, R., Z. Zhang, and A. Rao, 2000: Intelligent indexing and semantic retrieval of multimodal documents. *Information Retrieval, 2(2)*, 245–75.

[50] Stricker, M., and M. Orengo, 1995: Similarity of color images. *SPIE*, **SRIVD**, 381–92.

[51] Swain, M., and D. Ballard, 1991: Color indexing. *International Journal of Computer Vision*, **7(1)**, 11–32.

[52] Tamura, H., S. Mori and T. Yamawaki, 1978: Texture features corresponding to visual perception. *IEEE Trans. on SMC*, **8(6)**, 460–73.

[53] Teh, C., and R. T. Chin, 1988: On image analysis by the methods of moments. *IEEE Trans. on PAMI*, **10**, 496–13.

[54] Turtle, H. R., and W. B. Croft, 1982: A comparison of text retrieval models. *The Computer Journal*, **35(3)**, 279–90.

[55] Vleugels, J., and R. C. Veltkamp, 2002: Efficient image retrieval through vantage objects. *Pattern Recognition*, **35(1)**, 69–80.

[56] Yu, H., M. Li, H. Jiang Zhang and J. Feng, 2002: Color texture moments for content-based image retrieval. *IEEE Int. Conf. on Image Proc.*, New York, USA.

...

Significant Feature Selection Using Computational Intelligent Techniques for Intrusion Detection

Srinivas Mukkamala and Andrew H. Sung

Summary. Due to increasing incidence of cyber attacks and heightened concerns for cyber terrorism, implementing effective intrusion detection and prevention systems (IDPSs) is an essential task for protecting cyber security as well as physical security because of the great dependence on networked computers for the operational control of various infrastructures.

Building effective intrusion detection systems (IDSs), unfortunately, has remained an elusive goal owing to the great technical challenges involved; and computational techniques are increasingly being utilized in attempts to overcome the difficulties. This chapter presents a comparative study of using support vector machines (SVMs), multivariate adaptive regression splines (MARSs) and linear genetic programs (LGPs) for intrusion detection. We investigate and compare the performance of IDSs based on the mentioned techniques, with respect to a well-known set of intrusion evaluation data.

We also address the related issue of ranking the importance of input features, which itself is a problem of great interest. Since elimination of the insignificant and/or useless inputs leads to a simplified problem and possibly faster and more accurate detection, feature selection is very important in intrusion detection. Experiments on current real-world problems of intrusion detection have been carried out to assess the effectiveness of this criterion. Results show that using significant features gives the most remarkable performance and performs consistently well over the intrusion detection data sets we used.

11.1 Introduction

Feature selection and ranking is an important issue in intrusion detection. Of the large number of features that can be monitored for intrusion detection purposes, which are truly useful, which are less significant, and which may be useless? The question is relevant because the elimination of useless features (audit trail reduction) enhances the accuracy of detection while speeding up the computation, thus improving the overall performance of an IDS. In cases where there are no useless features, by concentrating on the most important

ones we may well improve the time performance of an IDS without affecting
the accuracy of detection in statistically significant ways.

The feature selection and ranking problem for intrusion detection is similar
in nature to various engineering problems that are characterized by:

- Having a large number of input variables $\mathbf{x} = (x_1, x_2,\ldots, x_n)$ of varying degrees of importance to the output $\mathbf{y}$; i.e., some elements of $\mathbf{x}$ are
  essential, some are less important, some of them may not be mutually
  independent, and some may be useless or irrelevant (in determining the
  value of $\mathbf{y}$);
- Lacking an analytical model that provides the basis for a mathematical
  formula that precisely describes the input–output relationship, $\mathbf{y} = \boldsymbol{F}(\mathbf{x})$;
- Having available a finite set of experimental data, based on which a model
  (e.g. a neural network) can be built for simulation and prediction purposes;
- Excess features that can reduce classifier accuracy;
- Excess features that can be costly to collect;
- Excess features that can reduce classifier operating speed independent of
  data collection;
- Excess features that can be costly to store.

Feature selection is typically viewed as a search for the feature subset resulting
in the best classifier error rate. Usually, the best error rate is equated with
the smallest magnitude, since we hope that the error rate is a measurement
of future classifier performance. The procedure is to use operators which map
from a feature subset to other feature subsets, analyze these subsets, and
select one of these to continue searching from. However, we immediately see
how difficult a problem this is; there are an exponential number of feature
sets to search through. Although for small numbers of features this search
is tractable, it does not scale. Many search algorithms sacrifice a "complete"
search and explore only a fraction of the space in order to find a "good"
feature set. Techniques include sequential search and best-first search with a
limited "queue" of states to expand to limit the search time.

Feature selection is designed to select important features and produce
better classifiers. However, the very process of feature selection can introduce
bias into the feature sets searched. Each time a new feature set is examined, we
must build a classifier and analyze it using the same data set. The more often
this data set is used, the more our results will be biased towards classifiers
which perform well on this data. Recent work has shown that we can create
operators which search the space more efficiently, thereby using the data less
often and creating better, unbiased feature sets which perform better on future
data.

Through a variety of experiments and analysis of different computational
intelligent techniques, it is found that, with appropriately chosen population
size, program size, crossover rate and mutation rate, LGPs outperform other
techniques in terms of detection accuracy at the expense of time. SVMs out-

perform MARSs and artificial neural networks (ANNs) in three critical aspects of intrusion detection: accuracy, training time, and testing time [9].

A brief introduction to SVMs and SVM-specific feature selection is given in Section 11.2. Section 11.3 introduces LGPs and LGP-specific feature selection. In Section 11.4 we introduce MARSs and MARS-specific feature selection. An experimental data set used for evaluation is presented in Section 11.5. Section 11.6 describes the significant feature identification problem for intrusion detection systems, a brief overview of significant features as identified by different ranking algorithms and the performance of classifiers using all features and significant features. Conclusions of our work are given in Section 11.7.

11.2 Support Vector Machines

The support vector machine (SVM) approach transforms data into a feature space F that usually has a huge dimension. It is interesting to note that SVM generalization depends on the geometrical characteristics of the training data, not on the dimensions of the input space [5, 6]. Training an SVM leads to a quadratic optimization problem with bound constraints and one linear equality constraint. Vapnik shows how training an SVM for the pattern recognition problem leads to the following quadratic optimization problem [14].

Minimize

$$W(\alpha) = -\sum_{i=1}^{l} \alpha_i + \frac{1}{2} \sum_{i=1}^{l} \sum_{j=1}^{l} y_i y_j \alpha_i \alpha_j k(x_i, x_j) \qquad (11.1)$$

subject to

$$\sum_{i=1}^{l} y_i \alpha_i \qquad (11.2)$$
$$\forall i : 0 \le \alpha_i \le C$$

where l is the number of training examples, α is a vector of l variables and each component α_i corresponds to a training example (x_i, y_i). The solution of Equation (11.1) is the vector α^* for which Equation (11.1) is minimized and Equation (11.2) is fulfilled.

In the first phase of the SVM, called the learning phase, the decision function is inferred from a set of objects. For these objects the classification is known *a priori*. The objects of the family of interest are called, for ease of notation, the positive objects and the objects from outside the family, the negative objects.

In the second phase, called the testing phase, the decision function is applied to arbitrary objects in order to determine, or more accurately predict, whether they belong to the family under study, or not.

Linear case SVM

The objects are represented by vectors in R^n where each coefficient represents a feature of the object: weight, size, etc. An example of a linear case SVM is briefly shown in Figure 11.1.

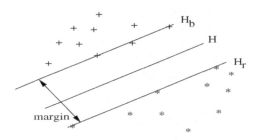

Fig. 11.1. Linear case SVM.

The positive examples form a cloud of points, say the points labelled "+" (referred to as a set X_b), while the negative examples form another cloud of points, say, the points labelled "*" (referred to as X_r). The aim is to find a hyper-plane H separating the two clouds of points in some optimal way.

Definition of Margin and Maximal Margin

Let H be a separating hyper-plane, H_b a separating hyper-plane parallel to H and passing through the points in X_b that are closest to H, H_r a separating hyper-plane parallel to H and passing through the points in X_r that are closest to H.

The margin, γ, is the distance between two parallel separating hyper-planes H_b and H_r (as shown in Figure 11.1). Vapnik's theory of risk minimization shows that hyper-planes for which γ is maximum have better generalization potential than others, and so the problem of a linear SVM is to find a separating hyper-plane with maximum margin.

There are many ways to represent mathematically such an optimization problem. We have two concerns here. The first is to find a formulation that can be handled by standard optimization techniques (quadratic programming in our case). The second concern is of major significance from an application point of view: is it indeed possible to find a formulation that will allow us to construct nonlinear separating surfaces while remaining in the previous computational framework of linear separation?

Quadratic Programming:

A constrained optimization problem consists of two parts: a function to optimize and a set of constraints to be satisfied by the variables. Constraint satisfaction is typically a hard combinatorial problem; while, for an appropriate choice of function, optimization is a comparatively easier analytical problem. Hence, we choose the design of formulations where the constraints are simple linear constraints and we use duality to move expressions from the set of constraints to the function we seek to optimize. In the maximum margin case, we want to maximize a distance. In order to express distances of points to a hyper-plane $W * X + b = 0$, we require that $||W||^2 = 1$. Equivalently we can divide the expression by $||W||^2$.

However either formulation gives us a nonlinear constraint, which does not lead to efficient computation. We will therefore formulate the problem to move the nonlinear constraint into the function to optimize.

Let $W * X + b = 0$ be the equation of a separating hyperplane, situated halfway between the two sets, so that for some $t>0$ we have all the points in X_b on one side and all the points in X_r on the other:

$$(W * X_r + b)/||W||^2 \quad >= t/||W||^2$$

and

$$(W * X_b + b)/||W||^2 \quad <= -t/||W||^2,$$

and there exist points in X_b and X_r for which the inequalities are replaced by equalities. Consequently we have the margin:

$$\gamma = g2t/||W||^2$$

Assume the maximum margin is reached for $W= W_0$, $b = b_0$, $t = t_0$. Dividing W_0 and b_0 by t_0 shows that the maximal margin is reached for hyper-planes such that $\gamma = 2/||W||^2$.

Without loss of generality we may therefore assume that $t = 1$. The problem of maximizing γ is replaced by the problem of minimizing the norm of W,

$$\frac{1}{2} * < W, W > \tag{11.3}$$

under the linear constraints:

$$Y_i * (W * X_i + b) \geq 1 \quad \text{for any } I \tag{11.4}$$

where X_i, is a data point and Y_i is the label of the data point, equal to 1 or −1 depending on whether the point is a positive or a negative example.

We now have a typical quadratic programming problem and we will change this formulation with nonlinear separability in mind.

Nonlinear Separation

It can be shown that if you have fewer points than the dimension, then any two sets are separable. It is therefore tempting, when the two sets are not linearly separable, to map the problem into a higher dimension where it will become separable. There is however a price to pay as quadratic programming problems are quite sensitive to high dimensions. SVM handles this problem very well, by simulating in the original space a computation in an arbitrarily higher (even infinite) dimension space.

Consider Figure 11.2 and Figure 11.3 of a mapping Φ from the original space to a higher-dimensional space.

Fig. 11.2. Nonlinear case SVM.

Fig. 11.3. Nonlinear case SVM.

Two conditions have to be met:

1. find a formulation such that the data appears only as vector dot products such as $<W, W>$.
2. find an appropriate function K, called a kernel function, such that $<\Phi(V), \Phi(W)> = K(V, W)$.

In such a case there is no need to represent the vectors in high dimension as the computation is performed by K in the original space. This might superficially appear as a contrived trick, so the reader is referred to Vapnik's books [14] in order to realize that there is in fact a very deep theory behind the design of kernel functions.

Wolfe's Dual
The preceding formulation can be transformed by duality, which has the advantage of simplifying the set of constraints, but more importantly, Wolfe's

dual gives us a formulation where the data appears only as vector dot products. As a consequence we can handle nonlinear separation.

Minimizing $1/2 * \|W\|^2$ under the constraint of Equation (11.4) is equivalent to maximizing the dual Lagrangian obtained by computing variables from the stationary conditions and replacing them by the values so obtained in the primal Lagrangian. Details can be found in [3].

$$Y_i * (W * X_i + b) \geq 1 \quad \text{for any} \quad I \tag{11.5}$$

The primal Lagrangian is:

$$L = \frac{1}{2}(W * W) - \sum \alpha_i * (Y_i * (W * X_i + b) - 1), \tag{11.6}$$

where the α_i is the Lagrange multiplier and Y_i is the label of the corresponding data point under the constraint:

$$\alpha_i \quad \geq 0 \quad \text{for any} \quad i \tag{11.7}$$

The stationary conditions are:

$$\partial L / \partial b = \sum \alpha_i * Y_i = 0 \tag{11.8}$$

$$\partial L / \partial w = W - \sum \alpha_i * Y_i * X_i = 0. \tag{11.9}$$

Substituting the value of w from Equation (11.8) in the primal Lagrangian (Equation (11.5)) gives us the Wolfe Dual Lagrangian:

$$W(a) = \sum \alpha_i - \frac{1}{2} * \sum \alpha_i * \alpha_j Y_i * Y_j * (X_i * X_j) \tag{11.10}$$

This must be maximized subject to the constraints of Equations (11.7) and (11.8). It is then straightforward to implement nonlinearity by simply replacing the vector products by kernel functions.

Support Vectors
It is clear that the maximum margin is not defined by all points to be separated, but by only a subset of points called support vectors. Indeed from Equation (11.9) we know that $W = \sum Y_i * \alpha_i * X_i$, and the data points X_i whose coefficients $\alpha_i = 0$ are irrelevant to W, are therefore irrelevant to the definition of the separating surface; the others are the support vectors.

Over-fitting and Soft Margin Trade Off
Figure 11.4 shows an example where, by choosing a kernel of sufficient degree we can find a surface complex enough to separate the two clouds of points. When there is noise we can make this surface extremely complex in order to fit the data. This phenomenon is called over-fitting, as perhaps some of these noisy points should be in fact ignored, leading to a simpler surface of

Fig. 11.4. Over-fitting an SVM.

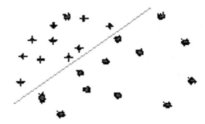

Fig. 11.5. Soft margin trade-off in an SVM.

separation. In Figure 11.5 we have a trade-off: a simple linear separation rather than a complex one at the cost of a training error, which could in fact be noise or erroneous data.

So there exists a trade-off between the degree of the kernel function and the extent to which training errors are allowed. This has a very important consequence as the algorithm we described will not work when the sets are not separable. Therefore to have the algorithm work we must increase the nonlinearity, and therefore the complexity of the surface, and therefore the risk of grossly over-fitting.

The problem is solved by relaxing the conditions in such a way that a certain degree of misclassification is allowed, leading to simpler solutions at the cost of some erroneous, or potentially erroneous, predictions.

We refer the reader to [3] for the description of the techniques involved. The user has to define the value of a parameter that controls the extent of misclassification allowed. This value is heavily dependent on the data at hand.

11.2.1 SVM-specific Feature Ranking Method

It is of great interest and use to find exactly which features underline the nature of connections of various classes. This is precisely the goal of data visualization in data mining. The problem is that the high-dimensionality of data makes it hard for human experts to gather any knowledge. If we knew the key features, we could greatly reduce the dimensionality of the data and thus help human experts become more efficient and productive in learning about network intrusions.

The information about which features play key roles and which are more neutral is "hidden" in the SVM decision function. Equation (11.11) is the formulation of the decision function in the case of using linear kernels.

$$F(X) = < W, X > + b \qquad (11.11)$$

The point X is predicted to be in class A or "positive class" if $F(X)$ is positive, and class B or "negative class" if F(X) is negative. We can rewrite Equation (11.11) to expand the dot product of W and X.

$$F(X) = \Sigma W_i X_i + b \qquad (11.12)$$

One can see that the value of $F(X)$ depends on the contribution of each factor, $W_i X_i$. Since X_i can take only $b \geq g_0$, the sign of W_i indicates whether the contribution is towards positive classification or negative classification. The absolute size of W_i measures the strength of this contribution. In other words if W_i is a large positive value, then the ith feature is a key factor of "positive class" or class A. Similarly if W_i is a large negative value then the ith feature is a key factor of the "negative class" or class B. Consequently the W_i, that are close to zero, either positive or negative, carry little weight. The feature, which corresponds to this W_i, is said to be a garbage feature and removing it has very little effect on the classification.

Having retrieved this information directly from the SVM's decision function, we rank the W_i, from largest positive to largest negative. This essentially provides the soft partitioning of the features into the key features of class A, neutral features, and key features of class B. We say soft partitioning, as it depends on either a threshold on the value of W_i that will define the partitions or the proportions of the features that we want to allocate to each of the partitions. Both the threshold and the value of proportions can be set by the human expert.

Support Vector Decision Function Ranking
The input ranking is done as follows: First the original data set is used for the training of the classifier. Then the classifier's decision function is used to rank the importance of the features. The procedure is:

1. Calculate the weights from the support vector decision function.
2. Rank the importance of the features by the absolute values of the weights.

11.2.2 Performance-Based Ranking

We first describe a general (i.e., independent of the modeling tools being used), performance-based input ranking (PBR) methodology [12]: One input feature is deleted from the data at a time; the resultant data set is then used for the training and testing of the classifier. Then the classifier's performance is compared to that of the original classifier (based on all features) in terms of relevant performance criteria. Finally, the importance of the feature is ranked according to a set of rules based on the performance comparison.

The procedure is summarized as follows:

1. Compose the training set and the testing set.
2. *For* each feature *do* the following:
   - delete the feature from the (training and testing) data;
   - use the resultant data set to train the classifier;
   - analyze the performance of the classifier using the test set, in terms of the selected performance criteria;
   - rank the importance of the feature according to the rules.

11.3 Linear Genetic Programming

Linear Genetic Programming (LGP) is a variant of the Genetic Programming (GP) technique that acts on linear genomes [1]. The linear genetic programming technique used for our current experiment is based on machine code level manipulation and evaluation of programs. Its main characteristics, in comparison to tree-based GP, are that the evolvable units are not the expressions of a functional programming language (like LISP), instead the programs of an imperative language (like C) are evolved. In the automatic induction of machine code by genetic programming, individuals are manipulated directly as binary code in memory and executed directly without passing an interpreter during fitness calculation. The LGP tournament selection procedure puts the lowest selection pressure on the individuals by allowing only two individuals to participate in a tournament. A copy of the winner replaces the loser of each tournament. The crossover points only occur between instructions. Inside instructions the mutation operation randomly replaces the instruction identifier. In LGP the maximum size of the program is usually restricted to prevent programs without bounds.

In genetic programming, an *intron* is defined as part of a program that has no influence on the fitness calculation of outputs for all possible inputs.

Ranking Algorithm using Evolutionary Algorithms
The performance of each of the selected input feature subsets is measured by invoking a fitness function with the correspondingly reduced feature space and training set and evaluating the intrusion detection accuracy. Once the required number of iterations is completed, the evolved high-ranking programs are analyzed for the number of times each input appears in a way that contributes to the fitness of the programs that contain them. The best feature subset found is then output as the recommended set of features to be used in the actual input for the classifier.

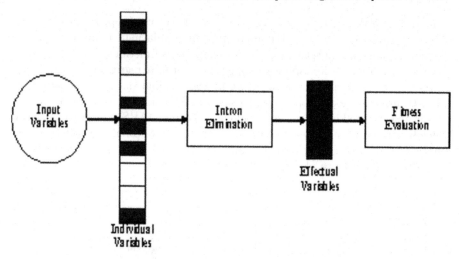

Fig. 11.6. LGP intron elimination and fitness evaluation.

In the feature selection problem the main interest is in the representation of the space of all possible subsets of the given input feature set. Each feature in the candidate feature set is considered as a binary gene and each individual consists of a fixed-length binary string representing some subset of the given feature set. An individual of length d corresponds to a d-dimensional binary feature vector Y, where each bit represents the elimination or inclusion of the associated feature. Then, $y_i = 0$ represents elimination and $y_i = 1$ indicates inclusion of the ith feature. Fitness F of an individual program p is calculated as the mean square error (MSE) between the predicted output (O_{ij}^{pred}) and the desired output (O_{ij}^{des}) for all n training samples and m outputs [2].

$$F(p) = \frac{1}{n \cdot m} \sum_{i=1}^{n} \sum_{j=1}^{m} (O_{ij}^{pred} - O_{ij}^{des})^2 + \frac{w}{n} CE = MSE + w \cdot MCE \quad (11.13)$$

Classification Error (CE) is computed as the number of misclassifications. Mean Classification Error (MCE) is added to the fitness function while its contribution is multiplied by an absolute value of weight (w).

11.4 Multivariative Adaptive Regression Splines

Splines can be considered as an innovative mathematical process for complicated curve drawings and function approximation. To develop a spline the X-axis is broken into a convenient number of regions. The boundary between regions is also known as a knot. With a sufficiently large number of knots virtually any shape can be well approximated. While it is easy to draw a spline in two-dimensions by keying on knot locations (approximating using linear, quadratic or cubic polynomial etc.), manipulating the mathematics in higher dimensions is best accomplished using basis functions. The multivariative adaptive regression splines (MARS) model is a regression model using basis functions as predictors in place of the original data. The basis function transform makes it possible to selectively blank out certain regions of a variable by making them zero, and allows the MARS model to focus on specific sub-regions of the data. It excels at finding optimal variable transformations and interactions, and the complex data structure that often hides in high-dimensional data [4, 13].

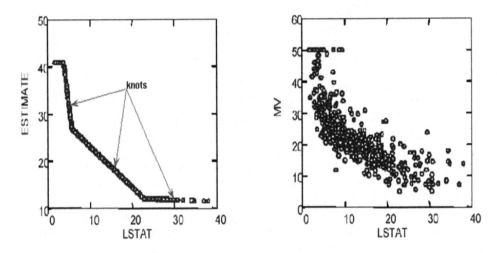

Fig. 11.7. MARS data estimation using splines and knots (actual data on the right).

Given the number of records in most data sets, it is infeasible to approximate the function $y = f(x)$ by summarizing y in each distinct region of x. For some variables, two regions may not be enough to track the specifics of the function. If the relationship of y to some x is different in three or four regions, for example, the number of regions requiring examination is even larger than 34 billion with only 35 variables. Given that the number of regions cannot be specified *a priori*, specifying too few regions in advance can have serious implications for the final model. A solution is needed that accomplishes the following two criteria:

• judicious selection of which regions to look at and their boundaries;
• judicious determination of how many intervals are needed for each variable.

Given these two criteria, a successful method will essentially need to be adaptive to the characteristics of the data. Such a solution will probably ignore quite a few variables (affecting variable selection) and will take into account only a few variables at a time (also reducing the number of regions). Even if the method selects 30 variables for the model, it will not look at all 30 simultaneously. Such simplification is accomplished by a decision tree at a single node, only ancestor splits being considered; thus, at a depth of six levels in the tree, only six variables are used to define the node.

Ranking Algorithm using MARS

Generalized cross-validation is an estimate of the actual cross-validation which involves more computationally intensive goodness of fit measures. Along with the MARS procedure, a generalized cross-validation (GCV) procedure is used to determine the significant input features. Non-contributing input variables are thereby eliminated.

$$GCV = \frac{1}{N} \sum_{i=1}^{N} \left[\frac{y_i - f(x_i)^2}{1 - k/N} \right] \qquad (11.14)$$

where N is the number of records and x and y are independent and dependent variables respectively. k is the effective number of degrees of freedom whereby the GCV adds penalty for adding more input variables to the model. The contribution of the input variables may be ranked using the GCV with/without an input feature [13].

11.5 The Experimental Data

A subset of the DARPA intrusion detection data set is used for off-line analysis. In the DARPA intrusion detection evaluation program, an environment was set up to acquire raw TCP/IP dump data for a network by simulating a typical US Air Force LAN. The LAN was operated like a real environment, but blasted with multiple attacks [7, 15]. For each TCP/IP connection, 41 various quantitative and qualitative features were extracted [8]. The 41 features extracted fall into three categories: "intrinsic" features that describe the individual TCP/IP connections can be obtained from network audit trails; "content-based" features that describe the payload of the network packet can be obtained from the data portion of the network packet; "traffic-based" features that are computed using a specific window (connection time or number of connections). Attack types fall into four main categories:

- Probing: surveillance and other probing
- DoS: denial of service
- U2Su: unauthorized access to local super user (root) privilege
- R2U: unauthorized access from a remote machine

As DoS and probing attacks involve several connections in a short time frame, whereas R2U and U2Su attacks are embedded in the data portions of the connection and often involve just a single connection, "traffic-based" features play an important role in deciding whether a particular network activity is engaged in probing or not.

11.5.1 Probing

Probing is a class of attacks where an attacker scans a network to gather information or find known vulnerabilities. An attacker with a map of machines and services that are available on a network can use the information to look for exploits. There are different types of probes (see Table 11.1): some of them abuse the computer's legitimate features; some of them use social engineering techniques. This class of attacks is the most commonly known and requires very little technical expertise.

Table 11.1. Probe attacks.

Attack Type	Service	Mechanism	Effect of the attack
Ipsweep	Icmp	Abuse of feature	Identifies active machines
Mscan	Many	Abuse of feature	Looks for known vulnerabilities
Nmap	Many	Abuse of feature	Identifies active ports on a machine
Saint	Many	Abuse of feature	Looks for known vulnerabilities
Satan	Many	Abuse of feature	Looks for known vulnerabilities

11.5.2 Denial of Service Attacks

Denial of service (DoS) is a class of attacks where an attacker makes some computing or memory resource too busy or too full to handle legitimate requests, thus denying legitimate users access to a machine. There are different ways to launch DoS attacks: by abusing the computer's legitimate features; by targeting implementation bugs; or by exploiting the system's misconfigurations. DoS attacks are classified based on the services that an attacker renders unavailable to legitimate users (Table 11.2).

11.5.3 User to Super user Attacks

User to super user (U2Su) exploits are a class of attacks where an attacker starts out with access to a normal user account on the system and is able to exploit a vulnerability to gain root access to the system. The most common exploits in this class of attacks are buffer overflows, which are caused by programming mistakes and environment assumptions (see Table 11.3).

Table 11.2. Denial of service attacks.

Attack Type	Service	Mechanism	Effect of the attack
Apache2	http	Abuse	Crashes httpd
Back	http	Abuse/Bug	Slows down server response
Land	http	Bug	Freezes the machine
Mail bomb		Abuse	Annoyance
SYN Flood	TCP	Abuse	Denies service on one or more ports
Ping of Death	Icmp	Bug	None
Process table	TCP	Abuse	Denies new processes
Smurf	Icmp	Abuse	Slows down the network
Syslogd	Syslog	Bug	Kills the Syslogd
Teardrop		Bug	Reboots the machine
Udpstrom	Echo/Chargen	Abuse	Slows down the network

Table 11.3. User to super user attacks.

Attack Type	Service	Mechanism	Effect of the attack
Eject	User session	Buffer overflow	Gains root shell
Ffbconfig	User session	Buffer overflow	Gains root shell
Fdformat	User session	Buffer overflow	Gains root shell
Loadmodule	User session	Poor environment sanitation	Gains root shell
Perl	User session	Poor environment sanitation	Gains root shell
Ps	User session	Poor temp file management	Gains root shell
Xterm	User session	Buffer overflow	Gains root shell

11.5.4 Remote to User Attacks

A remote to user (R2U) attack is a class of attacks where an attacker sends packets to a machine over a network, then exploits machine's vulnerability to illegally gain local access as a user. There are different types of R2U attacks; the most common attack in this class is done using social engineering (see Table 11.4).

11.6 Significant Feature Selection for Intrusion Detection

Feature selection and ranking is an important issue in intrusion detection [10, 11]. Of the large number of features that can be monitored for intrusion detection purposes, which are truly useful, which are less significant, and which may be useless? The question is relevant because the elimination of useless features (audit trail reduction) enhances the accuracy of detection while speeding up the computation, thus improving the overall performance of an IDS. In cases where there are no useless features, by concentrating on

Table 11.4. Remote to user attacks.

Attack Type	Service	Mechanism	Effect of the attack
Dictionary	telnet, rlogin, pop, ftp, imap	Abuse feature	Gains user access
Ftp-write	ftp	Misconfiguration	Gains user access
Guest	telnet, rlogin	Misconfiguration	Gains user access
Imap	imap	Bug	Gains root access
Named	dns	Bug	Gains root access
Phf	http	Bug	Executes commands as http user
Sendmail	smtp	Bug	Executes commands as root
Xlock	smtp	Misconfiguration	Spoof user to obtain password
Xnsoop	smtp	Misconfiguration	Monitor key stokes remotely

the most important ones we may well improve the time performance of an IDS without affecting the accuracy of detection in statistically significant ways.

The feature ranking and selection problem for intrusion detection is similar in nature to various engineering problems that are characterized by:

- Having a large number of input variables $\mathbf{x} = (x_1, x_2, \ldots, x_n)$ of varying degrees of importance to the output $\mathbf{y}$; i.e., some elements of $\mathbf{x}$ are essential, some are less important, some of them may not be mutually independent, and some may be useless or irrelevant (in determining the value of $\mathbf{y}$);
- Lacking an analytical model that provides the basis for a mathematical formula that precisely describes the input–output relationship, $\mathbf{y} = \mathbf{F}(\mathbf{x})$;
- Having available a finite set of experimental data, based on which a model (e.g. a neural network) can be built for simulation and prediction purposes.

Due to the lack of an analytical model, one can only seek to determine the relative importance of the input variables through empirical methods. A complete analysis would require examination of all possibilities, e.g., taking two variables at a time to analyze their dependence or correlation, then taking three at a time, etc. This, however, is both infeasible (requiring 2^n experiments!) and not infallible (since the available data may be of poor quality in sampling the whole input space). Features are ranked based on their influence towards the final classification. Description of the most important features as ranked by three feature-ranking algorithms (SVDF, LGP, and MARS) is given in Tables 11.5, 11.6, and 11.7. The (training and testing) data set contains 11,982 randomly generated points from the five classes, with the amount of data from each class proportional to its size, except that the smallest class is completely included. The normal data belongs to class 1, probe belongs to class 2, denial of service belongs to class 3, user to super user belongs to class

Table 11.5. Most important feature descriptions as ranked by SVDF.

Data class	Feature description
Normal	• destination bytes: number of bytes received by the source host from the destination host • dst_host_count: number of connections from the same host to the destination host during a specified time window • logged in: binary decision (1 successfully logged in, 0 failed login) • dst_host_same_srv_rate: % of connections to same service ports from a destination host • flag: normal or error status of the connection
Probe	• source bytes: number of bytes sent from the host system to the destination system • dst_host_srv_count: number of connections from the same host with same service to the destination host during a specified time window • count: number of connections made to the same host system in a given interval of time • protocol type: type of protocol used to connect (e.g. tcp, udp, icmp, etc.) • srv_count: number of connections to the same service as the current connection during a specified time window
DoS	• count: number of connections made to the same host system in a given interval of time • srv_count: number of connections to the same service as the current connection during a specified time window • dst_host_srv_serror_rate: % of connections to the same service that have SYN errors from a destination host • serror_rate: % of connections that have SYN errors • dst_host_same_src_port_rate: % of connections to same service ports from a destination host
U2Su	• source bytes: number of bytes sent from the host system to the destination system • duration: length of the connection • protocol type: type of protocol used to connect (e.g. tcp, udp, icmp, etc.) • logged in: binary decision (1 successfully logged in, 0 failed login) • flag: normal or error status of the connection
R2U	• dst_host_count: no of connections from the same host to the destination host during a specified time window • service: type of service used to connect (e.g. finger, ftp, telnet, ssh, etc.) • duration: length of the connection • count: number of connections made to the same host system in a given interval of time • srv_count: number of connections to the same service as the current connection during a specified time window

Table 11.6. Most important feature descriptions as ranked by LGP.

Data class	Feature description
Normal	• hot: number of "hot" indicators • source bytes: number of bytes sent from the host system to the destination system • destination bytes: number of bytes received by the source host from the destination host • num_compromised: number of compromised conditions • dst_host_rerror_rate: % of connections that have REJ errors from a destination host
Probe	• dst_host_diff_srv_rate: % of connections to different services from a destination host • rerror_rate: % of connections that have REJ errors • srv_diff_host_rate: % of connections that have the same service to different hosts • logged in: binary decision (1 successfully logged in, 0 failed login) • service: type of service used to connect (e.g. finger, ftp, telnet, ssh, etc.)
DoS	• count: number of connections made to the same host system in a given interval of time • num_compromised: number of compromised conditions • wrong fragments: number of wrong fragments • land: binary decision (1 if connection is from/to the same host/port; 0 otherwise) • logged in: binary decision (1 successfully logged in, 0 failed login)
U2Su	• root_shell: binary decision (1 if root shell is obtained; 0 otherwise) • dst_host_srv_serror_rate: % of connections to the same service that have SYN errors from a destination host • num_file_creations: number of file creations • serror_rate: % of connections that have SYN errors • dst_host_same_src_port_rate: % of connections to same service ports from a destination host
R2U	• guest login: binary decision (1 if the login is guest, 0 otherwise) • num_file_access: number of operations on access control files • destination bytes: number of bytes received by the source host from the destination host • num_failed_logins: number of failed login attempts • logged in: binary decision (1 successfully logged in, 0 failed login)

Table 11.7. Most important feature descriptions as ranked by MARS.

Data class	Feature description
Normal	• destination bytes: number of bytes received by the source host from the destination host • source bytes: number of bytes sent from the host system to the destination system • service: type of service used to connect (e.g. finger, ftp, telnet, ssh, etc.) • logged in: binary decision (1 successfully logged in, 0 failed login) • hot: number of "hot" indicators
Probe	• dst_host_diff_srv_rate: % of connections to different services from a destination host • dst_host_srv_count: : number of connections from the same host with same service to the destination host during a specified time window • source bytes: number of bytes sent from the host system to the destination system • dst_host_same_srv_rate: % of connections to same service ports from a destination host • srv_count: number of connections to the same service as the current connection during a specified time window
DoS	• count: number of connections made to the same host system in a given interval of time • srv_count: number of connections to the same service as the current connection during a specified time window • dst_host_srv_diff_host_rate: % of connections to the same service from different hosts to a destination host • source bytes: number of bytes sent from the host system to the destination system • destination bytes: number of bytes received by the source host from the destination host
U2Su	• dst_host_srv_count: number of connections from the same host with the same service to the destination host during a specified time window • count: number of connections made to the same host system in a given interval of time • duration: length of the connection • srv_count: number of connections to the same service as the current connection during a specified time window • dst_host_count: number of connections from the same host to the destination host during a specified time window
R2U	• srv_count: number of connections to the same service as the current connection during a specified time window • count: number of connections made to the same host system in a given interval of time • service: type of service used to connect (e.g. finger, ftp, telnet, ssh, etc.) • dst_host_srv_count: number of connections from the same host with same service to the destination host during a specified time window • logged in: binary decision (1 successfully logged in, 0 failed login)

4, remote to user belongs to class 5. Attack data is a collection of 22 different types of attack instances that belong to the four classes probe, denial of service, user to super user, and remote to local. A different randomly selected set of 6890 points of the total data set (11,982) is used for testing different intelligent techniques. Classifier performance using all 41 features and the six most important features as inputs to the classifier is given in Tables 11.8 and 11.9, respectively. SVM performance using performance-based feature ranking and SVDF are reported in Table 11.10.

Table 11.8. Performance of classifiers using all 41 features.

Class	LGP Accuracy (%)	MARS Accuracy (%)	SVM Accuracy (%)
Normal	99.89	96.08	99.55
Probe	99.85	92.32	99.70
DOS	99.91	94.73	99.25
U2Su	99.80	99.71	99.87
R2U	99.84	99.48	99.78

Table 11.9. Performance of classifiers using six most important features.

Class	LGP Accuracy (%)	MARS Accuracy (%)	SVM Accuracy (%)
Normal	99.77	94.34	99.23
Probe	99.87	90.79	99.16
DOS	99.14	95.47	99.16
U2Su	99.83	99.71	99.87
R2U	99.84	99.48	99.78

Table 11.10. Performance of SVM using important features.

Class	No of Features Identified		Training Time (sec)		Testing Time (sec)		Accuracy (%)	
	PBR	SVDF	PBR	SVDF	PBR	SVDF	PBR	SVDF
Normal	25	20	9.36	4.58	1.07	0.78	99.59	99.55
Probe	7	11	37.71	40.56	1.87	1.20	99.38	99.36
DOS	19	11	22.79	18.93	1.84	1.00	99.22	99.16
U2Su	8	10	2.56	1.46	0.85	0.70	99.87	99.87
R2U	6	6	8.76	6.79	0.73	0.72	99.78	99.72

11.7 Conclusions

Three different significant feature identification techniques along with a comparative study of feature selection metrics for intrusion detection systems are presented. Another contribution of this work is a novel significant feature selection algorithm (independent of the modeling tools being used) that considers the performance of a classifier to identify significant features. One input feature is deleted from the data at a time; the resultant data set is then used for the training and testing of the classifier. Then the classifier's performance is compared to that of the original classifier (based on all features) in terms of relevant performance criteria. Finally, the importance of the feature is ranked according to a set of rules based on the performance comparison.

Regarding feature ranking, we observe that

- The three feature-ranking methods produce largely consistent results. Except for the class 1 (Normal) and class 4 (U2Su) data, the features ranked as important by the three methods heavily overlap.
- The most important features for the two classes of Normal and DoS heavily overlap.
- U2Su and R2U are the two smallest classes representing the most serious attacks. Each has a small number of important features and a large number of insignificant features.
- Using the important features for each class gives the most remarkable performance: the testing time decreases in each class, the accuracy increases slightly for Normal, decreases slightly for Probe and DoS, and remains the same for the two most serious attack classes.
- Performance-based and SVDF feature ranking methods produce largely consistent results: except for the class 1 (Normal) and class 4 (U2Su) data, the features ranked as important by the two methods heavily overlap.

Acknowledgments: Support for this research was received from ICASA (Institute for Complex Additive Systems Analysis, a division of New Mexico Tech), and DoD and NSF IASP capacity building grant. We would also like to acknowledge many insightful suggestions from Dr. Jean-Louis Lassez and Dr. Ajith Abraham that helped clarify our ideas and contributed to our work.

References

[1] Banzhaf, W., P. Nordin, E. R. Keller and F. D. Francone, 1998: *Genetic programming: An introduction – on the automatic evolution of computer programs and its applications.* Morgan Kaufmann.

[2] Brameier, M., and W. Banzhaf, 2001: A comparison of linear genetic programming and neural networks in medical data mining. *IEEE Transactions on Evolutionary Computation,* **5 (1),** 17–26.

[3] Cristianini, N., and S. J. Taylor, 2000: *An introduction to support vector machines*. Cambridge University Press.

[4] Friedman, J. H., 1991: Multivariate adaptive regression splines. *Annals of Statistics*, **19**, 1–141.

[5] Joachims, T., 2000: Making large-scale SVM learning practical. *LS8-Report*, University of Dortmund.

[6] — 2000: SVMlight is an implementation of support vector machines (SVMs) in C. *Collaborative Research Center on Complexity Reduction in Multivariate Data (SFB475)*, University of Dortmund.

[7] Kendall, K., 1998: A database of computer attacks for the evaluation of intrusion detection systems. Master's Thesis, Massachusetts Institute of Technology.

[8] Lee, W., and S. Stolfo, 2000: A framework for constructing features and models for intrusion detection systems. *ACM Transactions on Information and System Security*, **3**, 227–61.

[9] Mukkamala, S., and A. H. Sung, 2003: A comparative study of techniques for intrusion detection. Proceedings of 15th *IEEE International Conference on Tools with Artificial Intelligence, IEEE Computer Society Press*, 570–579.

[10] — 2003: Feature selection for intrusion detection using neural networks and support vector machines. *Journal of the Transportation Research Board of the National Academics, Transportation Research Record*, No 1822, 33–9.

[11] — 2003: Identifying significant features for network forensic analysis using artificial intelligence techniques. *International Journal on Digital Evidence, IJDE*, **1**.

[12] Sung, A. H., 1998: Ranking importance of input parameters of neural networks. *Journal of Expert Systems with Applications*, **15**, 405–41.

[13] Steinberg, D., P. L. Colla and K. Martin, 1999: *MARS user guide*. Salford Systems, San Diego.

[14] Vapnik, V. N., 1995: *The nature of statistical learning theory*. Springer.

[15] Webster, S. E., 1998: The development and analysis of intrusion detection algorithms. Master's Thesis, Massachusetts Institute of Technology.

On-board Mining of Data Streams in Sensor Networks

Mohamed Medhat Gaber, Shonali Krishnaswamy and Arkady Zaslavsky

Summary. Data streams are generated in large quantities and at rapid rates from sensor networks that typically monitor environmental conditions, traffic conditions and weather conditions among others. A significant challenge in sensor networks is the analysis of the vast amounts of data that are rapidly generated and transmitted through sensing. Given that wired communication is infeasible in the environmental situations outlined earlier, the current method for communicating this data for analysis is through satellite channels. Satellite communication is exorbitantly expensive. In order to address this issue, we propose a strategy for on-board mining of data streams in a resource-constrained environment. We have developed a novel approach that dynamically adapts the data-stream mining process on the basis of available memory resources. This adaptation is algorithm-independent and enables data-stream mining algorithms to cope with high data rates in the light of finite computational resources. We have also developed lightweight data-stream mining algorithms that incorporate our adaptive mining approach for resource constrained environments.

12.1 Introduction

In its early stages, data-mining research was focused on the development of efficient algorithms for model building and pattern extraction from large centralized databases. The advance in distributed computing technologies had its effect on data mining research and led to the second generation of data mining technology – *distributed data mining (DDM)* [46]. There are primarily two models proposed in the literature for distributed data mining: collect the data to a central site to be analyzed (which is infeasible for large data sets) and mine data locally and merge the results centrally. The latter model addresses the issue of communication overhead associated with data transfer, however, brings with it the new challenge of knowledge integration [38]. On yet another strand of development, *parallel data mining* techniques have been proposed and developed to overcome the problem of length execution times of complex machine learning algorithms [53].

Recently, we have witnessed a new wave in data mining research, that of mining streams of data. The emergence of sensor networks and dissemination of mobile devices along with the increase of computational power in such devices have opened up new vistas, opportunities and challenges for data mining. The data generated from sensors and other small devices are continuous and rapid and there is a real-need to analyze these data in real-time. Examples of such data streams include:

- the NASA Earth Observation System (EOS) and other NASA satellites that generate around 1.5 TB/day [14],
- the pair of Landsat 7 and Terra spacecraft which generates 350 GB of data per day [46],
- oil drills that can transmit data about their current drilling conditions at 1 Mb/second [42], and
- NetFlow from AT&T that generates a total of 100 GB/day of data [14].

The transfer of such vast amounts of data streams for analysis from sensor networks is dependent on satellite communication, which is exorbitantly expensive. A potential and intuitive solution to this problem is to develop new techniques that are capable of coping with the high data rate of streams and deliver mining results in real-time with application-oriented acceptable accuracy [24]. Such predictive or analytical models of streamed data can be used to reduce the transmission of raw data from sensor networks since they are compact and representative. The analysis of data in such ubiquitous environments has been termed *ubiquitous data mining*(UDM) [20, 32]. The research in the field has two main directions: the development of lightweight analysis algorithms that are capable of coping with rapid and continuous data streams and the application of such algorithms for real-time decision making [34, 35].

The applications of UDM can vary from critical astronomical and geophysical applications to real-time decision support in business applications. There are several potential scenarios for such applications:

- Analyzing biosensor measurements around a city for security reasons is one of the emerging applications [13].
- Analysis of simulation results and on-board sensors in science has potential in changing the mission plan or the experimental settings in real time.
- Web log and web click-streams analysis is an important application in the business domain. Such analysis of web data can lead to real time intrusion detection.
- The analysis of data streams generated from the marketplace, such as stock market information [35], is another important application.

One-pass algorithms have been proposed as the typical approach to dealing with the new challenges introduced by the resource constraints of wireless environments. We have developed lightweight one-pass algorithms: *LWC* for clustering, *LWClass* for classification and *LWF* for counting frequent items.

These algorithms have proved their efficiency [20, 21, 28]. However, we realized that one-pass algorithms don't address the problem of resource constraints with regard to high data rates of incoming streams.

Algorithm output granularity (AOG) introduces the first resource-aware data analysis approach that can cope with fluctuating data rates according to available memory and processing speed. AOG was first introduced in [20, 28]. Holistic perspective and integration of our lightweight algorithms with the resource-aware AOG approach is discussed. Experimental validation that demonstrates the feasibility and applicability of our proposed approach is presented in this chapter.

This chapter is organized as follows. In Section 12.2, an overview of the field of data-stream processing is presented. Data-stream mining is discussed in Section 12.3. Section 12.4 presents our AOG approach in addressing the problem. Our lightweight algorithms that use AOG are discussed in Section 12.5. The experimental results of using the AOG approach are shown and discussed in Section 12.5.3. Finally, open issues and challenges in the field conclude our chapter.

12.2 Data Streams: An Overview

A data stream is a flow of rapid data items that challenges the computing system's abilities to transmit, process, and store these massive amounts of incoming elements. Data streams have three models:

- time series: data items come in ascending order without increments or decrements;
- cash-register model: data items increment temporally;
- turnstile model: data items increment and decrement temporally.

The complexity of stream processing increases with the increase in model complexity [41]. Most data-stream applications deal with the cash-register model. Figure 12.1 shows the general processing model for mining data streams.

Fig. 12.1. Mining data stream process model.

Stream-processing systems [26] deal with stream storage, mining and querying over data streams. Storage and querying [54] on data streams have been addressed in research recently. STREAM [5], Aurora [1] and Tele-graphCQ [37] are representative work for such prototypes and systems. STan-ford stREam datA Manager (STREAM) [5] is a data-stream management sys-tem that handles multiple continuous data streams and supports long-running continuous queries. The intermediate results of a continuous query are stored in a *Scratch Store*. The results of a query could be a data stream transferred to the user or it could be a relation that could be stored for re-processing. Aurora [1] is a data work-flow system under construction. It directs the input data stream using pre-defined operators to the applications. The system can also maintain historical storage for *ad hoc* queries. The Telegraph project is a suite of novel technologies developed for continuous adaptive query process-ing implementation. TelegraphCQ [37] is the next generation of that system, which can deal with continuous data stream queries.

Querying over data streams faces the problem of the unbounded memory requirement and the high data rate [39]. Thus, the computation time per data element should be less than the data rate. Also, it is very hard, due to un-bounded memory requirements, to have an exact result. Approximating query results have been addressed recently. One of the techniques used in solving this problem is the sliding window, in which the query result is computed over a recent time interval. Batch processing, sampling, and synopsis data structures are other techniques for data reduction [6, 24].

12.3 Mining Data Streams

Mining data streams is the process of extracting application-oriented accept-able accuracy models and patterns from a continuous, rapid, possibly non-ended flow of data items. The state of the art of this recent field of study is given in this section. Data-stream mining techniques address three research problems:

- Unbounded memory requirements due to the continuous feature of the incoming data elements.
- Mining algorithms require several passes and this is not applicable because of the high data rate feature of the data stream.
- Data streams generated from sensors and other wireless data sources are very challenging to transfer to a central server to be analyzed.

12.3.1 Techniques

There are different algorithms proposed to tackle the high speed nature of mining data streams using different techniques. In this section, we review the state of the art of mining data streams.

Guha *et al.* [29, 30] have studied clustering data streams using the K-median technique. Their algorithm makes a single pass over the data and uses little space. It requires $O(nk)$ time and $O(n\varepsilon)$ space where k is the number of centers, n is the number of points and $\varepsilon < 1$. The algorithm is not implemented, but the analysis of space and time requirements of it are studied analytically. They proved that any k-median algorithm that achieves a constant factor approximation can not achieve a better run time than $O(nk)$. The algorithm starts by clustering a calculated size sample according to the available memory into $2k$, and then at a second level, the algorithm clusters the above points for a number of samples into $2k$ and this process is repeated to a number of levels, and finally it clusters the $2k$ clusters to k clusters.

Babcock *et al.* [8] have used an exponential histogram (EH) data structure to enhance the Guha *et al.* algorithm. They use the same algorithm described above, however they try to address the problem of merging clusters when the two sets of cluster centers to be merged are far apart by marinating the EH data structure. They have studied their proposed algorithm analytically.

Charikar *et al.* [12] have proposed a k-median algorithm that overcomes the problem of increasing approximation factors in the Guha *et al.* algorithm by increasing the number of levels used to result in the final solution of the divide and conquer algorithm. This technique has been studied analytically.

Domingos *et al.* [16, 17, 33] have proposed a general method for scaling up machine-learning algorithms. This method depends on determining an upper bound for the learner's loss as a function in a number of examples in each step of the algorithm. They have applied this method to K-means clustering (VFKM) and decision tree classification (VFDT) techniques. These algorithms have been implemented and tested on synthetic data sets as well as real web data. VFDT is a decision-tree learning system based on Hoeffding trees. It splits the tree using the current best attribute taking into consideration that the number of examples used satisfies a statistical result which is "Hoeffding bound". The algorithm also deactivates the least promising leaves and drops the non-potential attributes. VFKM uses the same concept to determine the number of examples needed in each step of the K-means algorithm. The VFKM runs as a sequence of K-means executions with each run using more examples than the previous one until a calculated statistical bound is satisfied.

O'Callaghan *et al.* [43] have proposed STREAM and LOCALSEARCH algorithms for high quality data-stream clustering. The STREAM algorithm starts by determining the size of the sample and then applies the LOCALSEARCH algorithm if the sample size is larger than a pre-specified equation result. This process is repeated for each data chunk. Finally, the LOCALSEARCH algorithm is applied to the cluster centers generated in the previous iterations.

Aggarwal *et al.* [2] have proposed a framework for clustering data steams, called the CluStream algorithm. The proposed technique divides the clustering process into two components. The online component stores summary statistics about the data streams and the offline one performs clustering on the summarized data according to a number of user preferences such as the time frame and the number of clusters. A number of experiments on real data sets have been conducted to prove the accuracy and efficiency of the proposed algorithm. Aggarwal *et al.* [3] have recently proposed HPStream, a projected clustering for high dimensional data streams. HPStream has outperformed CluStream in recent results. The idea of micro-clusters introduced in CluStream has also been adopted in On-Demand classification in [4] and it shows a high accuracy.

Keogh *et al.* [36] have proved empirically that most cited clustering time-series data-stream algorithms proposed so far in the literature come out with meaningless results in subsequence clustering. They have proposed a solution approach using a *k*-motif to choose the subsequences that the algorithm can work on.

Ganti *et al.* [19] have described an algorithm for model maintenance under insertion and deletion of blocks of data records. This algorithm can be applied to any incremental data mining model. They have also described a generic framework for change detection between two data sets in terms of the data mining results they induce. They formalize the above two techniques into two general algorithms: GEMM and Focus. The algorithms are not implemented, but are applied analytically to decision tree models and the frequent itemset model. The GEMM algorithm accepts a class of models and an incremental model maintenance algorithm for the unrestricted window option, and outputs a model maintenance algorithm for both window-independent and window-dependent block selection sequences. The FOCUS framework uses the difference between data mining models as the deviation in data sets.

Papadimitriou *et al.* [45] have proposed AWSOM (Arbitrary Window Stream mOdeling Method) for interesting patterns discovery from sensors. They developed a one-pass algorithm to incrementally update the patterns. Their method requires only $O(\log N)$ memory where N is the length of the sequence. They conducted experiments on real and synthetic data sets. They use wavelet coefficients for compact information representation and correlation structure detection, and then apply a linear regression model in the wavelet domain.

Giannella *et al.* [25] have proposed and implemented a frequent itemsets mining algorithm over data streams. They proposed to use tilted windows to calculate the frequent patterns for the most recent transactions based on the fact that people are more interested in the most recent transactions. They use an incremental algorithm to maintain the FP-stream, which is a tree data structure, to represent the frequent itemsets. They conducted a number of experiments to prove the algorithm's efficiency. Manku and Motwani [40] have proposed and implemented approximate frequency counts in data streams. The implemented algorithm uses all the previous historical data to calculate the frequent patterns incrementally.

Wang *et al.* [52] have proposed a general framework for mining concept-drifting data streams. They observed that data-stream mining algorithms don't take notice of concept drifting in the evolving data. They proposed using weighted classifier ensembles to mine data streams. The expiration of old data in their model depends on the data's distribution. They use synthetic and real life data streams to test their algorithm and compare between the single classifier and classifier ensembles. The proposed algorithm combines multiple classifiers weighted by their expected prediction accuracy. Also the selection of a number of classifiers instead of using all is an option in the proposed framework without losing accuracy.

Ordonez [44] has proposed several improvements to the K-means algorithm to cluster binary data streams. He proposed an incremental K-means algorithm. The experiments were conducted on real data sets as well as synthetic data sets. They demonstrated that the proposed algorithm outperforms the scalable K-means in most of the cases. The proposed algorithm is a one-pass algorithm in $O(Tkn)$ complexity, where T is the average transaction size, n is number of transactions and k is number of centers. The use of binary data simplifies the manipulation of categorical data and eliminates the need for data normalization. The main idea behind the proposed algorithm is that it updates the centers and cluster weights after reading a batch of transactions which equals square root of the number of transactions rather than updating them one by one.

Datar *et al.* [15] have proposed a sketch-based technique to identify the relaxed period and the average trend in a time-series data stream. The proposed methods are tested experimentally showing an acceptable accuracy for the approximation methods compared to the optimal solution. The main idea behind the proposed methods is the use of sketches as a dimensionality reduction technique. Table 12.1 shows a summary of mining data stream techniques.

12.3.2 Systems and Applications

Recently systems and applications that deal with data streams have been developed. These systems include:

- Burl *et al.* [10] have developed *Diamond Eye* for NASA and JPL. They aim by this project to enable remote systems as well as scientists to extract patterns from spatial objects in real-time image streams. The success of this project will enable "a new era of exploration using highly autonomous spacecraft, rovers, and sensors" [3].
- Kargupta *et al.* [35, 46] have developed the first UDM system: *MobiMine*. It is a client/server PDA-based distributed data mining application for financial data. They develop the system prototype using a single data source and multiple mobile clients; however the system is designed to handle multiple data sources. The server functionalities in the proposed system are data collection from different financial web sites; storage; selection of active stocks using common statistics; and applying online data mining techniques to the stock data. The client functionalities are portfolio management using a mobile micro database to store portfolio data and user's

Table 12.1. Summary of mining data stream techniques.

Algorithm	Mining Task	Technique	Implementation
VFKM	K-means	Sampling and reducing the number of passes at each step of the algorithm	Implemented and tested.
VFDT	Decision trees	Sampling and reducing the number of passes at each step of the algorithm	Implemented and tested.
Approximate Frequent Counts	Frequent itemsets	Incremental pruning and update of itemsets with each block of transactions	Implemented and tested.
FP-Stream	Frequent itemsets	Incremental pruning and update of itemsets with each block of transactions and time-sensitive patterns extension	Implemented and tested.
Concept-Drifting Classification	Classification	Ensemble classifiers	Implemented and tested.
AWSOM	Prediction	Incremental wavelets	Implemented and tested. (This algorithm is designed to run on a sensor but the implementation is not on a sensor).
Approximate K-median	K-median	Sampling and reducing the number of passes at each step of the algorithm	Analytical Study.
GEMM	Applied to decision tress and frequent itemsets	Sampling	Analytical study.
CDM	Decision trees, Bayesian nets and clustering	Fourier spectrum representation of the results to save the limited bandwidth	Implemented and tested.
ClusStream	Clustering	Online summarization and offline clustering	Implemented and tested.
STREAM, LOCAL SEARCH	Clustering	Sampling and incremental learning	Implemented and tested against other techniques.

preference information, and construction of the WatchList and this is the first point of interaction between the client and the server. The server computes the most active stocks in the market, and the client in turn selects a subset of this list to construct the personalized WatchList according to an optimization module. The second point of interaction between the client and the server is that the server performs online data mining and represents the results as a Fourier spectrum and then sends this to the client, and the client in turn displays the results on the screen. Kargupta and his colleagues believe that a PDA may not be the right place to perform data analysis.

- Kargupta *et al.* [34] have developed a Vehicle Data Stream Mining System (*VEDAS*). It is a ubiquitous data-mining system that allows continuous monitoring and pattern extraction from data streams generated on board a moving vehicle. The mining component is located at the PDA. VEDAS uses online incremental clustering for modeling of driving behavior and road safety.

- Tanner *et al.*[48] have developed an environment for on-board processing (*EVE*). The system mines data streams continuously generated from measurements of different on-board sensors. Only interesting patterns are sent to the ground stations for further analysis, preserving the limited bandwidth.

- Srivastava and Stroeve [47] work in a NASA project for onboard detection of geophysical processes, such as snow, ice and clouds. They use kernel clustering methods for data compression to preserve limited bandwidth when sending image streams to the ground centers. The kernel methods have been chosen due to their low computational complexity.

- Cai *et al.* [11] are developing an integrated mining and querying system. The system can classify, cluster, count frequency and query over data streams. Mining alarming incidents of data streams (*MAIDS*) is currently under development and recently they had a prototype presentation.

The above systems and techniques use different strategies to overcome the three main problems discussed earlier. The following is an abstraction of these strategies [27]:

- **Input data rate adaptation:** This approach uses sampling, filtering, aggregation, and load shedding on the incoming data elements. Sampling is the process of statistically selecting the elements of the incoming stream that will be analyzed. Filtering is the semantics sampling in which the data element is checked for its importance, for example to be analyzed or not. Aggregation is the representation of number of element in one aggregated elements using some statistical measure such as the average. Load shedding, which has been proposed in the context of querying data streams [7, 49, 50, 51] rather than mining data streams, is the process of eliminating a batch of subsequent elements from being analyzed rather than checking each element that is used in the sampling technique. Figure 12.2 illustrates the idea of data rate adaptation from the input side using sampling.

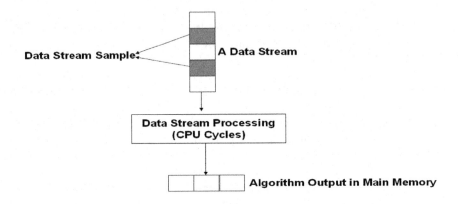

Fig. 12.2. Data rate adaptation using sampling.

- **Knowledge abstraction level:** This approach uses the higher knowledge level to categorize the incoming elements into a limited number of categories and replace each incoming element with the matching category according to a specified measure or a look-up table. This producs fewer results, conserving the limited memory. Moreover, it requires fewer processing CPU cycles.
- **Approximation algorithms:** In this approach, one-pass mining algorithms are designed to approximate the mining results according to some acceptable error margin. Approximation algorithms have been studied extensively in addressing hard problems in computer algorithms.

The above strategies have attempted to solve the research problems raised from mining streams of information; however the issue of resource-awareness with regard to high data rates has not been addressed. We have proposed algorithm output granularity *(AOG)* as a novel strategy to solve this problem. The details and formalization of the approach is given in the next section.

12.4 Algorithm Output Granularity

AOG uses data rate adaptation from the output side. Figure 12.3 [20] shows our strategy. We use the algorithm output granularity to preserve the limited memory size according to the incoming data rate and the remaining time to

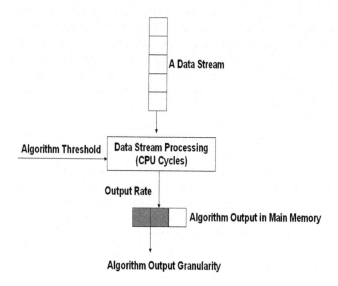

Fig. 12.3. The algorithm output granularity approach.

mine the incoming stream without incremental integration; this represents a sufficient time for model stability given that the more frequent the knowledge integration, the less the algorithm accuracy. The algorithm threshold is a controlling distance-based parameter that is able to change the algorithm output rate according to data rate, available memory, algorithm output rate history and remaining time for mining without integration.

The algorithm output granularity approach is based on the following axioms:

- The algorithm rate (AR) is a function of the data rate (DR), i.e., AR = f(DR).
- The time needed to fill the available memory by the algorithm results (TM) is a function of (AR), i.e., TM = f(AR).
- The algorithm accuracy (AC) is a function of (TM), i.e., AC = f(TM).

AOG is a three-stage, resource-aware, distance-based data-streams mining approach. The process of mining data streams using AOG starts with a mining phase. In this step, a threshold distance measure is determined. The algorithm can have only one look at each data element. Using a distance threshold in clustering has been introduced in BIRCH [32] for mining large data sets. In the mining stage, there are three variations in using this threshold according to the mining technique:

- Clustering: the threshold is used to specify the minimum distance between the cluster center and the data element;

- Classification: In addition to using the threshold in specifying the distance, the class label is checked. If the class label of the stored items and the new item that is similar (within the accepted distance) are the same, the weight of the stored item is increased along with the weighted average of the other attributes, otherwise the weight is decreased and the new item is ignored;
- Frequent patterns: the threshold is used to determine the number of counters for the heavy hitters.

The second stage in the AOG mining approach is the adaptation phase. In this phase, the threshold value is adjusted to cope with the data rate of the incoming stream, the available memory, and time constraints to fill the available memory with generated knowledge. This stage gives the uniqueness of our approach in adjusting the output rate according to the available resources of the computing device. The last stage in the AOG approach is the knowledge integration phase. This stage represents the merging of generated results when the memory is full. This integration allows the continuity of the mining process. Figure 12.4 [28] shows the AOG mining process.

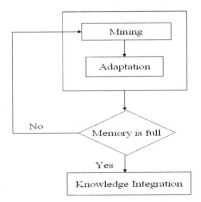

Fig. 12.4. The AOG mining approach.

12.4.1 Concept and Terminology of AOG

Algorithm Threshold
The algorithm threshold is a controlling parameter built into the algorithm logic that encourages or discourages the creation of new outputs according to three factors that vary over temporal scale:

- Available memory.
- Remaining time to fill the available memory.
- Data stream rate.

The algorithm threshold is the maximum acceptable distance between the group means and the data element of the stream. The higher the threshold, the lower the output size produced. The algorithm threshold can use Euclidean or Manhattan distance functions and a normalization process would be done online in the case of a multidimensional data stream.

Threshold Lower Bound

The threshold lower bound is the minimum acceptable distance (similarity measure) that can be used. As a matter of fact, the lower the threshold the higher the algorithm accuracy. If the distance measure is very small, it has two major drawbacks. It is meaningless in some applications, such as astronomical once, to set the distance measure to a very small value. The distance between some of data elements in such applications is relatively high. And the smaller the threshold, the greater the run time for the model use.

Threshold Upper Bound

The threshold upper bound is the maximum acceptable similarity measure that can be accepted to produce meaningful results. If the distance measure is high, the model building is faster; however it has the limitation of needing to produce meaningful results; that is, it should not group data elements that are totally different in the same class or cluster.

Output Granularity

The output granularity is the amount of generated results that are acceptable according to a pre-specified accuracy measure. This amount should be resident in memory before doing any incremental integration.

Time Threshold

The time threshold is the required time to generate the results before any incremental integration. This time might be specified by the user or calculated adaptively based on the history of running the algorithm.

Time Frame

The time frame is the time between each two consecutive data rate measurements. This time varies from one application to another and from one mining technique to another.

12.4.2 The Process of Mining Data Stream

i. Determine the frequency of adaptation and mining.
ii. According to the data rate, calculate the algorithm output rate and the algorithm threshold.
iii. Mine the incoming stream using the calculated algorithm threshold.
iv. Adjust the threshold after a time frame to adapt with the change in the data rate using linear regression.

v. Repeat steps 3 and 4 till the algorithm lasts the time interval threshold.

vi. Perform knowledge integration of the results

The algorithm output granularity in mining data streams has primitive parameters, and operations that operate on these parameters. AOG algebra is concerned with defining these parameters and operations. The development of AOG-based mining techniques should be guided by these primitives depending on empirical studies. That means defining the timing settings of these parameters to get the required results. Thus the settings of these parameters depend on the application and technique used. For example, we can use certain settings for a clustering technique when we use it in astronomical applications that require higher accuracy; however we can change these settings in business applications that require less accuracy. Figure 12.5 and Figure 12.6 show the conceptual framework of AOG.

AOG parameters:

- **TFi:** The time frame i
- **Di:** Input data stream during the time frame i
- **I(Di):** Average data rate of the input stream Di
- **O(Di):** Average output rate resulting from mining the stream Di

AOG operations:

- $\alpha(\mathbf{Di})$ Mining process of the Di stream
- $\beta([\mathbf{I(D1)}, \mathbf{O(D1)}], \ldots, [\mathbf{I(Di)}, \mathbf{O(Di)}])$ Adaptation process of the algorithm threshold at the end of time frame i
- Ω (**Oi, ...,Ox**) Knowledge integration process done on the output i to the output x

AOG settings:

- **D(TF)** Time duration of each time frame
- **D(Ω)** Time duration between each two consecutive knowledge integration processes

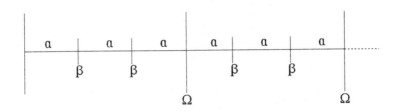

Fig. 12.5. AOG-based mining.

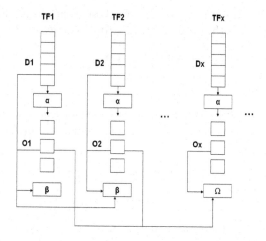

Fig. 12.6. AOG-based mining (detailed).

12.4.3 Mathematical Formalization

The following is a mathematical formalization of AOG-based data-stream mining. Table 12.2 shows the symbols used in the mathematical formulation.

Table 12.2. AOG symbols.

Symbol	Meaning
AAO	Atomic algorithm output size. The size of smallest the element produced from the mining algorithm. For example, in clustering, the AAO represents the size of storing the cluster center and the weight of the cluster.
D	Duration of the time frame.
M_i	Remaining memory size by the end of time frame i ($M_i = M_{i-1} - (AAO \times O(TF_i))$).
TF_i	Time frame i by which the threshold is adjusted to cope with the data rate.
$N(TF_i)$	Number of data elements that arrived during the time frame i.
$O(TF_i)$	Number of outputs produced during the time frame i.
AR_i	The average algorithm rate during TF_i ($O(TF_i)/D$).
DR_i	The average data rate during TF_i ($N(TF_i)/D$).
t_i	Remaining time from the time interval threshold needed by the algorithm to fill the main memory ($T_i = T_{i-1} - D$).
th_i	Threshold value during the time frame i.

The main idea behind our approach is to change the threshold value that in turn changes the algorithm rate according to three factors:

- History of data rate to algorithm rate ratio
- Remaining time
- Remaining memory

The target is to keep the balance between the algorithm rate and the data rate from one side and the remaining time and remaining memory from the other side.

$$[(AR_{i+1}/DR_{i+1})/(AR_i/DR_i)] = [(M_i/AR_i)/t_i] \qquad (12.1)$$

$$AR_{i+1} = (M_i/t_i).(DR_{i+1}/DR_i) \qquad (12.2)$$

Using the AR_{i+1} in the following equation to determine the new threshold value:

$$th_{i+1} = [(AR_{i+1}/DR_{i+1}).th_i]/(AR_i/DR_i) \qquad (12.3)$$

After a time frame we can use linear regression to estimate the threshold using the values obtained from the AR and th.

$$th = a.AR + b, b = \Sigma(th.AR)/\Sigma AR^2, a = (\Sigma th/\Sigma N) - (b\Sigma th/N) \qquad (12.4)$$

Linear regression is used because of the fluctuating distribution of the incoming data elements. Data stream distribution is an effective factor in determining the algorithm output rate.

12.5 AOG-based Mining Techniques

In this section, we show the application of the algorithm output granularity to clustering, classification and frequent items.

12.5.1 Lightweight Clustering (LWC)

LWC is a one-pass similarity-based algorithm. The main idea behind the algorithm is to incrementally add new data elements to existing clusters according to an adaptive threshold value. If the distance between the new data point and all existing cluster centers is greater than the current threshold value, then create a new cluster. Figure 12.7 shows the algorithm.

```
1.   x = 1, c = 1, M = number of memory blocks
     available
2.   Receive data item DI[x]
3.   Center[c] = DI[x]
4.   M = M - 1
5.   Repeat
6.       x = x + 1
7.       Receive DI[x]
8.       For i = 1 to c
9.           Measure the distance between Center[i]
             and DI[x]
10.      If distance > dist (the threshold)
11.      Then
12.          c = c + 1
13.          If (M <> 0)
14.          Then
15.              Center[c] = DI[x]
16.          Else
17.              Merge DI[]
18.      Else
19.          For j = 1 to c
20.              Compare between Center[j] and DI[x] to
                 find shortest distance
21.              Increase weight for Center[j] by the
                 shortest distance
22.              Center[j] = (Center[j] * weight + DI[x]) /
                 (weight + 1)
24.  Until Done.
```

Fig. 12.7. Lightweight clustering algorithm.

12.5.2 Lightweight Classification (LWClass)

LWClass starts with determining the number of instances according to the available space in the main memory. Once a new classified data element arrives, the algorithm searches for the nearest instance already stored in the main memory according to a pre-specified distance threshold. The threshold here represents the similarity measure acceptable by the algorithm to consider two or more elements as one element according to the element's attribute values. If the algorithm finds this element, it checks the class label. If the class label is the same, it increases the weight for this instance by one, otherwise it decrements the weight by one. If the weight becomes zero, this element will be released from the memory. Given that CL is the class label vector, Figure 12.8 shows the LWClass algorithm.

```
1. x = 1, c = 1, M = number of memory blocks available
2. Receive data item DI[x]
3. Center[c] = DI[x]
4. M = M - 1
5. Repeat
6.   x = x + 1
7.   Receive DI[x]
8.   For i = 1 to c
9.       Measure the distance between Center[i] and DI[x]
10. If distance > dist (The threshold)
11. Then
12.      c = c + 1
13.      If (M <> 0)
14.      Then
15.          Center[c] = DI[x]
16.      Else
17.          Merge DI[]
18. Else
19.      For j = 1 to c
20.          Compare between Center[j] and DI[x] to find
             shortest distance
21.      If CL[j] = CL[x]
22.      Then
23.          Increase weight for Center[j] with shortest
             distance
24.          Center[j] = (Center[j] * weight + DI[x]) /
             (weight + 1)
25.      Else
26.          Increase weight for Center[j] with shortest
             distance
27.Until Done
```

Fig. 12.8. Lightweight classification algorithm.

12.5.3 Lightweight Frequent Items (LWF)

LWF starts by setting the number of frequent items that will be calculated according to the available memory. This number changes over time to cope with the high data rate. The algorithm receives the data elements one by one, tries to find a counter for any new item and increases the item for the registered items. If all the counters are occupied, any new item will be ignored and the counters will be decreased by one till the algorithm reaches some time threshold. A number of the least frequent items will be ignored and their counters will be re-set to zero. If the new item is similar to one of the items in memory, the counter will be increased by one. The main parameters that can affect the algorithm accuracy are time threshold, number of calculated frequent items and number of items that will be ignored. Their counters will be re-set after some time threshold. Figure 12.9 shows the algorithm outline for the LWF algorithm.

```
 1. Set the number of top frequent items to k
 2. Set the counter for each k
 3. Repeat
 4.  Receive the item
 5.  If the item is new and one of the k counters are 0
 6.  Then
 7.      Put this item and increase the counter by 1
 8.  Else
 9.      If the item is already in one of the k counters
10.      Then
11.          Increase the counter by 1
12.      Else
13.          If the item is new and all the counters are full
14.          Then
15.              Check the time
16.              If time > Threshold Time
17.              Then
18.                  Re-set number of least n of k counters to 0
19.                  Put the new item and increase the counter by 1
20.              Else
21.                  Ignore the item
22.                  Decrease all the counters by 1
23. Until Done
```

Fig. 12.9. Lightweight frequent item algorithm.

12.6 Experimental Results

The experiments have been developed on an iPAQ with 64 MB of RAM and a strongARM processor, running Microsoft Windows CE version 3.0.9348. The data sets used are synthetic data with low dimensionality generated randomly with uniform distribution. Different domains were used in the experiments. The program was developed using Microsoft embedded Visual C++ 3.0. We ran several experiments using AOG with LWC, LWClass and LWF. The aim of these experiments was to measure the accuracy of the generated results with and without adding the AOG in addition to measuring the AOG cost overhead. Figure 12.10 and Figure 12.11 show that the AOG overhead is stable with the increase in data set size which indicates the applicability of this approach in such a resource-constrained environment. Figure 12.12 shows the feasibility of AOG using the concept of the number of generated knowledge structures. The number of generated clusters is comparable with and without AOG. Thus using AOG adds resource awareness to mining data-stream algorithms while maintaining a high degree of accuracy. The accuracy is measured as the number of created knowledge structures.

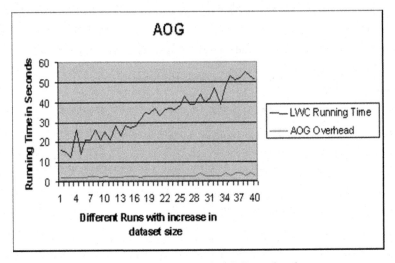

Fig. 12.10. LWC with AOG overhead.

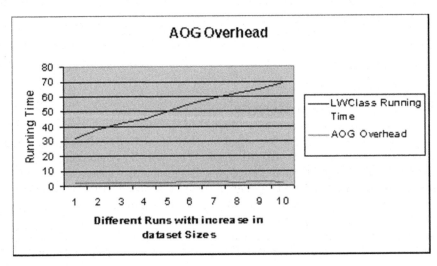

Fig. 12.11. LWClass with AOG overhead.

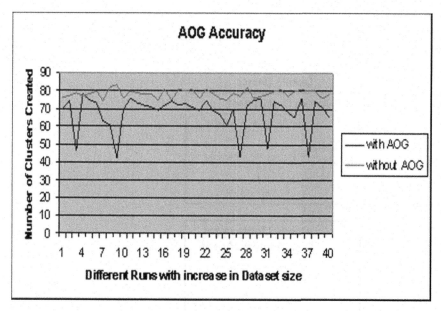

Fig. 12.12. Number of knowledge structures created with and without AOG.

12.7 RA-UDM

Having developed the theoretical model and experimental validation, we are now implementing a resource-aware UDM system (RA-UDM) [22, 27]. In this section, we describe the architecture, design and operation of each component of this system. The system architecture of our approach is shown in Figure 12.13 [27]. The detailed discussion about each component is given in the following.

Resource-aware Component
Local resource information is a resource monitoring component which is able to inform the system by the number of running processes in a mobile device, battery consumption status, available memory and scheduled resources.
Context-aware middleware is a component that can monitor the environmental measurements such as the effective bandwidth. It can use reasoning techniques to reason about the context attributes of the mobile device.
Resource measurements is a component that can receive the information from the above two modules and formulate this information to be used by the solution optimizer.
Solution optimizer is a component determines the data mining task scenario according to the available information about the local and context information. The module can choose from different scenarios to achieve the UDM process in a cost-efficient way. The following is a formalization of this task. Table 12.3 shows the symbols used.

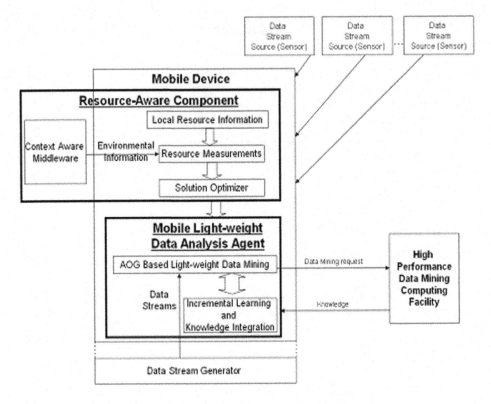

Fig. 12.13. RA-UDM system architecture.

In the UDM process, we have three main strategies:

- Fully distributed data mining, in which the DM processes are done locally:

$$
\begin{aligned}
Cost(UDM) = \quad & \Sigma_{i=1}^{n}DM_i + \Sigma_{j=1}^{m}DM_j + \Sigma_{z\in\{1,2,\dots,n+m-1\}}KI_z + \\
& \Sigma_{t\in\{1,2,\dots,n+m-1\}}(K_t/band_t) + (K_{Final}/band_{Final}) + \\
& \Sigma_{e\in\{1,2,\dots,n+m\}}(age_e/band_e) \qquad (12.5)
\end{aligned}
$$

- Central data mining, in which the DM process is done centrally:

$$
Cost(UDM) = \Sigma_{i=1}^{n+m}(D_i/band_i) + DM + KI + (K_{Final}/band_{Final})
$$
$$(12.6)$$

- Partially distributed data mining, in which the DM processes are done locally at some sites to which the other sites transfer their data:

$$
\begin{aligned}
Cost(UDM) = \quad & \Sigma_{i=1}^{c}D_i + \Sigma_{j=1}^{n+m-c}DM_j + \Sigma_{z\in\{1,2,\dots,n+m-c-1\}}KI_z + \\
& \Sigma_{t\in\{1,2,\dots,n+m-c-1\}}(K_t/band_t) + (K_{Final}/band_{Final}) + \\
& \Sigma_{e\in\{1,2,\dots,n+m-c\}}(age_e/band_e) \qquad (12.7)
\end{aligned}
$$

Table 12.3. Solution optimizer symbols.

Symbol	Meaning
DM	The time needed for the data mining process centrally
DM_i	The time needed for the data process at site i
n	Number of stationary data sources
m	Number of mobile data sources
KI	The time needed for knowledge integration process at the central site
KI_z	The time needed for KI at site z
$band_t$	The effective bandwidth between two devices
K_t	The generated knowledge at site t
ag_e	The mobile agent e transferred to a specific data source

Mobile Lightweight Data Analysis Agent

Lightweight data-mining agent is a component that incorporates our AOG methodology in mining data streams. The module has the ability to continue the process at another device in case of a sudden lack of computational resources. This is done by using mobile agents to perform this process.

Incremental learning and knowledge integration: is a component that can merge the results when the device runs out of memory. It also has the ability to integrate knowledge that has been sent from other mobile devices.

Data stream generator Most mobile devices have the ability to generate data streams. Sensors are a typical example. Handheld devices can generate data streams about the user context.

High performance data-mining computing facility is component that runs a grid computing facility. This is the manager for the whole process and can inform the mobile device of the solution if the solution optimizer can't achieve the required information to make a decision.

12.8 Conclusions

Mining data streams is in its infancy. The last two years have witnessed increasing attention this area of research because of the increase in sensor networks that generate vast amounts of data streams and the increase of computational power of small devices. In this chapter, we have presented our contribution to the field represented in three mining techniques and a general strategy that adds resource-awareness which is a highly demanded feature in pervasive and ubiquitous environments. AOG has proved its applicability and efficiency.

The following open issues need to be addressed to realize the full potential of this exciting field [18, 23]:

- Handling the continuous flow of data streams: Data items in data streams are characterized by continuity. That dictates the design of non-stopping management and analysis techniques that can cope with the continuous, rapid data elements.
- Minimizing energy consumption of the mobile device [9]: The analysis component in the UDM is local to the mobile device site. Mobile devices face the problem of battery life-time.
- Unbounded memory requirements: Due to the continuous flow of data streams, sensors or handheld devices have the problem of lack of sufficient memory size to run traditional data-mining techniques.
- Transferring data mining results over a wireless network with limited bandwidth: The wireless environment is characterized by unreliable connections and limited bandwidth. If the number of mobile devices involved in a UDM process is high, the process of sending the results back to a central site becomes a challenging process.
- Data mining results visualization on the small screen of mobile device: The user interface on a handheld device for visualizing data-mining results is a challenging issue. The visualization of data mining results on a desktop is still a challenging process. Novel visualization techniques that are concerned with the size of image should be investigated.
- Modeling changes of mining results over time: Due to the continuity of data streams, some researchers have pointed out that capturing the change of mining results is more important in this area than the mining results. The research issue is how to model this change in the results.
- Interactive mining environment to satisfy user requirements: The user should be able to change the process settings in real time. The problem is how the mining technique can use the generated results to integrate with the new results after the change in the settings.
- Integration between data-stream management systems and ubiquitous data-stream mining approaches: There is a separation between the research in querying and management of data streams and mining data streams. The integration between the two is an important research issue that should be addressed by the research community. The process of management and analysis of data streams is highly correlated.
- The relationship between the proposed techniques and the needs of real-world applications: The needs of real-time analysis of data streams is affected by the application needs. Most of the proposed techniques don't pay attention to real-world applications: they attempt to achieve the mining task with low computational and space complexity regardless of the applicability of such techniques. One of the interesting studies in this area is by Keogh *et al.*[36] who have proved that the results of the most cited clustering techniques in times series are meaningless.

- Data pre-processing in the stream-mining process: One of the important issues in data mining is data pre-processing. In data streams, data pre-processing is a challenging process, because the global view over the data set is missed. The need for real-time lightweight data pre-processing is an urgent need that should be addressed in order to come out with meaningful results.
- The technological issue of mining data streams: The real-time aspect of UDM raises some issues about the technologies that should be used. Tools that can be used for offline business applications are not sufficient to develop real-time applications.
- The formalization of real-time accuracy evaluation: There is a need to formalize the accuracy evaluation, so the user can know the degree of reliability of the extracted knowledge.
- The data-stream computing formalization: The mining of data streams could be formalized within a theory of data stream computation [31]. This formalization will facilitate the design and development of algorithms based on a concrete mathematical foundation.

References

[1] Abadi, D., D. Carney, U. Cetintemel, M. Cherniack, C. Convey, C. Erwin, E. Galvez, M. Hatoun, J. Hwang, A. Maskey, A. Rasin, A. Singer, M. Stonebraker, N. Tatbul, Y. Xing, R. Yan and S. Zdonik, 2003: Aurora: A data stream management system (demonstration). *Proceedings of the ACM SIGMOD International Conference on Management of Data.*

[2] Aggarwal, C., J. Han, J. Wang and P. S. Yu, 2003: A framework for clustering evolving data streams. *Proceedings of 2003 International Conference on Very Large Databases.*

[3] — 2004: A framework for projected clustering of high dimensional data streams. *Proceedings of International Conference on Very Large Databases.*

[4] — 2004: On demand classification of data streams. *Proceedings of International Conference on Knowledge Discovery and Data Mining.*

[5] Arasu, A., B. Babcock, S. Babu, M. Datar, K. Ito, I. Nishizawa, J. Rosenstein and J. Widom, 2003: STREAM: The Stanford stream data manager demonstration description – short overview of system status and plans. *Proceedings of the ACM International Conference on Management of Data.*

[6] Babcock, B., S. Babu, M. Datar, R. Motwani and J. Widom, 2002: Models and issues in data stream systems. *Proceedings of the 21st Symposium on Principles of Database Systems.*

[7] Babcock, B., M. Datar and R. Motwani 2003: Load shedding techniques for data stream systems (short paper). *Proceedings of the Workshop on Management and Processing of Data Streams.*

[8] Babcock, B., M. Datar, R. Motwani and L. O'Callaghan, 2003: Maintaining variance and k-medians over data stream windows. *Proceedings of the 22nd Symposium on Principles of Database Systems.*

[9] Bhargava, R., H. Kargupta and M. Powers, 2003: Energy consumption in data analysis for on-board and distributed applications. *Proceedings of the International Conference on Machine Learning workshop on Machine Learning Technologies for Autonomous Space Applications.*

[10] Burl, M., C. Fowlkes, J. Roden, A. Stechert and S. Mukhtar, 1999: Diamond Eye: A distributed architecture for image data mining. *Proceedings of SPIE Conference on Data Mining and Knowledge Discovery: Theory, Tools, and Technology.*

[11] Cai, Y. D., D. Clutter, G. Pape, J. Han, M. Welge and L. Auvil, 2004: MAIDS: Mining alarming incidents from data streams (system demonstration). *Proceedings of ACM-SIGMOD International Conference on Management of Data.*

[12] Charikar, M., L. O'Callaghan and R. Panigrahy, 2003: Better streaming algorithms for clustering problems. *Proceedings of 35th ACM Symposium on Theory of Computing.*

[13] Cormode, G., and S. Muthukrishnan, 2003: Radial histograms for spatial streams, *Technical Report DIMACS TR 2003-11.*

[14] Coughlan, J., 2004: Accelerating scientific discovery at NASA. *Proceedings of Fourth SIAM International Conference on Data Mining.*

[15] Datar, M., A. Gionis, P. Indyk and R. Motwani: Maintaining stream statistics over sliding windows (extended abstract). *Proceedings of 13th Annual ACM-SIAM Symposium on Discrete Algorithms.*

[16] Domingos, P., and G. Hulten, 2000: Mining high-speed data streams. *Proceedings of the Association for Computing Machinery Sixth International Conference on Knowledge Discovery and Data Mining* ,71–80.

[17] — 2001: A general method for scaling up machine learning algorithms and its application to clustering. *Proceedings of the Eighteenth International Conference on Machine Learning,* 106–13.

[18] Dong, G., J. Han, L. Lakshmanan, J. Pei, H. Wang and P. S. Yu, 2003: Online mining of changes from data streams: Research problems and preliminary results. *Proceedings of the ACM SIGMOD Workshop on Management and Processing of Data Streams. In cooperation with the ACM-SIGMOD International Conference on Management of Data.*

[19] Ganti, V., J. Gehrke and R. Ramakrishnan, 2002: Mining data streams under block evolution. *SIGKDD Explorations,* **3(2)**, 1–10.

[20] Gaber, M. M., S. Krishnaswamy and A. Zaslavsky, 2003: Adaptive mining techniques for data streams using algorithm output granularity. *Proceedings of the Australasian Data Mining Workshop, Held in conjunction with the Congress on Evolutionary Computation.*

[21] — 2004: Cost-efficient mining techniques for data streams. *Proceedings of the Australasian Workshop on Data Mining and Web Intelligence (DMWI2004), CRPIT, 32. Purvis, M., Ed. ACS.*

[22] — 2004: A wireless data stream mining model. *Proceedings of the Third International Workshop on Wireless Information Systems, Held in conjunction with the Sixth International Conference on Enterprise Information Systems ICEIS Press.*

[23] — 2004: Ubiquitous data stream mining, *Current Research and Future Directions Workshop Proceedings held in conjunction with the Eighth Pacific-Asia Conference on Knowledge Discovery and Data Mining.*

[24] Garofalakis, M., J. Gehrke and R. Rastogi, 2002: Querying and mining data streams: you only get one look (a tutorial). *Proceedings of the ACM SIGMOD international conference on Management of data.*

[25] Giannella, C., J. Han, J. Pei, X. Yan and P. S. Yu, 2003: Mining frequent patterns in data streams at multiple time granularities. H. Kargupta, A. Joshi, K. Sivakumar and Y. Yesha (eds.), *Next Generation Data Mining, AAAI/MIT.*

[26] Golab L., and M. Ozsu, 2003: Issues in data stream management. *SIGMOD Record*, Number 2, **32**, 5–14.

[27] Gaber, M. M., A. Zaslavsky and S. Krishnaswamy, 2004: A cost-efficient model for ubiquitous data stream mining. *Proceedings of the Tenth International Conference on Information Processing and Management of Uncertainty in Knowledge-Based Systems.*

[28] — 2004: Resource-aware knowledge discovery in data streams. *Proceedings of First International Workshop on Knowledge Discovery in Data Streams, to be held in conjunction with the 15th European Conference on Machine Learning and the 8th European Conference on the Principals and Practice of Knowledge Discovery in Databases.*

[29] Guha, S., N. Mishra, R. Motwani and L. O'Callaghan, 2000: Clustering data streams. *Proceedings of the IEEE Annual Symposium on Foundations of Computer Science.*

[30] Guha, S., A. Meyerson, N. Mishra, R. Motwani and L. O'Callaghan, 2003: Clustering data streams: Theory and practice. *TKDE special issue on clustering*, **15.**

[31] Henzinger, M., P. Raghavan and S. Rajagopalan, 1998: Computing on data streams. *Technical Note 1998-011, Digital Systems Research Center.*

[32] Hsu, J., 2002: Data mining trends and developments: The key data mining technologies and applications for the 21st century. *Proceedings of the 19th Annual Information Systems Education Conference.*

[33] Hulten, G., L. Spencer and P. Domingos, 2001: Mining time-changing data streams. *Proceedings of the seventh ACM SIGKDD international conference on Knowledge discovery and data mining*, 97–106.

[34] Kargupta, H., R. Bhargava, K. Liu, M. Powers, P. Blair, S. Bushra, J. Dull, K. Sarkar, M. Klein, M. Vasa and D. Handy, 2004: VEDAS: A mobile and distributed data stream mining system for real-time vehicle monitoring. *Proceedings of SIAM International Conference on Data Mining.*

[35] Kargupta, H., B. Park, S. Pittie, L. Liu, D. Kushraj and K. Sarkar, 2002: MobiMine: Monitoring the stock market from a PDA. *ACM SIGKDD Explorations*, **3**, **2**, 37–46.

[36] Keogh, E., J. Lin and W. Truppel, 2003: Clustering of time series subsequences is meaningless: implications for past and future research. *Proceedings of the 3rd IEEE International Conference on Data Mining.*

[37] Krishnamurthy, S., S. Chandrasekaran, O. Cooper, A. Deshpande, M. Franklin, J. Hellerstein, W. Hong, S. Madden, V. Raman, F. Reiss and M. Shah, 2003: TelegraphCQ: An architectural status report. *IEEE Data Engineering Bulletin*, **26(1)**.

[38] Krishnaswamy, S., S. W. Loke and A. Zaslavsky, 2000: Cost models for heterogeneous distributed data mining. *Proceedings of the 12th International Conference on Software Engineering and Knowledge Engineering*, 31–8.

[39] Koudas, N., and D. Srivastava, 2003: Data stream query processing: A tutorial. *Presented at International Conference on Very Large Databases.*

[40] Manku, G. S., and R. Motwani, 2002: Approximate frequency counts over data streams. *Proceedings of the 28th International Conference on Very Large Databases.*

[41] Muthukrishnan, S., 2003: Data streams: algorithms and applications. *Proceedings of the fourteenth annual ACM-SIAM symposium on discrete algorithms.*

[42] Muthukrishnan, S., 2003: Seminar on processing massive data sets. Available at URL: `athos.rutgers.edu/%7Emuthu/stream- seminar.html`.

[43] O'Callaghan, L., N. Mishra, A. Meyerson, S. Guha and R. Motwani, 2002: Streaming-data algorithms for high-quality clustering. *Proceedings of IEEE International Conference on Data Engineering.*

[44] Ordonez, C., 2003: Clustering binary data streams with k-means. *Proceedings of ACM SIGMOD Workshop on Research Issues on Data Mining and Knowledge Discovery (DMKD)*, 10–17.

[45] Papadimitriou, S., C. Faloutsos and A. Brockwell, 2003: Adaptive, hands-off stream mining. *Proceedings of 29th International Conference on Very Large Databases.*

[46] Park, B., and H. Kargupta, 2002: Distributed data mining: Algorithms, systems, and applications. *Data Mining Handbook, Nong Ye (ed.).*

[47] Srivastava, A., and J. Stroeve, 2003: Onboard detection of snow, ice, clouds and other geophysical processes using kernel methods. *Proceedings of the International Conference on Machine Learning workshop on Machine Learning Technologies for Autonomous Space Applications.*

[48] Tanner, S., M. Alshayeb, E. Criswell, M. Iyer, A. McDowell, M. McEniry and K. Regner, 2002: EVE: On-board process planning and execution. *Proceedings of Earth Science Technology Conference.*

[49] Tatbul, N., U. Cetintemel, S. Zdonik, M. Cherniack and M. Stonebraker, 2003: Load shedding in a data stream manager. *Proceedings of the 29th International Conference on Very Large Data Bases.*

[50] — 2003 Load shedding on data streams, *Proceedings of the Workshop on Management and Processing of Data Streams.*

[51] Viglas, S. D., and F. Jeffrey, 2002: Rate based query optimization for streaming information sources. *Proceedings of the ACM SIGMOD International Conference on Management of Data.*

[52] Wang, H., W. Fan, P. Yu and J. Han, 2003: Mining concept-drifting data streams using ensemble classifiers. *Proceedings of 9th ACM International Conference on Knowledge Discovery and Data Mining.*

[53] Zaki, M., V. Stonebraker and D. Skillicorn, eds., 2001: Parallel and distributed data mining. *CD-ROM Workshop Proceedings, IEEE Computer Society Press.*

[54] Zhu, Y., and D. Shasha, 2002: StatStream: Statistical monitoring of thousands of data streams in real time. *Proceedings of the 28th International Conference on Very Large Databases*, 358–69.

Discovering an Evolutionary Classifier over a High-speed Nonstatic Stream

Jiong Yang, Xifeng Yan, Jiawei Han and Wei Wang

Summary. With the emergence of large-volume and high-speed streaming data, mining data streams has become a focus of increasing interest. The major new challenges in streaming data mining are as follows: since streams may flow in and out indefinitely and at fast speed, it is usually expected that a stream-mining process can only scan a data stream once; and since the characteristics of the data may evolve over time, it is desirable to incorporate the evolving features of data streams. This paper investigates the issues of developing a high-speed classification method for streaming data with concept drifts. Among several popular classification techniques, the naïve Bayesian classifier is chosen due to its low construction cost, ease of incremental maintenance, and high accuracy. An efficient algorithm, called EvoClass (Evolutionary Classifier), is devised. EvoClass builds an incremental, evolutionary Bayesian classifier on streaming data. A *train-and-test* method is employed to discover the changes in the characteristics of the data and the need for construction of a new classifier. In addition, divergence is utilized to quantify the changes in the classifier and inform the user what aspects of the data characteristics have evolved. Finally, an intensive empirical study has been performed that demonstrates the effectiveness and efficiency of the EvoClass method.

13.1 Introduction

Data mining has been an active research area in the past decade. With the emergence of sensor nets, the world-wide web, and other on-line data-intensive applications, mining streaming data has become an urgent problem. Recently, a lot of research has been performed on data-stream mining, including clustering [12, 20], aggregate computation [5, 11], classifier construction [3, 15], and frequent counts computation [18]. However, a lot of issues still need to be explored to ensure that high-speed, nonstatic streams can be mined in real-time and at a reasonable cost.

Let's examine some application areas that pose a demand for real-time classification of nonstatic streaming data:

- Online shopping. At different times, shoppers may have different shopping patterns. For instance, some shoppers may be interested in buying a t-shirt and shorts while other shoppers would be interested in leather jackets and sweaters. In addition, new items may appear at any time. As a result, the classifier may evolve over time. Thus, it is necessary to devise an adaptive classifier.

- Target marketing. In business advertisement campaigns, mailing out coupons (or credit card pre-approval applications) is an expensive operation due to handling costs and mailing fees. If a coupon recipient does not use the coupon, the overhead is wasted. It is essential to identify the set of customers who will use the coupons for further purchases. To identify these customers, a classifier can be built based on the customer's shopping history to determine to whom a coupon should be sent. This classifier will have to evolve over time due to the change of economic environment, fashion, etc. As a result, it is important to find the best classifier for the current trend.

- Sensor nets. A sensor net continuously collects information from nearby sites and sends signals. The stream of sensor data can be used to detect the malfunction of sensors, outliers, congestions, and so on. For instance, based on the data from traffic sensors in a major city, a model has to be constructed dynamically based on the current traffic and weather situation, such as accidents, traffic jams, storms, special events, and so on.

The above examples show that there is a need to dynamically construct classifiers based on the history and current information of streaming data, which poses the following challenges:

- The classifier construction process should be *fast* and *dynamic* because the data may arrive at a high rate, with dramatic changes. For example, thousands of packets can be collected from sensor nets every second, and millions of customers may make purchases every day.

- The classifier should also *evolve over time* since the label of each record may change from time to time. As a result, how to keep trace of this type of evolution and how to discover the cause that leads to the evolution is an important and difficult problem.

- The classifier should not only be suitable for peer prediction, but also for future prediction. In some applications, the behaviors of one peer is not a good indication of another, but rather the behavior in the past is a better indication for the future. For instance, the price of stocks may not follow the same trend, but the previous fluctuation of the stock price may be a good indication of future stock price.

Let's first examine what kinds of classifiers may be good candidates for building fast, adaptive, and evolving classifiers in the data-stream environment. Classification is one of the most popularly studied fields in data mining, machine learning and statistics [13, 14, 19, 21]. There have been many well-studied classifiers, such as decision trees, Bayesian networks, naïve Bayesian classifiers, support vector machines, neural networks, and so on. In many studies, researchers have found that each classifier has advantages for certain types of data sets. Among these classifiers, some, such as neural networks and support vector machines, are obviously not good candidates for single-scan, very fast model reconstruction while handling the huge amount of data streams.

In the previous studies on classification of streaming data, decision trees have been popularly used as the first choice for their simplicity and easy explanation, such as [3, 13, 15]. However, it is difficult to dynamically and drastically change decision trees due to the costly reconstruction once they have been built. In many real applications, dynamic changes in stream data could be normal, such as in stock market analysis, traffic or weather modeling, and so on. In addition, a large amount of raw data is needed to build a decision tree. According to the model proposed in [15], it has to keep them in memory or on disk since they may be used later for updating the statistics when old records leave the window and for reconstructing parts of the tree. If the concept drifts very often, the related data needs to be scanned multiple times so that the decision tree can be kept updated. This is usually unaffordable for streaming data. Also, after detecting the drift in the model, it may take a long time to accumulate sufficient data to build an accurate decision tree [15]. Any drift taking place during that period either cannot be caught or will make the tree unstable. In addition, the method presented in this paper only works for peer prediction, but not for future prediction.

Based on the above analysis, we do not use the decision tree model, instead we choose the naïve Bayesian classifier scheme because it is easy to construct and adapt. The naïve Bayesian classifier, in essence, maintains a set of probability distributions $P(a_i|v)$ where a_i and v are the attribute value and the class label, respectively. To classify a record with several attribute values, it is assumed that the conditional probability distributions of these values are independent of each other. Thus, one can simply multiply the conditional probabilities together and label the record with the class label of the greatest probability. Despite its simplicity, the accuracy of the naïve Bayesian classifier is comparable to other classifiers such as decision trees [4, 19].

The characteristics of the stream may change at any moment. Table 13.1 illustrates an example of a credit card pre-approval database, constructed by a target marketing department in a credit card company. Suppose it is used to trace the customers to whom the company sent credit card pre-approval packages and the applications received from the customers. In the first portion of the stream, client 1578 is sent a pre-approval package. However, in the second portion of the stream, client 7887 has similar attribute values, but is not delivered such a package due to a change in the economic situation.

The above example shows that it is critical to detect the changes in the classifier and construct a new classifier in a timely manner to reflect the changes in the data. Furthermore, it is nice to know which attribute is dominant for such a change. Notice that almost all the classifiers require a good amount of data to build. If the data for constructing a classifier is insufficient,

Table 13.1. Example of credit card pre-approval database.

Client ID	Age	Salary	Credit History	Year	Approval
1578	30–34	25k–30k	Good	2000	Yes
1329	40–44	30k–35k	Bad	2000	Yes
2345	35–39	30k–35k	Good	2000	Yes
3111	25–29	25k–30k	Bad	2000	No
...	...	...	...	...	...
7887	30-34	30k-35k	Good	2002	No

the accuracy of the classifier may degrade significantly. On the other hand, it is impractical to keep all the data in memory especially when the arrival rate of the data is high, e.g., in network monitoring. As a result, we have to keep only a small amount of summarized data. The naïve Bayesian classifier can work for this scenario nicely, where the summarized data structure is just the occurrence frequency of each attribute value for every given class label.

Since the change of underlying processes may occur at any time, the stream can be partitioned into disjoint windows. Each window contains a portion of the stream. The summarized data (occurrence frequency) of each window is computed and stored. When the stream is very long, even the summarized data may not be able to fit in the main memory. With a larger window size, the memory can store the summarized data for a larger portion of the stream. However, this can make the summarized data too coarse. During the process of constructing a new classifier, we may not be able to recover much useful information from the coarse summarized data. To overcome this difficulty, a *tilted window* [2] is employed for summarizing the data. In the tilted window scheme, the most recent window contains the finest frequency counts. The window size increases exponentially for older data. This design is based on the observation that more recent data is usually more important. With this tilted window scheme, the summarized counts for a large portion of the stream can fit in memory. During the construction of the classifier, more recent information can be obtained, and the classifier can be updated accordingly.

Based on the above observation, an evolutionary stream data classification method is developed in this study, with the following contributions:

- The proposal of a model for the construction of an evolutionary classifier (e.g., naïve Bayesian) over streaming data.
- A novel two-fold algorithm, EvoClass, is developed with the following features:
  - A test-and-update technique is employed to detect the changes of conditional probability distributions of the naïve Bayesian.
  - The naïve Bayesian is adaptive to new data by continuous refinement.
  - A tilted window is utilized to partition the data so that more detailed information is maintained for more recent data.

- – Variational divergence and Kullback-Leibler divergence are used to discover the dominant attributes that contribute to the classifier changes.
- – The algorithm can also be adapted to future prediction in addition to the peer prediction.
- • An extensive performance study has been conducted on the proposed method using synthetic data, which shows the correctness and high efficiency of the EvoClass algorithm.

The remainder of the paper is organized as follows. Related work is presented in Section 13.2. We briefly describe the problem of streaming-data classification in Section 13.3. We formulate the EvoClass approach in Section 13.4 and report the experimental results in Section 13.5. Related work and comparison between EvoClass and decision-tree-based algorithms are given in Section 13.6. We also discuss other issues related to EvoClass in that section. Finally, we draw our conclusion in Section 13.7.

13.2 Related Work

Querying and mining streaming data has raised great interest in the database community. An overview of the current state of the art of stream data management systems, stream query processing, and stream data mining can be found in [1, 9]. Here, we briefly introduce the major work on streaming data classification.

Building classifiers on streaming data has been studied in [3, 15], with decision trees as the classification approach. In [3], it is assumed that the data is generated by a static Markov process. As a result, each portion of the stream can be viewed as a sample of the same underlying process, which may not handle well dynamically evolving data. A new decision-tree construction algorithm, VFDT is proposed. The first portion (window) of the stream data is used to determine the root node. The second portion (window) of the stream data is used to build the the second node of the tree, and so on. The window size is determined by the desired accuracy. The higher the accuracy desired, the more data in a window. According to [3], this method can achieve a higher degree of accuracy and it outperforms some other decision-tree construction methods, such as C4.5.

The algorithm proposed in [15], CVFDT, relaxed the assumption of static classification modeling in VFDT. It allows concept drift, which means the underlying classification model may change over time. CVFDT keeps its underlying model consistent with the ongoing data. When the concept in the streaming data changes, CVFDT can adaptively change the decision tree by growing alternative subtrees in questionable portions of the old tree. When the accuracy of the alternative subtree outperforms the old subtree, the old one will be replaced with the new one. CVFDT achieves better performance than VFDT because of its fitness to changing data. However, because of the inherent properties of constructing decision tree, CVFDT has the following difficulties in processing highly variant streaming data:

- CVFDT needs to store the records of the current window in memory or on disk. These records are prepared for reconstruction of the tree when concept drift takes place. When the window size is large, or when the concept drifts frequently, it often needs multiple scans over the records in order to partially rebuild the tree.
- In CVFDT, the window on which the decision tree is built is fixed, which means that the decision tree covers all the records in the window. If there is a concept drift in the middle of the window, it cannot discard the first part of the records in the window. Thus it may not reflect the newest concept trend accurately. The window size cannot be reduced further since there is a lower bound of necessary records to build a tree.
- The entire decision tree may become bushy over time due to the maintenance of a large number of alternative subtrees.
- If the alternative subtrees do not lead to replacements for old ones, the computation time spent on these subtrees is wasted.

EvoClass avoids the above problems using a tilted window scenario and naïve Bayesian classifier. Since naïve Bayesian needs only the summary information of records, EvoClass does not need to store data records, it is a truly **one-scan** algorithm. EvoClass can refine the minimum window size to small granularity without much loss of efficiency. Thus EvoClass can catch high frequency significant concept drifts. Furthermore, the additive property of the naïve Bayesian classifier makes the merging of two probability distributions simple and robust. Finally, the cost per record for EvoClass is $O(|V||A|)$, which is much cheaper than that for CVFDT, $O(dN_t|V|\sum_{\forall j}|A_j|)$ [15] (where d is the maximum depth of the decision tree and N_t is the number of alternate trees; the notation is introduced in the next section).

13.3 Problem Definition and Analysis

We assume that a data stream consists of a sequence of data records, $r_1, r_2, \ldots,$ r_n, where n could be an arbitrarily large integer. Each record consists of a set of attributes and a class label. Let $A = \{A_1, A_2, \ldots, A_m\}$ be a set of attributes. A data record, $r = \langle a_1, a_2, \ldots, a_m, v \rangle$, where a_j is the value of attribute A_j, and v is the class label of r.

Streaming Data Classification
The problem is to build a classifier based on streaming data in order to predict the class label of unknown, coming records. In this paper, we focus on the problem that the underlying process behind the streaming data may not be static, i.e., it may change over time. We call such changes *concept drifts*. It is

challenging to build an adaptive classifier over streaming data, as well as to represent how the concepts drift.

We assume that the values in each attribute are categorical values. In the case that an attribute has real values, we first discretize the data into bins via either equal-width or equal-depth binning techniques [17], which will not be elaborated here.

Comparing with other classification methods, the naïve Bayesian classification approach is an affordable solution for data stream classification due to the following characteristics:

- The construction cost and memory consumption are relatively low.
- It is easy to update the naïve Bayesian classifier with new data.
- Its accuracy is comparable to other classifiers, e.g., Bayesian network and decision trees [19].

We first introduce the concept of the naïve Bayesian classification. Let $V = v_1, v_2, \ldots, v_k$ be the set of target class labels. As we know, the conditional probability distribution, $P(v_i|a_1, a_2, \ldots, a_n)$, can be used to predict the class label of records where a_j is the value of the j-th attribute. By applying the Bayes theory, we can obtain the following formula.

$$P(v_i|a_1, \ldots, a_n) = \frac{P(a_1, \ldots, a_n|v_i) \times P(v_i)}{P(a_1, a_2, \ldots, a_n)}$$

$$\propto P(a_1, a_2, \ldots, a_n|v_i) \times P(v_i) \qquad (13.1)$$

$$\propto P(a_1|v_i) \times \cdots \times P(a_n|v_i) \times P(v_i) \qquad (13.2)$$

For a given record $\langle a_1, a_2, \ldots, a_n \rangle$, we compute the probability for all v_i. The class label of this record is that v_j (for some j where $1 \leq j \leq k$) which yields the maximum probability in Equation (13.1). The number of conditional probabilities that need to be stored is $|A_1| \times |A_2| \times \cdots \times |A_m| \times |V|$ where $|A_i|$ is the number of distinct values in the ith attribute. If there are 10 attributes and 100 distinct values for each attribute and 10 class labels, there will be $100^{10} \times 10$ conditional probabilities to be computed which is prohibitively expensive. On the other hand, the naïve Bayesian classifier assumes the independence of each variable, i.e., $P(a_i, a_j|v) = P(a_i|v) \times P(a_j|v)$. In this case, Equation (13.1) can be simplified to Equation (13.2). Then we need only track $\sum_{\forall i} |A_i| \times |V|$ probabilities. In the previous example, we only need to track 10,000 probabilities, a manageable task. The set of conditional probabilities that can be learned from the data seen so far is, $P(a_i|v) = \frac{P(a_i, v)}{P(v)}$, where $P(a_i, v)$ is the joint probability distribution of attribute value a_i and class label v, and $P(v)$ is the probability distribution of the class label.

Classifier Evolution

The problem is to catch the concept drifts and identify them. For discovery of the evolution of a classifier, one needs to keep trace of the changes of the data or conditions closely related to the classifier [8]. The naïve Bayesian classifier captures the probability distributions of attribute values and class labels, and thus becomes a good candidate for the task. It is important to capture and measure the difference between two probability distributions. There exist some methods which assess the difference between two probability distributions, among which the *variational distance* and the *Kullback-Leibler divergence* are the most popular ones [16].

- Variational Distance: Given two probability distributions, P_1 and P_2, of the variable σ, the variational distance is defined as $V(P_1, P_2) = \sum_{\sigma \in \Omega} |P_1(\sigma) - P_2(\sigma)|$.
- Kullback-Leibler Divergence: The Kullback-Leibler divergence is one of the well-known divergence measures rooted in information theory. There are two popular versions of the Kullback-Leibler Divergence. The asymmetric measure (sometimes referred as the *I*-directed divergence) is defined as

$$I(P_1, P_2) = \sum_{\sigma \in \Omega} P_1(\sigma) \log \frac{P_1(\sigma)}{P_2(\sigma)}.$$

Since the *I*-divergence does not satisfy the metric properties, its symmetrized measure, *J*-divergence, is often used to serve as a distance measure.

$$\begin{aligned} J(P_1, P_2) &= I(P_1, P_2) + I(P_2, P_1) \\ &= \sum_{\sigma \in \Omega} (P_1(\sigma) - P_2(\sigma)) \log \frac{P_1(\sigma)}{P_2(\sigma)} \end{aligned} \qquad (13.3)$$

In this paper, we also adopt the *J*-divergence to measure the difference between two probability distributions. One limitation to applying the Kullback-Leibler divergence is that the measure is undefined if either $P_1(\sigma) = 0$ or $P_2(\sigma) = 0$. To resolve this issue, a smoothing process can be performed on the probability distributions. Probabilities with zero value will be assigned to a small but positive probability after the smoothing process. A simple way to implement the smoothing probability is to slightly decrease the value of each non-zero empirical probability and uniformly distribute the small amount of probability to the zero probability virtually. The decrement of each non-zero probability is done in proportion to its value.

13.4 Approach of EvoClass

As discussed before, a naïve Bayesian classifier is essentially a set of probability distributions induced from data. The probability $P(a_i, v)$ and $P(v)$ are crucial to the accuracy of a classifier. In this section, we are to present a novel approach that dynamically estimates the probability distributions over the stream data, which may evolve over time. We first present a high level overview of our approach and then give the detailed description of each component in the algorithm.

13.4.1 Overview

As mentioned previously, the naïve Bayesian classifier is chosen for its efficient construction, incremental update, and high accuracy. Since data may arrive at a high rate and the set of overall data stream can be very large, it is expected that the computer system cannot store the complete set of data in the main memory, especially for sensor nets. As a result, only part of the raw data and some summarized data may be stored. Most of the raw data is only processed once and discarded. Thus, one needs to know the count of the number of records in which the value a_i and the class label v occurred together.

The stream is partitioned into a set of disjoint windows, each of which consists of a portion of the stream. The coming data is continuously used to test the classifier to see whether the classifier is still sufficiently accurate. Once the data in a window is full, the counts of the occurrences of all distinct $a_i \cap v$ are computed. After computing the counts, the raw data of the stream can be discarded. These counts are used to train the classifier, i.e., to update the probability distributions.

There are two cases to be considered. First, if the accuracy of the classifier degrades significantly, one needs to discard the old classifier and build a new one. In many occasions, the changes in the classifier are also interesting to the users because based on the changes, they may know what occurred in the data. Therefore, the major changes in the classifier will be reported. The procedure is depicted in Figure 13.1. Second, when the probability distribution does not change for a long time, there may be a significant amount of information accumulated on the counts. In this case, some of the windows will need to be combined to reduce the amount of information.

In the following subsections, we will present the details of each step.

13.4.2 Window Size

The size of the window is a critical factor that may influence the classification quality. The probability distribution is updated when the accumulated data has filled a *window*. When the window size is small, the evidence in a window may be also small, and the induced probability distribution could be inaccurate, which may lead to a low-quality naïve Bayesian classifier. However, when the window size is too large, it will be slow in detecting the change of probability distribution, and the classifier may not be able to reflect the true state of the *current stream*.

The summary information of a window includes the number of occurrences of each distinct pair of $a_j \cap v$, the number of occurrences of each v, and the number of records in the window. There are in total $|V| \times \sum_{\forall j} |A_j|$ counts (for

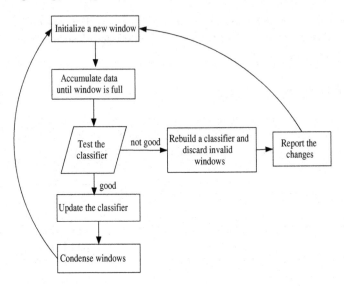

Fig. 13.1. Flowchart of EvoClass.

all distinct $v \cap a_j$) where $|V|$ and $|A_j|$ are respectively the number of class labels and the number of distinct values for attribute A_j. As a result, the number of counts for summarizing a window is $|V| \times \sum_{\forall j} |A_j| + |V| + 1$. First, let us assume that each count can be represented by an integer which consumes four bytes. Then the total number of windows (summary information), N_w, that can fit in the allocated memory is $\frac{M}{4 \times (|V| \times \sum_{\forall j} |A_j| + |V| + 1)}$ where M is the size of the allocated memory. Now the problem becomes how to partition the stream into N_w windows.

First, we want to know the minimum window size, w_{min}. Let us assume that each record has $|A|$ attributes. There are overall $|V| \times \sum_{1 \leq j \leq |A|} |A_j|$ counts that need to be tracked for the purpose of computing conditional probabilities. Each record can update $|A|$ counts. The minimum window size is set to $q \times \frac{|V| \times \sum_{1 \leq j \leq |A|} |A_j|}{|A|}$, where q is a small number. In Section 13.5, we experiment with various w_{min}. We found that with large w_{min}, the accuracy is low and the delay of evolution detection may be large. This is because the change of the data characteristics may take place at any time but the construction of a new classifier is done only at the end of a window. On the other hand, although a smaller w_{min} can improve the accuracy, the average response time is prolonged. After a window is full, we need to update the classifier. Since the cost of classifier update is the same regardless of window size, the per record cost of classifier updating can be large with a small w_{min}. In Section 13.5, we will discuss how to decide w_{min} empirically.

To approximate the exponential window growth, we use the following algorithm. When the summary information can fit in the allocated memory, we keep the size of each window as w_{min}. Once the memory is full, some windows may have to be merged, and the newly freed space can be utilized for the summary data of a new window. We choose to merge the consecutive windows with the smallest growth ratio i.e., w_i and w_{i-1} where $\frac{|w_{i-1}|}{|w_i|}$ is the smallest ratio. The rationale behind this choice is that we want the growth of the window size to be as smooth as possible. If there exists a tie, we choose the oldest windows to merge because recent windows contain more updated information than older ones. Figure 13.2 shows the process of window merging. At the beginning, there are four windows, each of which contains a record. For illustration, we assume the memory can only store the summary data for four windows (in Figure 13.2a). When a new window of data arrives, some windows have to be merged. Since the ratio between any two consecutive windows is the same, the earliest two windows are merged (as shown in Figure 13.2b). As a result, the size ratios between windows 3 and 4 and windows 2 and 3 is 1 while the size ratio between windows 1 and 2 is 2. Thus, windows 2 and 3 are merged when the new data is put in window 4 as illustrated in Figure 13.2c.

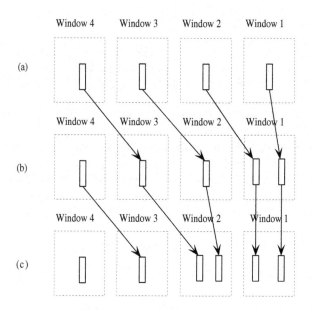

Fig. 13.2. Merging windows.

After the merge of two existing windows, some space is freed to store the new data. Once w_{min} new records have been obtained, the counts for the new window of data are calculated. For instance, assuming that the window consists of the first four records in Table 13.1, Table 13.2 shows the summary counts after processing the window of data. This structure is similar to AVC-Set (Attribute–Value–ClassLabel) in [7].

Table 13.2. Counts after processing first four records in Table 13.1.

Attribute	Value	Pre-Approval	
		Yes	No
Age	25–29	0	1
	30–34	1	0
	35–39	1	0
	40–44	1	0
	45–49	0	0
Salary	20k–25k	0	0
	25k–30k	1	1
	30k–35k	1	1
	35k–40k	0	0
	40k–45k	0	0
	45k–50k	0	0
Credit History	Good	2	0
	Bad	1	1

13.4.3 Classifier Updating

The classifier is updated once the current window is full and there is no significant error increasing (see Section 13.4.4). Let's assume that we have a naïve Bayesian classifier, i.e., a set of probability distribution $P(a_i|v)$ and $P(v)$ and a set of new counts $c(a_i \cap v)$ and $c(v)$ where $c(a_i \cap v)$ and $c(v)$ are the number of records having $A_i = a_i$ with class label v and the number of records having class label v in the new window, respectively. If there is no prior knowledge about the probability distribution, we can assume the uniform prior distribution which yields the largest entropy, i.e., uncertainty. Based on the current window, we can obtain the probability distribution within the window $P_{cur}(a_i|v) = \frac{c(a_i \cap v)}{c(v)}$. For example, based on the data in Table 13.2, $P_{cur}(25k–30k|yes) = \frac{1}{2} = 0.5$. Next we need to merge the current and the prior probability distributions. Let's assume that the overall number of records in the current window is w, and the number of records for building the classifier before this window is s. The updated probability distribution is

$$P_{new}(v) = \frac{\mu P_{past}(v) + P_{cur}(v)}{\mu + 1}$$

$$P_{new}(a_i|v) = \frac{\mu P_{past}(v) P_{past}(a_i|v) + P_{cur}(a_i|v) P_{cur}(v)}{\mu P_{past}(v) + P_{cur}(v)}$$

where $\mu = \frac{s}{w}$ if the importance of the current and past records are equal. μ can be used to control the weight of the windows. For example, in the fading model, i.e., the recent data can reflect the trend much better than the past data, μ can be less than $\frac{s}{w}$, even equal to 0.

13.4.4 Detect Changes

Due to noise and randomness, it is very difficult to tell whether a set of probability distribution has changed. In this paper, we adopt a *train-and-test* technique as follows. In each window, the training records are also used to test the model after their final class labels are known. If the accuracy of the classifier decreases significantly, e.g., by an amount of γ, then we may consider the data has changed, and a new classifier is needed. The main challenge is what the value of γ should take. If γ is too large, we may miss the concept change. However, since there may exist noise in the data set, the accuracy may vary from one test data set to another. On the other hand, if γ is too small, the system may *over-react* to the noise in the data set. Therefore, we want to set γ to the value that enables one to separate noise from the real changes of the underlying data.

We assume that whether a record is correctly classified by our classifier is a random variable X. $X = 1$ if the class label is correct, 0 otherwise. The accuracy of a classifier with a test data set is equal to the expected value of X in the test data set. Let $accuracy_0$ be the maximum accuracy of the classifier on recent test data sets, and ξ be the true mean (accuracy of our classifier). According to the Hoeffding bound [14, 15], the true mean ξ is at least $accuracy_0 - \epsilon$ with $1 - \delta$ confidence, where ϵ can be computed by the following formula:

$$\epsilon = R\sqrt{\frac{\ln(1/\delta)}{2N}} \tag{13.4}$$

where N is the number of records in the test data set, $1 - \delta$ is the confidence level, and R is the range of X which is 1 in this case.

Let $accuracy_1$ be the accuracy of the classifier on the current test data set. Based on the Hoeffding bound, with $1 - \delta$ confidence, $accuracy_1$ is at least $\xi - \epsilon$. Therefore, with $1 - \delta$ confidence, we can conclude that $accuracy_1$ is at least $accuracy_0 - 2\epsilon$. When $accuracy_1$ falls below $accuracy_0 - 2\epsilon$, we may consider that the concept has changed and it is time to construct a new classifier.

There is one drawback of this approach. When the change of the underlying process is gradual, it may lead to a situation in which accuracy of the classifier may also degrade gradually. For instance, if the accuracy of the classifier for window $i, i-1, i-2, i-3$ is $0.65, 0.7, 0.75, 0.8$, respectively, and the threshold 2ϵ is 0.06, then our scheme would not detect the gradual change. To overcome this problem, we compare the accuracy of the classifier for this window with the best accuracy yielded by the current classifier. In the same example, let us assume that 0.8 is the best accuracy achieved by the current classifier. Then we can detect the change at window $i - 1$.

13.4.5 Under-representing

There is one major drawback of the Bayesian classifier: *underestimation*. For example, if the joint probability of a_j and v is 10^{-6} and there exist 100,000 records, then it is very likely that there exists no record having a_j with class label v. Thus, it is natural to assign $P(a_j|v) = 0$. As a result, v will not be assigned to any record with attribute $A_j = a_j$ because the probability is zero. It can lead to a significant misclassification. This problem may become severe especially when the number of attributes and distinct attribute values is large. A *smoothing* technique is applied to remove zero probabilities. Let $P(a_i|v)$ be the probability value before smoothing and $P'(a_i|v) = \dfrac{P(a_i|v) + \frac{\omega}{|A_i|}}{1+\omega}$ be the probability after smoothing, where ω is a small constant, e.g., 10^{-10}.

13.4.6 Change Representation

As mentioned before, the naïve Bayesian classifier can be viewed as a set of joint probability distributions, $P(a_i, v)$. There exist several methods to qualify the difference between two probability distributions, e.g., mutual information, divergence, and so on. In this paper, the divergence is employed for this purpose because it is one of the most popular measures. However, from the divergence, one may know only that there exists a probability change, but not how the probability changes. As a result, we compute the Kullback-Leibler divergence for each individual conditional probability distribution. In other words, for each given class label v, we calculate the divergence of $P(a_i|v)$. The divergence of $P(v)$ is also computed to catch the class label distribution changes. In reality, the majority of the probability distributions does not change significantly during a short period. Only a small number of probabilities in $P(a_i|v)$ distribution may change dramatically, which finally leads to the change of the classifier and the record labels. It is meaningful to let the users know where the probability changes significantly. For instance, if the probability distribution for one particular class label changes largely, the user may conjecture that something related to this class label and its attributes has taken place and can investigate it further.

Because there are thousands of probabilities in $P(a_i|v)$, it is unaffordable to ask the user to check the divergences one by one. Thus we propose to present only the top-k probabilities which have the greatest divergence for a small k chosen by an expert or a user. Our experiments show that it can usually catch more than half of the major causes that contribute to the classifier changes.

13.4.7 Estimation of Processing Cost

By putting together all the techniques discussed so far, we present a general view of the cost for each step depicted in Figure 13.1. The total processing time can be partitioned roughly into four parts: accumulating records, testing the classifier, updating the classifier, and rebuilding a new classifier. Assume the minimum window size is w_{min}, the number of testing records in each window is T, and the number of windows in record is N_w. We have,

- Accumulating records: The cost to count each record (updating $c(a_i \cap v)$ and $c(v)$) is $O(|A|)$.
- Testing the classifier: The cost is $O(T|V||A|)$ per window.
- Updating the classifier: The cost to merge two windows is $O(|V| \sum_{\forall j} |A_j|)$. The cost to update the current probability distribution is $O(|V| \sum_{\forall j} |A_j|)$.
- Rebuilding a new classifier: Since each time we have to scan the history windows and build a best naïve Bayesian classifier based on the testing records, the cost is $O(N_w|V| \sum_{\forall j} |A_j| + N_w T|V||A|)$.

We set $w_{min} = q \frac{|V| \sum_{\forall j} |A_j|}{|A|}$ and $T = \sigma w_{min}$, where usually $q > 1$ and $\sigma < 1$. Based on the above analysis, we can calculate the lower bound and the upper bound of the amortized cost for processing one single record. To calculate the lower bound cost, one extreme case is that the concept does not change at all over time. Then it will not rebuild any classifiers except the initial one. Therefore, the lower bound for the total cost per record is

$$O\left(|A| + \frac{2|V| \sum_{\forall j} |A_j|}{w_{min}}\right) \sim O(|A|).$$

For the upper bound, the worst case is that the concept changes dramatically in each window. The cost is

$$O\left(|A| + \frac{2|V| \sum_{\forall j} |A_j| + N_w|V| \sum_{\forall j} |A_j| + N_w T|V||A|}{w_{min}}\right)$$

which can be simplified to $O(|V||A|)$ if q is larger than N_w, and σN_w is a small constant. Therefore, the amortized upper bound of processing cost for each record is $O(|V||A|)$, which is equal to the cost of classifying one record.

13.5 Experimental Results

We conducted an empirical study to examine the performance of EvoClass, which is implemented using C++ with the standard template library. The experiments were conducted on an Intel Pentium III PC (1.13GHz) with 384MB main memory, running Windows XP Professional. The result demonstrated the characteristics of EvoClass in terms of accuracy, response time, sensitivity, and scalability for varying concept drift level and frequency.

13.5.1 Synthetic Data Generation

We experimented on several synthetic data sets embedded with changing concept over time. The data sets are produced by a synthetic data generator using a rotating hyperplane. The general description of the generator can be found in [15]. Here, we briefly introduce the concept behind this generator. A d-dimensional hyperplane can be viewed as a set of points which satisfy

$$\sum_{i=1}^{d} w_i a_i = w_0 \qquad (13.5)$$

where a_i is the coordinate of the ith dimension. We can treat the vector $\langle a_1, a_2, ..., a_d \rangle$ as a data record, where a_i is the value of attribute A_i. The class label v of the record can be determined by the following rule: if $\sum_{i=1}^{d} w_i a_i > w_0$, it is assigned the positive label; otherwise (i.e., $\sum_{i=1}^{d} w_i a_i \leqslant w_0$), it is assigned the negative label. By randomly assigning the value of a_i in a record, an infinite number of data records can be generated in this way. One can regard w_i as the weight of A_i. The larger w_i is, the more dominant is the attribute A_i. Therefore, through rotating the hyperplane to some degree by changing the magnitude of w_i, the possible distribution of the class label vs $\langle a_1, a_2, \ldots, a_d \rangle$ changes, which is equal to saying the underlying concept drifts. This also means that some records are relabelled according to the new concept. In our experiments, we set w_0 to $0.1d$ and restrict the value of v_i in $[0.0, 1.0]$. We increase the value of w_i with $+0.01d$ or $-0.01d$ gradually. After it reaches either $0.1d$ or 0.0, it then changes in the opposite direction.

While generating the synthetic data, we also inject noise into the data. With the probability p_{noise}, the data is arbitrarily assigned to the class labels. p_{noise} is randomly selected from $[0, P_{noise,max}]$ each time the concept drifts. We do not use a fixed probability of noise injection such as that performed in [15] since we want to test the robustness and sensitivity of our algorithm. The concept drift from small changes of w_i cannot be detected since the drift and the noise are not distinguishable. The average probability of noise is around $P_{noise,max}/2$ for the synthetic data set. Because there are only two class labels in the data set, so with 50% probability (assume $P_{positive} = P_{negative} = 0.5$), the injected noise produces wrong class labels. Therefore, the error caused by the noise is around $P_{noise,max}/4$ on average. This is a background error that cannot be removed for any kind of classification algorithm. We denote $p_{ne} = P_{noise,max}/4$. In Table 13.3, we collect the parameters used in the synthetic data sets and our experiments.

13.5.2 Accuracy

The first two experiments show how quickly our algorithm can respond to the underlying concept changes by checking the classifier error of EvoClass after a concept drift.

We assume that the Bayesian classifier has an error rate p_b which means without the injection of any noise and concept drift, given a synthetic data set described above, the Bayesian classifier can achieve the accuracy of $1 - p_b$. Suppose the noise does not affect p_b significantly if the noise is not very large

Table 13.3. Parameters for the synthetic data set.

Symbol	Meaning
$|A|$	Number of attributes
C	Cardinality
N	Number of records
N_w	Number of windows
w_{min}	Minimum window size (records)
f_c	Concept drift frequency (per records)
$p_{noise,max}$	Max noise rate

(which is justified in Section 13.5.3), we can achieve the average error rate $p_{error} = p_b + p_{ne}$. We denote the new error rate p'_{error} for the classifier we build after the concept changes. We want to see how fast our algorithm can catch it. Drift level [15], p_{de}, is the error rate if we still use the old concept C_{old} (before one drift) to label the new data (after that drift). It is expected that p'_{error} should evolve from $p_{error} + p_{de}$ to some value close to p_{error}. The problem is how fast this procedure takes place.

In this experiment, we set $|A| = 30$, $C = 8$, $N = 4,800,000$, $N_w = 32$, $w_{min} = 12,000$, $f_c = 400,000$, and $p_{noise,max} = 5\%$. Figure 13.3a shows three kinds of errors: the error from concept drift (the percentage of records that change their labels at each concept drift point), the error from our EvoClass algorithm without any concept drift, and the error from our EvoClass algorithm with concept drift. It illustrates that the EvoClass algorithm can start of respond to the concept drift very quickly. The very start of Figure 13.3a shows that when a huge drift happens (> 10% records change their labels), EvoClass can respond with a spike and quickly adapt to the new concept. For the small concept drifts taking place in the middle of the figure, EvoClass struggles to absorb the drift. It takes much longer because it is more difficult to separate the concept drift from noise in the middle of a stream. Furthermore, since the ϵ-error tolerance (by Equation (13.4)) in this experiment is 0.034, it makes EvoClass oscillate around its average classifier error.

Figure 13.3b depicts the result of another experiment where f_c is set to $20,000$. It means the concept drifts in 20 times faster than in the first experiment. Again the curves show that the change of classifier error rate can follow the concept drift.

Next we want to test the model described in Section 13.3, which represents the set of attributes causing the concept drift. Here we use Kullback-Leibler divergence to rank the top-k greatest changes (Equation (13.3)) discovered in the distribution of $P(a_i|v)$. We vary the value of $w_1, w_2, \ldots, w_k$ simultaneously for each concept drift. Then the average recall and precision are calculated. Figure 13.4 shows the recall and precision from the top-k divergence list when k is between 1 and 5. The overall recall and precision are around 50–60%. It

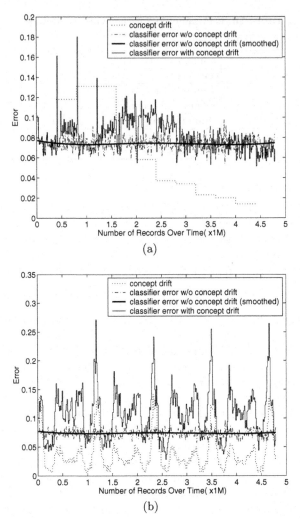

Fig. 13.3. Accuracy over time when the concept drifts over a)400,000 records and b) 20,000 records.

demonstrates EvoClass not only helps build an evolutionary classifier adapt to the concept drift but also discovers which attributes lead to the drift.

13.5.3 Sensitivity

Sensitivity is used to measure how the fluctuation of noise level may influence the quality of a classifier. Sensitivity is involved with the percentage of noise in the data set, the concept drift frequency, and the minimum window size. We use the same experimental setting mentioned previously. Figure 13.5a shows

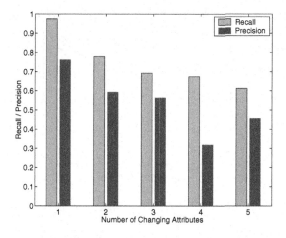

Fig. 13.4. Recall and precision vs number of changing attributes.

the relationship between the noise rate and the classifier error rate. The error rate of the classifier increases proportionally to the percentage changes of the noise. The dotted line shows p_{ne} caused by the average noise rate. The formula $p_{error} = p_b + p_{ne}$ holds very well based on the result in Figure 13.5a. That means that the performance of our EvoClass algorithm will not degrade even when lots of noise presents in the data set.

We next conduct an experiment to see the influence of the concept drift frequency in the classifier error rate. We set the minimum window size w_{min} to $10k$ and then vary the concept drift frequency f_c from 200 to $100k$. Figure 13.5b shows that the classifier cannot update its underlying structure to fit the new concept if f_c is below $10k$. This is because our minimum processing unit is $10k$, and the classifier cannot catch up with the changing frequency below that minimum processing unit.

In Figure 13.5c, we vary the minimum window size from 100 to $40k$ and fix the concept drift frequency to $20k$. It shows that when the minimum window size is below $10k$, the error rate will be in the range $[p_{opt}, 1.1p_{opt}]$, where p_{opt} is the best error rate achieved in this series of experiments. When the concept does not drift very frequently, the minimum window size can be selected freely in a very large range and EvoClass can still achieve a nearly optimal result. When w_{min} is close to 100, the error rate increases steadily because of over-fitting. Figure 13.5c also shows the processing time for a varying minimum window size: generally it will take a longer time to complete the task if we choose a smaller minimum window size.

We then check the performance of EvoClass when the total available number of windows, N_w, varies. We have the following experiment settings: $|A| = 30$, $C = 32$, $N = 480,000$, $w_{min} = 400$, and $f_c = 400$. We intentionally change w_0 to 0.001 and $p_{noise,max}$ to 0.10 such that in a long period, the con-

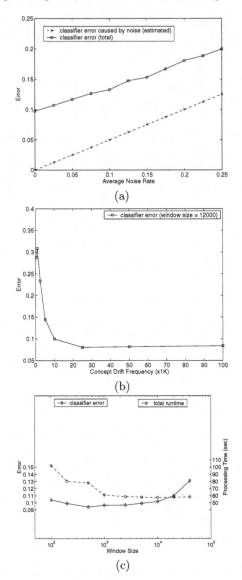

Fig. 13.5. Sensitivity: noise, concept drift frequency, window size

cept drift cannot be detected from noise. With the increase of cardinality (or number of attributes), one window is not enough to build an accurate classifier. The increment of minimum window size does not work because of the small concept drift frequency. The tilt window scenario performs well in this case. The result is depicted in Figure 13.6. As we can see, only maintaining one window will result in a significant increase of errors when compared with

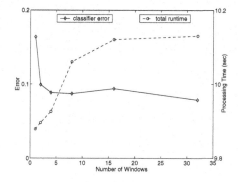

Fig. 13.6. Accuracy and run time vs number of windows.

maintaining several windows. In terms of processing time, a large number of windows does not affect the performance too much. In fact, the time spent updating the classifier is dominant when compared with that for completely rebuilding the classifier in this case. The former is unavoidable for all the situations where different numbers of windows are used.

13.5.4 Scalability

Finally, the scalability of our EvoClass algorithm is tested in our experiments. The scalability is measured in two aspects in terms of processing time and accuracy: when the number of attributes increases, and when the cardinality for each attribute increases.

First, we fix the cardinality of each attribute to 8, and vary the number of attributes from 10 to 200. Figure 13.7a shows that both the total processing time and the classifier construction time increase linearly as the number of attributes increases. The reason is obvious: naïve Bayesian classification, the processing time is proportional to the number of attributes as shown in Equation (13.2). Figure 13.7a also tells us that the average classifier error rate decreases from 15% to 9%. To some extent, this is because the independence assumption in naïve Bayesian classification becomes more realistic when the number of attributes increases.

Second, we fix the number of dimensions to 30 and vary the cardinality from 3 to 50. The minimum window size is 10,000. The result is depicted in Figure 13.7b. It shows that the processing time is basically unrelated to the cardinality. However, the cardinality affects the accuracy a little bit. In the case of $C = 3$, the error rate increases mainly because the discretization is too coarse. In this case, many cells cross the hyperplane defined in Equation (13.5), thus they cannot be labelled accurately.

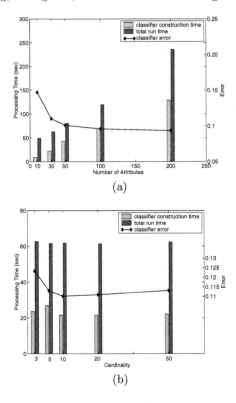

Fig. 13.7. Accuracy and run time as the system scales.

13.5.5 Path Length Measurement

Figure 13.7a also illustrates the computational time in different parts of the
EvoClass algorithm. We roughly divide the processing time into two parts:
classifier construction time, which includes classifier initialization, change detection, testing, and classifier updating; and the classification time, which
includes the time to predict the class label of each record when it arrives. The
experiments show that the first part occupies 1/6 to 1/2 of the total processing time. This ratio can be further reduced if the concept changes slow down
or the minimum window size is enlarged. We collect the data that shows the
number of records that can be processed each second. For a 200-attribute data
set, the processing speed is around 20,000 records per second. For 10-attribute
data set, it can achieve processing of 100,000 records per second. Since our
implementation is based on C++/STL, we believe that it can be further improved using a C implementation and a more compact data structure.

13.6 Discussion

We first discuss why we chose the naive Bayesian classifier as the base classifier for streaming data and then consider other issues for improvements and extensions of EvoClass.

13.6.1 Classifier Selection

There have been numerous studies on classification methods in the statistics, machine learning and data-mining communities. Several types of popular classifiers, including decision trees, neural networks, naïve Bayesian classifiers and support vector machines [6, 19], have been constructed and popularly used in practice. Here we first examine a few classification methods and see why we have selected the naïve Bayesian method for classification of stream data.

The decision tree is a widely studied classifier, where each node in a decision tree specifies a test of some attribute of the instance, and each branch descending from that node corresponds to one of the possible values of this attribute. An instance is classified by starting at the root node of the tree, testing the attribute specified by this node, then moving down the tree branch corresponding to the value of the attribute in the given examples. This process is then repeated for the subtree rooted at the new node. The time to construct a decision tree is usually high and requires multiple scans of the data. The recent decision tree construction algorithms (for large databases), such as BOAT [10], proposed a two-scan algorithm. It first uses a subset of data to construct an initial decision tree, then makes a scan over the whole database to build the final tree. BOAT can also be extended to a dynamic environment where the classifier may change over time. However, BOAT has similar problems to CVFDT [15].

A neural network is another popular method to learn real-valued, discrete-valued, and vector-valued target functions. A neural network is usually constructed by iteratively scanning the data, which is slow and is not suitable for the streaming data environment. The same problem exists for support vector machines and several other classification methods. Thus among several major classification methods, we have selected the naïve Bayesian classification method as the major candidate for extension to classification of streaming data.

13.6.2 Other Related Issues

In this subsection, we are going to discuss a few related issues, including choosing the window size, handling high frequent data streams, window weighting, and alternative classifiers.

Window Size

In the previous section, we mentioned that a window has a minimum size, $q \times \frac{|V| \times \sum_{1 \le j \le |A|} |A_j|}{|A|}$. When the cardinality of attributes is large, the minimum number of records in a window can also be quite large. Certainly, we can arbitrarily reduce the minimum size, in the extreme to 1. A smaller window size means updating the classifier more frequently, which degrades the performance a lot. A user can determine the window size based on the trade-off between processing speed and data arriving rate. Once the size of the minimum window is fixed, it may need to wait until a window is full before EvoClass can process the data. This may lead to longer delay in detecting the evolution of the classifier. To solve this problem, we test the classifier at the same time as data accumulating. Let $accuracy_1$ be the best accuracy of the classifier for all previous windows. A change will be detected if the accuracy falls below $accuracy_1 - 2\epsilon$. This means that we will detect a change if more than $w_{min} \times (1 + 2\epsilon - accuracy_1)$ records are mislabeled in the current window. Thus, we can keep track of the number of misclassified records. If the number of records exceeds this threshold, a change is detected and we will immediately build a new classifier. Under this scheme, the new classifier can be done much earlier.

High Frequent Data Stream

When the data arrival rate is extremely high, it is possible that our algorithm may not be able to process the data in time. In turn, more data have to be buffered. Over time, the system would become unstable. To solve this problem, we propose to use a sampling method. Let's assume that the time for processing a window of data is w_{min}, and w_{new} new records arrive in that time. If $w_{new} \le w_{min}$, it means that we are able to process the new data. Otherwise, we only can process a fraction of the new data. As a result, among the new w_{new} records, we use a random sample to pick w_{min} records, each having the probability $\frac{w_{min}}{w_{new}}$ of being chosen. The unchosen records are discarded because it is important to process the new data as soon as possible so that one can detect the changes as early as possible.

Window Weighting

In this paper, μ is the parameter that controls the weight that a new window carries. This value can easily be adjusted to fit the needs of different users. μ will be set to a smaller value if a user believe that the current data is a better indicator of the classifier. In the extreme case, we can set $\mu = 0$ when a user only wants a classifier that is solely built on the current window. On the other hand, if the user thinks that each record contributes equally to the classifier, we should set $\mu = \frac{s}{w}$ where s and w are the number of records in previous windows and the current window, respectively.

Alternative Classifiers

In this paper, we presented an algorithm for building a naïve Bayesian classifier for streaming data. However, the framework we proposed is not restricted to this specific classification algorithm, instead, it can be generalized to other classifiers, e.g., decision trees. To construct a decision tree on the evolving stream data, the new arrival window of data can be used first to test the accuracy of the decision tree. If the accuracy of the decision tree does not degrade significantly, then the new data will be used to refine the decision tree, e.g., building more leaf nodes. On the other hand, if the accuracy of the decision tree degrades significantly with respect to the current window of data, then it may signal the characteristics have changed and a new decision tree needs to be constructed. The new decision tree can be constructed in the same manner as the Bayesian classifier proposed in this paper. We trace back the previous windows of data, for a new set of windows, and a new decision tree is built. Among these new decision trees, the most accurate one (with respect to the current window of data) is chosen as the current decision tree.

13.7 Conclusions

We have investigated the major issues in classifying large-volume, high-speed and dynamically evolving streaming data, and proposed a novel approach, EvoClass, which integrates the naïve Bayesian classification method with titled window, boosting, and several other optimization techniques, and achieves high accuracy, high adaptivity, and low construction cost.

Compared with other classification methods, the EvoClass approach offers several distinct features:

- It is highly scalable and dynamically adaptive, since it does not need to buffer streaming data in memory, and it integrates the newly arriving summary information smoothly with the existing summary, which makes it especially valuable for dynamic model re-construction for streaming data.
- The introduction of tilted windows facilitates the effective maintenance for flexible weight/fading adjustment of historical information.
- The usage of Kullback-Leibler divergence provides us with the power to catch the important factors that are likely lead to concept drifts.

EvoClass represents a new methodology for effective classification of dynamic, fast-growing, and large volume data streams. It works well with low dimensional data. However, classification of high-dimensional streaming data (such as web documents, e-mails, etc.) is an interesting topic for future research.

References

[1] Babcock, B., S. Babu, M. Datar, R. Motwani and J. Widom, 2002: Models and issues in data stream systems. In *Proceedings of ACM Symp. on Principles of Database Systems*, 1–16.

[2] Chen, Y., G. Dong, J. Han, B. W. Wah and J. Wang, 2002: Multidimensional regression analysis of time-series data streams. In *Proceedings of International Conference on Very Large Databases*.

[3] Domingos, P., and G. Hulten, 2000: Mining high-speed data streams. *Proceedings of ACM Conference on Knowledge Discovery and Data Mining*, 71–80.

[4] Domingos, P., and M. J. Pazzani, 1997: On the optimality of the simple bayesian classifier under zero-one loss. *Machine Learning*, **29**, no. 2–3, 103–30.

[5] Dobra, A., M. N. Garofalakis, J. Gehrke and R. Rastogi, 2002: Processing complex aggregate queries over data streams. In *Proceedings of ACM Conference on Management of Data*, 61–72.

[6] Duda, R., P. E. Hart and D. G. Stork, 2000: *Pattern Classification*. WileyInterscience.

[7] Gehrke, J., R. Ramakrishnan and V. Ganti. RainForest: A framework for fast decision tree construction of large datasets, 1998: In *Proceedings of International Conference on Very Large Databases*, 416–27.

[8] Ganti, V., J. Gehrke, R. Ramakrishnan and W. Loh, 1999: A framework for measuring changes in data characteristics. In *Proceedings of ACM Symp. Principles of Database Systems*, 126–37.

[9] Garofalakis, M., J. Gehrke and R. Rastogi, 2002: Querying and mining data streams: you only get one look. Tutorial in *Proc. 2002 ACM Conference on Management of Data*.

[10] Gehrke, J., V. Ganti, R. Ramakrishnan and W. Loh, 1999: BOAT: optimistic decision tree construction. *Proceedings of Conference on Management of Data*, 169–80.

[11] Gehrke, J., F. Korn and D. Srivastava, 2001: On computing correlated aggregates over continuous data streams. In *Proceedings of ACM Conference on Management of Data*, 13–24.

[12] Guha, S., N. Mishra, R. Motwani and L. O'Callaghan, 2000: Clustering data streams. In *Proc. IEEE Symposium on Foundations of Computer Science*, 359–66.

[13] Han, J., and M. Kamber, 2000: *Data Mining Concepts and Techniques*. Morgan Kaufmann.

[14] Hastie, T., R. Tibshirani and J. Friedman, 2001: *The Elements of Statistical Learning: Data Mining, Inference, and Prediction*. Springer-Verlag.

[15] Hulton, G., L. Spencer and P. Domingos, 2001: Mining time-changing data streams. *Proceedings of ACM Conference on Knowledge Discovery in Databases*, 97–106.

[16] Lin, J., 1991: Divergence measures based on the Shannon entropy. *IEEE Tran. on Information Theory*, **37**, **1**, 145–51.

[17] Liu, H., F. Hussain, C.L. Tan and M. Dash, 2002: Discretization: An enabling technique. *Data Mining and Knowledge Discovery*, **6**, 393–423.

[18] Manku, G., and R. Motwani, 2002: Approximate frequency counts over data streams. In *Proc. 2002 Int. Conf. on Very Large Databases*.

[19] Mitchell, T., 1997: *Machine Learning*. McGraw-Hill.

[20] O'Callaghan, L., N. Mishra, A. Meyerson, S. Guha and R. Motwani, 2002: High-performance clustering of streams and large data sets. In *Proceedings of IEEE International Conference on Data Engineering*.

[21] Witten, I., and E. Frank, 2001: *Data Mining: Practical Machine Learning Tools and Techniques with Java Implementations*. Morgan Kaufmann.

Index

Printed in the United States
By Bookmasters